THE EPIC OF RUSSIAN LITERATURE

MARC SLONIM

The Epic of Russian Literature

FROM ITS ORIGINS THROUGH TOLSTOY

OXFORD UNIVERSITY PRESS

NEW YORK

OXFORD UNIVERSITY PRESS

Oxford London New York
Glasgow Toronto Melbourne Wellington
Cape Town Salisbury Ibadan Nairobi Lusaka Addis Ababa
Bombay Calcutta Madras Karachi Lahore Dacca
Kuala Lumpur Hong Kong Tokyo

Foreword

THIS PAPERBACK edition reproduces
with slight revisions *The Epic of Russian Literature,* published by Oxford
University Press in a cloth edition in 1950, reprinted with some corrections in 1959, and now out of print. As the first volume of my history
of Russian literature, it deals with the great classics and the literary
evolution from the eighteenth century to the 'seventies of the nineteenth
century. Its sequel, *From Chekhov to the Revolution,* dealing with the
period between the 'eighties of the past century and 1917, is already
available in Galaxy Books. It reproduces the first ten chapters of
Modern Russian Literature, also out of print. The third part of the
whole work, *Soviet Russian Literature,* is scheduled for publication by
Oxford University Press at the end of 1964.

In this work the author tried to present literary events in their
continuity of historic development, and establish the relation of the
past to the present. He has availed himself of materials and biographical and critical treatises published in the Soviet Union since 1918,
thus bringing fact and interpretations up to date. He also attempted
to fill the gaps that exist in many old surveys of Russian literature in
English, and therefore devoted a large part of his exposition to poets
who had not hitherto been given the place they truly deserve, and to
critics, such as Belinsky, Dobroliubov, Grigoriev, and others, whose
ideas and activity contributed so much to Russian artistic and intellectual life. The statements of Herzen, or of Slavophiles and Westernizers,
made a hundred years ago, seem strangely prophetic today and shed
an illuminating light on the contemporary scene. It is the author's firm
conviction that a comprehensive study of Russian literature is more
helpful for a dispassionate and real understanding of the Russians than
all the political guesses and travelers' tales. At any rate one of the
aims of this book is to present a portrayal of Russian mentality and to

assist the reader in his efforts to grasp that impalpable and elusive thing called national character.

For centuries the search for truth, the ideological controversies, the social longings of the Russian people found expression in their literature. It would be futile to attempt to separate Russian writers from the spirit of their times and the various trends of national thought. The author consequently felt the urgency to give to the American reader some notions of the political and cultural backgrounds against which the Russian literature evolved during the last century and a half, yet without sacrificing the critical interpretation and aesthetic evaluation of each writer treated. This purpose made it often necessary for the author to function both as historian and critic. It also accounts for the structure of the book, in which chapters on the historical setting, on various trends of thought, and the development of literary schools alternate with chapters devoted to the creative personalities of the most prominent writers, to the uniqueness of their temperaments, their respective approaches to reality, and the means and techniques of their artistic expression.

Since this work is the result of several decades of study and research, the references and bibliography — for the most part in Russian — would in themselves form a small volume, and it has been deemed advisable to omit them from the present edition and to mention instead, in the Notes, only a selection of helpful texts in English.

Sarah Lawrence College   M.S.
Bronxville, New York
Spring 1964

Contents

Contents

THE EPIC OF RUSSIAN LITERATURE

INTRODUCTION: THE BEGINNINGS

THE WESTERN world discovered Russian literature only in the second half of the nineteenth century. That discovery came as a great surprise. Before that time Russia's contribution to the cultural life of mankind had seemed almost nonexistent. Throughout the eighteenth and nineteenth centuries, translations of Russian authors had been rare and casual in Europe and America, arousing as little interest among critics as among the general reading public. The prevailing opinion was that the Empire of the Czars was not blessed by the Muses. There was in the East, an enormous and silent land of luxury, misery, oppression, revolutionary plots, strange customs, few printers, and fewer writers. Then, in the course of a decade, the Western world became acquainted with Turgenev, Tolstoy, and Dostoevsky. Other Russians followed: an awe-impelling procession from Gogol to Chekhov and Gorky.

The suddenness of this unexpected and triumphant revelation produced a series of prejudiced and erroneous opinions concerning Russian letters; some of these opinions are still widely current among our contemporaries. Many Europeans and Americans continue to compare the great Russian novelists and poets to giant trees that have miraculously sprung full grown in a desert. Those who try to understand and to study the golden age of the Russian classics often attribute their originality, the boldness in their approach to life, and the freshness of their style, to a lack of tradition. After the well-kept gardens of European art, Russian literature holds a charm somewhat like that of fields of wild flowers.

Unfortunately this theory, like so many other ideas concerning Russia, is totally unfounded. Russian literature is over a thousand

3

years old. It is true, it did not become international in fame and influence before the nineteenth century, but its maturity had been preceded by a long and painful evolution, and its artistic and ideological originality is the result of a slow, centuries-long process. Special conditions of growth explain the peculiarities or qualities of modern Russian writers; tradition has determined many of the traits that superficial observers ascribe to 'the Slavic soul' or other such trite generalities.

Russian literature has a long and complicated history, and no study of the main trends of the nineteenth and twentieth centuries can be profitable or comprehensive without at least a short survey of the primary currents of the past. Hence this introduction to a book devoted to *modern* Russian writers.

I   It is usually accepted that written literature began in Russia immediately after the introduction of Christianity, in the tenth century, by Prince Vladimir of Kiev. By then Russian, as a spoken language, had already become highly developed and widely accepted, along with other Slavic dialects, among the peoples inhabiting the vast quadrangle bound by the Carpathian Mountains in the west, the Volga River on the east, the Baltic Sea on the north, and the Black Sea on the south. Slavic songs, incantations, folk rhymes, war ballads, and fairy tales had existed in oral tradition since time immemorial. This vast folklore had not grown around strictly local themes and motives. By way of the Scythians and the Greeks, Byzantine influences had reached the primitive inhabitants of the plains in the south—a country which toward the seventh or eighth century had given birth to the State of Kiev (today, the Ukraine). In the southeast and the east the Russians were in permanent contact with the peoples of the Caucasus and the Asiatic tribes, from whom they had borrowed many tales that had originated in Persia, the Middle East, China, and India. And, finally, in the west the European influence, although lacking in strength, was infiltrating through neighboring Galicia, Poland, and Lithuania, while in the north the Scandinavians and the Germans had left their impress, especially in the regions ruled by the Principality of Novgorod, the ancient and powerful state guarding the gateway of the Baltic.

The introduction of the Christian faith under the form of Byzantine Orthodoxy raised the problem of a written language. This concerned not only the State of Kiev, which had been converted by A.D. 988, but also the Western Slavs of Bohemia, Moravia, and Bulgaria, where Greek missionaries had been active since the sixth century. Two of these, Cyril and Methodus, are believed to have laid the foundations of a written Slavonic language in Bulgaria as early as A.D. 863. Its phonetic alphabet, corresponding to the sounds of certain Bulgarian dialects, had been supplied mostly by Greek characters; its grammar was also borrowed mainly from the Greek. This alphabet, called the Cyrillic (slightly differing in appearance from another derived from a simplified Greek cursive) was successively adopted by Russians, Bulgarians, Serbs, and other Slavic tribes. Despite a few modifications and later typographic adaptations, it remains today basically the same as it was a thousand years ago.

The creation of the alphabet had an obviously practical purpose: to provide the Church with a popular medium for the propagation of its doctrine and ritual among the newly converted people and the recently ordained priests, since the services in all countries under the jurisdiction of the Greek Eastern Church of Byzantium were invariably conducted in the native tongues.

In Bulgaria, as far back as the tenth century, especially under Czar Simeon (893-927), the disciples of Methodus had made a number of translations from Greek and Latin into a sort of composite Slavonic. This was the beginning of the Church-Slavonic language, which served as the main literary vehicle in Russia from the eleventh to the eighteenth century. One of the first books designed for the converted Russians was the New Testament, copied from the Bulgarian original for Ostromir, ruler of Novgorod (1056-7).

Christianity had been introduced into Russia from Constantinople. This fact was responsible for the great influence of Byzantium upon Russian culture. The Byzantine Empire considered itself the heir of the Hellenic-Roman civilization, and Byzantine books, as well as scholars, priests, and artists, brought to Russia some of the spirit of the ancient philosophers, historians, and poets. This Hellenic-Roman trend was counterbalanced, however, by the doctrinary intransigency of the Byzantine Church, its exclusiveness, its sectarianism and rigid formalism, combined with its pompous hierarchy. Byzantine theocracy was based on the identification of secular with religious power, a dogma that was transplanted to Russia, where the Church was called upon to assist and to strengthen the State. The struggle between Emperor and Pope, which determined the course of European events in the Middle Ages, was unknown in Russia, at least until the end of the sixteenth century. From its very beginnings the Russian Church worked hand in glove with the Princes, backing their conflicts against external foes and, in general, acting as a strong and faithful ally of autocracy.

No less decisive was the impact of Byzantine influence on the structure of Russian administration, social life, and family organization.

Manners, fashions, speech, arts, and letters imitated the Byzantine pattern.

In the eleventh and twelfth centuries the books, written or translated almost exclusively in the monasteries of Kiev, Suzdal, and Novgorod, were all of a strictly religious character. In the Old and New Testaments, in the Lives of the Saints, or in certain works of the Fathers of the Church, the Russian reader found specimens of various literary forms, which monks and priests tried to imitate: historical narratives, sermons, prophetic revelations, songs and psalms. The influence of Biblical style lasted for many generations and survived in popular literature until our times. The treatises of John of Damascus, sermons of Greek bishops, and prophetic books (the Book of Daniel and, especially, the Apocalypsis) were widely disseminated in Russia; the Lives of the Saints were also very popular. All these books (for the most part the productions of the Bulgarian school of translators) helped to shape the style of Russia's first writers. Some original texts of that period present a peculiar mixture of solemn, heavy, artificial Church-Slavonic with colloquial Russian, the language spoken by the people. As the religious content decreased, the number of 'Russisms' increased, although all theological treatises were still being composed in high-flown and often stilted Church-Slavonic. In all cases the tradition of Greek rhetorics weighed heavily upon the writers, filling the books with Biblical metaphors, flowery turns of phrase, and intricate circumlocutions. A special place in popular reading was occupied by the Apocrypha—legends and myths lacking the official approval of the Church and therefore on the verge of cryphia or hidden literature. Many heretical opinions were promulgated in such apocrypha as *A Tale of Heaven and Hell, The End of the World, The Calvary of the Mother of God,* and a few others, which show similarities with Dante's *Commedia.* Some of these legends clearly indicate their Egyptian origin (identification of the Virgin Mary with the goddess Hera, Mistress of the Sun, or the cult of Osiris as in the *Tale of Vassily Novy*); others can be traced back to Iranian myths and the Arian heresy, their conception of good and evil as two separate principles of the universe. The clergy and the higher circles of Russian society preferred the *Pateriki* (miscellanies of stories from the lives of saints and pious monks) and sermons by great preachers of the period, such as Ilarion, Kiril Turovsky, Feodosy Pechersky,[1] Clement Smoliatich.

The religious character of all these works in Church-Slavonic is best shown by a few statistical data: out of 708 manuscripts of the eleventh to fourteenth centuries, described by Russian scholars at the end of the last century, only 20 were of non-clerical content (including some travel

[1] The first monastic saint canonized by the Russian Church.

books, such as *Daniil's Pilgrimage to the Holy Land* (twelfth century). The Church was the driving force of written literature, and the monasteries with their schools were the main sources of cultural education for the whole land. The language created by the Church was accepted as the only medium of true literary expression, and its use for profane purposes was frowned upon. Thus Church-Slavonic became identified with books of 'high' (moral or religious) subject matter.

But the spoken language of the people, of the peasants, artisans, merchants, townfolk, and military men, existed before the birth of Church-Slavonic, and between the eleventh and thirteenth centuries this colloquial speech was definitely formed and fully developed. Its rich life continued independently of the evolution of Church-Slavonic. The writers of legal acts, of family precepts, or of secular tales were using it widely. Sometimes, when they dealt with such matters as Divine Justice or the exploits of magnificent princes, they would intersperse their vernacular with ornate words borrowed from 'serious' books in Church-Slavonic. An example of such an admixture is to be found in *The Russian Truth* (or *Law*) of Yaroslav the Wise, one of the outstanding Kiev princes of the eleventh century, who tried to sum up in precepts and instructions his own experiences in life and statesmanship.

Like most works of that time, *The Russian Truth*—as well as the *Testament* written for the instruction of his sons by another prince, Vladimir Monomachos (1125), a bluff warrior and a kind, wise man— had a distinct moral significance. The aim of all written literature was strictly instructive. The translations of religious books were made for the purpose of spreading the 'true religion'; friars and priests of the Kiev-Pechersk, the Kiev-Vydubets, or the Novgorod cloisters were transcribing sermons with this same end in view; princes were instructing their heirs and statesmen how to rule the land; heads of families taught the organization of households. This emphasis on religious and moral usefulness became and has remained the basic trait of Russian literature.

Even the most important historical works of Russia's Middle Ages, *The Chronicles,* have a definite didactic flavor. The best known and the most valuable as a historical source is that of Friar Nestor (1120). Friar Nestor, usually called the first Russian chronicler, probably assembled and edited the writings of his predecessors, besides utilizing various Greek materials. Written in lively style, remarkable for its simplicity as well as for the dramatic quality of its exposition, it is not merely a document providing the basic facts for the study of Russian history; its literary value is such that it forms a bridge between purely didactic works and the legends, books of travel, and apocrypha which took the place of fiction in the twelfth and thirteenth centuries.

The double source of literary creativity corresponded to the duality of language: colloquial Russian and Church-Slavonic. Along with the religious, semi-religious, and moral works pervaded by the Christian spirit and expressed primarily in Church-Slavonic or in a curious blend of official and colloquial styles, there was a powerful and deep-rooted strain of folklore. It belonged to the people as the Church-Slavonic literature belonged to the clergy, the princes, the noblemen, and the rich merchants. The pagan tradition had not been entirely broken by the conversion to Christianity: it co-existed with the new religion. Sometimes it adapted itself to the doctrines of the Church; sometimes the Church, trying to absorb and modify the pagan beliefs, included them under various guises in its own ritual. This intermingling of pagan and Christian elements persisted among the Russian masses until recent times. Cyclic feasts linked to the ritual of seasons, of work, of sex, together with dances, songs, and games, found a place on the Church calendar. Many pagan ceremonies, including those pertaining to birth, marriage, and burial, became blended with Greek Orthodox rites. Belief in ghosts and familiar spirits was interwoven into the cult of saints; Russian stories of the life and deeds of the most popular saints, such as St. Nicholas and St. George, present a patchwork of religious tradition and folk tales.

This interpenetration of Christian and pagan elements added a special poetic quality to the religious practices of the Russian people: their faith was, and still is, devoid of gloomy asceticism; it preserved the naive traits of spontaneity and a strong attachment to nature. The writers of the nineteenth and twentieth centuries were delighted to find strong traces of animism and magic even in contemporary popular tales and customs. Russia is one of the few European countries where this treasury of ancient times remained almost intact even after the era of industrial revolution. This phenomenon is extensively reflected in the novels and short stories of Russian classics (Turgenev's 'Bezhin Meadow,' in his *Hunting Sketches,* is but one example of many).

The poetic imagination of the Russians manifested itself in fairy tales, legends, songs, riddles, proverbs—even spells. The most striking of all this oral poetry are, no doubt, the folk chants or lays, the *byliny*— epic songs of the Men of Might. The term *byliny* (tales-of-things-that-have-been) was introduced in 1830 by the Russian scholar Sakharov: it covers any kind of folk ballad. Most of them were probably created about the eighth to tenth centuries, when the Russians of the south and of the north were passing from tribal to feudal conditions, and when the states of Kiev and Novgorod were emerging as the main centripetal forces of the country. Originating in several regions (they can be classified according to geographical principles) the *byliny* followed at first the tradition of war songs, passed on to the people by the Court minstrels. In many instances these chants reflected the popular evaluation of current events and various aspects of national life, such as the reign of Vladimir of Kiev, the initiator of Christianity; the struggle against the Asiatic raiders, the Polovetz, and the Pechenegs; Novgorod's trading with the West, and so on. But gradually historical reality was obscured, sublimated by generations of popular bards, singing these ballads during village feasts, fairs, and weddings. Regional songs, mythological reminiscences, symbolic images, political allusions, and even literary influences—both native and foreign—overcrowded the *byliny*.

The chief hero of these songs is Ilya of Murom, the grandiose symbol of Russia's might and of the undying forces of its people, the champion of the war against the Asiatic invaders, the defender of his land, of religion, and of the common man. The symbolic significance of Ilya of Murom is clearly indicated in the ballad telling about the supernatural origin of his strength:

He sat, never stirring, for three-and-thirty years; they of the begging brotherhood came unto him, Jesus the Christ himself, and His Apostles two.
'Go, thou, Ilya, and fetch us somewhat to drink'
'Begging brethren, I can stir neither hand nor foot'
'Get thee up, Ilya, do not us deceive.'
Ilya heaved and rose, all unkempt and dazed; he brought back a bowl bigger than a pail—to the begging brethren he did offer it; but the begging men made him drink himself, and when he had drunk they did question him:
'Dost thou feel, Ilya, much of strength in thee?'
'If there were a pillar reared to the very sky, if a ring of gold were to that pillar fixed, I would seize that ring, all Holy Russia heave.' [2]

Almost as popular as Ilya are Dobryna (Good Fellow) Nikitich, the brave and adventurous, and Mikula Selianinovich, the peasant, who personified the Russian soil and had all the virtues (and defects) of a tiller of the soil. The heroes of the Kiev Cycle are centered around Prince Vladimir and his comrades-in-arms—not unlike the Arthurian Cycles. The Northern Cycle portrays the Novgorod Men of Might: the irresponsible and gay Vassily Buslaev, or Sadko, the shrewd trader, and others.

The musical rhythm of the *byliny,* the richness of their rhymes and alliterations, the freshness of their metaphors, the majestic pace of their

[2] B. G. Guerney, *A Treasury of Russian Literature,* copyright 1943 by Vanguard Press, N. Y.

descriptions, and the breadth of their style rank them with the world's greatest epic poetry. Many poets and novelists of modern times have looked for inspiration to these ancient chants, which reflect the true mentality of the Russians more than any other literary document of the Middle Ages. Modernized transcripts of these ballads were found in the seventeenth and eighteenth centuries, but a number of them were collected quite recently in certain remote villages of northern and eastern Russia, where they were still being narrated in an amazingly well-preserved form by old men or women. *Skaziteli,* or reciters, still declaim these tales of the times of old, and the folk epos is by no means extinct in the Russian countryside. The ballads, songs, and tales expressed the feelings and dreams of the people in a poetic style of their own, in a free language that evolved independently from Church-Slavonic.

These two tendencies—the popular, stemming for the most part from folklore and vernacular Russian, and the religious, based on Byzantine-Bulgarian books, with Church-Slavonic as its medium of expression—remained apart until the eighteenth century, when all literary discussions hinged on the problem of their unification.

The most important example of medieval written literature in Russia, belonging exclusively to neither tradition, yet revealing the highest degree of poetic fulfilment, is *The Lay of the Host of Igor,* composed probably by the end of the twelfth or the beginning of the thirteenth century. The *Lay* was discovered in 1795 in a sixteenth-century manuscript, and was translated into modern Russian in 1800. The original manuscript was destroyed in 1812 during the burning of Moscow, a misfortune that only intensified the scholarly battle about the sources and authenticity of the poem. This magnificent epic relates the grievous defeat of Igor, Prince of Novgorod Seversk, who was captured during his campaign against the Polovetz invaders. The plaint of Yaroslavna, Igor's wife, filled with vivid imagery, is one of the best pieces of Russian lyrical poetry before the nineteenth century: its opening lines are familiar to every educated Russian:

> 'Tis not spears
> Humming through the air over the Danube;
> 'Tis the voice of Yaroslavna,
> Igor's wife, I hear;
> Like a linnet unseen, at early morn
> She sends forth her call:
> 'I shall fly like the linnet,'
> She utters,
> 'Over the Danube,
> That I knew as a maid;

> I shall dip my sleeve,
> Trimmed with beaver pelt,
> In the Kayala;
> I shall cleanse the wounds and blood
> On the stiffened body
> Of my prince. . .[3]

The artistic value of the *Lay,* its sensitivity to nature, to human emotions, and to historic events, its deep national awareness, its appeal for unity in the face of common danger, as well as its harmonious form and the cumulative effect of its rhythmic lines, place it above any other literary work of that period and among the greatest Russian poems. It testifies that in the thirteenth century, at a time when towns like Kiev, Rostov, Suzdal, Novgorod, Pskov, and others had set high standards in architecture, painting, and statesmanship, Russian poetry had also attained stature. Further development of that poetry was unfortunately handicapped by the collapse of the Kievan States and finally arrested by the Mongolian invasion, which enslaved the country for more than two hundred years.

II   Kiev had already declined by the twelfth century, and cultural interests shifted to southwestern Russia, to the principalities of Galicia and Volynia, with their interesting historical chronicles, their western way of life, and progressive political thinking, and to northern Russia where Alexander Nevsky (1120-63), prince and saint, had repelled the Livonian and Teutonic knights. His deeds were celebrated in a cycle of ballads comparing him to the heroes of Rome and Athens. Some literary activity was also preserved in northeastern regions: Serapion of Vladimir (d.1275) gives in his sermons a striking picture of Russia's political plight and describes her mores under the Mongolian yoke; Daniil the Incarcerated, or the Immured (probably about the first quarter of the thirteenth century), in a supplication to his prince, blends realistic observation with scholarly quotations.

By 1240 Russia had been definitely conquered by the Tartars. The Mongolians of the Golden Horde found the country they had subdued divided into many small principalities with a social structure similar to that of European feudalism. Rivalry of rulers, strife, intrigues, conflicts, and assassinations prevented any serious opposition to the invaders. After Byzantium, the Tartar invasion was the second great shaper of Russian history. Its influence manifested itself in many ways and left

[3] B. G. Gurney, *A Treasury of Russian Literature,* copyright 1943 by Vanguard Press, N. Y.

innumerable imprints on Russian customs, social and political organization, language, and mentality. But it did not help cultural life in general,
or literature in particular: the sufferings and material damages caused
by the Tartar domination had a disastrous effect on Russian literature.
It was almost completely cut off from Western influence, while in the
south the Byzantine Empire had undergone a process of disintegration.
Although there is a school of modern historians that questions whether
the Mongolian intervention in Russia had such negative results, there is
no doubt that the Tartar yoke, which deprived Russia of its independence and thwarted its normal growth, retarded the development of
the country and was responsible for its cultural backwardness.

Some signs of literary awakening in Russia coincide with another
main event of that period—the rise of Moscow. The process of unification was concurrent with the enslavement of the country. Economic
relations between various parts of Russia were constantly growing, and
in the fourteenth century two cities, Tver and Moscow, asserted themselves as new and rival political centers. Both principalities, less de-
vastated than the south of Russia and the regions along the main paths
of Mongolian invasion, had strategic sites at the intersection of land
and river routes. Moscow succeeded in becoming the seat of the Greek
Orthodox Russian Metropolitan and was characterized by its diplomacy,
ruthlessness, and stubbornness. Gradually it rose to first place, and
under Ivan Kalita (Money-Bag), Grand Prince (or Duke) of Moscovy
(1325-41), the Muscovite expansion became a factor of national importance, despite the continuation of struggle among rival princes who
were more or less assisted by the Khans of the Golden Horde. The
feudal parceling of northern Russia was halted and later abolished.
Moscow rallied around her princes the best religious, political, and
cultural forces of the period. Literary productivity of any importance
in the fourteenth and fifteenth centuries (mostly chronicles, tales, and
lives of the saints) shifted to Moscow from Tver and Novgorod (where
some interesting works had appeared). New translations were made in
this capital (including the semi-fantastic *Tale of an Indian Kingdom*
and *The Twelve Dreams of Cha-Hai-Ishi,* told in the form of questions
and answers—both of Far Eastern origin). Asiatic, and especially
Turko-Mongolian influences, are in general more and more evident in
Russian manuscripts.

The period of unification (1380-1480) began with the victory over
the Tartars on the field of Kulikovo, won by a coalition of princes under
the leadership of Dimitri, ruler of Moscow. This battle did not liberate
Russia from the Mongolian yoke, but it did hearten the people and raise
their hopes. Many manuscripts of that period, dealing with the life of

Dimitri or the lives of monks and Church dignitaries, mention this battle and evince a growing national feeling. In the epic poem *Beyond the River Don,* created by Cossack warriors in the fifteenth century and often favorably compared with *The Lay of Igor,* the hope of national unity and independence under the leadership of Moscow is expressed with great poetic force. Another striking work is the *Journey Beyond Three Seas* by Athanasy Nikitin (d.1472), a merchant of Tver who wrote his impressions of India and other far lands in a vivid, spontaneous style.

In 1480 the Tartar domination was definitely overthrown and, although wars against the Mongols continued for many decades, a united national State was established with Moscow as its capital. The rulers of Moscow called themselves Czars and after the fall of Constantinople assumed the prerogatives of the Byzantine Emperors with whom Ivan III (1440-1505) had become related by marrying a Greek princess. Moscow still carried on a struggle against rebel provinces or free cities, such as Novgorod and Pskov, where the spirit of local independence favored political and religious heresies, which are reflected in Novgorod chronicles, apocrypha, and tales. The rise of Moscow gave a new impetus to the arts; the ties with the West were resumed. Foreigners helped the Russians to build their churches and palaces. The Kremlin with its walls and towers was built by Italian architects, and the Palace of the Czars resembles the Castle of Milan. The rulers of Moscow lived in magnificence, the ceremonial of the Russian court carried on the traditions of Byzantine pomp and luxury. The fifteenth century also saw the blossoming of the Russian school of painting (with the masterpieces of Rublev), which blends the pictorial trends of the iconography of Novgorod and Rostov-Suzdal with the first influence of the Italian Renaissance. Moscow art spread all over central and northern Russia and formed the style that was to prevail for centuries in architecture, religious painting, and ornamentation.

A new era began for literature as well. Scattered productions (translations, popular tales and songs, chronicles) proclaimed the rising tide of cultural life and steadily increased in number. There was also an increase in works in Church-Slavonic. The unification of the country and the consolidation of the autocratic central power was backed by the Church, but new conditions raised new problems. Would the triumphant State allow the possession of vast territories, and even towns, by convents, monasteries, and Church institutions? This practical question was extensively debated by two distinguished writers: Joseph Volozky (1439-1515), well known for his eloquent sermons against the Novgorod heretics, defended the right of the Church to own secular property; while the ascetic and mystical Nil Sorsky (1433-1508) dreamt of the primitive poverty of the early days of Christianity.

But whatever the discussions on practical matters, the Church supplied the State with an orthodox philosophy and offered to the Czars a doctrine for the justification of their deeds. This doctrine was fully formulated by the Abbot Philothei, whose *Letter to the Czar* (1510-11) is one of the most curious and significant documents of the time. Philothei had his own deterministic theory of history, according to which only three great empires had been planned by the Almighty. Two of them, Rome and Byzantium, had already collapsed. Now the time had come for the Third Rome: Russia, the land of promise, the guardian of true religion, had been chosen by Providence to be the last Universal Empire, by whose means history and mankind would be guided to the apocalyptic days of the Last Judgment. 'Moscow is the Third Rome, and there will be no Fourth'—this conclusion definitely sanctioned Moscow's expansion, her complex of superiority, and her scornful attitude toward the Western heretics, both Catholic and Protestant. This theory, taken by Philothei in part from various sources, became very popular in Moscow in the sixteenth and seventeenth centuries. Under Ivan the Terrible (or more correctly Ioann the Awesome) (1533-84), the Russian national State became a multi-national empire, expanding in all directions and incorporating the territories of old rivals, such as Novgorod and Pskov, of Russia's recent masters, such as the Tartars of Kazan and Astrakhan, and of the remote, newly conquered regions of the Urals and Siberia. Ivan pushed on toward the Baltic, waged interminable wars against the Poles and Lithuanians, and consolidated the southern borders of his land in the direction of the Caspian and Azov seas. He also fought the descendants of those feudal princes who wanted to limit the privileges of autocracy. Shrewdly and ruthlessly he accomplished the unification of the country under the absolute rule of a sovereign who was responsible only to the King of Heaven.

The formation of a centralized and autocratic empire, the liquidation of the feudal opposition, and the oppressive status of the serfs and the lower strata of society created a new cultural and literary climate. It coincided with another great event—the beginning of printing. Through the zeal of Ivan Fedorov, the 'Father of Russian Printing,' who was later forced to leave Moscow, the first printed book, *The Apostle,* came off the press in 1564. The new craft did not put an immediate stop to the transcription of manuscripts, but it did create new readers and new writers; and gradually it supplanted the slow toil of monkish and other copyists.

The desire for codification and the establishment of definitive forms of life and thought determined most of the literary productivity under Ivan the Terrible. The Russian Metropolitan Makary edited a revised text of the *Lives of the Saints,* the *Chetii Minei,* which remained one of the favorite books of the Russian folk for ten generations. The Congress of high Church dignitaries compiled a book of resolutions, *The Hundred Chapters,* which gives an exhaustive picture of clerical life. *Domostroy (On the Ordering of a Household)* was in the nineteenth century always cited as an example of Russian obscurantism, and even barbarism, which is not quite correct; rather it is both a book of morality and an anthology of the household arts; it contains the norms of social, domestic, and economic life, as conceived by a representative of the Russian *petite bourgeoisie;* it also advises its readers on the relations of the sexes and points out the way to improving the family atmosphere through 'moderate wife-beating!'

Historical and political pamphlets carrying on the Church tradition of social service have a place of their own. They throw a singular light on the ideas and the way of life in the sixteenth century. The Awesome Czar proved to be a keen polemicist and a gifted writer in his correspondence with Prince Kurbsky, his former friend, who had fled from Moscow and become an exile and an ally of Russia's enemies, the Poles. These letters (1563-4 and 1577-9) are filled with vehemence, passion, recriminations, and violent accusations; yet despite their highly personal character they constitute a defense of two political ideals. While Kurbsky accuses the dread Czar of cruelty, breaking his word, and despotism, which in his opinion are but the natural result of persecuting the boyars, Ivan tries to justify all his hateful measures by protesting the interests of the country and the supreme rights of an autocrat.

Two other writers had dealt in different ways with the same problems: Ivan Peresvetov, who came to Russia from Lithuania around 1538 and who summed up the experience of his European travels and missions in a semi-poetic, semi-didactic form; and Maxim the Greek (1480-1556), an eloquent defender of Christian ideology against foreign heretical deviations, who at the same time took a strong stand, in his various pamphlets, in favor of autocratic secular power and displayed a genuine literary gift.

III   The strenuous efforts of unification and expansion toward the end of the sixteenth century had exhausted the forces of the Russians, while internal strife between the Czar and the boyars, the economic misery of the masses, and their political oppression had created conditions favorable to uprisings, intrigues, and social upheavals. Such conditions prevailed for a quarter

of a century after Ivan's death: Russia was in the throes of civil war
and various pretenders exploited the credulity and the discontent of the
peasants, while the Western foes of Moscow, such as Poland and
Sweden, predicted her immediate collapse and invaded the country.
This perilous period lasted until the beginning of the seventeenth century. Owing to the patriotic efforts of a few men from different social
groups and to the resolute action of the people, the invaders were driven
out and some degree of order was finally established. In 1613 a body of
delegates from all parts of the country elected a new Czar, Mikhail, the
first of the Romanov dynasty.

While Mikhail was attempting the task of reconstruction, cultural
activity, badly shaken by three troublous decades, sought to reassert
itself in a contradictory and complex situation. The Church, at least
formally, was still maintaining its intellectual and artistic dictatorship,
but its position was in jeopardy. Its part in the creation of the Muscovite
state was completed, and when the Patriarch Nikon attempted to put
the authority of the Church above the power of the Czar he was defeated
by the latter. His failure marks the beginning of the decline of the
Church in Russia. Furthermore, it had been shattered from within by
the Great Schism. The reforms of the ritual undertaken under Mikhail
and the revision of liturgical books, into which many errors had crept
through the ignorance of copyists and translators, had provoked con-
tumacious opposition by part of the lower clergy and great numbers
of the laity. The partisans of the old ritual would have nothing to do
with any reforms. They stubbornly clung to the old books and the
ancient rites, refusing to make the sign of the cross with three fingers
(after the Greek usage) instead of the usual two, rejecting the new
icons painted according to the Greek pattern, and defending the faith
of their forefathers. These Old Ritualists (or Old Believers or Schismatics) were cruelly persecuted by both the ecclesiastic and the secular
authorities. In order to escape imprisonment and torture many of them
migrated to the Far North, to Siberia, to the Caucasus, or even to
foreign lands. Subsequently they were broken down further into numerous sects. Despite the persecutions, however, they succeeded in preserving their own ways of life, and their communities, sometimes hidden in
the forest wildernesses of the Urals and Siberia, have preserved down to
our times strange survivals of the seventeenth century, with the language,
the customs, the mentality, and even the physical appearance of the
Sectarians of three hundred years ago. (Many modern writers, such as
Melnikov (Pechersky), Leskov, and Gorky, attracted by the originality
and integrity of these Old Believers, have studied and described their
lives in novels and short stories.)

The Great Schism found its most vivid literary reflection in an extraordinary work, *The Life of Arch-Presbyter Avvacum*. Avvacum (or Habakkuk, 1620-82) was a violent opponent of the ecclesiastic reforms and attacked them publicly in Moscow. Exiled to Eastern Siberia, he suffered greatly from the injustice and persecutions of local authorities. Upon his return to Moscow he resumed his struggle, was again exiled, and was immured in an underground cell for fourteen years. But no torture could change this fiery priest who continued exposing the prelates and their corruption, criticizing the abuses of the administration, and fighting for the old faith. He was finally burned at the stake in 1682 together with three other Schismatics.

Avvacum was a prolific writer, but his autobiography is by far the most important of his works. It would be difficult to put a label on this highly original, pathetic, racy, and witty book. It is a narrative of facts and events, a gallery of character sketches, a study in religious polemics, the credo of an Old Believer, and the work of a natural raconteur who loved the simple expressive language of the people and was able to use it effectively. Avvacum describes with coarse realism and a great sense of humor how he expelled from a village certain mountebanks and their trained bears, or how he denied a blessing to the son of Cheremetev, a boyar who had shaved off his beard; or he writes with poetic tenderness of his wife, who shared all the sufferings of her intransigent husband; or after a series of salty remarks, jests, and biting characterizations, he suddenly attacks the patriarch with fury, inventing abusive terms, quoting the prophets of the Bible, and reverting to the oratorical devices of the Church-Slavonic tradition. Idealism and realism, passion and slyness, fanaticism and triviality are combined in a most surprising manner in this book, which breathes the indomitable spirit of its author.

The spirit of this autobiography was transmitted to several minor writers. Popular anonymous literature followed in the wake of Avvacum's works, especially by the Old Ritualists, as in 'The Tale of Kitezh,' which later supplied the libretto for an opera by Rimsky-Korsakov, or in 'On Potatoes and Tobacco,' a pamphlet assailing two of the many things the Schismatics detested and spurned. Nothing, however, approaches the variety, profundity, and richness of the *Life*. It has a distinguished place in the evolution of Russian letters, in so far as it is written in the living, spoken language and shows all its flexibility, resources, and literary qualities—a striking contrast to the Church-Slavonic literature.

The latter, although on the decline, was still considered the only real literature and had a wide audience. In the seventeenth and eighteenth centuries the presses were busy publishing old books. The Byzantine *Prologue,* a religious text, had 20 reprints, the *Sermons of John of Damascus,* 40, and the *Chetii Minei,* 70. The Old Believers clung to their fifteenth- and sixteenth-century manuscripts. All this theological literature had, of course, undergone many changes, particularly under the influence of the southern school of learning, established in Kiev in the Ukraine. In 1631, the Metropolitan Peter Moguila had founded there an academy for the purpose of training Othodox priests and laymen to lead the struggle against Roman Catholicism. Special attention was given in the curriculum to the refutation of the arguments of Rome, to rhetoric, and to the composition of sermons and speeches. In 1701 it took the name of the Kiev Academy, when a Slavonic Greek-Latin Academy was founded in Moscow.

Through Poland Western culture, especially Latin literature and Roman-Catholic theology, had a strong influence in the Ukraine. Many Ukrainians brought new ideas and literary forms to Moscow. Their most noteworthy representative was Simeon Polozky (1629-80), a Byelorussian, who lived as monk and teacher in the town of Polozk (hence his surname). In 1667 he moved to Moscow and was appointed tutor to the children of the Czar Alexis the Most Pacific, whose reign, nevertheless, was among the most turbulent. Simeon, a man of great erudition and well-read in Latin classics, wrote poetry for various Court occasions (collected in two anthologies in 1678) as well as comedies and dramas. The most important contribution he and his disciples made to Russian literature was the introduction of the syllabic system of versification. Polozky's solemn and lyrical poetry was usually concerned with current events. Half secular, half religious, it clung to the Church-Slavonic tradition as far as the choice of words and turns of speech were concerned, and was slow in pace and pompous in style. These lines found few readers; their circulation was limited to the Court circles, to groups of literati, and certain learned clerics, but they did distinctly mark a stage in the history of Russian poetry and created a medium that was to be perfected within the next hundred years.

Under Mikhail (1613-45) and, particularly, under Alexis (1645-76), the ties between Russia and Europe were strengthened, and the number of translations and adaptations from foreign languages increased. Most of them lacked any religious intent but simply sought to satisfy the general reader's desire for entertainment—in tales of chivalry, which were circulated widely, for example. Some of the heroes, such as Prince Bova, or Franzel the Venetian with his beloved Persiana, had quite startling careers: they enjoyed wide popularity among peasants and burghers until the end of the nineteenth century (see Gorky's *Child-*

hood). Despite the scorn of critics and serious writers, these cheap books prepared the ground for the 'precious' French romance and the sentimental German novel of the succeeding era. They teemed with adventures, involved situations, deeds of bravery and cunning, and occasionally with amorous exploits (*The Tale of Peter of the Golden Keys*), and, on the whole, appealed to the imagination. These profane tales were innocent of the Byzantine spirit or of any Church-Slavonic style. Without attaining the color or force of Avvacum's prose they were, nevertheless, written in a similarly plain, even coarse, vernacular. Side by side with these were translations of stories about unfaithful wives and credulous husbands, jest books, collections of quibbles and riddles, and so forth, generally deriving from the Renaissance fabliaux and facetiae.

The folklore tradition likewise flourished and preserved the songs and tales of the Middle Ages (or even earlier) of Russian history. Current events gave rise to new ballads and stories; the Cossacks in the south, for instance, produced narratives of the capture of Azov and of the conquest of Siberia. Extremely popular were *Frol Skobeyev* and *Savva Grudcyn,* two seventeenth century novels, and *Eruslan* (borrowed from the Iranian epic *Shah-nameh* whose hero, Rustam, became Arslan the Lion in Turkish and Eruslan in Russian), a Russified version of Eastern legends and adventures. All these stories as well as the *Tale of Yuliania* portraying a faithful wife and tender mother, found thousands of readers and were reprinted in pulp editions for over two centuries.

As before, however, the folklore tradition had practically no connection with polite letters, and the educated class either ignored it or regarded it as of no value in the development of literature.

The new phenomena—syllabic poetry, romances of chivalry, popular tales, and the appearance of such a work as Avvacum's autobiography in colloquial Russian—are the slight and scattered signs of a movement to reform Russian literature. Its development would have taken many decades had not Peter the Great intervened with his revolutionary methods, forcing Russian writers to adopt a new and firm attitude.

IV   The enormous impact of Peter's reforms resulted from the accelerated Westernization of Russia and the secularization of the State and society. The growth of Western influence, which had become perceptible under Peter's father, Alexis, was, historically speaking, an inevitable process of evolution. But Peter detested slow and organic changes. He tried to whip up the steady pace of time into a frantic gallop. Breaking with traditions that were centuries old, he accelerated the transformation of his country by revolutionary methods. Nothing could stop him: he crushed the opposition of the Church dignitaries, drowned in blood the resistance of the old aristocracy and their military hirelings, put to death Alexis, his own son, who had conspired with the enemies of reform, persecuted the Old Believers, who saw him as the Anti-Christ, sacrificed the common man, enslaved and mercilessly taxed the peasants, and waged wars and built cities at the cost of thousands of human lives. To carry out his designs he acted as a tyrant and resorted to violence and force. But his aims were lofty and his despotism was never selfish. This great Czar worked and sweated harder than any of his downtrodden subjects. A man of broad vision, remarkable statesmanship, and vast knowledge, he devoted all his energies to what in his opinion was the welfare of his country. He himself declared during the war against the Swedes that he never cared for anything but the greatness of Russia.

The old Muscovite State with its sluggish manners and solemn traditions had suddenly been shaken and awakened to a new life. Peter threw it into the current of Western civilization and ruthlessly taught it to swim. The iron grip of the Czar was bruising and wounding, but Russia was compelled to obey his commands and to follow where he led.

It is well known that Peter's reforms included every aspect of Russian civilization. He not only organized an army and a navy to conquer the shores of the Baltic and to 'break a window through into Europe,' but also took a hand in changing the fashions in women's dress and arranging programs of social entertainment. He was absorbed in the conduct of military campaigns and in international alliances, yet found time to introduce such innovations as watches and to keep an eye on the furnishing of the houses of the nobility. He was not only the publisher but the editor of and a contributor to the first Russian newspaper. Fully aware of the necessity of a real cultural revolution, he realized that it could not be brought about merely by sending young noblemen abroad, as he so freely did; he had to create an enlightened society permeated with Western ideas and capable of supporting and continuing his reforms. That could be achieved only by education, and to this Peter, with his usual boldness, turned his attention.

His reign marks the end of the Church's mortmain over learning and literature. Not only was the State secularized and the Church assigned a part subservient to it (something the Russian Orthodox thinkers never forgave), but science and the arts were abruptly freed from religious domination. The schools and presses were no longer in the hands of the clergy. A reform of great symbolic and practical implications opened a new era: the alphabet was simplified and, while religious texts were still printed in Church-Slavonic, all other books were (from 1708 on) issued in the new faces. This meant that the new alphabet was intended for science, literature, art, and State documents, regardless of ancient tradition. Peter made a list of the translations to be undertaken: it included European philosophers, scientists, and statesmen, but barred the theologians. Of course all of Peter's educational activity bore a distinctly functional character: books were for him a means of transforming life; they had to instruct, to be useful. However, the impact of all these reforms went beyond the strictly utilitarian aim of the reformer. Together with textbooks on mathematics or ship building, works of fiction were translated or read in the original by those who obeyed the Czar's ukase to study foreign languages. For the first time in centuries the ties between Russian and European literatures became organic and firm. Russian writers made a conscious effort to raise their work to the level of French or German poetry and prose—English influence was at that period less pronounced. The Russian historian Kliuchevsky remarked that Russia had started by borrowing the techniques of the West, but had ended by transplanting its cultural values. The Russians 'started with foreign soldiers and German cannon and ended with the German ballet and Latin grammar.' Dutch sea captains, French military engineers, and German artillerists, all greatly favored by Peter, were followed by Leibniz, Diderot, and Lessing.

This process of rapid Westernization created, however, a dangerous and paradoxical state of affairs. The Czar's program contained many contradictions and its consequences were no less conflicting. Peter was directing Russia toward progress and enlightenment, yet he was accomplishing these aims through despotic and almost barbaric means. With the creation of a modern state as his goal, he was nevertheless maintaining serfdom, exploiting the peasants, and deepening the gulf between the upper and lower classes. In need of men who could carry on his work, he strove to form an educated class from which he could draft public servants. He succeeded in forcefully amalgamating this new bureaucracy and nobility. In obedience to his orders they shaved off their beards, that symbol of the good old days, took to wearing jackets of a German cut instead of Muscovite kaftans, imitated French *politesse,* and followed European patterns in speech and thought. But this new ruling class of Westernized Russians found themselves more and more isolated from the large masses of the people. Before Peter the Great the landowners had differed from their peasants in wealth and their way of life, but the social and economic inequality had seldom been aggravated by a cultural difference. Master and serf had spoken the same language, observed the same religious rites, read (or listened to the reading of) the same books, shared the same superstitions, wore clothes and beards of the same cut. With Peter this situation changed entirely, and the conservatives accused the Czar of having sacrificed the organic unity of national life.

The evolution of the customs and mentality of the upper classes was very rapid. By the middle of the nineteenth century they dressed, talked, and behaved very much like Frenchmen or Germans, despite all their national characteristics. Their homes, their furniture, their entertainments (such as the theater and the ballet), their luxuries, their education and books, all bore the impress of the West. On the other hand, the Europeanization of the great masses was a slow and painful process, handicapped by serfdom, economic inequality, and political backwardness. The gulf between the common man and the educated elements, the latter issuing almost exclusively from the nobility, was not only social but cultural as well. The peasant, the artisan, and the small merchant preserved the purity of the spoken language and the traditions of their folklore. The upper classes, whose language had undergone many changes through the influence of foreign tongues, spoke and wrote in such a manner that their conversation and books seemed strange and far too highfalutin to the average Russian. These two influences—the Western current and the popular tradition—struggle or intermingle in the Russian literature of the eighteenth and nineteenth centuries. In *War and Peace* Tolstoy gives a startling example of the two systems of language (and thought): the Frenchified drawl of the upper nobility and the plain, straightforward talk of the peasants.

It took almost a century after Peter the Great for writers to rise above the limitations of a purely Western aristocratic culture and look for inspiration in the sources of popular tradition. Before Peter Church-Slavonic and popular tradition had been developing on separate and parallel lines; in the same way after Peter, the cultural life of the upper classes and that of the people formed two independent currents, which occasionally met but did not merge completely until the Revolution of 1917.

During the reign of Peter the Great (1682-1725) only a few writers reflected the spirit of the new times. One of them was a churchman, Theophan Prokopovich (1681-1736), who had been trained at the same school as Simeon Polozky. He received his education in Rome, was well acquainted with the ideas of the Renaissance and the Reformation, and gave his wholehearted support to Peter. Preacher, poet, and publicist, Prokopovich exalted Peter's activities in speech and verse. His poetry is the first attempt at a literary interpretation of Peter's reign. Although conceived in the artificial style of Church-Slavonic and adapted to the demands of syllabic verse, it nevertheless contains some elements of the vernacular.

While Prokopovich was fighting the 'high aristocracy among the clergy and throughout the land,' his main literary opponent, Stephen Yavorsky, was defending the integrity of Greek Orthodoxy and of the ancient traditions. His writings are an amazing mixture of Byzantine pomposity and Latin rhetoric.

Two other writers stand out among the literary supporters of the reforms: Posochkov and Tatishchev. Ivan Posochkov (1670-1726), a self-made man of peasant origin, was an economist, and publicist. He dealt with many social problems and gave a most valuable picture of Russia's everyday life in his simply written work on *Poverty and Wealth*. Arrested and thrown into the fortress of SS. Peter and Paul, he died in prison. His complete works were not published until 1892. Vassily Tatishchev, an aristocrat and a high Imperial official, was a man of vast knowledge and excellent classical education, who wrote four volumes of *Russian History*, the first Russian work in this field executed according to a scientific method and comparable to the best European histories of the time.

While the secularization of literature remained one of the main accomplishments of Peter's reign, the full effect of his reforms on the cultural life of the country became apparent only under his successors. After his death in 1725, Russia was governed by a succession of rulers, mostly women (five empresses and three emperors in three decades), whose lovers and mistresses assumed leading positions. The old feudal aristocracy challenged the work of the Great Czar; military plots, foreign intrigues, and wars endangered the Empire; cabals, rivalries of ministers, and the clash between the old and the new nobilities, interspersed with assassinations, threatened the throne and created a feeling of instability among the upper classes. But despite this unscrupulous struggle for power and a certain stigma of decadence, the fundamental ideas of Peter's policy still dominated the whole period. Absolutism as the leading force of the State was preserved against any attempts at domination displayed by the old aristocracy or the Church. The State compelled the nobility to serve in the Army and to fill public offices; the Westernization of society continued at an undiminished pace; the splendor of the Russian Court, replacing the austerity of Peter, now equaled that of Versailles and St. James's, and the arts flourished in the northern capital; successful military expeditions and diplomatic activity expanded the borders and made Russia a powerful factor in European politics. At the same time European culture had spread extensively among the upper

classes, and a score of Russian noblemen of that period seem to have
reached a high degree of intellectual and artistic refinement.

One of these was Prince Antioch Kantemir (1708-44), poet and
diplomat, who acted as Russian ambassador to France and England
when these great powers, frightened by the sudden growth of Peter's
Empire, plotted to oust their dangerous rival from the European scene.
Widely read in Greek and Latin authors and a great admirer of Italian
art and poetry (especially Tasso), Kantemir belonged to the Neo-
Classical school and believed that the ode and satire were the highest
achievements of literary form. His writings have a strong personal
touch—which was a novelty—and an easy style full of colloquialisms
and realistic details. Although strongly influenced by Horace, La
Bruyère, and Boileau, Kantemir portrayed Russian life; his caustic
humor, philosophy, and images are distinctly national. A hundred years
later the great Russian critic Belinsky was correct in saying that Kantemir was the founder of the new Russian literature, inasmuch as he was
the first to 'blend life and poetry in his works.' The *Satires* were
originally published (1750) in London and in a French translation.
The first Russian edition was printed in 1762, but they were well known
before that time, and had circulated in manuscript copies. Kantemir,
like most of his contemporaries, wrote in the syllabic verse introduced
in Russia by scholars who had formed their poetic theory from Latin,
French, and Polish models. This system, however, based on a definite
number of syllables in each line and on fixed accents (in French on the
ultimate, and in Polish on the penultimate syllable) was not the most
appropriate medium for poetic expression in the Russian language,
which belongs to the group of accent tongues. Russian folklore did not
use the syllabic system but resorted to the rhythm of tonic prosody.
Russian poets soon discovered that the syllabic system was artificial and
that the tonic verse, based on accent and allowing great freedom in the
number and the order of unaccentuated syllables (as it does in German
or English), was in greater keeping with the character and the traditions
of the Russian language.

The first to realize this and to introduce tonic verse in his poems
was Vassily Trediakovsky (1703-69), translator, philologist, and poet.
His *Solemn Ode on the Occasion of the Surrender of the Town of
Gdansk* (1735), inaugurated 'a high poetical style in keeping with the
noble, delicate and lofty subject.'

However right Trediakovsky's ideas may have been they were expressed in a heavy and clumsy fashion. Today it is impossible not to
acknowledge his valuable and beneficial influence on Russian poetry,
but his contemporaries made a laughingstock of this man of humble

origin, who disgusted the snobs with his shabby clothes, rough manners, and barbarous verse. They treated him meanly, occasionally cruelly, and let him starve. He died in misery after a series of failures and humiliations. But the poetic reform he initiated was carried out by another plebeian who succeeded in becoming one of the most famous Russian writers of the eighteenth century.

Mikhail Lomonossov (1711-65), born in a northern village near the city of Arkhangelsk, had to hide his peasant origin in order to register at the Slavonic Greek-Latin Academy in Moscow. He studied there for five years, struggling with poverty and often living on nothing but weak tea and black bread. His brilliance in his studies won him a scholarship in Germany, where he spent another five years of intense activity. Upon his return to St. Petersburg in 1741 he already had the reputation in European universities of being an outstanding scholar. Physicist, mathematician, chemist, and geographer, he displayed the quality of his analytical mind in various treatises. But he did not limit himself to scientific research. His chief aim was to promote education in Russia, and for a quarter of a century he took the lead in every field of knowledge and arts. He infused new spirit into the Russian Academy—a newly established institution for the promotion of science. He founded schools, built laboratories and plants, and erected industrial or experimental shops; and in 1756 the University of Moscow was founded through his unceasing efforts. All this activity was inspired by a lofty and rationalistic philosophy very similar to that of Leibniz.

The cultural influence of Lomonossov was enormous. He was the answer personified of the Russian people to the appeal made by Peter the Great: he showed that the Russians were able to reach the highest standards set by European thought. As a scientist he initiated the great tradition of Russian pre-eminence in physics, chemistry, mathematics and biology.

No less valuable, however, were his contributions to literature. In the wake of the reform of the alphabet initiated by Peter, Lomonossov decided to lay solid foundations for the Russian language as distinct from Church-Slavonic. The first work of this kind was his *Grammar* (1757), which was followed by his *Rhetorics* (first written in 1748). Earlier, in his *Letter Concerning the Rules of Russian Prosody* (1739), he had formulated his theory of the three literary styles. The Lofty Style was designated for heroic poems and all works dealing with serious matters requiring 'force, abundance, magnificence, impressiveness.' In these cases the use of Church-Slavonic locutions was recommended. The Middle Style was assigned to satires, eclogues, plays, and prose writings. It proposed to limit the use of Church-Slavonic without, however, lapsing into the banality of 'low words.' And, finally, there remained the Low Style for epigrams, songs, comedies, and descriptions of trivial incidents. It corresponded to the spoken language of the common folk. This classification formed the recognized beginning of the era of Russian Pseudo-Classicism, for which Lomonossov himself supplied the standards.

The odes he wrote in tonic verse played a great part in the development of Russian poetry. According to his theory the ode was the appropriate form for lofty emotions and solemn subjects. Lomonossov wrote his odes for various events occurring during the reign of the Empress Elisabeth (eight pieces) and of Catherine the Great (two). All of them are definitely eulogistic: they glorify the sovereigns and exalt the deeds of generals and statesmen. A battle, the taking of a Turkish fortress, an anniversary, a royal birth, all afforded the poet occasion for writing an ode. In most instances the event served merely as a pretext for a free flow of poetic imagination. Although all of them praise the Empress to the skies, they deal with many other themes, of which the greatness of Russia is considered the most important. In his first ode, 'On the Capture of Khotin' (1739), celebrating a victory over the Turks, Lomonossov expresses his patriotic fervor and evokes the image of Peter the Great, the real hero of all his poetry.

All these odes might be called court poems, or occasional verse (the first description is probably the most applicable). Yet Lomonossov never wrote like a courtier and his works lack a personal note. He treats monarchs as symbols, and uses abstract and hyperbolic images bound up with the general patriotic theme. However, the odes of Lomonossov, which delighted his contemporaries by their loftiness, eloquent metaphors, and majestic structure, today appear rather cold and conventional to us. A more lasting effect was achieved in his 'Evening and Morning Meditations on the Grandeur of our Lord,' in which he evinces his genuine emotions, inspired by visions of nature. Here his pathos is convincing, his Biblical intonations are powerful, and his images are striking. Many lines from these poems are still living poetry.

The great success of Lomonossov's poetic work signified the ultimate victory of tonic verse, and at the same time denoted the self-assertion of Russian Pseudo-Classicism. It is well known that individual, historical, and national diversifications made French Classicism as unlike the English or German as Racine was unlike Pope or Gottsched. The Russians learned a good deal from Malherbe, Boileau, or Günther (the latter obviously influenced Lomonossov); they accepted the rules set by European classicists for every literary form—tragedy, comedy, ode, or satire—and saw in poetry the highest expression of art. But transplanted to Russian soil, the principles of classical style grew strange offshoots. The character and the short duration of Pseudo-Classicism were determined by traditions of Russian literature and conditions of Russian life. Starting later in Russia than elsewhere, it was of short duration (roughly between 1747 and 1780) and contained more realistic elements than in other countries. It is extremely significant that its greatest exponent, Sumarokov, imitated the Russian folklore in his songs (a thing inconceivable for a Racine) and represented contemporary life in his other poetic works.

Sumarokov (1718-77) was a typical scion of the Europeanized intelligentsia that was forming among the nobility of Russia in the middle of the eighteenth century. He had received his education in an aristocratic military school founded in 1732 by the Empress Anna Ivanovna. The teachers and students of this college cultivated the liberal arts, especially literature and the theater. Sumarokov was by no means a radical; he firmly believed in aristocracy and the monarchy, based on serfdom and autocracy. But he had a high idea of the mission of a true nobleman, who, according to his theory, was chosen by the Almighty for patriotic and cultural tasks. He nurtured a cult of public service, honor, and civic virtue, and demanded from the well-born great qualities of mind and heart. Sumarokov found many obstacles in his path when he attempted to live up to these high standards. He was too sensitive, nervous, self-conscious, and proud to cope successfully with the intricate realities of the Court and the administration. For five years he was the director of Russian theaters (1756-61) and played an outstanding part in the development of the theater in Moscow. Although Catherine paid him a salary and published his works at the Treasury's expense, he died in neglect and poverty.

His main contribution was to the theater. His nine tragedies were so famous that contemporaries called him the Northern Racine and compared him to Shakespeare. His *Horev* (1747) was the first Russian 'regular' tragedy, strictly observing the three unities of time, place, and action imposed by the classicists. But in only two of Sumarokov's 'tragedies' does the hero die—an ending prescribed by the rules. The other seven have happy endings—a thing quite unusual in French literature, for instance. The subject matter of the majority of his plays was taken from real or legendary Russian history, and the main theme was the conflict of honor and duty (identified with reason) against egotism, the passions, and folly. Sumarokov's princes are caught between their obligations to the state and their personal interests, and all his heroes are highly moral in both sentiment and deeds. They act exactly as Sumarokov's ideal nobleman would act. This idealization of aristocracy definitely appealed to his select audiences and flattered its class pride.

Sumarokov also wrote 2 operas and 12 comedies, the latter being closely connected with Italian popular plays and the *commedia dell' arte* (Italian theatrical companies played in Russia almost every year between 1735 and 1760). Even though most of them were farces and burlesques, they definitely tended toward comedy of character, which was destined to triumph on the Russian stage.

Much more interesting than his comedies, however, are Sumarokov's poetic works, in which he definitely breaks with the manner of Lomonossov. His keen fables introduced this form into Russian literature; his Anacreontics created a school; while his love songs and lyrics blend elements of folklore and of classical literature. Throughout the eighteenth century his imitators were to follow the trend he had set.

Sumarokov's style was clear and refined in his tragedies, and pure, simple, and graceful in all his other poetry. Although a classicist, he did not believe in a strict division of styles and had no respect for the stiff grandeur of the Lomonossov school. Even under the Empress Elisabeth Russian Pseudo-Classicism was divided into two factions: the disciples of Lomonossov, like Vassily Petrov (1736-99), wrote pompous odes full of eulogies and patriotic enthusiasm; while the followers of Sumarokov advocated simpler forms and were inclined to express in popular language the intimate emotions of love, anxiety, or grief. Sumarokov's son-in-law, Yakov Knyazhnin (1742-91), author of seven tragedies in verse, acquired great popularity as a playwright of comedies (*The Boaster, The Eccentric*).

Pseudo-Classicism received its most serious setback during the reign of Catherine the Great, when Russian letters seemed at the peak of their development. Between 1725 (the death of Peter) and 1762 (the beginning of Catherine's reign) literature had covered vast ground. With surprising rapidity it had got into the stride of Western development and had tried all the forms and tendencies existing in Europe. Of course, this progress was accompanied by the usual diseases of quick growth: blind imitation of foreign models, the simplification of artistic devices, a certain crudity of style, and so on. But the work of Russian writers had, even in those times, a strong national flavor, and was coming closer to Russian life. This tendency became prevalent in the second half of the eighteenth century, when the foreign influence had been absorbed and assimilated, and new and original works sprang up from the European seeds planted in Russian soil.

1

POETS, PLAYWRIGHTS, AND SATIRISTS OF THE EIGHTEENTH CENTURY

I IN THE FIRST years of the eighteenth century Peter the Great transferred the capital of Russia to St. Petersburg, a newly created city on the shores of the Baltic Sea at the mouth of the Neva River. Thus the Moscow period of Russian history came to a close and that of St. Petersburg began. Under Catherine II the new Empire definitely asserted itself as a great European power. Within thirty years of her ascension to the throne Russia scored numerous diplomatic and military successes. A contemporary historian has summed up this resplendent period in a few eloquent figures: 80 victories on the battlefields, 30 peace treaties and international agreements, 144 newly founded towns, 29 new provinces established in conquered territories. Access to the Black Sea had been won at last: the Russians had defeated the Turks and taken possession of the Crimea, of the northern shores, where Odessa was to be founded, and of the mouth of the Danube (Bessarabia). In the West, Byelorussia and the Ukraine were re-integrated into the Empire, while the partition of Poland extended Russia's borders to Austria and Prussia. Under Peter Russia had but thirteen million inhabitants; by the end of the eighteenth century its population was close to forty million. The Empire's military might, enhanced by such brilliant generals as Rumiantzev, Potemkin, Suvorov, assured her a place of honor in European affairs. Her foreign policy, guided by such an outstanding diplomat as Panin, was firm and maintained an independent attitude toward France and England, especially after the Act of Armed Neutrality (1780), whereby Russia favored the struggle of the American colonies against the British Crown.

Paralleling Russia's territorial and diplomatic gains was an energetic advance in all the fields of national life. Catherine never overlooked an opportunity for stressing the link between her efforts and those of Peter the Great. She appointed herself heiress of his work and caused the words *Petro Primo—Catharina Secunda* to be graven on the pedestal of the Bronze Horseman, the famous statue of the Great Czar erected in St. Petersburg on the shores of the Neva. Like Peter, she intended to direct the progress of the country—in politics, economics, and culture.

In the early years of her reign she had been strongly influenced by French Enlightenment and endorsed the ideas of Diderot, Voltaire, and Montesquieu. Russia was the only country in the world that had published their works in government-sponsored editions, at the expense of the State Treasury. Special commissions appointed by the Empress revised the judicial system and reformed local administration in accordance with the principles of the Philosophers of Reason. A consultative body was entrusted with the task of working out a new code, and Catherine wrote her instructions for this body in a truly liberal spirit. For a time she behaved as if the dream of many Encyclopedists were about to come true: she seemed to personify Enlightened Absolutism based on a union of monarchs and philosophers. But social and economic conditions in Russia, as well as events abroad, soon cooled her enthusiasm. She became more practical and more conservative—a change in attitude her liberal pretences could hardly conceal.

Catherine had been raised to power by the nobility. Officers of the Guards had dethroned and later killed her husband, Emperor Peter III. She could rule only by complying with the interests of the nobility, especially of its military elements, who had lent her their support, and to some extent with the interests of a steadily growing upper middle class. She was therefore, compelled to grant privileges to the nobles and to extend the rights of certain groups of the burghers. The obligatory public service of the nobility, introduced by Peter the Great, was abolished. Serfdom, the main economic basis of the nobility, was reaffirmed. Large tracts of land with their peasant populations were distributed to nobles as rewards for their services. The brothers Orlov, who had helped her in her *coup d'état* in 1762, received huge estates with 50,000 serfs, and Field-Marshall Potemkin got an entire province with 40,000 peasants. More than 800,000 peasants were 'donated' in this way to old or new members of the ruling class.

This trend of her domestic policy had been strengthened by two events: the Pugachev Rebellion (1773-5) and the French Revolution of 1789.

Emelian Pugachev was an illiterate Cossack who claimed to be none other than Peter III, miraculously saved from death. He found thousands of followers willing to rebel among Cossacks, persecuted Old

Believers, discontented peasants, the Kirghiz, Kalmucks, and other Mongolian tribes. The rebellion flared up along the Volga River and in the southeastern regions of the Caspian Sea. The pretender issued a manifesto proclaiming the abolition of serfdom and launched a merciless war against the nobility. His ragtag army succeeded in defeating governmental troops, seized important towns, and established a peasant dictatorship over vast territories. Catherine was compelled to send a regular army under General I. Michelson to quell this dangerous revolt, which reflected the social unrest and the discontent of the lower classes. The memory of Pugachev's daring attempt to overthrow the rule of the landowners remained for generations among the common folk, who made up songs and legends about the Cossack pretender. After 1917 the Bolsheviks came to consider him one of the forerunners of their revolution. The Pugachev uprising has been commemorated in many literary works, from Pushkin's delightful tale, 'The Captain's Daughter' (1836), to *Emelian Pugachev,* a bulky novel by the Soviet writer V. Shishkov (1938-45).

The French Revolution and the beginning of the Terror had another chastening effect on Catherine. The ideas she had toyed with in her youth proved to be dynamite menacing her throne. More resolutely than ever she adopted a policy of conservative defense of the Russian monarchy. She divided the formula of Enlightened Absolutism into two separate parts—admitting enlightenment in education, art, and literature, but enforcing absolutism is politics and economics. This brought about a paradox that determined the relation between educated society and the government for many generations.

The cultural advancement of the country under Catherine was enormous. Efforts were made to spread education not only among the nobles, who were the first to profit from the newly founded lyceums, colleges, and universities, but also among the middle classes. Catherine believed, together with the philosophers of Enlightenment, that 'education is the most difficult but surest means for the betterment of men.' Although hardly anything had been done for the elementary education of the lower classes, the effect of Catherine's reforms even reached to them and there were a number of notable self-educated peasants.

Institutions of higher education were actively supported by the government. The Academy of Science became a center of research and manifold theoretical and practical studies. In 1783 a special Academy of Russian Language and Literature was founded under the auspices of the Empress, who appointed Princess Catherine Dashkova, her friend, the chairman of the new body. Other scientific and literary societies (such as the Free Economic Society) were established during

Catherine's reign and enjoyed a glorious career in the nineteenth century.

Another facet of this educational activity was the extensive development of printing. The right to establish presses was granted to all citizens by a governmental decree (which was, however, revoked toward the end of Catherine's reign). Following this liberal measure, presses mushroomed in many provincial towns and even on some private estates. Catherine herself launched the first of the many humorous periodicals, *Mish-Mash,* to which she contributed some of its best writings. Nicholas Novikov (1744-1818), publisher and editor of satirical magazines (*The Drone, The Chatter Box, The Painter, The Puree*) and an outstanding educator, founded the Printing Company, a non-profit organization with the sole aim 'of combating ignorance and spreading the light of education.' Within a few years Novikov, helped by the Freemason Schwartz, published a thousand titles (among them the first *Survey of Russian Literature,* by Novikov himself). He was also very active as a founder of schools and lending libraries. With Schwartz he established the Society of Friends of Science, launched various charity institutions, and contributed greatly to the spread of Freemasonry in Russia.

Translations from foreign languages increased in both number and quality. Even in the first decade of Catherine's reign the literary productivity became five times greater than during the previous decade. Periodicals also showed an amazing growth. There were only 8 periodicals in Russia between 1703 (when Peter started the first newspaper) and 1762; by the end of the century more than a hundred periodicals were being brought out in Russia, and 69 of them were publishing fine prose and poetry. Writers had found a new and steadily growing audience.

Other arts were expanding. Catherine was embellishing the capital. Foreign masters were still coming from Italy, France, and Germany to erect public buildings and private dwellings and to adorn them with pictures and sculptures. Working next to them, however, and frequently surpassing them in skill and genius were Russian architects, such as Bazhenov and Kasakov, builders of cathedrals and palaces; Russian portrait painters such as Levitzky, Borovikovsky, Rokotov; Russian sculptors such as Kozlovsky and Martos. The Academy of Fine Arts, with a large staff of instructors, was preparing a new generation of artists. Bortniansky, Fomin, and other composers had begun a renaissance of Russian religious and secular music. In 1779 the first comic opera *The Miller-Magician, Cheat, and Match Maker* (with music by Sokolovsky) was written by Alexander Ablesimov (1742-83), an imitator of Sumarokov. It had been preceded (in 1772) by the 'popular' opera *Aniuta* by Popov (with music by Fomin).

More than any other art literature reflected this blossoming of national consciousness. During the preceding period it had been reflected in only a few isolated authors. Now there was a considerable number of writers—poets, playwrights, publicists. They belonged to various social strata—from the Empress herself to a serf, Matinsky, author of an interesting comic opera. Literature was becoming richer and more diversified. Although Pseudo-Classicism was officially accepted as the perfect expression of thought and sentiment, new forms and tendencies were developing freely, indicating that a turning point in the Russian literary evolution was at hand. This is amply illustrated by the work of Gavriil Derzhavin, the greatest Russian poet of the eighteenth century.

II   GAVRIIL DERZHAVIN was born of
an impoverished noble family, in 1743, in the province of Kazan, on the Volga, where an important Tartar kingdom had existed until the sixteenth century, and Derzhavin himself had Tartar blood in his veins. After a few years of school he joined the Regiment of the Transfiguration in St. Petersburg as a private. There he was forced to sweat and toil for ten years before getting his commission, for a poor provincial youth could not compete with the rich and distinguished young men who held all the better posts. During this hard struggle he found his only consolation in reading books and writing poems. In 1772 when he was finally promoted, he served with General Bibikov, commander-in-chief of the troops fighting against Pugachev. In putting down the uprising Derzhavin displayed unusual energy, courage, and administrative ability. His efforts, however, were not sufficiently appreciated; he was too headstrong, sensitive, and straightforward to be welcomed by his superiors. Frequent clashes between the quick-tempered, sharp-tongued young officer and the old, crafty bureaucrats handicapped Derzhavin's career. It was then that his gifts as a poet suddenly turned the tables. In 1782, almost in his forties, he addressed to Catherine his ode, 'To Felicia,' which instantly made him famous. Within a short time he became the poet laureate, and the Empress granted him many favors. Derzhavin devoted but a part of his time to literature, however, public service remained his main concern. Patronized by Catherine and flattered by the Court, he rose quickly in the bureaucratic hierarchy: Governor-General of the provinces of the north and of Tambov; private secretary to the Empress; Senator; assistant secretary of the Treasury; and finally (under Alexander I) Secretary-Minister of Justice. This long career was hazardous and uneven. Derzhavin's violent and quarrel-

some character, his integrity, his blind and somewhat embarrassing (for others!) devotion to truth, his fighting spirit and his frankness, made him a tiresome and difficult official. He provoked scandals and aroused bitter opposition among the complacent, well-educated, and suavely diplomatic dignitaries.

The Empress herself complained that her secretary was rude and boring and she finally dismissed him. As a matter of fact she preferred his odes to his endless reports. Not until he became old and had retired to Zvanka, his country estate, did Derzhavin give up his activities as an administrator. He died in 1816, four years after the Napoleonic invasion, at the age of 73.

For thirty years Derzhavin continued to be the supreme figure in Russian literature. He was acclaimed as Russia's greatest poet, and the odes and poems in which he glorified the Empress and her military victories embodied the glamor of a brilliant epoch. Under Catherine the magnificence of the Court at St. Petersburg eclipsed even Versailles. The Court aristocracy led a life of luxury and splendor. There were theatrical entertainments that blended in a fantastic vision of light and gold the prodigality of the new Empire and the traditions of Byzantine majesty. At the Court or in the palaces Asiatic colorfulness met with French grace, and the abundance of wealth combined with the refinement of the *siècle galant*. This was the background of Derzhavin's poetry. His poems have a sonority, a fullness of tone, a richness of metaphor, and an oratorical swing that evoke the spacious rooms of the Imperial palace where these odes were read to an audience of gold-braided generals and magnificently gowned ladies-in-waiting. Occasionally Derzhavin's works may seem long, verbose, or uneven, but they all possess a distinct sensual quality; they are specific and graceful, full of vitality and humor. Derzhavin may overwork the drums and brass, yet they do contribute to the impression of force and intensity. One hundred and fifty years later Mayakovsky, the Soviet poet, was, in spite of all their vast dissimilarities, to exhibit the same oratorical dynamism and concreteness as Derzhavin.

Derzhavin differed from his predecessors in his repudiation of the abstract and scientific loftiness that burdened the odes of Lomonossov. No poetic revolutionary, he followed the precept of Classicism that the ode was the highest poetic form; yet actually his works combined the characteristics of a eulogistic style with satirical elements and realistic descriptions. For example, the subject matter of his famous ode 'To Felicia' is the traditional praise of the sovereign. But what Lomonossov would have made a solemn piece of grandiloquence with earnest references to God, Motherland, and Duty, Derzhavin, renouncing the monotonous unity of Pseudo-Classicism, made a polyphonic composition sparkling with wit, gaiety, and fancy.

In general, the didactic-satirical trend in his poetry is very strong. Not only is he 'smilingly telling the truth to Czars,' as he had himself described his work, but he castigates evil wherever it appears—he always remains 'the servant of truth.' He presents a whole gallery of his contemporaries, with bold allusions. Some of his portraits are deeply and sharply etched, as is 'The Dignitary,' in which he points out that kindness is more important than gold or pearls, and recalls the nefarious practices of the Roman emperors. No less revealing is his ode 'To Potentates and Judges,' with its passionate appeal to the Lord to judge the kings of this earth and put an end to universal crimes and injustices. (This ode was banned by the censors, while another, 'On the Capture of Warsaw,' was suppressed by Catherine herself.)

Despite his conservative political opinions Derzhavin is obviously one of the great pioneers of Russian civic poetry, which grew into a large movement in the nineteenth and twentieth centuries (from Ryleyev to Nekrassov, to Mayakovsky and Blok.) Dostoevsky considered 'To Potentates and Judges' beautiful poetry, permeated by a spirit of independence and moral courage, and he often read it aloud to confound those who considered Derzhavin merely a courtier-poet.

In his leaning toward the grandiose Derzhavin often lapses into pomposity, ponderous images, and rhetoric or he piles up bombastic words and archaic expressions. He deliberately seeks grand effects in his verse, yet his lyrics reveal that he could 'coo as well as roar.' Gogol described him as the poet of grandeur and admired such odes as 'On the Capture of Izmail,' with its impressive battle scenes and its epic portraits of Russian military leaders—Rumiantzev, Repnin, and Suvorov. In 'The Waterfall' the grandeur of his vision of nature is evoked in metallic lines of extraordinary sound and tonality. Derzhavin's verbal exaggerations are seldom shallow; they are in keeping with the exuberance and force of his temperament.

A man of strong vitality and a disciple of the materialistic and sensual philosophy of his century, Derzhavin claimed to be an Epicurean. He loved movement, color, nature, the pleasures of the flesh, the luxury of feasts, as well as the idyllic leisure of country life, which he pictured so well in his 'Life in Zvanka.' He described good food with amazing, almost Flemish realism (as in the poem 'Invitation to Dinner'); his landscapes have a vividness that was later echoed in Gogol's descriptions of nature; and his Anacreontics vie with Sumarokov's eulogies of love, wine, and gaiety. Despite all his vitality and exuberance, however, Derzhavin was subject to spells of depression, when the vanity of all earthly things seemed overwhelming to him. The image of Death, casting her shadow over all things we are attached to, haunts many of his best poems, particularly 'On the Death of Prince Mestchersky' and 'The Waterfall,' the latter a lyrical masterpiece, in which he speaks of 'the river of time which engulfs kingdoms, rulers, and peoples,' and of eternity, 'which devours all things that lyre and trumpet strive to preserve.'

Some of his religious poems, particularly 'God,' were proclaimed the most powerful of his poetic achievements. Pushkin did not share this opinion, and today the critics definitely prefer Derzhavin's less flamboyant, but more realistic, works.

Although in different ways Lomonossov and Sumarokov had tried to assert the classical order in Russian poetics. Derzhavin, too, is a classicist—in his didacticism, in his allegories, in his lofty purpose to 'serve the truth.' But at the same time he breaks away from the fundamental rules of the school. The range of his poetry is unusually great, extending from the solemnity of the ode in the Lomonossov tradition (mostly in his religious poems) to the lightness of Anacreontics; but in every form he blends the High and the Low styles, the epic and the lyric, the sublime and the satirical. Gogol remarked that Derzhavin has used an extraordinary mixture 'of high-flown expressions and of the most idiomatic words—sometimes regional or dialectic in origin.' Church-Slavonic terms sometimes appear under a popular disguise, and colloquialisms acquire under his pen an archaic, Church-Slavonic resonance.

This duality of style determines Derzhavin's place in Russian literature. He belongs to the classical school, yet at the same time his poetry is a negation of classicism. He depicted the colorful and splendid world of his contemporaries not only with powerful artistry but also with sensual concreteness, looking at it from the point of view of his own temperament and giving free play to his caprice, humor, and emotions, in a language that appears at once strong, flexible, and highly expressive. Thus did he break a trail for Karamzin, Batiushkov, and Zhukovsky—the predecessors and teachers of Pushkin.

Other poets of the same period also prove that Pseudo-Classicism was on the decline. Some turned to sentimental themes or wrote in a light vein to amuse the readers, who were by that time tired of heroic and serious subjects. One of these poets was Ippolit Bogdanovich (1743-1803), translator of Voltaire and other French authors. In 1775, under the influence of La Fontaine's *Les Amours de Psyché* (based upon *The Golden Ass* of Apuleius), he wrote a poem relating the adventures of Psyche in the palace of the god of love. It was light, brilliant, and graceful, in the style of the *poèmes galants* of the Versailles Court, and it found so many admirers among the aristocrats of both sexes that within a very short time fifteen printings of *Dushenka* (*Little Psyche*) were brought out in St. Petersburg.

More indicative of the change in literary taste, however, was the increasing number of satires, fables, and comedies.

III   The satirical tendency was significant of the awakening of liberal forces in Russia and it played an important part in the moral and civic education of cultivated society.
Catherine encouraged it as a means of combatting the ignorance and
backwardness of the country. She put her own not inconsiderable
literary talent at the service of the cause and wrote tales, comedies, and
comic operas expressing her views on education, on Freemasonry
(which she ridiculed in *The Sorcerer* and in *The Secret of the Anti-
Absurd Society*), on the superficial radicalism of intellectuals, and on
the callousness of the aristocracy. She also contributed to satirical newspapers and magazines, one of the most characteristic features of her
reign, which waged a campaign against bad manners, prejudices, and
the lack of culture among the nobility as well as against the indis-
criminate imitation of foreigners. In the second half of the eighteenth
century many young men and women sincerely believed that Parisian
fashions, a few words of French, and some notion of modern dances
were the only marks of social distinction. Catherine made them a laughing stock in her comedies of *The Birthday of Mrs. Querulous, Mrs.
Gossip and Her Family,* and so on.

This movement, which had its eminent forerunners in Kantemir and
Sumarokov and had also been influenced by the French (particularly
by Voltaire, Diderot, and the *Persian Letters* of Montesquieu), found
its main expression in certain periodicals (*The Artist, The Ghostly,
Post-Office, The Drone, Citizens' Discourse,* and so on), edited by Emin,
Novikov, Krylov, and many others. It is revealing that this satirical
tendency is one of the earliest and most striking features of Russian
literature. The writers of the nineteenth and twentieth centuries, such as
Gogol, Saltykov-Shchedrin, Leskov, Chekhov, and Mayakovsky, no
matter how different from one another, all stem from this same tradition,
which has its roots in the eighteenth century.

The fables of Ivan Khemnitzer (1745-84), written in a simple style
and published in 1779, formed a bridge between the works of Sumarokov and the later writers of fables, such as Ivan Dmitriev (1760-1837),
a high dignitary, who published his collected fables, odes, and epigrams in 1805, and Krylov. The satire of Vassily Kapnist (1757-1823)

and his comedy in verse, *Chicane* (1798), were typical of the trend.

Under Catherine satire colored all literary forms—odes, fables, essays—but was most effective in the drama, and Catherine herself strove to become a leading playwright. Although they often contained wit, humor, and realistic details (usually supplied by her literary collaborators) her comedies were thoroughly didactic and rationalistic. They were in no way better than the works of many minor writers whose names are found only in footnotes, but their importance lay in the fact that their author was the ruler of Russia. With her support the satirical tendency flourished like the green bay tree and gained wide popularity.

Many comedies were written and produced during this period. Most of them had but slight literary merit, with the possible exception of *The Profligate Reformed by Love,* by Vladimir I. Lukin (1737-94), who attempted to 'adapt' foreign plays by transposing them into the idiom of Russian life. All these playwrights were, however, overshadowed by a truly outstanding satirist and the founder of the Russian national dramatic repertoire, Denis Fonvizin.

Before the seventeenth century Russian drama had been reduced to religious plays presented in schools, to morality plays, and to coarse farces performed by motley bands of Skomorokhi (Scaramouches) who wandered about with bears and other trained animals, amusing the crowds at fairs and hard put to escape the persecutions of the ecclesiastic and secular authorities. Moscow's ukases against them were issued at the same time as the ordnances adopted by the English Puritan Parliament in 1642-55 made the English actors subject to corporal punishment. The Russian theater was officially born when, in 1672, Czar Alexis ordered the building of a theater in his Court residence near Moscow. In the main its repertoire was borrowed from Germany, where traveling companies of English players had always enjoyed popularity. Alexis' Court theater came to an end in 1676 after the death of Father Gregory, its director. In 1702 Peter gave orders that the German actor Kunst be brought to Russia, and the latter, helped by German and Russian aides, directed the theater for a few years. Peter's sister Nathalie also established two theatrical companies on her estates in the suburbs of Moscow. German and Italian companies often gave performances at the Czar's Court and at the homes of his rich aristocrats. But no permanent theatrical organization existed in Russia until the middle of the eighteenth century.

In 1749 the students of the aristocratic Cadet School played Sumarokov's *Horev,* a tragedy, with such success that the Empress Elisabeth asked the performance to be repeated at Court. These students formed an amateur company and went on acting (mostly in Sumarokov's plays) at their school and in the Imperial Palace. During a chance visit to the capital Fedor Volkov (1729-63), the son of a provincial merchant, happened to see one of these performances from the wings, and became an enthusiastic theatrophile. Upon his return to Yaroslavl, his home town on the upper Volga, he organized a company, collected money for a provisional theater building, and inaugurated a series of regular performances. This was the first Russian theater founded through private initiative, and Volkov was called the Lomonossov of the Russian Stage. The news of his successful undertaking reached the Court and Elisabeth commanded him to come to St. Petersburg. Actors of the capital joined Volkov's group, and in 1756 by Elisabeth's order a permanent public theater was established under the title of the Russian Theater for the Performance of Tragedies and Comedies. Sumarokov was appointed its director. From then on theatrical life flourished not only in Moscow and St. Petersburg but in the provinces as well. Rich landowners assembled companies of serf-actors on their estates, while in the cities foreign and Russian actors presented numerous plays, mostly translated from the French and German, and Italian ballet also became popular.

Denis Fonvizin (1745-1792), who came from an obscure but cultured family of Muscovite nobles, tells us in his remarkable *Memoirs* that a theatrical performance he attended as a child had impressed him so greatly that it determined the course of his life. In his youth he became the friend of Dmitrevsky, one of the foremost actors of the period, translated the plays of Ludwig Holberg, the Danish dramatist, and occasionally acted himself. After a short period as a translator at the Foreign Office, Fonvizin obtained a secretarial post with Elaghin, the Imperial Minister, a highly educated man, a well-known prose writer, and, since 1766, the official Inspector-General of Russian Theaters. In Elaghin's drawing-room Fonvizin met the Russian admirers of Voltaire and the Encyclopedists.

He was a welcome guest in many other of the capital's salons, and met Sumarokov, Bogdanovich, and other prominent writers. His witty conversation and spirited jests made him popular, but those who resented his barbed *mots* gave him the nickname 'the Vulture.' He held a distinguished place among the literati for his satirical writings, one of which was the caustic *Letter to my Servants* (1763), a comico-philosophical conversation, in the manner of Voltaire, on the purpose of the universe. His first important work, however—*The Brigadier*— came six years later. After a public reading of this comedy in the presence of the Empress and Paul, the heir apparent, Fonvizin was offered

a post with Count N. Panin. He stayed for many years with this progressive dignitary and worked on Panin's political testament advocating
a liberal constitution for Russia. He also contributed to numerous magazines and wrote scores of journalistic articles.

'A friend of freedom' (as Pushkin called him), Fonvizin contended
that a writer should be 'the guardian of general welfare, and raise his
voice against abuses and prejudices.' He therefore refused to separate
his activity as a civil servant from that of a playwright. All his comedies, including his masterpiece, *The Hobbledehoy,* had a definite social
significance. In 1783, encouraged by the great success of this play, he
published twenty questions addressed to the Empress and dealing with
various political or social problems and, in particular, with the hypocrisy
at Court. Catherine's angry reply marked the end of her friendly attitude
towards Fonvizin. He was declared a dangerous dreamer in a high
place, his articles were banned, and the publication of a periodical he
had planned and advertised was forbidden by the authorities. With all
his literary projects thwarted, the playwright turned to religion and
travel. His *Letters from Abroad* (France, Germany, and Italy) are excellent writing and of great historical interest. He suffered a stroke of
paralysis and after some years of ill health, died in 1792.

The Brigadier, partly inspired by Holberg's *Jean de France,* is an
early attempt at a genuinely Russian comedy. His five protagonists represented well-known types: the rough old Brigadier (a rank between
colonel and general); his thrifty wife Akulina, who believes that all
women ought to fear God and their husbands; the hypocritical councilor, who preaches virtue but has made his fortune through bribes and
grafts; the councilor's brainless and coquettish wife; and, finally, the
simpleton Ivan, the Brigadier's son, who never stops talking about Paris
and is ashamed of not having been born in France. All of these characters were so vivid and true to life that, despite the skimpiness of plot
and lack of action, the comedy delighted Fonvizin's contemporaries,
while his realism and style greatly influenced the comedies of Sumarokov and Catherine.

It was in *The Hobbledehoy,* however—the first truly national play of
the Russian drama—that Fonvizin's gift for realism and satire found its
full expression. He had worked for years on this comedy, which was
first performed in 1782, two decades after the first draft was written.
As in *The Brigadier,* the main theme was the problem of education, but
while Ivan, the Brigadier's son, reflects the evil consequences of a
superficial imitation of Europe, of a faulty Europeanization, Mitrophanushka, the Hobbledehoy, is a product of national backwardness.
His ignorance and vulgarity stem from the way of life of despotic land-

owners whose welfare was based on serfdom. The central figure of the comedy is Prostakova (Simple Soul), the Hobbledehoy's mother. She treats her peasants like cattle and is indignant when her sick maid goes to bed. 'In bed, is she? Like a noblewoman?' Eremeievna, the old nurse, describes her own situation in one incisive sentence: 'I get five roubles a year—and my face slapped five times a day.' Prostakova is a domestic tyrant as well as a cruel mistress. When Starodum (Old Raisonneur) comes to Prostakova's house, he is met by three men who introduce themselves: 'I am my sister's brother,' 'I am my wife's husband,' 'I am my mother's son.' Her brother, the stolid Skotinin (Beastly), is as ignorant and caddish as Prostakova herself. He is interested only in pigs, for whom he cares much more than for his peasants. His nephew, the sixteen-year-old and half-witted Mitrophanushka, the Hobbledehoy, is coarse, greedy, and illbred. He does not want to study, because a nobleman has no need of learning. His mother shares his opinion about the uselessness of science: Why should one, for instance, learn geography, when there are enough postmen and coachmen who know everything there is to know about roads?

The plot is very simple. Prostakova has robbed Sophie, an orphan, of her estate and, in order to hide her machinations, wants to marry the young girl off to Skotinin. But when Sophie inherits a large legacy, Prostakova suddenly changes her plans: she now wants Sophie to marry her son. The uncle and the nephew vie desperately for the desirable prize. Their distasteful love-making and the brutal insistence of Prostakova horrify the girl, who dreams of Milon, a well-educated young man from St. Petersburg. Prostakova is about to use violence on Sophie when the arrival of a government investigator, Pravdin (the Just), and the intervention of the good old man, Starodum, frustrate all her evil schemes.

Within the framework of this flimsy plot Fonvizin displays brilliant characterization and a mastery of comic situations and witty dialogue. His humor is forceful, sometimes approaching a sarcastic indignation. Despite some farcical notes and the grotesque characterization (typical of Russian humor in general), the action moves in a perfectly realistic atmosphere. This 'true-to-life' quality, as well as the lusty naturalness of the characters, was a novelty. Fonvizin observed the rules of Pseudo-Classicism and never departed from the unity of place, time, and action, but he abandoned the rationalistic and schematic generalizations of the school and wrote a vigorous work drawn from observation of life. He exposed the evils and prejudices of provincial Russia, revealed the ignorance of his own class, and, as Kliuchevsky put it, offered 'an inimitable mirror of his time.' He presented a penetrating picture of the

social scene, and the broad range of his comedy made it national in
implication.

His didactic tendency is quite obvious: the positive types, such as
Starodum, Pravdin, or Milon, ape the *raisonneurs* of French comedy.
But audiences of the eighteenth century did not find their speeches as
prosaic as we do; they heard in them hints and allusions to the burning
problems of the day.

The success of the comedy was not, however, a result of realism
alone. It has continued to be played in the Russian theater for more
than a century and a half because it is a powerful and lively representation of a nation's life and characters, expressed in simple and colloquial
language by a great playwright. *The Hobbledehoy* soon became a
classic; even today the names of its protagonists serve as bywords in
the Soviet Union, while many of its lines have become popular sayings
in current speech. Fonvizin inaugurated a long series of realistic types
in Russian literature; he also introduced the tradition of social satire
and, in particular, of social comedy, which was so successfully followed in the nineteenth century by Griboyedov's *'Tis Folly to be Wise,*
Gogol's *Inspector General,* and the plays of Ostrovsky, Chekhov, and
others.

IV   By the end of the eighteenth century the exposure of the abuses and evils of contemporary society carried on by the satirical journals and the stage took on a political character. The Russian followers of the Encyclopedists inevitably arrived
at the same conclusions as their French brethren.

The news of the fall of the Bastille in 1789 was received in St.
Petersburg with such enthusiasm that according to the *Memoirs* of the
Count de Ségur, young liberals embraced one another in the streets.
However, these liberals, who passionately discussed Rousseau's *Social
Contract* and the problem of the equality of men, formed but a small
minority. The majority of the nobility and the Empress herself had not
misread the ominous message of the French Revolution. Relying on the
support of the Army, the landowners, and the bureaucracy, Catherine
initiated the most reactionary period in domestic policy and reasserted
the inviolability of autocracy in Russia. When ideas of education and
public service, which she herself had favored in the first decade of her
reign, began to have political implications, she challenged them in a
series of restrictive measures. Liberalism was declared the great enemy
of the State. Freemasons were persecuted and their lodges closed.
Novikov's printing plants were banned, while their director himself was
arrested and sentenced to fifteen years of solitary confinement in the

fortress-prison of Schlüsselburg. Derzhavin was censored, and Fonvizin was not allowed to publish his articles. The intellectuals, whose radicalism Catherine feared, were fettered and put under surveillance. Actually these fears had been grossly inflated and exaggerated by the reactionaries; the liberalism of a part of the nobility and of the educated middle class was a rather mild affair. Those whom the police labeled 'the Opposition' would have been perfectly satisfied by some moderate reforms. Nevertheless, there did exist a minority that was aware of the results of the social and political defects of the autocratic regime and that demanded radical measures and bold action. The ideas of this left wing of the Russian intelligentsia were made articulate by the celebrated author Alexander Radishchev (1749-1802) in a book that marked the beginning of the literature of Russian radicalism.

Like so many noblemen of his time, Radishchev studied abroad, mostly in Germany, where he was sent by the Empress herself. He returned an enthusiastic believer in the natural rights of man and soon realized the contradiction between his idealistic theories and the realities of Russian life. As a customs official he had ample opportunity to come into close contact with peasants, artisans, and provincial bureaucrats and to realize the gap between the liberal talk of the Empress and the conditions of the serfs and the lower middle class. His wealth of personal experience and the incessant torments of his conscience impelled him to write a book that, while it was to assure his fame, was also to bring about his undoing. In his *Voyage from St. Petersburg to Moscow,* published in 1790, he related the many adventures, observations, and thoughts of a traveler who has met people from all classes and witnessed all sorts of incidents. Among those he encountered were a landlord who sold at auction his wet nurse, his mistress, and their child; a judge whose verdict depended only on the amount of money offered him by the parties involved; an officer who sacrificed human lives in order to satisfy a momentary whim; peasants mistreated by ruthless masters and weak from malnutrition; poor wretches beaten by the police; ignorant officials deciding the fate of thousands of frightened citizens. Radishchev did not limit himself to merely reporting facts, he analyzed the whole social system in an effort to find out what was wrong with it. In his allegoric tale about the Empress he presents her blindfolded and unaware of the truth; thus putting the blame not on the monarch but on her servants. Radishchev seemed to believe that his mission was to reveal the truth to the hoodwinked ruler, who would then proceed to put her house in order.

The main idea of Radishchev was that serfdom, 'this monster of a hundred snouts,' was the cause of all the evils. Russia, enslaved by poverty, injustice, and ignorance, could evolve into a modern state only if the peasants were emancipated and political freedom was granted to all citizens. Education or the moral betterment of man was not sufficient: what was sorely needed in Russia were actual social reforms aimed at a radical transformation of the regime.

Such a program, formulated with vigor and precision, corresponded to the outspoken or hidden demands of the democratically minded intelligentsia. Although Radishchev in his *Voyage* spoke of a constitutional monarchy similar to England's, he evinced a more revolutionary spirit in his odes, which prophesied the day of revolt 'when the peoples would wash off the abuses against them in the blood of tyrants and would send the rulers to the scaffold—thus achieving a rightful vengeance in the name of the natural rights of man.' These poems, written under German rather than French influence, were still inspired with Pseudo-Classical eloquence; nevertheless the *Voyage* reflects new literary tendencies. Its scenes were sketched with surprising naturalness; the comments of the author had strong emotional overtones. These are signs not only of pre-Romantic sentimentalism but also of Russian humanitarianism, which since its earliest days had assumed a highly emotional character. Radicalism in Russia was growing on moral and sentimental grounds far more than on economic or political ones—a tendency that was going to be a revealing aspect of Russian revolutionary theory and practice for more than a hundred years.

Curiously enough the publication of Radishchev's 'Ode to Freedom' and the *Voyage* was permitted by the censors (despite a violent attack against censorship in the *Voyage*). The officials probably felt that the author's ideas were not so very different from those the Empress herself was apparently regarding benignly. But they erred. Times had changed. Catherine had ceased her flirtations with Voltaire, Diderot, and Rousseau; their works were now called pernicious propaganda. Radishchev's book fell into this dangerous category and provoked a tempest at Court. Catherine took the *Voyage* very badly: Radishchev was thrown into prison and after a brief trial was condemned to death. The Empress, however, who loved to demonstrate her clemency, commuted the sentence to hard labor in Siberia.

The ill fate of Radishchev put a close to the period of liberal dreams. Now the government was ready to extirpate with violence whatever remained of the ideas it had itself helped to spread in Russia. Peter had acted as a progressive force in creating a Westernized educated society for the welfare of the Empire. At that point the governmental circles had advanced more rapidly than the society they tried to enlighten. When these efforts had borne their fruit and an intelligentsia, mostly drafted from the nobility, had absorbed the ideas of culture, freedom, and human dignity, there came a period, particularly under Catherine, when collaboration between the autocracy and the educated society seemed possible. This had been followed by a rift between the government, which saw the danger of Russia's realizing that absolutism was based on serfdom, and the intelligentsia, who continued to follow the road opened by its rulers. Now the two groups were confronting each other as rivals and, on occasion, even enemies. The symbolic significance of Radishchev's fate was a grim warning to the young liberals.

Paul I freed Radischev, and later Alexander I made him member of the Committee for the Revision of the Civil Code. Faithful to his ideas, the author of the *Voyage* set to work with great zeal. But he soon realized that the times were not yet ripe for the fulfilment of his dearest dream—the abolition of serfdom. Broken physically by the Siberian prisons, frustrated morally, ridiculed by his colleagues for his old-fashioned humanitarianism, he could not bear the struggle any longer and, in 1802, committed suicide by taking poison.

His influence was wide and lasting. The new generation read his work in clandestine copies, and admired them. His ideas were taken up at the beginning of the nineteenth century by the members of the Free Society of Lovers of Literature and Science. The political fables and odes of Panin, the lyrics of Born, Popugaiev, Izmailov, Vostokov (who made good verse translations of German and English poets), all followed Radishchev's tradition. The Decembrists, Pushkin, Lermontov, and many others knew and were greatly impressed by Radishchev—the first revolutionary writer of Russia.

v   Three main trends determined the rapid development of Russian literature in the eighteenth century. In the first place, its secularization, which had started as far back as the sixteenth century, had been completed under Peter and his successors. However deep the influence of Orthodox religion and Christian dogma, the Church had lost its spiritual and practical domination over the arts. Literature had torn itself free from the Church ideologically as well as stylistically and moved forward as an independent secular development. Church-Slavonic had a very limited use, while the language of educated society and the people was officially recognized as the literary medium.

But this process of secularization created a new bondage. The State took the place of the Church; ecclesiastical control was supplanted by governmental censorship. Instead of the pressures exerted by theocracy, literature now submitted to those exerted by autocracy. In addition, secular power to some extent identified itself with the literary movement. That Peter the Great was Russia's first newspaperman and that Catherine wrote comedies and articles are of almost symbolic significance. The State did not merely grant favors to writers and play Maecenas, as was the case all over Europe. In contrast to other countries, the Russian rulers and their governmental agencies took a genuine interest in literature, directing and trying to integrate it into the network of the Empire as a useful social enterprise. The publication of an ode or a book of prose was the State's concern. Literary productions were utilized for the practical purposes of education. Art became incorporated into the program of the Imperial policy. It was the government that launched magazines, founded publishing houses, organized theaters, established literary societies, simplified the alphabet, or imported the works of foreign authors. Whoever attempts to understand the intricate conditions of literary life in the Soviet Union should not overlook the particular auspices under which modern Russian literature with its traditions began in the eighteenth century.

It is highly significant that almost all Russian writers of this period were State officials of one sort or another. Poets and playwrights belonged to the bureaucracy and occupied prominent positions in the administration. With the exception of Trediakovsky they were cabinet ministers, ambassadors, dignitaries, governors, or generals. Literary and governmental circles were closely aligned. The cleavage did not materialize before the end of the century, when Radishchev, a customs official, tried to assert his independence as a writer. Until this daring venture the union of autocratic administration and literature was almost perfect. A book of portraits of eighteenth-century Russian writers would have shown many high officials in brilliant uniforms covered with medals and decorations.

It is quite obvious that the didactic, moral, and utilitarian brand the Church had placed on Russian literature remained practically unchanged during the eighteenth century. The ideology was new, of course; instead of spreading pious ideas of the True Faith and Christian virtue, Russian writers were propagating secular enlightenment, Voltairian skepticism, and the philosophy of the Age of Reason. Basically, however, they never questioned whether literature should have a social purpose. Like the laymen of the sixteenth century, who had regarded themselves as servants of the Church, they acted as servants of the State and proclaimed that art ought to teach and guide. Thus the tradition of social significance was firmly preserved under a new disguise. The realistic exposés of a Fonvizin, the initiator of a trend Gorky called 'magnificent and most fruitful,' are but a part of this general current.

Most of the works of imagination and entertainment belonged to folklore or popular literature, which continued to produce love songs and tales. But this kind of poetry and fiction was still an isolated phenomenon. The merging of the socially conscious literature of the educated classes with the spontaneous creativeness of the people had not yet been accomplished, even though several writers of the century felt the necessity of moving in that direction.

The second main tendency of eighteenth-century literature was its rapid Westernization. The expansion of the Empire had broken down the Chinese Wall of national isolation. The isolationist attitude of Moscow as the Third Rome was eventually abandoned. The arts in Russia caught up with the West, and European literary patterns and schools were quickly absorbed and Russified. Pseudo-Classicism found Russian admirers and followers; all the literary forms perfected abroad—ode, tragedy, heroic poem, comedy, fable, satire, philosophical tale, travelogue, essay—were successfully practiced by the Russians. However, Russian literature did not lose its own flavor; in becoming an organic part of the European whole it nevertheless preserved its national traits.

While this process of adaptation and imitation was under way, all the literary genres were flourishing. Russian poetry found its medium—tonic verse—which was developed into a forceful and flexible means of expression by Lomonossov, Derzhavin, and their disciples. The Russian theater had its birth; its surprising growth is evidenced by Sumarokov and Fonvizin. The political essay flourished in periodicals and in Radishchev's works.

The third feature of this period is not the least noteworthy. Although the prevailing theory of stylistic discrimination and the Church-Slavonic legacy still encroached on the writer's mind, the discussions of form, language, and esthetic principles were intensified. Conflicting artistic attitudes presaged the imminent formation of opposing movements. The interest in folklore and Russian medieval literature was intensified by historical research, which led to many valuable discoveries and the publication of the book of songs by Kirsha Danilov, of ballads, of *The Lay of Igor,* and many other books. Certain young writers were asking themselves whether Pseudo-Classicism answered the needs of Russian literature, and whether the popular tradition would not be a better foundation for further artistic development. One of the main problems haunting them was the creation of a literary language that would be nationally accepted and would express the thinking not of the educated society alone but of the Russian people as a whole. Thus basic issues of a purely literary, formal kind were having a more general impact and were indicating the approach of a new phase of literary evolution. These problems were more or less clearly formulated by the end of the century; their solution was to be attempted in the next few decades.

2

THE NEW ERA

I   RADISHCHEV was a sentimental revolutionist. Most of the Russian writers at the end of the eighteenth and the beginning of the nineteenth centuries were sentimentalists without being revolutionists. Even those who called themselves classicists indulged in melancholic emotions and abandoned the strict canon of accepted Pseudo-Classical forms for Gothic tales.

By 1800 the Russian reader was acquainted with such works as Rousseau's *Nouvelle Héloïse,* Sterne's *Tristram Shandy* and *A Sentimental Journey,* Young's *Night Thoughts,* Goethe's *The Sorrows of Young Werther,* the poems of Ossian, and other pre-Romantic literature. The romantic trend was also apparent in the native productions of Sumarokov and Derzhavin; in 'The Rossiad,' an epic poem describing the conquest of Kazan by Ivan the Terrible, written by Michael Kheraskov (1733-1807), who never missed the opportunity of analyzing the sentiment of his heroes; and particularly among minor writers, such as Lvov, Emin, and Neledinsky-Meletsky (1751-1828), who filled the magazines with melancholy tales and unhappy love stories. But it remained for Karamzin to collect all these *disjecta membra* of the new sentimentalism. He easily out-distanced his timid followers. His talent and his awareness of the definite aim he had set himself made him the chief exponent of the new school. He dealt a mortal blow to Pseudo-Classicism, already in decline, and introduced a new conception of fiction to the masses of the reading public.

Nicholas Karamzin (1766-1826), of the provincial nobility, had received an excellent education. He served for a short time in the army and, after a brief association with Novikov and Radishchev, took a long journey abroad. He saw Paris shortly after the fall of Bastille, traveled extensively in various European countries and, upon his return home, settled down to earn his living by his pen. His *Letters of a Russian Traveler* and especially his novelette, *Poor Liza,* made him famous. He founded a monthly, *The Messenger of Europe,* which was one of the most important Russian reviews up to 1917, and he took an active part in the literary movements of his time. After his appointment as Court Historian by Alexander I in 1802, he devoted the rest of his life to his monumental *History of the Russian State,* twelve volumes of which he wrote in twenty years. The first eight volumes, published in 1816, had an enormous success.

The first part of his literary activity lasted slightly over a decade (1791-1802), but this comparatively short period sufficed to establish his reputation as a great author and a reformer of Russian letters. His influence was so vast that the younger generation of writers unanimously recognized him as their leader. Most writers of the first half of the nineteenth century, including Pushkin, Gogol, and Tiutchev more or less admired Karamzin and felt the influence of his works.

He was a great admirer of Rousseau and described his own journey to the Lake of Geneva as a pilgrimage, but he disliked *The Confessions* and could never appreciate *The Social Contract.* Rousseau's egalitarian and revolutionary ideas were completely alien to Karamzin. The Russian also remained indifferent to the emotional tension of the German 'storm and stress' period, to the heroic reconstructions of MacPherson or Klopstock, or to the caustic irony of Sterne. He felt more at ease with Goldsmith's *Vicar of Wakefield.* Karamzin's sentimentalism was of a delicate, idyllic nature, full of gentle melancholy, heavy sighs, a few occasional tears mitigated by a philosophy of resignation. He revealed this sentimentalism for the first time in his *Letters of a Russian Traveler,* the publication of which he had begun in 1791 in his own monthly, *The Moscow Journal.* This work was different from other books of travel— from the sharp and critical letters of Fonvizin, for instance, who had voiced his hopes that Russia, thanks to the peculiarities of her history, would avoid many of the ills of Western civilization. Karamzin wrote as a first-rate journalist and a highly educated man, taking great care to give the reader a variety of informative material. The pages of his book, depicting the chambers at the English Court, the aristocratic salons or popular suburbs of Paris, German students or Swiss mountains, had a vividly descriptive quality. He was at home with European history, law, art, and customs, and he utilized freely his vast knowledge of the West. But his report on the situation of various countries at the end of the century was accompanied by a detailed portrayal of the moods and emotions of the writer. Exterior reality was expressed through a 'good and tender heart.' Karamzin adopted a highly subjective attitude; he talked intimately to his audience, his chief aim being to convey 'sweet and melancholy thoughts and emotions.' Today we study the *Letters* as a historical document which shows how an educated Russian saw and interpreted Europe at a given period. They certainly throw light on the everlasting problem of the relations between Russia and the West. But for his contemporaries the most enlightening part of the book was its sentimental atmosphere, its emotional content. This was a novelty—and the public, accustomed to the rationalism of classical odes or the didactic spirit of satires, responded enthusiastically to Karamzin's writings.

The success of *Poor Liza,* which was also published in *The Moscow Journal,* surpassed even that of the *Letters.* This story of a peasant girl who is driven to despair by her unhappy love affair with Erast, a nobleman, and who finally throws herself into a lake at the Simonov Monastery in Moscow, was one of the first Russian best-sellers. It was written in Karamzin's usual style—graceful, gentle, and melancholic. Despite its unhappy ending this narrative, 'permeated by a voluptuousness of tears,' was not tragic or overwhelming in its effect. The subject matter of the novelette was of but minor importance to the author as well as to his readers: both primarily enjoyed what seemed to them a delightful gamut of emotions running from sensitiveness to affectation.

In some of his other stories Karamzin also attempted to describe grim islands, medieval castles, mysterious heroes, a sense of guilt weighing upon somber lovers, but he soon renounced all these paraphernalia of pre-Romanticism and returned to his favorite roseate tales (*Julie* and others), with their 'tearful kindness of simple hearts,' their noble sentiments, and melancholy landscapes.

His *History of the Russian State* was conceived in the same spirit. Although he aimed at scientific accuracy and spent years studying documents, his series of volumes, unlike the monographs of his predecessors Tatishchev, Lomonossov, Shcherbatov, Schloetzer, and Boltin was primarily a work of art. 'Sweet estheticism' inspired this smooth narrative which at times becomes melodramatic without ever losing its eloquent fluency. Karamzin's characterization of military lords and princes was based on psychological analysis and picturesque details. In general, the imaginative and sentimental side of historical events attracted him most. He hardly ever referred to the life of the common people and stated with utter seriousness that 'the history of the people belonged to the Czars.' The liberals and the future Decembrists maintained that 'history belongs to the people' (N. Muraviev), but even those who disapproved of the conservative tendency of Karamzin's work were entertained by it. His contemporaries have noted that women read *The History of the Russian State* as if it were a novel.

Karamzin's short stories—and he was the first to introduce the short story as a genre in Russian literature—were narratives of human interest describing the intimate life of the main characters and stressing their feelings and passions. This marked a major change in literary taste. Even more important were the changes brought about by Karamzin's style. He fashioned the language into a polished, elegant, and rhythmic medium. Disregarding the division into three styles introduced by Lomonossov, he formulated the idiom of educated society. He never hesitated to introduce neologisms, derived for the most part from French or German words, and he invented new terms or figures of speech for the new ideas or sentiments about which he wrote. His goal was to create a literary language corresponding to the elegant colloquial speech of the nobility. To the great surprise of critics and readers he proved that a Russian writer was capable of producing a refined easy prose fully as rounded and supple as the best examples of French literature. No wonder that his contemporaries became ecstatic about his flowing periods and the rhythmic organizations of his pleasant well-balanced narrative. Today it may be said that Karamzin's language was not only too elaborate but even arty and prettified. Its monotonous fluency and snobbish exclusiveness alienated it from the folklore tradition or the spoken language of the common man. But in 1800 it was a revelation and aroused violent controversy.

Karamzin lacked the fighting spirit. His philosophical pessimism, his tenderheartedness, his quietism, and estheticism kept him aloof from action. A man of great moral integrity, he preferred privacy and solitude to the dubious tactics or violence of conflict. However, his position as the leader of the new school compelled him to take part in the literary disputes that raged in Russia before the Napoleonic invasion of 1812.

Traditionalists and conservatives were greatly upset by Karamzin's new literary language. The campaign against it was led by A. Shishkov, an influential and prominent bureaucrat (Minister of Education, head of the Censorship Department, President of the Russian Academy, member of the State Council, and so on). In his *Considerations on the Old and New Styles of the Russian Language* (1803) Shishkov pleaded for a strict discrimination between the Simple, Middle, and Lofty styles. Some of his remarks were valid. He was right in his laudatory evaluation of folklore and contemporary popular poetry, which he praised as sources for the Simple Style. His criticism of Karamzin's mannerisms also sounds sensible (instead of saying, like Karamzin, 'traveling had become a need of my soul,' Shishkov proposed 'I liked traveling'). He understood that certain literary forms require their own idiom and that literary styles are only differing systems of word arrangements, each one creating its own type of language. Not without reason he felt the usefulness and beauty of archaisms. But, on the other hand, he had no conception of the evolution, of the pulsating life of language, which ever brings about new changes, abrupt advances, and even revolutions. He did not realize the necessity of creating a new literary idiom in Russia that could become a vehicle of national unity and would fill the gap between the tongue spoken by small privileged groups and that spoken by the vast masses of the people. He wanted to preserve Church-Slavonic as the only basis for the High Style, he fought desperately against any neologisms of foreign origin, and, being a purist, aimed at what in practice was a sort of mummification of the language. This defense of the old traditions was not without a deep political meaning. 'Glory to thee, O Russian tongue,' he chanted, 'for thou dost not possess that vile and foul word—Revolution!' New words and styles reflected, in his opinion, the pernicious spirit of French Republicanism. On the contrary, the purity of the old language was, as he saw it, in keeping with loyalty to the principles of autocracy and Orthodoxy. In the name of conservative nationalism Shishkov was defending the sanctity of the past in literature.

Thus a literary problem was, as is always the case in Russia, assuming the character of an ideological clash. And the amusing part of it was that Karamzin, whom Shishkov accused of subversive activity in literature, was no less conservative politically than his incensed opponent. The great sentimentalist and reformer of the language belonged to the group of Monarchists who fully supported the established order, including its absolutism and serfdom. In 1811, in his *Memorandum on Ancient and New Russia,* Karamzin took a very reactionary attitude toward the constitutional reforms planned by Alexander I. It is true that his independence, his civic dignity, his reluctance to justify administrative abuses, and his proud frankness in the face of the smug aristocrats, as well as his innate kindliness and humanity, made him the friend of many liberals. Besides, being a thoroughly educated man, well-read in European literature, he felt more at ease with young radicals, who were avidly learning from Europe, than he did with old dignitaries, who feared the influence of the West.

Karamzin won many followers, old as well as young. Some of them, like Dmitriev, admired him as a stylist; others, like K. Izmailov and Prince Shalikov, imitated his sentimentalism. A few women writers also took Karamzin's part in the struggle and in Russia, as elsewhere, sentimentalism acted as godfather to feminine literature. From the very beginning of the new school women became more frequently the main characters in fiction, and more and more books were written by them.

Some of Karamzin's disciples, such as Vassily Pushkin (1767-1830), the uncle of the great poet, carried on the struggle against the Shishkov clique. Vassily Pushkin, a man-about-town, offered an easy target to his opponents, who ridiculed his vanity, pretentiousness, and other weaknesses. But aside from his stanzas for the albums of pretty ladies, his puns, and all his small talk in verse, Pushkin was a rather keen polemicist. He directed his witty epigrams mainly against the Forum of the Lovers of the Russian Word—a society organized by Shishkov. Most of the members of the Forum belonged to the higher bureaucracy and represented in the eyes of their liberal opponents the stuffed shirts of literature.

Another distinguished follower of Karamzin was Merzliakov (1778-1830), a professor at the University of Moscow, whose wistful songs and romances had been greatly influenced by folklore. Some of his songs found their way back to the people and became popular among peasants and workmen (his famous 'Among the Level Valleys,' for instance).

Sentimentalism conquered the stage, also, in the person of Vladislav Ozerov (1769-1836). This playwright had studied in the same military academy as Sumarokov and owed his love for the theater to the atmosphere and traditions of their alma mater. After graduation he began an administrative career, but devoted more time and attention to reading than to the Ministry of Finance, where he held a post. The last four years of his life were darkened by a mental disorder.

Ozerov won his fame between 1804 and 1807 with his tragedies. He pictured Oedipus (in *Oedipus in Athens*) as a sentimental Christian of the eighteenth century; his *Fingal,* inspired by Ossian, was based on melancholy love; in *Dmitri Donskoy* the lack of historic truth was compensated for by a passionate love story. In their structure these tragedies, obviously written under the influence of French writers (particularly Voltaire), displayed a peculiar variation of Russian Pseudo-Classicism. But, in perfect keeping with the tenets of the Karamzin school, the content of his dramas emphasized sentimental psychology. The audiences of that time were also fond of frequent political allusions (against Napoleon or for Alexander I) of which Ozerov's heroes recited mouth-filling lines. Ozerov kept to the middle course between Classicism and Romanticism, but his attempt to create sentimental drama helps to explain his short-lived success.

II   The literary movement launched by
Karamzin had manifold ramifications, all of which sooner or later
converged in the vast current of Romanticism. The gradual transformation of the Karamzin school into new patterns took but a few years
and was identified with the activity of Zhukovsky. Vassily Zhukovsky,
outstanding poet and first representative of Russian pre-Romanticism,
was born in 1783, the son of a rich landowner and a Turkish captive,
and derived his name from an obliging hanger-on of his real father.
He studied in the boarding school for the nobility at the University of
Moscow, and soon showed an interest in German and English literature.
An excellent linguist, he mastered five European languages and made
his literary debut as a translator. In 1802 he published, in Karamzin's
Messenger of Europe, a remarkable adaptation of Gray's 'Elegy in a
Country Churchyard.' This marked the beginning of Zhukovsky's long
list of translations from Ossian, Southey, Byron, Scott, Schiller, Goethe,
Uhland, Lenau, Chamisso, La Motte-Fouqué, the Brothers Grimm, and
other Romantics.

His incessant labors brought the best works of contemporary European poetry to the Russian reader. Zhukovsky's translations were veritable masterpieces of re-creation. He had once said that 'translators
of prose are the slaves of their original text, whereas the translators of
the poets are the rivals of the poets themselves.' He firmly believed that
only a poet of stature is able to find in his own tongue a poetic equivalent for the works he is translating, and thus to render their beauty, their
stylistic peculiarities, and their inner spirit. He regarded his own undertaking as a highly difficult and responsible one and established a
tradition of unique importance: all the great Russian poets have since
then made their translations the touchstone of their own skill. As a
result Pushkin, Lermontov, Fet, and many other first-rate poets have
made translations from foreign languages. Throughout the nineteenth
century, and even today, Russian readers were—and are—fortunate in
making the acquaintance of non-Russian poetry through outstanding
versions. A Russian college student has a knowledge of Byron, Shelley,
Poe, or Schiller derived from texts in his own language, yet of such high
poetic quality as to rival the originals. The American or European
reader is much less fortunate in so far as, for example, Russian literature
is concerned. Pushkin, Lermontov, and Nekrassov have been translated
into English or French by dilettantes or pedants rather than by great
poets, which explains the fact that the verbal richness, the charm, and
the rhythm of Russian poetry have hardly ever been rendered adequately
in any foreign language. It also accounts for the rather inexact evaluation

of Russian poetry by European and American critics, who are unable
to read it in the original.

In his translations Zhukovsky did not evince merely his unusual
gift of versification and a capacity for poetic transmutation. His choice
of authors and poems reflected his own personality and his literary
inclinations. He was attracted chiefly by poems of melancholic moods
and universal sorrow, so dear to the heart of the pre-Romanticists of
France and England, and of the early Romanticists of Germany. Certain
circumstances of his own life had strengthened this tendency. He was
a delicate dreamer whose heart had been broken (or at least he thought
so) by an unhappy love for his niece, Maria Protassova. Her parents
objected to their union; Maria, after a painful separation from her lover,
married another man, and died in 1823. For many years Zhukovsky
remained a lonely bachelor, worshiping her memory. He did not marry
until he was fifty-eight.

In his youth and early manhood he was, above all, a poet of suffering
and sadness. In melodious elegiac verse he sang of the frailty of human
life, of premonitions of doom, of the languor of love, or the forebodings
of death. Like so many of his contemporaries, he wandered among
melancholy ruins or pastoral landscapes, in a perpetual mood of wistfulness, sighing for the 'land of heart's desire.' Later he became interested in ballads and folklore and, as a true exponent of Romanticism,
appointed himself, according to his own statement, 'the godfather of
German and English witches.' He translated Buerger and more of
Ossian. Weird figures writhed in his poems: phantoms, the spirits of
the dead, demon bridegrooms galloping in the moonlight to abduct the
bride at the witching hour, felons selling their souls to the Evil One,
skeletons rising from yawning graves amid the swirling mists of eerie
nights—the usual paraphernalia of Gothic novels and Romantic ballads.
Zhukovsky replaced his former 'joy of grief' by the 'voluptuousness of
fright,' or the 'poetry of horror.' During this period he again did a great
service to Russian literature by associating it with one of the prevailing
currents of European letters. Zhukovsky's real temperament, however,
was rather placid; his lack of strong passions prevented him from becoming a Romantic in the Byronian or French style. He readily abandoned his ghouls, demons, and fiendish spirits for meditations and
reveries. At this period he certainly preferred Wordsworth's poems to
Coleridge's 'Rime of the Ancient Mariner.'

From the eighteen-twenties on Zhukovsky fell under the influence
of the German mystics and idealists. He replaced his early definition of
poetry, 'Art combines truth and goodness; poetry is virtue,' with the
Kantian concept, 'Esthetics are pure contemplation.' He often quoted

Plato's definition of inspiration as remembrance and, following Schelling and Schlegel, asserted that art was the intuitive perception of the ideal essence of nature.

Only that which is on the ebb is beautiful. Beauty is evanescent; it is not of this earth. What we hear is but a voice, a message of perfection; we feel a delightful longing for *home*—an obscure remembrance of the Beauty of the past and its promise for the future.

Individual emotions—the intimate world of the heart—form the center of his highly subjective creativeness. 'The lofty realization of being human exalts my soul,' he exclaims in his philosophical poem 'Theon and Æschines.' Sentiments are all that matter, and the inner life is incomparably more important than riches, nobility, glory, or success. This idealistic individualism is blended with resignation: the poet accepts man's condition and preaches conformity to existing reality.

These ideas run through all his writings. It may be said that three-quarters of his output consists of translations or was inspired by other books. His originality lay not so much in his subject matter as in the general merit of his verse. Instead of the logical concrete terms of the Classicists, he used words as symbols, aiming at the creation of moods or of fleeting impressions. He never sought to give an illusion of rationality to his fancies or meditations; he cherished the unconscious as the true substance of poetry, and his melodious lines contain vague allusions, strange overtones, and purely musical values. They always seem to flutter on a double plane, and remind one of Keat's line: 'Heard melodies are sweet, but those unheard are sweeter.' By the end of the nineteenth century and at the beginning of the twentieth Russian symbolists considered Zhukovsky as one of their predecessors and, like Alexander Blok, found a source of inspiration in the 'enchanting sweetness' (as Pushkin put it) of his poetry.

As a craftsman Zhukovsky discovered many rhythms unknown or hardly used in Russian poetry before him. His unrhymed iambic pentameters sounded so unusual that the administration of the Imperial Theaters rejected all plays written in this new form.

The even flow of his verse was like a melody played on a harpsichord, and Polevoy, one of his contemporaries, remarked that the word 'harmonious' could not be applied to Zhukovsky, inasmuch as harmony required poetic counterpoint, a blending of dissonances, a resolution of contradictions, while the somewhat monotonous songs of the author of 'Theon and Æschines,' had a remarkable evenness of tone and sound.

In 1812 Zhukovsky wrote a famous patriotic ode, 'A Bard Among Russian Warriors'—one of the best depictions of the Napoleonic invasion in the poetry of that period. A few years afterward he was compelled to renounce his bucolic retreat; he was appointed instructor of Russian to Princess Charlotte, the future Czarina Alexandra Fedorovna. With this appointment and later as tutor to Alexander, the son of Nicholas I and his heir apparent, Zhukovsky had to spend many years at the Court of St. Petersburg. Life in the intimacy of the Czar's family, while strengthening his conservative political views, did not at all affect his character. He remained self-effacing, kind, and humanitarian, and never failed to use his influence in behalf of his liberal friends. His many interventions alleviated the fate of various writers—among others Pushkin, Baratynsky, and Shevchenko, an artist of considerable merit and the greatest Ukrainian poet. The intellectuals saw him as a sort of ambassador of the republic of letters at the Court of the Czars. This situation actually gave rise to certain misunderstandings: the French representatives reported to Paris that Zhukovsky was the leader of the liberal opposition to the throne. Nicholas I became suspicious of the poet: on one occasion when Zhukovsky, as usual, interceded for some writers who had fallen victim to administrative repression, and offered to vouch for them, the Czar interrupted him, 'Aye, but who will vouch for thee?' In 1838, the situation had reached such a dismal point that Zhukovsky could no longer cope with it and resigned.

He spent the rest of his life on his estate or traveling abroad, where he had many friends, particularly among the German Romantics. More and more inclined toward mysticism, he refused to share many of their literary judgments. In a conversation with Tieck he declared that *Hamlet* was 'monstrous and incomprehensible.' He also disagreed with Goethe's judgment of Byron. The sage of Weimar in his conversations with Zhukovsky highly praised the English poet, while the Russian called Byron's revolt childish and futile. From 1841 on, after his marriage to the twenty-one-year-old Elizabeth Reutern, he lived in Germany, translating epics (among them the *Odyssey,* still one of the best of all translations although not done from the original), and studying Catholic and Protestant theology. 'I am a strict Christian,' he wrote shortly before his death. 'There exists but one philosophy, that which is based on the Revelation.' He died in 1852 at Baden-Baden.

In 1824, on the publication of Zhukovsky's collected works, Pushkin wrote: 'I have received his three volumes. The late Zhukovsky was a good man. May the Almighty grant peace to his soul.' Times were moving fast, and the young generation considered Zhukovsky dead almost thirty years before his actual passing. Nevertheless they had learned a great deal from him, and his poetic achievements had beaten a trail for them. A year later, when new attacks were launched against the poet, Pushkin himself corrected his former judgment, with the *bon mot:* 'Why should we bite the breasts of our common wet-nurse?' As a matter of fact, Zhukovsky had nursed many Russian poets, including Pushkin himself, and one of these, Kuechelbecker, acknowledged his role in these terms: 'Zhukovsky had a decisive influence on our poetic style, and hence we ought to be grateful to him; however, his influence on the *spirit* of our literature was bad: too much mist, mysticism, dreaminess, and vagueness.'

III   Karamzin, the reformer of style, championed sentimentalism in prose. Zhukovsky did the same for verse, and opened to Russian poets the enchanted land of Romantic idealism. Both were moving within the area of contemporary European fiction, while two other poets, Batiushkov and Gnedich, usually considered Pushkin's forerunners, represented another tendency connected with classical studies. Konstantin Batiushkov (1787-1855) was mainly interested in Latin and Greek authors, as well as in the poets of the Italian Renaissance. This functionary of the Foreign Office, and later an officer in the army that fought Napoleon in Russia and Europe, called himself 'the bard of earthly happiness.' His light verse is something more than merely Epicurean or hedonistic. It acclaims the luxurious fullness of life, the joy of being, and the sensual perception of the world, and it points out that happiness is attainable only when the individual possesses the twin blessings of youth: capacity for enjoyment and intensity of emotion. Batiushkov sought all earthly pleasures, but he was even more eager for a state of mind that gives one an ecstatic vision of reality. Pushkin was to follow this line, although his conception of the fullness of life was to acquire a broader meaning.

Batiushkov's paganism (partly influenced by the French erotic poetry of the eighteenth century, particularly by Parny and his *Erotic Poems*) was too tense and feverish to approach the rounded balance of Hellenic beauty. His art could never be Apollonian. Even at the peak of his apotheosis of human joys, as opposed to Zhukovsky's wan spiritualism, in the midst of his triumphs of love and lust (as in the poem 'The Bacchantes' and in his hymns to Venus and Bacchus), there was always a shrill note of tragic premonition; it resounds in his most riotous affirmations of sensual delights. The image of death is ever present in all the joyous pictures of Batiushkov. With the passing of the years this dualistic character of his poetry became more and more striking. It indicated a profound schism within the poet himself, to which he finally fell victim.

A man of rapidly changing moods, subject to fits of despair, melancholy, or enthusiasm, Batiushkov started his literary career with the firm belief that 'earthly happiness is possible.' His personal life, as well as international events, was a bitter denial of this theory. Lonely and ill, Batiushkov became appalled by what he had seen in Europe during his service in the Russian Army between 1812 and 1815. The reaction that gripped Europe after the Congress of Vienna made him question not only the possibility of human progress but also the rationality of the order of the universe. 'History proves,' he wrote, 'that men kill one another to found a State; States, in their turn, are destroyed by time; whereupon men have to start and kill one another all over again—and thus it goes on, *ad infinitum*.' Starting from these pessimistic premises he criticized the hopeful rationale of enlightenment and took a firm stand against the French Revolution. Its utter futility, according to Batiushkov, had been demonstrated by Napoleon and his wars. Russia was fortunate in being so far removed from the land where revolutionary passions had run their maddening and useless course. His final conclusion was that 'mortals need a morale based on Divine Revelation.' In this he agreed with Zhukovsky, whom he had opposed in his youth but who became his best friend in his later years. However, this new philosophy did not give Batiushkov that peace of mind he had vainly sought all his life. His poems described (before Byron's *Childe Harold*) a disillusioned young man who leaves his country and travels round the world without finding happiness or peace. His elegies, the lofty style of which was inspired not only by old Tibullus but by the Italians of the Renaissance as well (such as Tasso and Ariosto), betray the despondency of their author. They all have one main theme: the tragic undoing of this world and its beauty, the vision of which had charmed and elated the poet in his youth. He no longer sang of the ecstatic joy of life. One of his heroes, on his deathbed, sums up the experience of life in these terms: 'Man is but a slave from his birth to his grave, and even death does not reveal to him why he has traversed this vale of tears, why he failed, why he wept, why he loved and vanished.'

In his *Greek Anthology* (1817-18) Batiushkov collected his Hellenic poems. He mourned the irreparable loss of the supreme Hellenic harmony; the charm and beauty of this imaginary world of ancient glory is described by a poet who notes with tragic lucidity the discord and ugliness of his own times.

In 1821 Batiushkov became seriously ill. A nervous breakdown was followed by mental prostration and twenty years of madness, from which he never recovered. He died in 1855.

Batiushkov introduced Greece and the Hellenic concept of earthly life and its fullness into Russian literature. Before him Greece, 'that universal workshop of the world's art' as Belinsky put it, was hardly known to Russian letters, and his presentation of the variety of ancient rhythms and verse forms in his *Anthology* was quite a novelty. His contemporaries were greatly impressed by the fervor of this poetry, and saw him as the bard of Epicurean joy and of youth. The poems and philosophical elegies of the second period of Batiushkov's life initiated quite a different current—that of Romantic despondency. Yet, despite his inner duality Batiushkov preserved a unity of style. A master of mellow and melodious verse, he reflected in his beautifully ordered lines the clarity and harmony of the great Italians.

Paralleling Batiushkov's introduction of Greek influence was the work of Nicholas Gnedich (1784-1833), whose original poetry was obscured by the greatest achievement of his life—his translation (probably the best in the world) of the *Iliad*.

A nobleman of moderate means and an official in the Ministry of Education, Gnedich led a lonely, orderly, and uneventful life, broken only by a series of illnesses and the death of his beloved sister. As a young man he was introduced to and made a member of the circle presided over by his friend A. Olenin, the director of the St. Petersburg Public Library, a connoisseur of ancient art, and a man of immense wealth. He represented in Russia the same movement that Lessing and Winckelmann did in Germany. Their Greece was much more of an esthetic concept than a historic reality. To them Greek poems or statues were 'the highest achievements of art,' and Olenin always pointed out their 'noble simplicity, their calm, grandeur, proportionality, and harmony.' Gnedich, who had an excellent classical background and was a scholar by training, decided to introduce to the Russians what he believed was the most beautiful specimen of all these virtues—the *Iliad*. He did not confine himself to a mere translation of Homer, but supplemented his work with comments and notes explaining the specific characteristics of Hellenic civilization. He also used a Russian hexameter which proved most appropriate in rendering Homer's rhythms into a new tongue. He worked on his translation for more than twenty years. Its publication in 1829 was more than a literary success: it was a milestone in the evolution of Russia's cultural society. In the 'twenties and 'thirties of the last century Gnedich's work exercised a strong influence on the formation of literary taste. Today, more than a hundred years after his death, his magnificent version of the poem is still read and memorized by Russian schoolboys and girls.

IV   Despite the many differences in their
personalities and literary tendencies, all the poets at the beginning
of the nineteenth century wrote for a restricted audience. They were
known and read only by the upper classes; none of them ever acquired
a nation-wide reputation; none of them even dreamt of becoming a
national writer. They therefore looked askance at any author whose
popularity passed beyond the confines of a class group. Since a circulation of 5000 copies signified in 1800 a great success for a book of
poetry, the 75,000 copies of Krylov's *Fables* represented a new and
surprising fact. It was a first step toward the democratization of literature, of which many of his contemporaries heartily disapproved.
'Krylov,' remarked Prince Vyazemsky, 'is too popular; he smells.'

Ivan Krylov (1769-1844), the son of an army officer, had a very
hard time of it even in his childhood and was compelled to earn his
living by all sorts of odd jobs. Under Catherine he wrote comedies and
operas (one entitled *The Americans*) without much success. He did
slightly better as the editor of various satirical periodicals, but found
his true vocation in writing fables. His first collection of these, published
in 1809, proved a hit, and from then on his fame grew steadily. In the
eighteen-twenties he was a celebrity, and the people of St. Petersburg
used to greet 'good old grandpa Krylov' whenever the corpulent poet
ventured out for a walk.

In 1812 he was appointed to the Public Library, where he served
for twenty-nine years. Knowing from bitter experience that the path of
a satirist was full of thorns, Krylov, who in his youth had attacked
officialdom, nobility, and serfdom, now avoided committing himself to
any political or literary struggle. He took the attitude of a distant, im-
partial, and kindly onlooker, gained the favor of the Court, was elected
member of the Academy, and led the peaceful life of an Epicurean,
praising 'golden mediocrity' and 'small deeds.' His philosophy of social
and political conformism became distinctly conservative, and he seldom
deviated from his stand of common sense and quietism. Nevertheless
some of his witty remarks aroused the suspicion of the authorities, and
he had to make changes in several of his fables in order to placate the
censors.

Out of his 205 fables only 45 are derived from La Fontaine, Florian,
Gellert, Æsop, and so on. But even these borrowings are so utterly
Russified as to fit perfectly into the rest of his work. His fables resemble
so many scenes of one great comedy of manners. Whether their subject
matter is taken from the world of animals or from that of men,
they have the dramatic sharpness of dialogue, dynamic situation, and
concise comment of a play. Their range is wide—from the lion, King

of the forest, to the frog who bursts in trying to imitate a bull; from the silly potentate to the tailor who patches a coat and collar by cutting off its tails. The symbolism of the animals serves the satirical purposes of the fabulist: the wolf caught in the kennel of hunting dogs to whom he addresses eloquent declarations of friendship represents Napoleon in Russia; the bear who loves the anchorite so dearly that he smashes the fly on the forehead of his sleeping friend with a huge stone is a broad dig at the excessively zealous defenders of absolutism; other fables about foxes, swine, eagles, or hens reflect various aspects of society. Krylov laughed at human frailties, social customs, and political blunders, usually aiming at some actual condition of contemporary society, but he always spoke as a moralist and advanced a philosophy of common sense and sound rationalism. He was concrete, precise, earthy, and—although he told his fables simply and directly with an air of innocence—infinitely sly. This union of slyness and straightforwardness was not the only national trait reflected in Krylov's satirical miniatures. He surprised and delighted his contemporaries with his truly Russian humor, his wisdom, and his style. He judged men and events exactly as would a sage old peasant who knows the price of flattery, pretensions, and human folly, without ever losing his fundamental optimism and horsesense. Whatever Krylov wrote was strongly permeated with this typically Russian spirit. The smell that shocked Prince Vyazemsky was the smell of Russian soil, which had not become fashionable in the salons of the aristocracy.

For the nobility as for the middle class Krylov embodied the popular spirit, the essence of the national character. This spirit was intensified by the language of his fables. He wrote as millions spoke, employing the verbal richness, the semantics, and the logic of popular language. Hence his constant recourse to folk proverbs, which have an organic rather than an ornamental function. His own sentences became part of the popular speech as current sayings. In his works the animistic tradition of folklore, the realistic spirit of the Russian people, and the idiom of the masses rejoined the satirical tendency of the eighteenth century, and the fabulistic form widely developed by the Pseudo-Classicists.

'Dmitriev introduced Fable into the salons and palaces,' a contemporary commented; 'Krylov led it into the common dwellings.' This moralist of manners, who was also a penetrating observer of the realities of his time, wrote for all mankind and was equally admired by old and young, by common folk who felt at ease with him and by literati who admired the bold simplicity with which he raised the fable from a low to a high form and made the popular idiom, instead of Karamzin's elaborate language, the medium for successful literary experiment.

This is the true significance of Krylov. At a period when literature was in danger of becoming a luxury for the fortunate few, he reminded Russians of the immeasurable resources within the people themselves and became one of the first writers to attain popularity through all of Russia.

3

From the Napoleonic Invasion to the Decembrists

I   The reaction that set in during the
last years of Catherine's reign did not stop with her death in 1796.
Paul, her son and successor, established a capricious kind of despotism
over the country. Half mad and subject to sudden fits of despair or
anger, he would shed tears over a simpering French novel—and immediately afterwards would order the brutal punishment of some poor
devil whose only crime was a slight breach of the innumerable rules
and regulations. His subjects bestowed upon this suspicious, sleek, and
unaccountable Czar the nickname of the 'Sentimental Tiger.' Paul
wanted to fix the whole of Russia's life in a strict military pattern as
the best method of preventing the propagation of revolutionary ideas,
which he feared and loathed. He introduced rigid discipline in the Army
which was maintained through flogging and executions. He himself
worked out special regulations for the length of the soldiers' hair and
of the officers' wigs. Whoever had the misfortune of erring in the prescribed width of the brim of his cocked hat or the placement of the
buttons on the tunic ran the risk not only of being broken to the ranks
but also of being sent to Siberia on foot. A succession of restrictive
measures enslaved all cultural life. No passports were issued to noblemen who wanted to travel abroad or to study there. The importation of
books and musical scores was banned. All unlicensed presses were
summarily suppressed. Every line intended for publication in Russia
was subjected to a double censorship—secular and religious.

The cruelty and inconsistency of his rule provoked a growing discontent among the nobles and finally led to a conspiracy of high dignitaries and officers of the Guards, with the tacit moral support of Alexander, the heir apparent, who hated his father and was mistreated by

him. At night on 11 March, 1801, the plotters entered the Emperor's bedroom and assassinated him.

The end of Paul's regime and enthronement of Alexander I were greeted with joy by the upper classes. Brought up under the dual influence of Catherine and of Paul, and compelled to compromise with them and to hide his true feelings, Alexander I had developed many contradictory traits of character. The hypocrisy, slyness, and vengefulness he displayed toward the end of his reign stemmed beyond any doubt from his unhappy youth. At the same time he possessed great personal charm, which he used as skilfully as any actor. Napoleon, who during the negotiations at Tilsit in 1807 had learned how evasive and deceiving Alexander could be, called him 'the cunning Byzantine.'

At any rate, the beginning of his reign was happy and promising. All of Paul's restrictions were lifted; torture as a method of criminal investigation was abolished; the administration of the State was reorganized. A new blueprint for education comprised three types of schools: the parish school, for one year; the county school, for two years; and the *gymnasia,* with a course of four years. Outside the general network of schools, special restricted lyceums for the nobility were opened in St. Petersburg, Odessa, and other towns. Universities were granted academic autonomy with rectors, deans, and heads of departments elected by the faculty.

The liquidation of Paul's reactionary regime and the liberal era inaugurated by Alexander had a stimulating effect on literature. In the years 1802 to 1812 there was a sharp rise in book production; annuals, reviews, journals were being published all over Russia. Second to the growth of the interest in literature among the privileged classes was the startling increase of readers from other walks of society. Representatives of the middle class, artisans, and freed peasants joined the ranks of the intelligentsia. Literature and education were directed, as before, however, by the nobility, and the main body of writers and readers belonged to the aristocracy, the bureaucracy, the Army, and the gentry. Of the prominent Russian writers before Pushkin, most (Zhukovsky, Gnedich, Krylov, for example) had belonged to the minor nobility—somewhat different from the background of eighteenth-century writers. There was also another trend, which was to become still more obvious in the 'thirties and 'forties: the writers were more and more infrequently connected with the civil service or the Army. Their emancipation from the State coincides with the increase in number of those who earned a living by their writing. The feeling of professional solidarity grew into a desire to join forces, and poets, novelists, and journalists formed groups and circles. At the beginning of the nineteenth century there was an extraordinary blossoming of literary clubs and societies all over Russia. Each review, each magazine with its staff of regular contributors, became a literary chapel or the organ of a school; artistic factions were active and waged great wars of words.

Shishkov's society, the Forum of the Lovers of the Russian Word, was the citadel of literary conservatism. It drew together senators, Court chamberlains, and ministers. Among its members were Count Zavadovsky, the Czar's aide-de-camp, Count Razumovsky, the Minister of Education, Dmitriev, the Minister of Justice, Admiral Mordvinov, and so on. (Derzhavin was also a nominal member of this society.) The members of the Arzamas Society, which in 1815-18 led an ironic and burlesque offensive against the Forum, claimed that the sessions of Shishkov's group had a closer resemblances to those of the State Council than to those of a literary gathering. The evenings of the Arzamas Society were certainly lacking in solemnity or formality, but their participants—all bearing facetious nicknames—had a great deal of wit and humor, duly helped along by good wine. Prince Vyazemsky (1792-1878), a liberal dignitary, Romantic poet, and witty critic, Zhukovsky, Vassily Pushkin, and his glorious nephew, who was nicknamed 'the Cricket,' were among the most distinguished Arzamas members.

The Free Society of Lovers of Literature, Science, and Art represented another type of literary assembly. It had a definite political character, and its members were mainly interested in social and economic problems. Some of them—Kamenev, Pnin, and particularly Gromval and Bobrov—were quite active as poets.

The struggle between the various groups contributed to the development of literary satire, and epigrams, fables, and parodies flourished as never before. Some satirical works provoked heated discussions, such as the one that raged over *The Lipetski Spa,* a successful comedy by Alexander Shakhovskoy (1777-1846), a stage director and writer of 52 original and adapted plays. In it he had attacked Zhukovsky and made rather broad allusions to Karamzin and his school. The indignant supporters of the new tendency did not fail to answer, and bitter arguments lasted for a considerable time. One of the most popular satires of the period was *The Madhouse,* a poem by Alexander Voyeikov (1778-1839), which compared literature to a bedlam and portrayed the writers as lunatics.

On the eve of the Napoleonic invasion literary polemics became more and more colored by politics. Shishkov's group represented the right wing of Russian aristocracy and bureaucracy. Their defence of the division of literary styles corresponded to the established division of social classes. In their support of absolutism, Orthodox religion, and the existing social inequality and in their constant attack on modern writers for looking to Europe for knowledge and inspiration, they showed a tendency toward nationalistic smugness and cultural isolationism. On the other hand, despite many points in common, their opponents had no ideological unity.

The acknowledged leaders of the new school—Karamzin, Zhukovsky, and to some extent, Krylov—were conservatives, acclaimed the autocratic regime, and did not venture to attack serfdom. The majority of their followers, however, were liberals, and the young generation identified liberalism with the new literary trends. This fact, which brought about a split between fathers and sons, had its full impact during and after the Napoleonic wars.

The invasion of Russia by Napoleon in 1812 and the War for the Fatherland waged against him proved the real test of political ideology. The conservatives defined the purpose of this struggle 'against the scion of Revolution' as a 'restoration of the lawful authorities throughout Europe.' In 1812 the Czar asked Shishkov to write all his official proclamations, appeals, and manifestos, and the president of the Forum did not miss the opportunity of hitting out at the 'infernal sophistication of French enlightenment' or of accusing those who wanted to strengthen culture of flirting with France, 'that land of disorder and pernicious anti-Christian doctrines.' Shishkov's friends declared that Napoleon was the Antichrist foretold by St. John in his Apocalypse and proclaimed the Russian resistance of the invader a defense of Christian principles. The patriotic odes of this group (by Karpov, Golenishchev-Kutuzov, and others), widely read during the war, were expressions of this point of view.

On the other hand, the liberals stressed the popular character of the war, in which Russia was fighting for her territorial integrity and for independence against the foreign invader. Alexander Kunitzyn (1783-1841), one of Pushkin's professors at the Lyceum of Czarskoye Selo and author of the treatise on *Natural Right,* spoke in his writings of a war against despotism and for the freedom of the country. He also emphasized the active part taken by the Russian peasants in fighting Napoleon's troops and attributed the defeat of the enemy to the people's efforts. This interpretation was adopted by all liberal circles and was expressed in many ways in the literature of the eighteen-twenties. An example is the book that in its English translation was the delight of Walter Scott—*A Diary of Partisan Operations* by Denis Davydov (1784-1839). Davydov was an officer in the Hussars, one of the organizers of the guerrillas, the leading Russian poet of wine, woman, and song, author of popular love lyrics and epicurean verse, and a close friend of Pushkin.

Many young Russians, mostly Army officers, were deeply aware of the paradoxical situation: the peasants and the soldiers, the vast majority of whom were also of peasant stock, had saved the country, while that country continued to treat them as slaves and refused to grant them the rights they so well deserved. This contradiction became even more striking after 1815, at the end of the campaign, when the Russian troops, after their victorious march through Europe and the occupation of Paris, came home. A contemporary reports that, at the landing of the Army detachments in a Baltic port, the crowd assembled to greet these 'liberators of the Fatherland' was brutally dispersed by the police. The first things the soldiers saw on setting foot on their native soil after three years of fighting were clubs, sabers, and fists freely used by the gendarmes against the peaceful population. 'We saved Russia and the whole West—what for? To find slavery and despotism in our own country?' This sense of bitter disappointment grew stronger as the Army officers took stock of the political situation in Russia.

Even before 1812, Alexander I had shaken off the liberal dreams of his youth. Now he believed in his mission as the chief supporter of the Holy Alliance of emperors, which had been born at the Congress of Vienna. He considered himself elected by the Lord to prop up the thrones and altars of Europe. The reactionary trend in international politics personified by Metternich was followed by the strengthening of autocracy in Russia. After 1815 the Czar, increasingly mystical, fell under the influence of such 'exalted prophetesses' as the Baroness Kruedener and entrusted the affairs of State to his devoted servant and righthand man, General Arakcheyev. The latter, an uneducated trooper, administered the country as if it were an infantry regiment. To him order was identical with blind obedience and general welfare with strict discipline, and he maintained the regime with bayonets and horsewhips. Russia was returning to the times of the mad Czar Paul. The only 'reform' introduced by Arakcheyev was the transformation of thousands of villages in five provinces into 'Military cantonments' subject to Army regulations and allotted one third of the Army's regulars. Instead of drilling, soldiers were set to cultivating the land. These military peasants were awakened by drums and marched to the fields in files. Bugles called them to mass, sounded lights-out and taps. All the houses—both within and without—were supposed to be arranged in an identical way. Life was regimented down to the minutest detail. Arakcheyev regulated even the number of children in each family. Any infringement of the rules meant a severe flogging.

The Army was reorganized according to a Prussian pattern. The privates, drafted from the peasantry and the lower classes, had to serve twenty-five years, with the prospect of getting a plot of land in one of the military settlements after the expiration of their term. It was Arakcheyev who favored the notorious punishment of the 'Green Lane,' or running the gantlet, which for fifty years was one of the nightmares in the Russian Army. The condemned soldier, naked to the waist, made his way as best he could between two long ranks of his comrades who whipped him incessantly from both sides with sticks cut from green wood. The length of the 'lane' depended on the seriousness of his offense. Sometimes it was formed by five hundred to a thousand men. At the end of his *Via Crucis* the victim usually fainted; he was then put face downward on a cart and hauled away. The men in the ranks were watched by special officers; those who did not seem to hit out with sufficient zeal were marked with chalk—slated for a flogging in their turn. There are several descriptions of this 'Green Lane' in Russian fiction—one in *After the Ball,* a posthumous story by Leo Tolstoy.

After the uprising in the military cantonments of the Chernigov Province two hundred of the rebels were sentenced to pass from six to twenty-four times through a 'Green Lane' of five hundred soldiers. Most of the victims, of course, died before the end of their punishment.

For several years Arakcheyev, this 'brutal and treacherous hangman of freedom,' as Pushkin called him, held Russia in his grip. His dictatorship firmly entrenched serfdom, ruined the liberal measures promulgated at the beginning of Alexander's reign, and harrassed the educated classes. Arakcheyev shared the opinion of the then-influential Metropolitan Seraphim, who declared that 'education was the Devil's tool.' Universities and schools fell under strict bureaucratic control. A ruthless and arbitrary censorship overshadowed the publication of books and periodicals; for instance, a pamphlet on poisonous mushrooms was banned under the pretext that 'mushrooms were used by the faithful during Lent.' A. Herzen, the great publicist of the 'forties has described Arakcheyev's rule as follows: 'Servility, coercion, injustice everywhere. . . Serfdom solid as a rock, military despotism, silence and whips. . . Men and women mortgaged or sold as mere chattels, girls raped, soldiers tortured.' Even the conservatives, such as Karamzin, were disgusted with the dictator, but could not dislodge him. Alexander, completely spellbound by his mystical practices, gave his minister a free hand.

Even Arakcheyev's retirement from public office (he was so afflicted by the violent killing of his mistress by the peasants that he renounced all political activity) did not, however, bring about any great improvement: the reactionary regime was so firmly entrenched that a change in leaders could not transform the system. The liberals were now perfectly convinced that the only means of combating reaction and assuring the progress of Russia was a fundamental reform of all existing institutions, and the opposition to the regime was intensifying along with the enforcement of despotism. As under Catherine, it was chiefly a movement among the nobles, but the successors of the free-thinkers and Voltairians of the eighteenth century were more politically conscious and eager for action than their fathers.

A great number of the young noblemen of this period had served with the army that in 1812-15 had fought in Germany, Austria, and France. During this campaign they had often come into contact with ideas and institutions introduced to Europe by the French Revolution. They had read stirring books and met people who preached the necessity of political reforms. Some officers had also become particularly interested in various secret societies that at that time were flourishing in Italy and Germany, where political radicalism had combined with romantic patriotism, and the struggle for freedom had coincided with the struggle for national independence. They wanted to apply all they had learned to Russia—but there they found Arakcheyev.

The situation of the young people of that period was unbearable [commented a writer of the day]. For three years we have taken part in events that have changed the destiny of mankind, and after such an experience we could no longer endure living the empty, frivolous life of St. Petersburg, or listening to old fools who praised the past and abhorred progress. We were a hundred years ahead of them.

Discontented youth began criticizing the social and moral backwardness of its own society. This was the first phase of a growing liberal movement, whose main feature was a revolt of words in a country where silence was compulsory. The liberals talked—too much, perhaps, attaching an exaggerated significance to the power of speeches; yet this flood of words provided the needed self-expression and release. It was useful, even important. And it found its artistic embodiment in a comedy that became one of the masterpieces of Russian literature. *'Tis Folly to be Wise,* by Alexander Griboyedov (1795-1829), portrayed the conflict between the two generations and dealt with this outburst of words through which new ideas and emotions were trying to assert themselves.

II   Griboyedov wrote this comedy in 1823 and read it in 1824 at various literary and political gatherings at the capital. Its success was immediate and it circulated throughout

Russia in hundreds of manuscript copies. It was not published or produced before the 'thirties, after the death of its author, but it was a
real part of the spirit of the years preceding the Decembrist uprising
of 1825.

Chatsky, a young nobleman and the hero of the play, comes, after
a long stay abroad, to Moscow to see Sophie, the girl he loves. She is
the daughter of Famussov, a rich and fussy landowner who is hardly
distinguished for his intelligence, interested only in parties and gossip,
desirous of being 'like everybody else,' of doing the 'right things,' and
of being respectable, and observing the social standards of the wealthy
nobility. Another important character is Molchalin (the name indicates
that he is a 'yes-man'), who has made his way in the bureaucratic
world by groveling, by fawning before not only his superiors but even
their dogs, and by never daring to formulate a personal opinion. Next
comes Famussov's friend, Colonel Skalozub (Teeth-bared-in-a-grin),
the 'faithful old soldier' who curtly dismisses all literature and art.
Skalozub declares that books are the source of all evil . . . they ought
to be burned . . . a corporal would be a much better teacher for young
folks than that fellow Voltaire, and so on. The ball given by Famussov
is adroitly used by Griboyedov to exhibit a whole gallery of hypocritical
prigs, greedy old women, featherbrained young ladies in search of husbands, and no less featherbrained fops and dandies. Chatsky is horrified
and revolted by all these representatives of aristocratic society. He is
forever quarreling with all the important guests and openly declares that
old wrecks have no right to pass judgment on morals and ideas. The
odds are all against him, and finally he discovers that his attempts to
gain Sophie's love are as futile and preposterous as his speeches aimed
at reforming society. Hurt and desperate, he leaves Famussov's house.
The comedy closes with his outcry: 'My carriage! My carriage! I will
roam the world over to salve my injured feelings!'

Chatsky is powerless to act—and there lies his tragedy. He is bound
to remain futile, unable to change the environment he despises and
criticizes. Confined to verbal protests, he does not fight; he escapes—
probably abroad—and the people whom he so hurriedly abandons consider him no more than a fool, and not even a dangerous one. Chatsky
is a personification of the type of intellectual (so frequently portrayed
in Russian literature) whose brains and idealism serve no practical
purpose. He belongs to the category of 'superfluous men'—as Russian
critics have labeled various such heroes—later described by Turgenev,
Goncharov, Leskov, and many others.

The vivid portrayal of aristocratic society and the dramatic conflict
between the progressive intellectual and his retrograde environment

were not the only merits of Griboyedov's comedy. It was surprisingly realistic; all its characters had been taken from life, and they spoke of well-known facts and events. It was written in sharp, epigrammatic verse, with an ironic *brio* that gave pace and dynamic force to the dialogue. Each line rang with wit or echoed with underlying meaning, and the sarcastic formulas or funny definitions uttered by various characters have long since become proverbial in Russian society. Like so many of Molière's *mots,* hundreds of Griboyedov's lines were quickly incorporated into the colloquial speech of Russia and were repeated throughout the length and breadth of the land. But while Molière, whose *Misanthrope* may have had some influence on Griboyedov, used broadly burlesque situations, the Russian playwright paid little attention to the incidents of plot or to the comic *quid pro quo.* His intellectual comedy of manners was principally based on realistic presentation, ideological content, and a unique poetic form. Its perfect verbal texture made it a great literary achievement, and, despite many subsequent attempts at imitation, it stands alone in Russian letters. Today, as in Griboyedov's time, it is a vital and successful part of Russia's theatrical repertoire.

In comparison with Fonvizin it was a great step forward. Griboyedov had not sacrificed the realism of his exposé to any didactic aims. He had no need of a happy ending or of the intervention of some virtuous scion of morality, inasmuch as he was not afraid to display the triumph of vulgarity and stupidity over the idealism of his hero. There is something ruthless in Griboyedov's humor, and Belinsky, the great critic, who had not liked the comedy at first, had to recognize its beauty and strength:

What a lethal power of sarcasm, what biting irony, what pathos in the lyrical confessions of outraged feelings, what an analysis of society, what characters, and what language, what verse—energetic, compressed, lightning-like and so very Russian. . . It is a most noble humanitarian work, a powerful (and a first) protest against infamous Russian reality, against grafting officials, against dissolute aristocrats, against an onanistic society, against ignorance and voluntary servility. . .

Most surprising was the fact that this highly realistic work had been written by a man whose personality revealed so many romantic traits.

Unlike other Russian writers, Griboyedov was a man of one book. He must have put all his genius into *'Tis Folly to be Wise;* he seems to have spent himself in this one great effort. His life was no less extraordinary than the fate of his comedy. Born in 1795, the son of a Moscow military officer, Griboyedov was a *Wunderkind.* At the age of thirteen, when he entered the University, he was already an outstanding musician and an accomplished linguist: he spoke faultless French, German, and English, and was an excellent Latin scholar. He graduated in law at sixteen, but stayed on at the University to study the natural sciences. Later he learned Sanskrit and Persian, read widely in all sorts of subjects, and acquired the reputation of being one of the most educated men in Russia. For several years he served as an officer in a regiment of Hussars, leading the usual dissipated life of a nobleman of the Guards. Afterwards he joined the Foreign Office and advanced rapidly in his diplomatic career in the Russian embassies in the Near East. In appearance he was a glib, cold, and cynical bureaucrat; in speech and behavior he was a dandy; but fundamentally he was passionately attached to poetry. Literature was the source of all his dreams and joys. It could not, however, dispel his innate despondency and his profound pessimism. This typical representative of a certain group of sophisticated noblemen had an extremely complex personality. A friend of those revolutionary plotters who were later called Decembrists, he sympathized with their purpose, yet did not believe that 'a hundred young officers could change the regime in Russia.' This skepticism helped him when, after the unsuccessful uprising, he was arrested in the Caucasus and brought to the capital: he could prove easily that, although he was an intimate of all the leaders of the movement, he had not participated in the conspiracy. After his liberation he wrote: 'What a world—and what sort of inhabitants—and what an idiotic history it has!' He has summed up his feelings in one of his letters: 'What a torment it is to be an ardent dreamer in a land of eternal snow!'

The production of his play was banned. His closest friends were imprisoned, exiled, or hanged. He was dissatisfied with his life as well as with his work. All around him was nothing but stagnation, reaction, and stupidity. Russia was governed by the Skalozubs. The Famussovs, the Molchalins, and other nonentities lorded society. Griboyedov felt suffocated. Like his own Chatsky he wanted only to flee, to escape, and he gladly accepted the appointment as Russian minister to Persia. In Teheran he fought against political intrigues and feudal superstitions and fell victim to his powerful enemies: in 1829 he was killed by a mob that had been mysteriously incited. Pushkin, who was at that time traveling in the Caucasus, met the cart in which the mortal remains of Griboyedov were being brought to his birthplace for burial.

III   The feeling of loneliness, of isolation amidst a hostile world, which Chatsky had experienced during his visit to Moscow, acted as a powerful factor in unifying the liberal forces.

After a short period of discontent, criticism, and talk came a phase of political pathfinding and secret societies. At first young officers and their friends formed groups and circles where they could speak freely and feel themselves in a congenial atmosphere. Freemasonry, brought for the most part from France and Germany, became very popular among the nobility. Masonic lodges increased in number and assumed a more definitely political tinge. In St. Petersburg, in Moscow, in the south of Russia the Masons discussed ways and means of improving the general situation through good example and moral action. Simultaneously, some of them proceeded to organize secret societies on the pattern of the German patriotic groups (such as the *Tugendbund*). In 1817 a few young officers of the Imperial Guard, under the leadership of Prince Trubetskoy, Colonel Muraviev, and Colonel Pestel, formed a secret Union of Salvation, or the True Sons of the Fatherland. Its aim was the change of Russian constitutional laws, but it lacked a concrete program of reforms. Most of its members were inspired by a vague idealism and a desire to cure the 'plagues of Russian life' by honest administration, humanitarian influence, and a gradual education of the public. Not unlike Radishchev, they still hoped to 'reveal the truth' to the Czar and believed that the whole trend of Russia's domestic policy could be transformed if the 'right persons' were placed around the throne. Thus was born the movement that was destined to lead to the uprising of 14 December 1825.

The Decembrists were the intellectual élite at the end of the second decade, and in the early years of the third, of the nineteenth century. A number of officers in the Imperial Guard, who constituted the bulk of the movement, were men of great culture, widely read in literature and the social sciences. Almost all the young writers of the period were more or less connected with Decembrism: Alexander Pushkin, Griboyedov, Prince Odoevsky, the poet Ryleyev, the novelist Bestuzhev, the publicist Nicholas Turgenev, and many others. At the sessions of the Union of Salvation political discussions alternated with the reading of poems and the works of contemporary writers.

In 1819 the Union of Salvation was transformed into the Union for Public Welfare. This was no mere change of name, however, for the members of the society grouped themselves according to the two prevailing tendencies—moderate and radical. The leader of the moderates, Nikita Muraviev, wrote a projected constitution for a Russian 'Democratic Monarchy,' along the lines of the British system and the Constitution of the United States. It foresaw the emancipation of the serfs, equality of rights for all citizens, freedom of the press, speech, and religious worship, as well as the inviolability of private property. Russia was supposed to become a constitutional hereditary monarchy, with a government responsible to the elected legislative body. All the theories of Russian moderate liberalism throughout the nineteenth century had their origin in this document, the final version of which was prepared by 1822.

The radical wing, directed by Pavel Pestel and later by Kondraty Ryleyev, advocated the abolition of monarchy and the establishment of a democratic republic, as well as democratic freedoms and the emancipation of the serfs; and it added an important social measure— the distribution of land to the peasants and any citizens desiring to become farmers. In *The Russian Truth,* which remains one of the most remarkable and important works of Russian political literature, Pestel laid down his program for the reorganization of Russia on the basis of 'political and social democracy.' A freely elected constituent assembly, said Pestel, would abolish all privileges, 'whether originating in the nobility or in wealth. In the modern state no privilege should be granted to a citizen on account of his wealth. The aristocracy of money is worse than feudal aristocracy.' Pestel went even further than Muraviev in his solution of the problem of nationalities. He favored a Polish Republic, united to Russia by a federative link. This was quite a revolutionary proposal, when one considers that Poland was then no more than a province of the Russian Empire. Some friends of Pestel formed connections with Polish secret societies, while others dreamt of a vast Slav Federation, with Constantinople as its capital. One of the offshoots of the Union among certain infantry regiments in the south took the name of The United Slavs.

Having no faith in any evolution or self-improvement of Russian autocracy, Pestel advocated the overthrow of the regime by revolutionary methods, which naturally meant military insurrection.

Although Nikita Muraviev and his moderate friends disagreed with the political and social radicals of the left wing, they gradually became more and more inclined to accept Pestel's revolutionary tactics. In 1820-25 reactionary government in Russia was worse than ever, and while the members of the Union were discussing the advantages and disadvantages of constitutional monarchy and a democratic republic, the only reality they were confronted with outside of their meetings was despotic autocracy. In 1821 the government, getting wind of the activity in liberal circles, ordered the immediate dissolution of all Masonic lodges and non-registered societies. For reasons of safety, the leaders of the Union announced its liquidation. But immediately after this sham dissolution a new secret organization took the place of the Union. It had two central bodies: the Society of the North, led by Ryleyev,

Muraviev, Prince Obolensky, and Prince Trubetskoy, with headquarters in St. Petersburg and a branch in Moscow; the Society of the South, headed by Pestel, Bestuzhev-Rumin, and Muraviev-Apostol, established itself in the town of Tulchin in the Ukraine, where the Second Russian Army with its general staff was then quartered.

The actual membership of the two societies was relatively small, but they had hundreds of sympathizers and exerted a considerable intellectual, political, and literary influence. The majority of the Decembrists—such as the Princes Trubetskoy, Obolensky, Odoevsky, Volkonsky, and Bariatinsky—belonged to the old aristocracy or, like the millionaire Davydov, to high and wealthy nobility, while others held important positions in the Army—such as General Yushnevsky, Major-General Fonvizin, Colonels Pestel, Batenkov, Bulatov, Lieutenant-Colonels Lunin and Muraviev-Apostol. The rank and file of the Decembrists consisted mostly of officers in the Guards and a few civil servants. It is this composition of the conspirators that explains their confidence in a military coup d'état. They all belonged to the ruling classes and they could easily stage a palace revolution—a tradition that had proved to be a success in the case of Catherine and Paul. The only difference was that, while previous coups d'état had been carried out by groups of dignitaries or military men who wanted to replace one sovereign by another, the Decembrists wanted to abolish the sovereignty altogether.

Between 1821 and 1825 the movement entered its final phase. All hopes in reforms from above, moral suasion, and gradual education were abandoned. Insurrection was now the order of the day. But the sudden death of Alexander I and the ensuing confusion that delayed the enthronement of Nicholas compelled the Decembrists to take action before they were quite ready. They realized their lack of preparedness and organization, but events left them no choice. At the reunion of the Society of the North in St. Petersburg, Ryleyev declared, 'Revolutionary tactics can be summed up in one word: audacity. Even if we fail, our failure will serve as a lesson for others.' Later he added, 'Our fate is sealed. I am sure we will perish, but our example will survive.'

On 14 December 1825, the day the Army had to take their oath of allegiance to the new Czar, the conspirators led their companies, battalions, and regiments into Senate Place in St. Petersburg and raised the flag of insurrection. Kahovskoy, a member of the Society of the North, shot the military governor of the capital as he attempted to harangue the mutinous troops. Unfortunately the rebels did not know what to do next, and their indecision resulted in the fatal outcome of the whole affair. At the start of the rebellion Nicholas felt lost, but one of his generals rallied a few loyal batteries and put down the insurrection with artillery fire. An attempt at rebellion in the south, where a regiment led by Decembrists marched on Kiev, was also quickly crushed. Nicholas I, Czar of Russia, immediately ordered severe reprisals. Hundreds of Decembrists were arrested, tried, and sentenced to various punishments. Most of them were exiled to Siberia; their sympathizers were broken to the ranks and sent to infantry regiments in the Caucasus, where a war was raging against rebellious mountaineer tribes. Five of the leaders, including Pestel and Ryleyev, were hanged in the courtyard of the Fortress of SS. Peter and Paul in St. Petersburg.

The impression made by the tragic end of the Decembrist movement was overwhelming. 'The cannons on Senate Place awakened a whole generation,' Herzen recalled some twenty years later. The ideas of the Decembrists, their lives, and their fate became material for more or less hidden allusions and reflections in Russian literature. The writings of the Decembrists, together with the poems by their contemporaries who exalted or mourned their friends, circulated in manuscript or privately printed copies and initiated that underground press destined to be an important feature of Russian life for almost a hundred years.

Besides a series of strictly political books and pamphlets, such as *The Russian Truth* by Pestel, *The Project of a Constitution* by Nikita Muraviev, and *Russia and the Russians* by Nicholas Turgenev, the Decembrists left a considerable heritage of civic poetry. Its most distinguished exponent was Kondraty Ryleyev (1795-1826), the heart and soul of the movement, as Pestel had been its brains. Ryleyev was one of the few Decembrists who had not belonged to the army. He had served as an official of the Russian-American Company, which administered the Russian possessions in Alaska and California.

In the eighteen-twenties he had become renowned as a poet and was the chief contributor to *The Polar Star,* an influential literary annual of the Decembrists. Ryleyev's fiery poems were primarily devoted to freedom and rebellion, or they were irate attacks against despotism and, in particular, against Arakcheyev. Some of them possessed unusual force, and all had the charm of perfect sincerity. Ryleyev, a man of rare moral rectitude, hated injustice and oppression and was elated when faced with examples of idealistic sacrifice or courageous struggle for the common welfare. He transformed social and political concepts into emotions of patriotic sorrow or civic enthusiasm. The idea of freedom aroused in him a romantic passion, and he gave up everything for his goddess—including his family and his life.

'I saw Russia enslaved,' he wrote. 'With her head bowed, her chains rattling, she prayed for her Czar—because our heart does not feel the misery of our state, and our mind does not understand it.' In his long historical poems, conceived in an early Romantic spirit ('Nalivaiko' and 'Martha') he exalted the virtues and the democratic spirit of the ancient Slavs and the Ukrainian Cossacks. One of them contains the prophetic lines: 'I know that death awaits those who are the first to fight the despots, yet self-sacrifice is the price of freedom.'

Ryleyev's poetry reflected the moral nobility of the movement. The Decembrists were inspired by an ideal of right that made them forsake their class privileges. They possessed wealth, titles, enviable positions; they could attain to high military and administrative honors; they were in the upper hierarchy of the system they had decided to destroy. But, although their activity had as its supreme goal the welfare of the people, they did not try to carry out their program through or with the people. Martyrs, heroes, or utopians, they were relying only upon themselves and never dreamt of arousing a revolutionary movement among the broad masses of the population. They planned a revolution by the nobility against the autocracy, which was itself based on the nobility. There lay their fault—or their tragedy. This small group of idealistic, self-sacrificing noblemen tried to change the course of history through their own strength and were crushed by the juggernaut of autocracy. But it was they who initiated the Russian revolutionary movement; the liberals, radicals, and socialists of the nineteenth and twentieth centuries were to recognize them as their forerunners. The ruthless, complex, and long history of the struggle against Czarism in Russia stems from the thwarted rebellion on Senate Place.

The Decembrists represented Romanticism in politics. They corresponded to similar movements of Young Europe in Germany, Italy, France, and Poland. It was but natural that in their literary productions they should support the new Romantic school and reflect its tendencies. One of the exiled Decembrists, Alexander Bestuzhev (1797-1837), known under his pen name of Marlinsky, played an important part in the creation of the Romantic novel. A captain of the guards and aide-de-camp to the Duke of Wittgenstein, he made a brilliant military career, won fame as a duellist and a social lion, enjoyed spectacular success with women, and became sensationally successful as a writer. His many novels, the best of which are *Ammalat-Bey* (1832) and *The Frigate Hope* (1833), lack any sense of proportion but reveal rich imagination, a whimsical spirit, a contagious wistfulness, and an *élan* in their plots and style that overwhelmed his contemporaries. They were wild, unreal, dynamic, complicated—and thousands of readers fell under the spell of their rather easy eloquence. Bestuzhev was killed at the age of forty by the mountaineers in the Caucasus, where he had spent twelve years in exile.

The serious, awkward poems of Wilhelm Kuechelbecker and the airy poetry of Prince Alexander Odoevsky and of the pleiad around the annual *Mnemosine,* reflected the religious and mystical tendencies of Romanticism, chiefly the German brand. They were rather a link with Zhukovsky's later manner, but hardly had the same influence or popularity as the works of Ryleyev or Bestuzhev.

Decembrism as a movement signified the awakening of national consciousness among the intelligentsia. After the Napoleonic invasion, educated society became aware of the enormous potentialities of the country and tried to take part in shaping its future. From then on the development of the intellectuals in the direction of political awareness and social activity was inevitable.

Parallel to this phenomenon was the self-affirmation of literature as a national force. In the atmosphere of the great intellectual revival of the eighteen-twenties writers became aware of the significance and possibilities of literary movements. They merely needed someone able to formulate this process and to bring it to culmination. That someone was Pushkin.

4

PUSHKIN

I   THOSE who are unable to read Pushkin in the original are always somewhat puzzled over the unbounded enthusiasm of the Russians for their supreme poet. There are many reasons why Pushkin is the key figure of Russian nineteenth-century literature, and most of them are quite understandable even to foreign students. But as far as the main point is concerned—Pushkin's poetic genius—no convincing proof can be offered in English, French, or German translations, for, with a few rare exceptions, they are rather disappointing and to non-Russians do not justify the reputation Pushkin enjoys in Russia. Hardly anything in these translations is striking or particularly beautiful, and the European or American reader has to take for granted that Pushkin was a marvelous poet.

Russians usually claim that Pushkin is 'untranslatable.' But the only true translations of real poetry are made by poets who create in their own tongue an equivalent of the original—a general practice in translations of poetry into Russian. Unfortunately no English or American poet of stature has ever attempted to translate Pushkin, and the available translations are not only pale, but not always even scholarly or honest—for the most part second-rate versions that make Pushkin appear almost trivial.[1]

To the general difficulties inherent in translating poetry, Pushkin adds some special ones. One of the main characteristics of his poetry is its perfect marriage of sound and meaning. Pushkin's poems do not merely follow Arnold's definition in presenting the best words in the

---

[1] There are some passable translations in various collections and anthologies; they are all very useful and rather indispensable for the study of Russian literature, even though they fail to convey the full charm of Pushkin's verse.

best order. They endow the plainest, almost trivial words with poetic meaning. The simplicity and naturalness of Pushkin's lines turn into platitudes in translations, because the latter fail to convey their musical lucidity, their freshness and melodious quality. Pushkin had the magic power of extracting poetic resonance from colloquialisms, of instilling emotional intensity into the simplest sentences, of expressing profound thought in easy and concise statements. What is called the perfection of Pushkin's form is the complete coalescence of sound, rhythm, image, and meaning. Another aspect is Pushkin's clarity and directness of style, as well as his ability to obtain unobtrusive enduring effects—with economy, sober directness, and a sense of measure and balance; these do not exclude subtlety and a wide range of technical devices, which the poet— an astonishing master of versification—used with superb craftsmanship. He also had the gift of giving the same word—placing it in another context or qualifying it by varying the epithets or enhancing it by a diversified rhythmic and melodical movement—a solemn, an intimate, or a pensive value, according to the inner spirit of the individual poem. A poem by Pushkin in Russian creates the impression that what he says could never be said otherwise, that each word fits perfectly, serving as a necessary part of a whole, and that no other words could ever assume a similar function. And still these words are, for the most part, the plain words we use in our daily talk.

With Pushkin the Russian modern literary style was born, which was undoubtedly a phenomenon of national importance. He liberated Russian literature from the heavy legacy of Church-Slavonic, as well as from the artificial mannerisms prevailing at the beginning of the nineteenth century. His was not the language of any particular class (although he knew how to employ the linguistic mannerisms of each social group and was fully aware of the differences between them) but that of contemporary Russia—alive, rich, expressive, blending popular colloquialisms with the achievements of literary evolution. The entire development of Russian letters in the eighteenth century and at the beginning of the nineteenth was in the direction of a fusion of folklore and literary tradition, but only Pushkin succeeded in accomplishing this task.

Pushkin had easy access to popular sources for his reformation of literary language since he had a vast knowledge of folk tales, songs, and legends. He was brought up by French governors and French was his second tongue, but he learned his Russian from peasants, simple artisans, country squires, from old men and women of Moscow who had preserved intact the true flavor of the idiom, unspoiled by any foreign influence; and from his old nurse, who had first made the young nobleman aware of the wealth of national folklore. He wrote a series of fairy tales and legends and songs in the style and rhythm of folklore, which sound like genuine popular creations. At the same time, in some of his works the poet used Church-Slavonic archaisms most adroitly, thus perfecting the fusion of all the media of artistic expression in Russian.

The role played by Pushkin in this process explains the importance of one of his first (but not best) poems, *Russlan and Liudmila* (1820), a fairy tale in a light vein, a parody of solemn epic poems, filled with humor and bold colloquialisms. The conservatives were horrified by the impudence of a twenty-year-old youth who laughed at the sanctified forms of Classicism and took as the subject matter for his poem the old folk story of Eruslan. They were also shocked by the 'vulgarity' of the details, such as the hero's pulling the beard of the dreadful dwarf Chernomor (Black Death) who had kidnapped the beautiful Liudmila and was about to rape her. The popular atmosphere of the tale, the erotic boldness in the portrayal of Liudmila, the lusty descriptions of Chernomor's gardens and of knightly jousts, were done in an easy, almost nonchalant and somewhat ironic manner, in a conversational tone that provoked both indignation and acclaim. Despite all its weaknesses, *Russlan and Liudmila* marked the beginning of a new way of writing—free, lively, and colloquial. At the same time by its opposition to the remnants of Classicism and its distinct avoidance of sentimentality or the Romantic 'poetry of horror,' it inaugurated a new literary and stylistic movement. Pushkin became its natural leader and the 'liberals of literature'—from such venerable writers as Zhukovsky to the Decembrists—rallied around him. Zhukovsky after reading this poem presented Pushkin with his own portrait inscribed: 'To the victorious disciple from the vanquished master.'

In the ensuing years Pushkin proved that his new language could be successfully adapted to all literary forms. With surprising versatility, achieving the widest range ever known in Russian letters, he produced lyrics, novels in verse, historical and philosophical poems, dramas, short stories, novelettes, essays, critical and historical studies, to say nothing of translations, fairy tales, and epigrams. A fundamental unity of style and spirit integrates this diversity of genres, making their division into categories seem somewhat artificial.

II   Some critics believe that Pushkin gave the full measure of his genius in his lyrics. Most of these are records of his intimate feelings—love, recollection, joy or sadness, meditation, repentance—conveyed in limpid and melodious lines, usually in iambic verse, although Pushkin often resorted to other meters. This highly subjective poetry with all its romantic or sentimental implications has two distinct features that give it its inimitable character. First of all, these intensely emotional lines are never vague or misty. The imagery, the rhythm, and the melodious movement of each stanza are perfectly amalgamated with the actual idea, reflecting the activity of a lucid and penetrating mind. Whether they capture a fleeting mood, unfold an image, or express a thought, they are plastic, precise, unmistakably clear even in their conciseness, and all this without sacrificing the slightest nuance or relapsing into academic aloofness. Secondly, whatever the actual theme of these lyrics may be, even the most despairing ones, they are filled with potent vitality, with a sense of life that accepts reality and masters it. Whether he recalls his past and is disillusioned with his own errors, while the night spreads its diaphanous shadow over a silent city; whether he evokes the vision of death in crowded streets, or in a temple, or at a feast; whether he describes the departure of the beloved who had died under foreign skies; whether he longs for refuge from the world in some peaceful hermitage (since happiness is impossible and tranquillity and freedom are the best that mortals may hope for)—even these pensive lyrics never stress despair and are balanced by a positive attitude toward reality. But Pushkin's 'healthy optimism' is no mere acceptance of reality. He does not shut his eyes to the horrors and contradictions of life; he is extremely conscious of death, pain, injustice; and he does not attempt to hide anything or to play with illusions—but his attachment to the earth and his desire of experiencing everything, of living life fully in every way, give his poems intensity and power. 'No, I do not want to die,' he exclaims in one of his lyrics, 'I want to live, to think and to suffer. I would be delighted again by harmony, or weep over some tale, and perhaps the last smile of love will brighten the dreary days of my old age.' He 'exists'—as some modern French philosophers would say—and his sense of being is triumphant and self-asserting despite adversity or circumstance. Here lies the main difference between Pushkin and, for example, Batiushkov. Pushkin also wrote a score of sensual and erotic poems in a pagan and Epicurean tone. But sensuality and eroticism are no more than a facet of his Apollonian genius. His delight in life embraces the subtle joys of the mind, the exaltation of spirituality, the simple pleasures of nature, as well as the raptures of the flesh and the voluptuousness of love. A coined phrase labels Pushkin's poetry as 'sunny,' and a bright and warm light as of midday does illumine his poems. However, such a definition is too constrained, for Pushkin also knew how to explore and present the nocturnal and ambiguous side of life. He was perfectly aware of the 'devil's part' in the scheme of things. In 'A Feast during the Plague' he tells us that 'there is an ecstasy in battle or on the brink of a dark precipice,' and he asserted that 'all things that threaten ruin conceal inexplicable rapture for the heart of a mortal.' Pushkin's poetry expresses a passionate desire for being, a courageous acceptance of the world, with all its illusions and disillusions, with all its peaks and lowlands. And this fullness of life, this organic vitality are illuminated by his ever-present awareness, by his mind, which delights in thought and acclaims reason —'the sun of reason, that makes night's shadow flee.'

Pushkin's poetry in its emphasis on the dignity of man is profoundly humanistic. It extols man—in all his aspects. Man, freedom, action, love, art, are for Pushkin the true values.

This supreme poet reveals himself as both human and humane, not only in his serious works but also in his light ones. Abhorring anything flat, stilted, and dull, he attacked pretentiousness, academic solemnity, and artificiality, in both life and literature. He wrote biting epigrams, which made him many enemies; blasphemous facetiae (such as his 'Gabrieliad,' in 1821, in which the Virgin Mary is seduced by the Serpent, the Archangel Gabriel, and the Holy Ghost, all in one day), rather indecent but decidedly droll; erotic poems (such as 'Czar Nikita' and 'Count Nulin' in 1825, the latter a version of *The Rape of Lucrece*). 'The House in Colomna' (1830), in this vein, is the story of a widow who holds her daughter's virtue at a great price, but suddenly discovers that the woman cooking for her is a man in disguise. These poems had a definite literary and psychological importance. They were weapons with which Pushkin fought against the rigidity of established forms and canons, demolishing the restrictions of Classicism and effecting a reunion of life and literature. This was one of his main aims—to bring art down to earth, to make poetry realistic, alive, capable equally of creating laughter or treating serious problems. The obviously 'profane,' light, 'un-poetic' subject matter and treatment of these tales in verse, objected to by many of his contemporaries, were a challenge. They widened the range of poetic creation and introduced a freshness, whimsy, and spontaneity in striking contrast to the hitherto-accepted rules.

It was with precisely this intent—of bringing realism to art—that Pushkin began his long novel in verse, *Eugene Oneghin,* the writing of which took eight years (1823-31). But this masterpiece grew and deepened in the process of creation, and its actual effect surpassed the initial purpose of its author.

III   It was undoubtedly the Byron of *Childe Harold,* of *Beppo* and *Don Juan* who in this instance inspired Pushkin. Unlike the epic poem, the novel in verse, popularized by the

English poet, was exempt from any set rules; it was a loose form the Romantics fancied, since it offered vast possibilities for unhampered poetic self-expression and for their favorite blend of lyricism, description, adventure, and exaltation with an admixture of the comic and the sublime.

Eugene Oneghin, like all of Pushkin's poems, has a diversity of elements, a peculiar structure: the narrative is interrupted by long lyrical passages devoted to the poet's personal feelings or memories; the author converses with the reader, discusses his own work, indulges in intimate confessions or jests, and, in general, creates an atmosphere of ease and intimacy. While the lyrical passages of the poem are subtle and suggestive, the pictures of Russian autumn and winter, the countryside, or Moscow society are among the highest achievements of Russian descriptive art.

The facile, almost nonchalant, and—at first glance—loose manner in which this long work is written (it was published serially, each chapter arousing almost unanimous enthusiasm) did not prevent Pushkin from imparting a deep meaning to his apparently aimless poem. Begun as a mere fanciful imitation of the Romantic pattern, this light novel turned out to be a serious and realistic representation of Russian life, with social and psychological portraits of Pushkin's contemporaries which assumed the proportions of all-Russian types.

The hero of the novel, Eugene Oneghin, is a young nobleman of the eighteen-twenties, intelligent, well read, yet superficial. A man-about-town, he spends his days in futile occupations. Leisure and lack of any useful activity easily lead him to boredom and cynicism. Like Chatsky, he is a 'useless individual' and belongs to the vast group of 'Russian Europeans' who had neither character nor passion enough to make something of their lives. Oneghin's innate indolence and the blasé air he assumes preclude his voicing any such verbal protest as Chatsky's. He is but mildly liberal and is much more concerned over the cut of his clothes or his love affairs than over any social issues. At twenty, already tired of all his various experiences, he feels aged and barren.

The death of a rich uncle compels him to spend a few months on the latter's estate, where he is annoyed by country life—he does not enjoy nature or the simple pleasures of rural Russia. His only entertainments are his meetings with his neighbor, Lensky, a young poet who had studied in Germany and had brought home romantic dreams and idealistic yearnings. Lensky's poems are vague and nebulous and his idealism is rather childish, yet Oneghin likes him and the two become friends. Lensky is madly in love with Olga Larina, daughter of good, old-fashioned landowners, and he introduces Oneghin into this family. Olga's sister, Tatiana, loses her head over Oneghin, who seems to her the hero of her dreams. She is a simple, straightforward girl with a strong romantic strain in her character, and she takes her first love affair seriously. With the boldness of innocence she opens her heart to Oneghin in a letter as charming as it is passionate. But the St. Petersburg dandy, hardly touched by the freshness of her sentiments, does not care for this provincial miss and her follies. He talks to her in a cold and superior way, amusing himself by posing as a Childe Harold, a disenchanted man incapable of love and attachment. Then, from pure malice, he flirts with Olga, makes Lensky violently suspicious and jealous, offends him, and is faced with a challenge to a duel, which ends with Lensky's death; and having killed his friend, destroyed Olga's happiness, and crushed Tatiana's love, he returns to the capital. All but unaware of the unhappiness he has caused, he is more than ever bored with himself and his existence. Years pass—he travels about Russia and looks in vain for some novelty. One day at a social gathering in St. Petersburg, he meets the young wife of a wealthy prince and recognizes her as Tatiana. She is no longer a little provincial dreamer but a beautiful woman of the world, and Oneghin, piqued by her cold indifference, falls in love with her. Now Tatiana talks to him the same rationalistic language he had used in his answer to her letter. Her attitude toward life is not as frivolous as his; for she believes in truth and honesty and intends to remain faithful to her husband. Oneghin, defeated and disappointed, resumes his fruitless wanderings.

Eugene Oneghin is the first Russian realistic novel. Its main protagonists—the intelligent but egotistic nobleman whose energies are wasted, the spontaneous, great-hearted idealist, the romantic girl who develops into a woman of decision and moral integrity—as well as all the minor characters, belonged to the Russian soil and were projected against the background of their environment. There are startlingly true pictures of St. Petersburg and Moscow, the Russian countryside, the way of life in Russia's provincial towns, and the mentality of Russia's petty nobility. A national poem not solely because of its descriptions of Russian landscapes or its portraits of Russian types, it also raised, although in a very subtle and indirect way, the fundamental problems of Russian society. The issue of civic integrity in connection with Oneghin's wasted existence, the impact of European patterns on Russian life (in his own case as well as in Lensky's), the problem of moral conduct (solved by Tatiana in a manner that aroused discussion among the readers)—all these themes greatly impressed the poet's contemporaries. In *Eugene Oneghin* Pushkin opposed two points of view embodied in two types—Oneghin, the proud, sophisticated, and artificial, and the deep, genuine, but simple Tatiana. This contrast heralded one of the most popular trends in Russian literature of the nineteenth century. In the eighteen-eighties Dostoevsky commented on the moral significance of the poem and said that Tatiana's victory over Oneghin symbolized the triumph of an organically Russian sense of truth over an intellectual emptiness resulting from lost faith and conviction.

Pushkin's contemporaries did not at once perceive all the implications of the poem. They were most impressed by two things: that a simple plot taken from every-day life and deliberately devoid of exciting adventures could provide enough material for a long poem, and that the author's purpose had been fulfilled through the great variety of poetic devices, with such clarity, freshness, *brio,* humor, and feeling. The success of *Eugene Oneghin* was unique in Russian literature. It became so popular that everybody felt obliged to memorize at least some of its lines. Many quotations from the poem passed into sayings current in educated society and the Russian press. In it Pushkin said 'everything about everything'—ballet and philosophy, love and education, gambling and literature; he described the seasons of the year, social events, provincial balls, ancient customs, and modern dances; he analyzed the most diversified moods and feelings of widely differing temperaments.

Eugene Oneghin which soon became a classic, is still the most beloved work in Russian literature. Despite numerous imitations and subsequent long narrative poems, it remains the sole great Russian novel in verse: nobody has ever created a work of similar national significance and literary perfection.

IV   When Pushkin was twenty-two he wrote a few poems 'under the sign of Byron.' The influence of the English poet was, however, superficial and evanescent. Pushkin was too lucid, too fond of reason, logic, and reality, and far too fond of balance and measure in art to become a true disciple of the author of 'The Corsair' and 'Manfred.' Nevertheless Byron's influence, mitigated by these tendencies of Pushkin, is apparent in certain early poems, such as *The Caucasian Captive* (1821), a tale of a Russian prisoner who forsakes a mountain maid so passionately in love with him that after his departure she commits suicide. And in *The Gypsies* (1823) another Byronic hero, Aleko, while fleeing the 'thralldom of the stifling city,' joins a band of wandering gypsies and falls in love with Zemphira —a beautiful daughter of the 'prophetic tribe'—but fails in his attempts to lead a romantically free life. After Aleko kills Zemphira, who has betrayed him, and her lover, he is rejected by the chief of the gypsies.

'Leave us, proud man,' the old man tells him. 'You are not born for a free life; you look but for your own fancy, you are wicked and bold—whereas we are kind and peaceful; no need have we of bloodshed and groans.' This juxtaposition of the 'noble savage' to the forceful intellectual is far from the Byronic idealization of the 'dark hero.' The simplicity and kindness of the gypsies (somewhat in the Russian tradition) triumph over the evil sophistication of the city dweller.

In his fragmentary 'The Brigand Brothers' (1822) and the delightful 'Fountain of Bahchisarai' (1823), which evokes a vision of Tartar khans and their harems and wives captured in battle, the Byronic influence has been assimilated to such an extent as to appear completely transformed. Despite the ardor and tempestuousness of his own temperament, Pushkin disliked exaggeration in art and carefully avoided the unbelievable or supernatural in his non-folkloristic poems. The protagonists of his most Romantic works are far from being mysterious or wild: they are simply disenchanted souls like the Caucasian captive whose aloofness from life is the result of precocious experiences that have seared his heart. Pushkin's attitude to this sort of hero changes rapidly: at first he treats him seriously (the Caucasian captive, or Aleko in *The Gypsies*), then, more critical of this representative of a prematurely aged generation, he makes him the target of satire and parody (Eugene Oneghin).

Pushkin's departure from the Romantic pattern marks his liberation from Byronic influence. By 1825, when he was fully aware of Byron's affectations and other faults, he reproaches the English poet for making each of his heroes merely the personification of some one trait of his own personality: one of his pride, a second of his scorn, a third of his melancholy—'thus out of a sombre, energetic and full character Byron has created several insignificant ones.' And, in the same year Pushkin began his poem on the French poet André Chénier, who had been executed during the French Revolution, with these words: 'While the world contemplates Byron's urn in amazement, and his shade, by Dante's side, harkens to the chorus of European lyres, it is another's shade that beckons me.'

Pushkin joined Romanticism and fought as a Romantic, but in much the same way as Stendhal, for whom Romanticism meant only 'modern literature *versus* old literature.' Pushkin's chief debt to Romanticism was the idea of freedom. He wrote in the forms adopted by the school—the novel, the short story, historical chronicle, drama, light verse—and he evinced a certain interest in dramatic situations and in the clash of strong emotions. He utilized freely the Romantic blend of diverse elements—serious, comic, sublime, ironic—in the same work. He also

voiced repeatedly that supreme longing for things beyond reality that
is the essence of Romanticism, but he could never accept the Romantic
lack of proportion and haphazard, whimsical, and fantastic way of
writing. His style, therefore, scarcely touched by Romanticism, is pure,
sober, classically perfect; its richness never lapses into luxuriance, its
originality never becomes a pose. He always opposed and exposed
Romantic heroes, and in all his work, with the exception of a very few
early pieces, the stress is on simplicity of character, on kindheartedness,
and lack of pretensions. Dostoevsky attached great importance to *The
Gypsies* (written when Pushkin was twenty-four) because the proud
Aleko was taught a lesson by the illiterate vagabond: 'Submit, proud
man, be humble'—this is one of the main elements of Pushkin's philosophy. He often confronts the predatory man with the humble, and his
sympathy is always on the side of the latter. Here again his attachment
to the concept of the 'measure of a man' is clearly apparent.

   Without the slightest attempt at didacticism or moralizing, Pushkin
returns to this point, particularly in his poems and dramatic scenes, in
which he represented not only Russian life but the European as well.
Many are studies of man's demoralization under the influence of some
passion. *The Covetous Knight* (1830; a purported translation from
Shenstone) is more than a psychological study: the knight, drunk with
avarice, lives only for his money and repudiates his own son; the money
gives him a wonderful sense of power which kills any sense of pity and
all human understanding. *A Feast during the Plague* (1830) is also
no mere psychological study, with its hints of the delight a man may
take in danger and folly, its grim depiction of sensual lust in the face
of death, and its startling revelation of the power of evil over the mind.

   The best example of those of Pushkin's poems in which the structure
passes from the two-dimensional world to the three-dimensional is
Mozart and Salieri (1830). Salieri, a musician who has 'verified harmony through algebra,' had to work all his life in the sweat of his brow.
He knows everything about music, is an excellent pianist, a highly
skilled technician, and is deeply serious about his art. But he envies
Mozart, that 'idle roisterer' who creates sublime pieces almost in jest,
without effort or the least awareness of his achievements. Salieri adores
Mozart's music and hates the facility, the good fortune, and the thought-
lessness of his rival. The mere existence of this lucky, frivolous, and
inspired competitor seems to him a cruel unjustice—and he poisons
Mozart. But this drama of envy as a passion has another, and a deeper,
meaning. By killing Mozart Salieri adjusts an error in the universal
order, for it is unjust that beauty and fame should be the lot of an
indolent, thoughtless individual, while the earnest plodder is denied

recognition. The allotment of fortune's favors and spiritual gifts seems as faulty as the distribution of earthly goods. Salieri knows that there is no justice here on earth, but he wonders whether there is any justice even above. Worse still—and at this point the drama reveals a new aspect—the doing away with Mozart does not remove Salieri's excruciating doubts of his own talent. He believed himself to be superior to the composer of *The Requiem* and therefore entitled to act freely; he had committed a crime—but are crime and genius compatible? Michelangelo (so they say) had also killed a man. But what if that was just a legend, and the great artist has never been a murderer in reality? With this question the drama ends.

Now the incompatibility of crime and genius is not merely a moral problem or the issue of a given set of circumstances: it deals directly with the essence of art. What is the relation between art and morality? What part does the conscious effort of an artist play in his creativity?

In this philosophical issue, as interesting to his contemporaries as it is to us today, Pushkin took sides with the Romantics, accepting their concept of unconscious inspiration as the true essence of art. He has, in various poems, pointed out that a poet may seem 'the pettiest among the petty sons of the world,' who concentrates on futilities—until he hears the 'divine word.' Thereupon his soul trembles 'like an awakening eagle' and he seeks solitude where he may sacrifice to Apollo. In his act of creation he must be completely free. He should not care for public opinion, for friends or enemies, for lords and sovereigns. Nothing should curb the unleashed flow of his inspiration. Pushkin proclaims the unlimited spiritual independence of the artist, whose supreme happiness and highest rights are 'to depend on nobody, to serve and please none but himself.' This faith in absolute artistic freedom and the scorn Pushkin had for works of an obviously moralistic character, did not, however, coincide with the theory of art for art's sake. Pushkin was convinced that a true poet was a sounding board responsive to the voices of contemporary life. He wanted the poet to be actively interested in the ideas and events of his time. A series of his poems on political themes proves that he put this theory into practice. He was also of the opinion that a free, independent writer was bound to produce works of social and moral significance. In his justly proud poem 'A Monument I Reared' (inspired by Horace's 'Exegi monumentum aere perennius,' also imitated by Derzhavin), he foretells his future fame and explains why his name will be cherished by the people, over all of great Russia: 'Because I awakened kind feeling with my lyre, because in my ruthless age I glorified freedom and called for mercy for the vanquished.' These lines are no mere generalities. Pushkin had a definite political stand and he was the poet of freedom. In his youth he was associated with the Decembrists and had shared their opinions. Later, in the 'thirties, apparently reconciled with the monarchy, he tried to become a conformist, but in the last years of his life he resumed his critical attitude toward the autocratic regime. These changes in his political views, however, did not affect the core of his ideas. Throughout his life Pushkin remained a Westernizer and a liberal. He belonged to the progressive tradition of the educated nobility, which owed its beginnings to Peter the Great, and he therefore attached prime importance to the reforms initiated by the Great Czar.

v   Pushkin's admiration for Peter the Great was not based on political considerations alone. He loved Peter the man, he felt a genuine attraction for this tireless 'toiler on the throne,' and he portrayed him in various poems and in the unfinished novel about his own Negro ancestor, *The Blackamoor of Peter the Great*. Pushkin may, in fact, be called the bard of Russia's greatest Czar. He represented his beloved hero as a strong, violent, impetuous man who was aware of his goal and of Russia's future, and whose reforms were inspired by a single ideal. Pushkin fully approved Peter's policies and glorified them accordingly. In 'Poltava' (1828), which describes the perfidy of the Ukrainian Hetman Mazeppa in siding with the Swedes, Peter is represented at the peak of his triumph; at the Battle of Poltava the Czar has routed Charles XII of Sweden, from whom he has wrested the Baltic, and a new era is opening for the Russian Empire. In this poem Peter is pictured as a demigod, with hyperbolic description—something rarely found in any other work by Pushkin. During the battle Peter's countenance is 'awesome'; he is 'magnificent'; he is all 'like God's tempestuous wrath.'

Pushkin condones the oppression and violence Peter had used in order to lead Russia toward the West, and he hails his will power indomitable energy, and grandiose vision. He describes the builder of St. Petersburg in the prologue to *The Bronze Horseman* (1833): 'Filled with grandiose thoughts he stood upon the shore where broke the lonely waves, and gazed into the distance. . . . "Here will a great city be founded . . . Nature has decreed that a window into Europe is to be made at this spot." ' Pushkin was the first Russian poet who consciously accepted the Empire and the St. Petersburg period of Russian history. And he was also the first rhapsodist of the new capital, of that beautiful and fantastic metropolis built on marshes and buffeted in winter by frosts and winds, veiled in the spring by thick fogs hanging over the marble palaces, the church spires, and the golden needles of the Admiralty; languishing in summer under its white nights with their eerie twilight lasting from sunset to sunrise; and threatened in autumn by recurring inundations of the wrathful sea.

Pushkin knew the pricè the common man had to pay for the splendor of this artificial and proud capital. It was a price paid by the Russian people for the consolidation and expansion of the Empire, for its military conquests, and for its glorious position among other nations. He was fully aware of the fundamental conflict between the fate of an individual and the destiny of the State: the individual longings for peace and happiness were crushed by the merciless progress of the nation. This tragic and universal paradox is the theme of *The Bronze Horseman,* which, in my opinion, is the most beautiful and haunting of Pushkin's poems, written in vigorous, sweeping, and supple verse. Its title refers to the colossal equestrian statue of Peter on a pedestal of reddish granite, sculptured by E. Falconet and erected on the bank of the Neva; the pedestal is engraved: *Petro Primo—Catharina Secunda MDCCLXXXII.* The Emperor is on his rearing steed at the edge of a precipice.

The prologue of the poem is a miniature epic of the city's creation. The narrative shifts to a later day and describes the flood of 1824—hostile nature in elemental revolt against the works of man. During the flood the hero of the poem, Eugene, a minor official, loses all his dreams of happiness—his betrothed, his home, and all his belongings. Overwhelmed by the horror of the catastrophe, his mind becomes unhinged. In a fit of frenzy he threatens Peter, the Bronze Horseman, the cause of all his ills, the cruel builder of this unreal city that defies God and nature. The Bronze Horseman and horse leap down from the pedestal and pursue the offender through the empty streets of a silent city. Wherever Eugene turns he hears at his heels hoofs thundering over the reverberating pavement.

The symbolism of the poem is all too obvious. The Bronze Horseman 'on the height, at the very edge of the abyss, with his bridle of iron, has made Russia rear'—and none can tell which way he will go. In his flight over cliffs and precipices many lives will inevitably be sacrificed. But the acceptance, and even the justification, of this historic necessity does not prevent Pushkin from feeling sympathy and compassion for the victims. The Eugene of this poem is portrayed as a lonely 'little man' whose misfortune, misery, and madness affect us deeply. The lot of the 'little man' was to become one of the main themes of Russian literature, from Gogol (directly influenced by Pushkin) and Dostoevsky to Chekhov and the Soviet writers.

One of the most striking features of *The Bronze Horseman* is the portrayal of Eugene's madness, which is so vivid that the grim pursuit of the minor official by an equestrian statue becomes a reality. In this romantic fusion of realism and fantasy, devoid of exaggeration, Pushkin is again a forerunner of Gogol and Dostoevsky. The delirium of his hero is depicted by Pushkin in a simple, succinct, matter-of-fact manner.

He used the same device in his prose. His short stories, told in an efficient, brisk style free of adornment or grandiloquence (they are on a par with those of Mérimée and Stendhal), often treat romantic or fantastic situations in a soberly rational way (*The Coffin-Maker* has a ghastly nightmare after a celebration, the *Queen of Spades* brings about the ruin of Hermann, a gambler with *Übermensch* notions, and so on). The economy of artistic devices and the directness of the style make alive and concrete the episodes and characters in Pushkin's short stories and novelettes. They were the most important phenomenon in Russian prose since Karamzin, but they are far removed from the affected sentimentality and artificiality of the author of *Poor Liza*. Here again he is a pioneer, leaving for posterity perfect specimens of the short story (*The Shot, The Blizzard*), the novelette (*The Queen of Spades*), and the short historical novel (*The Captain's Daughter*).

Pushkin was most attracted by the more tempestuous periods of Russia's history. The dramatic scenes of *Boris Godunov* describe the troublous times after the death of the awesome Ivan IV, the intrigues of Dimitri, the mock pretender, and the civil strife fomented by enemies from without and faithless boyars from within. Next Pushkin turned his attention to the revolutionizing activity of Peter the Great, to the times when Muscovy ceded its place to the Empire born amid the flame and noise of battles and campaigns. And, finally, he composed *A History of the Pugachev Uprising,* for which he had been given permission to consult the State archives and to journey to the regions where this vast popular movement had taken place. The Pugachev uprising also forms the background of *The Captain's Daughter*. It may be claimed that in his choice of historical subject Pushkin merely followed the Romantic tendency of his own times. However, his work reveals something more profound than a literary eagerness for bright colors and the clash of intensified emotions. Pushkin's numerous essays and letters reveal that he was constantly concerned with what would today be called the problem of national awareness. He endeavored to determine the main trends of Russian history and character and to connect them with contemporary events.

In *Boris Godunov,* that romantic tragedy in which the Byronic influence is definitely supplanted by the Shakespearean, the reader is engrossed not only by the masterful characterization, the swiftly moving plot, and the suspense, but also by the vision of the hidden springs of Russian history and by the interpretation of the national psychology. The true hero of the tragedy is the people, but they are silent when the boyars, after their murders and uprisings, announce their new Czar—none other than Dimitri, the mock pretender. It is a silence pregnant with symbolic significance: sooner or later the people will make themselves heard—at first clamorously, as during the Pugachev rebellion, but the day will inevitably come when it will be in an articulate voice. Pushkin dreamt of education through freedom and tolerance, enabling the Russian people to take the place that was rightly theirs. He well knew the merits and deficiencies of the Russian national character; he nurtured no illusions, admitting that a Russian revolt was always senseless and cruel, but at the same time he could not help but feel and think as a typical representative of Russia. Although on many occasions he talked as a nationalist (he said he would never permit a foreigner to rail at Russia), he nevertheless exclaimed: 'Why the devil should any man with a heart and talent be born in such a land as Russia!' When the Polish insurrection of 1831 broke out, he wrote his ode 'To the Calumniators of Russia,' defending the reprisals against the rebels and expressing his faith in the leading role of a unified Russian Empire in the Slavic world. This was of utmost importance: in the person of Pushkin educated society (and not merely high officials such as Derzhavin) identified itself with Russia—even with the Empire—and asserted that the destiny of the State and of the people was its concern. Whatever Pushkin wrote about the past and present of his land was interpreted as a contribution to the development of national awareness. The Decembrists, in their way, had worked toward the same end.

Pushkin's national awareness, his feeling for Russia as a unit, did not affect his fundamental liberalism. He suffered from political oppression and exposed the evils of the autocratic regime. What was more, he never lapsed into chauvinism, and combined his national pride and patriotism with a strong leaning towards Western Europe. This combination formed one of the many complexities of the Pushkin phenomenon in Russian culture. His self-assertion as a Russian was coincident with his acceptance and assimilation of the Western legacy.

Pushkin himself was so very Russian—in his upbringing, his way of life, his love of his country and of the common man. He traveled widely in Russia, lived for years in provincial towns and on estates where he could come into close contact with peasants, artisans, and the lesser nobility; and in Moscow and St. Petersburg he was a familiar at Court, in aristocratic circles, and among the intelligentsia. His love of Russia was no blind emotion: he knew her history and was well acquainted with the folklore and local customs of Russia; he possessed an extraordinary sense of the Russian language and an uncanny perception of the Russian heart and mind. And at the same time this untranslatable Russian poet spoke and wrote French like a Frenchman; read and translated German, English, and Italian; knew the Greek and Latin classics; and was amazingly well read in the European authors of his day. There is proof that Pushkin knew American writers also; for instance, the germ of his popular fairy tale, 'The Golden Cockerel' (1834), so inimitably Russian in its folklore style, was borrowed from *The Alhambra* of Washington Irving, a French translation of which was found in Pushkin's library. Few Westerners were so *au courant* in contemporary European art and thought as this Russian writer who never had the opportunity of leaving his native land. 'I love Europe with all my heart,' said Pushkin, and he displayed his love and his intuitive understanding of Europe in his poems and dramatic pieces, which involve Scotland (*A Feast during the Plague*), Spain (*The Stone Guest,* dealing with Don Juan), Italy (*Angelo* and numerous lyrics), the Balkans (*Songs of the Western Slavs*), and which range in time from the Middle Ages (*The Covetous Knight*) to the eighteenth century (*Mozart and Salieri*) and Pushkin's own day (his lyrical poems). In his translations or 'imitations' he rendered the spirit of various periods and countries in the most striking fashion. He so absorbed the spirit of various forms of European civilization that he was right in proclaiming himself as much a Westerner as a Russian. He was at once a national and a European writer without ever being inconsistent, for in this, as in so many other things, Pushkin presented a oneness, an organic unity seldom found among great poets. According to Dostoevsky, his universality was not only the main feature of Pushkin's work and mentality, but it made him the most typical representative of the Russian spirit in so far as the latter always tends to transform the national into the universal.

Whatever this universality may be, one fact remains certain: Pushkin's work, for all its unmistakably national flavor, is part and parcel of world literature. It was Pushkin who won for Russian letters a place in European art, and this came about at the very moment Russian literature acquired, also through Pushkin, an awareness of its national peculiarities and asserted its formal and spiritual individuality. The whole importance of Pushkin's role is contained in this statement. The curious part of it is that Pushkin himself was conscious of what he was doing and had set precise objectives for himself and for his fellow writers. Despite all the romantic aura about his conception of the poet as the beloved child of the Muses and the inspired disciple of the gods, Pushkin acted as a man of great intellectual power and understanding.

He said once that 'poetry should be rather on the silly side'—probably wishing to stress the intuitive, irrational aspect of creativeness. But his own work, unlike that of so many Romantics, is marked for its rational clarity and its sparkling intelligence. Pushkin was an extremely intelligent man, of strong analytical judgment, a keen critical sense, and an utterly logical mind. Those who might be inclined to take too seriously his statements on the unconscious nature of poetic inspiration ought to examine his manuscripts and then scan the catalogue of his private library.

Pushkin had an astounding gift of spontaneous versification and he often enlivened informal gatherings with his dazzling improvisations. But, once in his study, he worked hard at polishing his verse, intent on finding the best word or compressing his thought into an artistically precise sentence. He constantly revised and rewrote his poems, and his manuscripts, with their innumerable blottings, corrections, and emendations, bear witness to his conscientious toil. Pushkin also needed to visualize his images and, being a gifted draughtsman, drew amazingly good and revealing sketches on the margins of his manuscripts or on separate sheets of paper. In general, he contended that inspiration should be carefully checked by the intellect; in his own case this process was backed by a superb memory and vast knowledge.

Pushkin's private library of four thousand volumes included books in many languages on science, medicine, philosophy, esthetics, law, ethnography, history, and literature, all well thumbed by their owner. Dante, Cervantes, Milton, Shakespeare (whom he studied systematically), Voltaire, Goethe, Scott, Byron, Musset, Stendhal, and Mérimée were among his favorite authors. In his essays and letters he discussed widely diversified problems of art, history, politics, and psychology, and his judgments are always witty, original, and wise, revealing his vast range of intellectual interests.

This Russian-European, whose Russian traits were as striking as his truly European spirit, possessed a rare combination of intuitive and rational qualities. His artistic and intellectual versatility was in keeping with his eagerness for life and knowledge and reflected the richness of his nature. In his work he succeeded in integrating the varied and frequently contradictory drives of his nature and in modifying his passionate outbursts. But the balance and harmony, the formal perfection and Olympian vigor which enhance his verse and prose are not to be found in the details of his biography. The life story of Pushkin is more turbulent and adventurous than any of his most romantic poems or tales.

VI   Pushkin's father, Serghei, the elegant and frivolous scion of an aristocratic but practically ruined family,
was a very well-educated but superficial and egotistic man, primarily
interested in his pleasures and social successes. His beautiful and tem-
peramental wife, Nadezhda—the granddaughter of the Abyssinian
princeling Hannibal who had been the favorite of Peter the Great—had
a passion for dancing and entertaining. Social life absorbed this brilliant
and thoughtless couple to such an extent that they had neither time nor
desire to bother about their children. Alexander, born 26 May (6 June,
new style) 1799 in Moscow, was brought up by English nurses, French
tutors, German servants, and that kindhearted Russian nurse, Arina,
who talked to the child in her native tongue and kept him spellbound
for hours with her fairy tales and songs.

In Moscow and on the family estate of Zaharovo, governors and
tutors taught him four foreign languages and the miscellany of various
fields of knowledge. The awkward, homely, obstinate, and frequently
ill-tempered child, whose parents paid him little attention, was an avid
reader and by the age of ten had devoured innumerable French books
definitely not intended for children, such as Voltaire's tales, the comedies
of Molière, and the *Erotic Poems* of Parny. He wrote verse (also in
French), but his sister and the rest of the family can hardly be said to
have appreciated it.

In 1811 he was accepted as one of the thirty pupils in the Lyceum
at Czarskoye Selo (Czar's Hamlet), recently established to prepare
young aristocrats for high governmental posts. The spirit of the place
was fairly liberal, and students were taught history, literature, philosophy, science, languages, arts, and sports by outstanding instructors.
Pushkin, who loved the Lyceum, acquired an excellent education there,
but the reports of his teachers, far from being eulogistic, picture him as
a 'brilliant, loquacious, kindhearted but conceited youth, full of passion
and pride, often frivolous and of a quick temper.'

In 1815, at a public examination in the presence of Derzhavin, the
sixteen-year-old youth recited one of his own poems, for which the old
man wanted to embrace him. Pushkin never forgot this episode; he was
proud that 'Derzhavin noticed us and, as his steps were leading him
to his grave, he bestowed his blessing upon us.' It was like a solemn
transmission of the poetic torch. Other representatives of the older
generation, such as Zhukovsky and Karamzin, both of whom Pushkin
knew personally, were also struck by the freshness and mellifluousness
of Pushkin's verse (first published in 1815) and predicted a great future
for him. Most of Pushkin's poems of the Lyceum period were inspired
by Parny and Voltaire, or by the precocious eroticism of the young

author. He learned early what he called (in *Eugene Oneghin*) 'the science of the tender passion' and by sixteen he had already had affairs with sundry actresses, maids, or demi-mondaines, while still maintaining a platonic love for those beautiful women of the world he met at Karamzin's house. He made friends with the officers of the regiment of Hussars stationed in Czarskoye Selo: they liked 'the Frenchman' or 'the Monkey-Tiger,' as his schoolmates had nicknamed him and taught him how best to 'sacrifice to Bacchus and to Venus.'

Graduating from the Lyceum in 1817, Pushkin was appointed to the Foreign Office. His post was a purely nominal one, and for almost three years his life was one long succession of parties, love affairs with demi-mondaines and noble ladies, gambling, drinking, and all sorts of dissipation. Although he participated in various literary societies, such as Arzamas or the Green Lamp, and wrote and read a great deal, his main purpose was to be a man-about-town and to move among others like him. He loved this senseless, futile, tense existence, with its intrigues, challenges, duels, and surprises, in which he could display his 'African' temperament, his daring spirit, and his lust for pleasure. What distinguished him from the other easygoing profligates was his lack of vulgarity and his ability to make clear, straightforward judgments. The pleasure-seeker never actually lost his head.

Pushkin's best friends during this turbulent period belonged to the aristocratic circles where the ideas of Decembrism abounded. He lived in an atmosphere of liberalism and gay parties, which started with cards and wine and ended in passionate discussions of political and social problems. This spirit is reflected in numerous poems that were greatly admired by the young critics of the autocratic regime. In 'The Countryside' (1819) he made a frontal attack on serfdom: 'When, O my friends, shall I see serfdom abolished and the people freed—when shall the desired dawn of enlightened liberty rise over my fatherland?' In his 'Ode to Freedom' (1819), inspired by Radishchev, he called the late Emperor Paul an 'autocratic malefactor,' at whom heaven was horrified and who was a 'disgrace to nature.' In popular epigrams he mercilessly ridiculed Arakcheyev and even Alexander I was not spared.

The 'Ode' and various political squibs were finally intercepted by the secret police, and only the intercession of such prominent personalities as Karamzin and Zhukovsky saved Pushkin from real disaster; he was sent to serve under General Inzov in the wilds of southern Russia.

This exile was the first blow life had ever dealt Pushkin. It came at the peak of his career as an erratic man-about-town and also at the point of his completion of his fairy-tale poem, 'Russlan and Liudmila.'

Toward the end of 1820, on his way south, Pushkin fell ill in Ekaterinoslav and was rescued by his friend Nicholas, a son of General Raevsky. The Raevsky family was traveling to the Caucasus and the Crimea, and the general, a doughty hero of 1812, won Inzov's permission to take the convalescent poet along. This experience was a happy one for Pushkin. After his superficial and dissipated life at the capital he found himself in the midst of a charming and cultured family with high moral standards; young Nicholas Raevsky was Pushkin's friend; Nicholas' elder brother, the wilful and eccentric Alexander, later revealed to Pushkin the inner meaning of Byron; the three Raevsky sisters were bright and pretty, and Pushkin fell in love with each in turn. There is a legend that Marie Raevskaya, later Princess Volkonskaya, was the poet's secret 'grand passion.' The wild scenery of the Caucasus, the semi-tropical luxuriance of the Crimea with its traces of Tartar domination, greatly impressed Pushkin and inspired many of his lyrics and poems.

The change from the Crimean shores to dull and dusty Kishinev, the semi-Asiatic capital of Bessarabia where Inzov had established his headquarters, was thoroughly disheartening: Pushkin now realized for the first time all the dreariness of his exile. It is true that Inzov was more like a father to him than an exacting superior: the general had liberal views, like Pushkin, and he was a member of a Masonic lodge and winked at the poet's whims and extravagances. Pushkin was granted a furlough and spent four months in the Ukraine on the estate of the millionaire Davydov. Members of various secret societies met there in the spring of 1821, while the host and his attractive and not too virtuous wife entertained high officials from St. Petersburg. Pushkin divided his time between 'aristocratic dinner parties and demagogic discussions.' The plotters became friendly with the poet but prevented him from joining in their conspiracies.

On his return to Kishinev he had to endure the monotonous provincial life, the boredom of which could hardly be relieved by light amours with Moldavian women or by the rows with jealous husbands which now and then led to duels. There was plenty of time to read and write, and Pushkin worked hard. This was the period when he was most strongly under Byron's influence and wrote such romantic pieces as 'The Caucasian Captive,' 'The Brother Brigands,' and 'The Gypsies,' the delightful Crimean fantasy of 'The Fountain of Bahchisarai,' many excellent lyrics, and the first chapter of *Eugene Oneghin,* in which he described his own experiences in St. Petersburg before his exile. By 1822 this young man of twenty-three had been definitely formed as a poet, and the maturity and profundity of his new works astounded those accustomed to see him as a firebrand or as a god of conviviality. Literary successes could not, however, compensate him for the heavy burden of exile. Pushkin complained of wasting his time out in the Bessarabian steppes, where he felt stifled and cut off from the world. After all sorts of wirepulling by influential friends, he was finally transferred in 1823 to Odessa, where he joined the staff of Count Vorontzov, the Governor-General of the New Russia province.

Odessa, a newly-built town on the Black Sea, possessed enormous advantages over Kishinev: it had an interesting international society and, as a foreign-trade port, was permeated by Western influences. Pushkin soon became very popular in local society. He was a frequent guest at the house of Countess Vorontzova, of whom he was very fond; he also met the beautiful Amalia Risnich, the wife of a Dalmatian merchant, to whom he dedicated some of his most poignant love lyrics. This young man of medium height but of a strong build, jerky in movement and brusque of manner, with an oversize head, irregular features, full 'African' lips, curly chestnut hair, short side whiskers and deep-set blue eyes, was far from handsome, yet the most beautiful women were easily attracted by his passionate personality, his irresistible vitality, and his brilliant and witty conversation.

In Odessa Pushkin shed the Byronic influence completely and started to study Shakespeare and the Italian writers. He kept on with *Eugene Oneghin,* while his lyrics and poems, published in various St. Petersburg periodicals, increased not only his fame but his income. The sale of 'The Fountain of Bahchisarai' alone brought him three thousand rubles. But, while lovers of literature and the fair ladies of Odessa admired the poet, Count Vorontzov took a dislike to this odd functionary, who wrote epigrams instead of formal reports and made love to his chief's wife. At the same time some of Pushkin's letters, in which he praised atheism and asserted his radical opinions, were intercepted by the secret police. The authorities, instigated by Vorontzov, decided to take new measures against the turbulent poet. In the summer of 1824 Pushkin was ordered to leave Odessa and proceed immediately to his mother's estate of Mikhailovskoye, in the northern province of Pskov, where he was to remain indefinitely. This house-arrest amounted to exile. After a violent quarrel with his father, Pushkin was left alone in Mikhailovskoye in the company of his old nurse Arina. Amid this isolation, feeling that the best years of his life were being foolishly sacrificed, he even thought of flight abroad, but gradually became resigned to his fate. His neighbors, the Wulf family, helped him a great deal: on their estate he met intelligent men and attractive women—particularly Ann Kern, to whom he became very attached. He wrote continuously; *Eugene Oneghin* was progressing well, while *Boris Godunov* was nearing completion.

He was exhilarated by the news of the Decembrist uprising of 1825. Subsequently, when Nicholas I asked him what he would have done if he had been in the capital on 14 December, he answered candidly that he would have joined the rebels. His exile had saved him from arrest and jail, but, as his own poems had been found among the papers of each defendant in the great Decembrist trial, he had to walk warily. All his friends were imprisoned; Pestel, whom Pushkin knew well and whom he had called 'the most intelligent man in Russia,' was hanged, together with Ryleyev and three other young men.

When the sensation provoked by the uprising subsided, Pushkin made desperate efforts to lift the ban on his return to the capital. Finally, in 1826, Zhukovsky and others succeeded in obtaining the Czar's consent to meet the poet in Moscow. Of course this favor was granted not so much to Pushkin the poet as to Alexander Pushkin the scion of an old aristocratic family. Pushkin gained Nicholas' confidence by his outright frankness and, in his turn, was charmed by the monarch's affability and particularly by his offer to become the poet's sole censor. Pushkin was also allowed to reside in Moscow and St. Petersburg. This graciousness, however, did not mean freedom, as Pushkin was to learn shortly through bitter experience. He had no right to travel without a special permit from the authorities, and was compelled to account for his every move. The Czar's censorship, which had seemed a blessing at first and had made Pushkin utterly happy, proved to be a tiresome jest: the poet, bound to submit to the Czar every line he had ever written, had to endure the imperial criticism. Thus Nicholas I was of the opinion that *Boris Godunov* ought to be changed from a drama into a novel *à la* Sir Walter Scott; that *Songs about Stenka Razin* was too vulgar to be published, and so on. And, despite the Emperor's promises, all of Pushkin's writings were also reviewed by the regular censors after passing the Emperor's desk. Worst of all, however, was the special favor the Czar bestowed upon the poet: Nicholas I entrusted Count Benckendorff, Chief of the Gendarmerie, with the 'surveillance, guidance, and counseling' of Pushkin. Although Benckendorff pretended to be the only governmental good angel at Pushkin's side, secret police agents were busy spying on the poet and registering his every word and act (their reports were unearthed in the State archives after the Revolution of 1917). Benckendorff proved a most exacting guide: his correspondence with the poet (always in exquisitely polite French) shows that Pushkin was obliged to justify his smallest action. Until his death Pushkin was treated like a suspect on bail and continually reminded of the fact that, as a 'suspicious character,' he would do well to be careful.

In 1826 Pushkin was granted permission to reside in Moscow. When he went to the theater for the first time, the whole house stared at him rather than the stage. In the streets he was followed by crowds. He soon became the central figure in Moscow society and lived up to his reputation for lively wit: he knew how to fascinate women and to interest men. At the salons of the Princesses Volkonskaya and Rimskaya-Korsakova, he met and made friends with Mickiewicz, Poland's greatest poet, and the outstanding men of letters of his time. As usual he had numerous love affairs and was twice on the point of marrying. The album of one of his future fiancées, Catherine Ushakova, contains his 'Don Juan list': two columns of feminine names, often disguised, to enumerate those he loved 'a little—much—passionately.' This list is still racking the heads of Pushkin's biographers, although the great majority of the names can be identified.

In 1826-8 new chapters of *Eugene Oneghin* were published, together with some delightful lyrics and poems. But his growing literary success did not seem to make Pushkin happy. He was bored by his dissipated life, his considerable losses at gambling, and his easy victories over actresses and titled ladies. He declared that 'Moscow and St. Petersburg, although they differ, are on a par when it comes to triviality and stupidity.' His dissatisfaction with life and society was aggravated by the liberals' censure of a poem he dedicated to the Czar, in which he wanted Nicholas I to emulate Peter the Great. At the same time the conservatives were shocked by his Epistle to the Decembrists exiled to Siberia:

> Mid ores deep in Siberia's soil
> Your patience proudly maintain;
> Not wasted is your grievous toil,
> Your lofty thoughts are not in vain,
> Your heavy shackles ye shall spurn,
> Your dark cells open, and liberty
> Shall greet your coming joyfully,
> Your brethren shall your sword return. . .

To cap everything else, the police found the inscription of 'To December 14th' on his 'Andre Chenier,' and, although there was nothing revolutionary in the poem, the authorities managed to make his 1828 sojourn in St. Petersburg unpleasant. Only the Emperor's order to suspend the investigation saved the poet from serious complications, but he was keenly aware of his bondage because of his 'debt to the Czar.' This period is marked by lyrics of a melancholy strain. 'Why was life, this useless and casual gift, ever granted me? And why has mighty fate condemned it to death?'

In the same year while passing through Moscow, he first saw at a ball a sixteen-year-old girl, Nathalie Goncharova and, struck by this 'purest example of purity,' he fell violently in love with her. His proposal was, however, not acceptable to the young beauty's mother, so Pushkin, after having secured the necessary authorization, went to the Caucasus, where he took part in the campaign against the Turks and enjoyed a life of danger, freedom, and adventure. He had always needed to be in close touch with reality. While other poets seem to depend on themselves and are satisfied with their inner resources, Pushkin looked to the experiences of life to furnish the material for his inspiration. He was continually hunting for impressions, sensations, events, to be used in his writing. His work was therefore quite inseparable from his eager desire for knowledge, love, experience, and suffering. The usual Romantic distinction between a poet's art and his life does not apply to Pushkin: he always believed that art gained directly from the intensity and multiplicity of the personal experiences of the artist. To be alive was for him as important as to write.

The shift from the Caucasian mountains to the society of St. Petersburg was painfully unpleasant. Upon his return Pushkin was immediately reminded of his servitude: Benckendorff rebuked him for having worn civilian evening dress instead of the prescribed uniform of the nobility at the French Embassy ball, and for having gone to Moscow without previous authorization. To avoid the repetition of these annoyances Pushkin again fled to the country and sought refuge in work. In 1829-31 his literary productivity reached its peak.

Pushkin's love for Goncharova increased during these months of retirement. Although he was somewhat apprehensive of losing his independence through marriage, he renewed his courtship. In the spring of 1830 Goncharova's mother finally yielded, although the uncertainty of Pushkin's income, his reputation as a 'mad lover,' his age, and especially his ambiguous position with the authorities, did not make him a desirable husband. On the other hand, the Goncharovs belonged to the lesser nobility, while Pushkin came of the old aristocracy and his name was on all lips.

However, his bride-to-be, now seventeen, was hardly impressed by literary fame. She was a reserved, cold, and none too intelligent girl, much more interested in dress and dances than in poetry. But her loveliness was undisputable. Count Vladimir Sollogub wrote in his *Memoirs:*

I have known many beautiful women, but none had her classic perfection of face and body. She was tall and slender, with a delightfully slim waist, a marvelous bosom, a fine head looking like a lily, a wonderfully regular profile—and what a complexion, what eyes, teeth, ears! All other women paled next to her.

In February, 1831, Pushkin married his 'Madonna' and settled down in St. Petersburg. The first happiness of his domestic life was soon obscured by numerous worries. Nathalie created a sensation in the capital's society; the Emperor himself paid attention to the beautiful lady, and the Pushkins were frequently invited to Court functions. This meant increased expenses, and yet the poet was always short of money. To meet his social obligations he had to take a post in a government bureau and was granted authorization to work in the State archives for his historical writings on Peter the Great and the Pugachev rebellion.

For the next three years his time was divided between his writings, his family (he became the father of two children), and his social life. He wrote a great deal: lyrics, poems ('Angelo,' 'The Bronze Horseman'), novelettes (*The Queen of Spades, Dubrovsky*), fairy tales—but not as much as he wanted to write. Dances and entertainments, to which he had to accompany his wife, and the struggle for money absorbed most of his energy. In 1834 Pushkin was appointed Chamberlain. This rank, usually given to young people, was hardly suitable to the poet's age, but the Court wanted his wife at the dances, and the new rank gave her husband an official standing. Pushkin raged over this 'favor'; whenever he had to put on his Court uniform he called it a buffoon's motley. The courtiers met him with scorn or hostility, and he repaid them by ridiculing them in his epigrams and describing the Court as a sewer. At the Court receptions he yawned or sulkily ate ices while his glamorous wife enjoyed herself. His personal resentment contributed to his resumption of opposition to the government: having lost all his illusions about the Emperor he bitterly criticized his regime. He attempted to resign from the Foreign Office and leave the Court, but all his plans of retirement were thwarted by the opposition of Benckendorff and other high officials.

The only course left to him was to go alone for a rest on his estate and to work in the seclusion of the country. These were his happiest moments, though even then he could not regain his serenity. His nerves were on edge.

The Emperor compels me to stay in St. Petersburg but does not leave me the possibility of earning money by literary work. I am wasting my time and my energy; I am throwing money out of the window, and

I expect nothing from the future. . . For creative work one should have serenity of spirit—and I am not serene.

His independence, added to his sharp tongue and sharper pen, made him many enemies among the aristocrats. They retaliated by spreading all sorts of vicious rumors about his wife, which greatly exasperated him. In 1836 anonymous letters informed Pushkin that Nathalie was betraying him with Baron d'Anthès, a Frenchman and the adopted son of the Dutch ambassador, von Heckeren. The latter played an ambiguous and probably infamous role in the net of intrigue woven around Pushkin. Although he was convinced of his wife's innocence, he challenged d'Anthès. The affair proved abortive, however, since von Heckeren declared that his adopted son was really in love with Nathalie's sister and wanted to marry her. Although this marriage actually took place, the rumors did not cease, and von Heckeren continued his whispering campaign in favor of d'Anthès, whom he now pictured as a victim of his desperate passion for Nathalie. This maddening imbroglio proved too much for Pushkin. In a fit of fury he wrote an insulting letter to von Heckeren—and this time the duel with d'Anthès could not be avoided. It was fought on 27 January (old style) 1837, and Pushkin was mortally wounded. Two days later he was dead.

VII   Pushkin was one of the few great writers who won true fame during their lives. His contemporaries acclaimed his genius. The 'School' of Pushkin included practically all the poets of his period, and even such original writers as Lermontov could not entirely escape his influence. The national significance of Pushkin's work, however, became fully apparent only after his death, when the growth of his popularity assumed extraordinary proportions; he became the symbol of national and artistic perfection. 'He is an astounding and perhaps a unique phenomenon of the Russian spirit,' proclaimed Gogol, 'He embodies what the Russian may become two hundred years hence.'

The founder of the modern Russian literary language, who fulfilled the hopes of the past and opened the roads for further development, Pushkin appealed equally to realists like Nekrassov, to idealistic esthetes like Fet, to the symbolists of the 'nineties like Briussov, or to the Soviet poets who still strive to imitate his clarity, directness, and simplicity and willingly employ his metric forms. Although anti-Pushkin revolts took place in the 'sixties and in 1920, it is safe to say that all Russian poetry of the last hundred years advanced under the aegis of Pushkin, and can never shed his spell. He determined its development, established its standards, formulated its idiom, and even shaped its main forms.

His influence upon Russian prose was no less profound. He laid the foundations of Russian realism in the short story, in the novel, in the historical narrative, and in the drama, not counting his contributions to the essay and literary criticism. Gogol considered himself his disciple; Dostoevsky worshiped him with a kind of superstitious awe; Leo Tolstoy advised young writers to take Pushkin's short stories as models and spoke of their lasting and beneficial effect on his own prose; Chekhov and Gorky placed Pushkin above all other Russian writers—even as Soviet poets and novelists do today.

Some indication of Pushkin's status in Russian culture may be gained from the extent of his influence on music and the graphic arts. His lyrics and poems inspired all the outstanding Russian composers. More than twenty of the most widely known Russian operas are based on Pushkin's works, from *Eugene Oneghin* and *The Queen of Spades* by Tchaikovsky, and *Boris Godunov* by Mussorgsky, to *Aleko* by Rachmaninov and *Mavra* by Stravinsky. Pushkin and his works have also inspired sculptors and painters, such as Repin, Serov, and Wrubel; and the illustrators, such as Bilibin, Kanevsky, A. Fonvizin, Mogilevsky, and Rerberg.

The cult of Pushkin is a part of Russian life; it manifests itself in hundreds of ways: monuments, portraits, names of libraries, schools, institutions; there is hardly a Russian town without a Pushkin Street or Avenue. Anniversaries connected with the poet's life are observed on a nation-wide scale. The editions of his individual or collected works, ranging from pamphlets costing a few kopecks to items for the bibliophile, are innumerable, while Pushkin scholarship flourishes in the U.S.S.R.

Pushkin's prophecy has come true: his name has resounded throughout his vast land and been taken to the hearts of millions. The number of his readers has grown steadily. In the two decades preceding the Revolution of 1917 almost ten million copies of his works were printed in the Empire; under the Soviets these figures have almost trebled: in the span of thirty years (1917-47) over thirty-five million copies of Pushkin's writings have been published in Russian, as well as in seventy-six languages and dialects of the main nationalities and tribes constituting the U.S.S.R. At the present time Pushkin is the most popular and widely read classic in the Soviet Union.

More than a century has gone by since Pushkin's death. In that span of time revolutions have broken out, regimes have changed, wars and ruin have raged over Russia—but Pushkin and Russia's love for Pushkin have remained unchanged.

5

Lermontov

I   On 29 January 1837, the day Push-
kin died, an anonymous poem was being circulated in manuscript copies
among the university students and young officers at St. Petersburg.
Its incisive lines expressed the thoughts and emotions of many educated
Russians to whom the death of Pushkin was a terrific blow, almost a
national catastrophe. The government officials, however, did not view
the event with the same eyes. When a St. Petersburg newspaper appeared with black border, announcing that 'The sun of Russian poetry
has set; Pushkin has died at the half-mark of his magnificent career,'
Count Benckendorff, the acting head of the political police, chided the
publisher: 'Why do you make such a fuss about an individual who did
not even hold any important post?' In certain aristocratic salons the die-
hards and titled snobs defended d'Anthès as a 'perfect gentleman' and
dismissed Pushkin's works with a shrug. The author of the poem, after
having listened to several opinions of Pushkin's fate, quarrelled with a
member of the smart set and added sixteen lines to his original text.[1]
These, too, made the rounds of the capital, heartening the liberals and
shocking the conservatives. A dowager who saw the frightful signs of
Decembrism everywhere made a copy of the poem and sent it to the
Emperor anonymously with the notation: 'Here is an appeal to revolu-

---

[1] Ye sons of sires for evil deeds notorious,
  A hungry throng who crowd the Royal Court,
  Downtrodden lie beneath your heels inglorious
  The wrecks of noble houses,—Fortune's sport.
  Ye dare to strangle Freedom, Genius, Glory,
  And hide within the shelter of the Laws;
  Base lovers of Corruption! Mute before ye
  Stand Justice, Truth and every righteous Cause.
                 (translated by Mary Grace Walker, *Free Russia*, London 1899 v. 10)

tion.' Nicholas I ordered an immediate investigation, and the police had no difficulty in finding and arresting the culprit. He proved to be Michael Lermontov, twenty-three years old and an officer of the Imperial Guard Hussars. His name was far from familiar to the small group of literati, who knew only that this young man was writing poetry in whatever leisure hours he could spare from wild sprees, balls, gambling, and military duties.

The affair was closed by the Emperor's order to reduce Lermontov in rank and to transfer him to an infantry regiment in the Caucasus. The relative mildness of the punishment was owing to the intervention of Arsenieva, Lermontov's grandmother, a wealthy landowner of old aristocratic stock.

Before starting for the Caucasus, Lermontov went to report to the commander of the Hussar regiment. 'Why do you write poems?' the old soldier chided him. 'Leave that to scribblers, buffoons and other bohemians. You are a nobleman.' He was completely ignorant of the fact that 'A Poet's Death' and the consequent banishment had made Lermontov extremely popular. The best poets of the day, such as Zhukovsky and Odoevsky, had found the poem remarkable, while the great literary critic Belinsky had given it high praise.

Although the transfer from the Guards to an ordinary infantry regiment had hurt Lermontov's pride, he left the capital without regret and almost with relief. The life he had been leading was far from satisfactory.

He was born in Moscow in 1814. His mother, Mme Arsenieva's only daughter, had died before he was three. His father, the handsome and frivolous Captain Yuri P. Lermontov, was neither rich, nor a member of the upper ten thousand, although he claimed that his ancestors, who had appeared in Russia only in the seventeenth century, were descended from the Scottish lairds of Learmont and the Spanish dukes of Lerma. Mme Arsenieva hated her son-in-law; she accused him of having ruined her daughter's life and causing her premature death, and she fought tooth and nail to keep her grandson with her. As a result of this family squabble, Michael was separated from his father, whom he saw only on rare visits to his shabby estate. His grandmother transferred all her affection to him, giving him all that wealth and love could command, but, although he reciprocated this love, he could not forget his father. His rich maternal relatives did not hide their contempt for the impecunious Captain, and this the child resented deeply. He felt pity and something like shame for his father. This relation between son and father brought about one of the main psychological complexes in Lermontov's contradictory nature; it is reflected in several of his poems and, in particular, in his first dramas.

In his early childhood Michael was in poor health, and Mme Arsenieva took him twice to the sun-flooded resorts of the Caucasus. The picturesque wildness of the country, the variety of customs among the native tribes, the haughty independence of the mountaineers and their romantic tales of bravery and banditry all left indelible marks on Lermontov's imagination: it was inevitable that he should become the Poet of the Caucasus.

He was extremely precocious, writing poetry at the age of eight, falling violently in love at ten, and showing signs of an unusual feeling for language and a surprising intensity of emotion. His intellectual development was also outstanding. At the age of twelve, surrounded by tutors, he spoke faultless French and German, was good in Greek and Latin, and read at random all sorts of books, including the French poets of the eighteenth century.

A year later, in 1827, Mme Arsenieva moved to Moscow intending to complete the education of her beloved Michael. The adolescent spent his first months in Moscow reading, day and night, the works of Zhukovsky and Pushkin, who filled him with rapture. He was also an avid reader of Chateaubriand and of books on Napoleon, whom he began to worship as a superman. Later he learned English and was able to read in the original the novels of Scott and the poetry of Shelley, Moore, and Byron, the last making a particularly deep and lasting impression upon him.

By fifteen he had already written scores of poems, tales, and dramas, and was at this point a finished poet. He had conceived his most famous dramatic poem, 'The Demon,' had planned 'Mtsyri,' had written 'The Circassians,' 'The Corsair,' the plays *Men and Passions* and *The Spaniards,* and had in his notebook many lines and stanzas that were to be included later in his best works and to become anthology pieces. (For more than a hundred years Russian school children have been learning 'The Angel' by heart—a poem Lermontov composed at the age of fifteen.) Even more astonishing is the fact that in all these early productions he displayed his characteristic versification, his metric originality, and all the peculiarities of his language—in short, all the main features of his style.

Not the least surprising is the development of his personality. This adolescent showed all the eccentricities that were to mark him as a man: he was morbidly sensitive, shy and aggressive, passionate and sarcastic, sensual and idealistic. His contemporaries knew his fits of frenzy as well as his strong logic, his perfect control of his feelings and his capacity for dissimulation. His kindness of heart was constantly hidden under a mask of irony and despondency. He produced the impression of extraordinary vitality and was obviously agitated by forces that could not find a proper outlet. The problem presented by these contradictions of Lermontov's personality has aroused many discussions in Russian critical literature: did they develop from his life or were they just part of a Byronic pose?

There is no doubt that for several years (between 1826 and 1834) Byron was Lermontov's most admired master. Lermontov's demoniac spirit and his feeling of revolt and *Weltschmerz,* however, were no mere Byronic apings. They stemmed from the depth of his own temperament. Lermontov did not become Byron-like by choice; he was simply made like that. He loved and imitated Byron because he found in him the same passions that were rending his own mind and heart, yet he emphasized the difference between himself and the English poet: 'No, I am not Byron; like him I am a persecuted wanderer, but mine is a Russian soul. . . I began earlier, and earlier shall I end. . . Whoever will communicate my thoughts to the world? Either myself—or God—or nobody.'

Life intensified the complexities of Lermontov's character. He was a clumsy, rather ugly youth, and girls laughed at him or refused to take him seriously when he talked of love. We still do not know who the young woman was who made him most unhappy: Nadezhda Ivanova, the daughter of a Moscow playwright, who inspired most of his love lyrics but who, not reciprocating his feeling, married another man in 1833; or Varenka Lopukhina, who had been Michael's close friend and had roused many hopes in him, but also ended by making a more suitable match? While the latest Russian biographers support the theory that Nadezhda Ivanova was Lermontov's muse between 1827 and 1835, the more traditional sources contend that Varenka Lopukhina was the only woman to whom he ever gave his heart. Whoever was the cause of Lermontov's emotional disillusionment, there is no doubt that the unhappy love experiences of his youth are responsible for his embittered and almost cruel attitude toward women. His many love affairs seem to follow the same pattern: he pretended to be madly in love and eventually seduced women from the sheer desire for self-assertion; he did it coldbloodedly, calculating his strategic moves, displaying the shrewdness and skill of a professional hunter—and was disenchanted, bored, and aloof as soon as the conquest was attained.

Another important psychological factor in Lermontov's life was his complex of social inferiority. In his early writings (and by 1830-31, at the age of 17, he had produced 15 poems, 3 dramas, a novelette, and

300 lyrics) he had affirmed that he was concerned solely with 'the dreams and wonders of poetry.' But he was vain; social life held for him an irresistible fascination, and he attached great importance to birth, social standing, and worldly success. Through his grandmother he had entrée into the families of the old nobility, but he wanted to mingle with the higher and more brilliant circles of the Court and the titled aristocracy. His morbid and continually hurt pride prodded him to make desperate attempts to display wit and elegance at balls and parties. He sincerely believed that being a good dancer was far more important than becoming a good poet. Of one thing he was perfectly certain: lovely women preferred empty-headed dandies to a seventeen-year-old dreamer who knew how to write sonnets but was plain and slightly stoop-shouldered. Of course, the ladies he courted could hardly suspect that after a dance he wrote in the solitude of his chamber. 'I know my fate, I see my end; grief has set its mark upon me; God only knows all my pains, which the world will ignore!'

The attempts made by Lermontov (in his adolescence and later) to lead a social life occasionally took the form of an escape from his dreams, from the yearning and passions of his soul. Throughout his whole life he tried to become 'like everybody else,' and his behavior was always distorted by straining and artificiality. Only in his poems was he sincere and free, revealing his real self—but he showed them to hardly anybody and did not want to get them published. Occasionally he would write one in the album of some fair debutante—and this seemed to him the best use he could make of his poetic genius.

II   During a brief period at the Moscow University Lermontov got in touch with the circles of radically inclined students who were cherishing the political tradition of Decembrism and criticizing the reactionary regime of Nicholas I. There is no doubt that Lermontov shared their liberal views; the violent attacks against serfdom in his unfinished novels (especially *Vadim*) as well as his epigrams, plainly prove where his sympathies lay. He dedicated fiery verses to the French Revolution of 1830, and hailed freedom. Later, under the influence of Ryleyev, whose works he obtained in a clandestine edition, he wrote a few pieces impregnated with the revolutionary spirit. In one of them he predicted the future collapse of absolutism: 'The dark day of Russia will come when the crown of the Czars will fall, when the mob, oblivious of its former allegiance, will spread death and blood far and wide.'

The maturing of his political ideas kept pace with his intellectual growth. He studied the German philosophers (especially Schelling and

Fichte), read the European poets, and made excellent progress in mathematics, music and design (his drawings show that he had artistic talent). All these achievements, however, did not seem to satisfy him. He did not want to spend his life merely thinking of freedom and slavery, of nature and the essence of things, and of art and poetry. He was ashamed of the fact that his head was overflowing with rhymes, with visions of demons and angels, images of sorrow and beauty. He wanted to follow the usual life of the younger members of the smart set who valued horses, gambling, wine, and women above all the Byrons in the world. Fleeing from himself into the triviality of life, Lermontov left the university and went to St. Petersburg, where in 1832 he joined the Imperial Guard Hussars. At first he could not help feeling depressed in the capital, where the burden of the autocratic regime and of the secret police was heavier than in Moscow. He tried to forget 'this nonsense about freedom, and infinity, and poetry'; his sole aim now was to become a model officer of the Guards. He ceased to write—except for bawdy puns and erotic poems, the only kind of literature his fellow officers would accept. Lermontov was surrounded by a gay and frivolous crowd, and they cared not at all for the problems of love, death, and freedom, which tormented Lermontov. They gambled, drank, bedded with women of easy virtue, and indulged in practical jokes. In all these worldly pursuits Lermontov behaved with a wild brilliance that gained him a certain reputation among the firebrands of the Guards. He also took part in the social life of the capital: he danced at all the balls and appeared at all the first nights and receptions, displaying his usual mixture of impertinence, affectation, and eccentricity. On one occasion he ostentatiously courted a red-headed beauty, poaching on what the Tsar regarded (so the rumor went) as his private preserve. Another time he turned the head of a girl who used to laugh at him when he was fourteen and, after having almost ruined her reputation by his assiduity, he suddenly walked out on her, thus taking his revenge and leaving his victim, Sushkova, completely crushed and heartbroken.

A psychologist would say that his failure to win the love of Ivanova or Lopukhina, his lack of self-confidence, and his feeling of isolation were responsible for his efforts to win a series of useless amorous victories, which tickled his vanity without granting him any real gratification. This cruel and voluptuous, almost sadistic game with women was interrupted in 1835, when Lermontov got the news that his current love had married another man. By this time he was tired of all his extravagances and utterly bored by his successes. He again turned to writing and composed various poems, ranging from a historical epic, 'Orsha the Boyar,' to the romantic 'Hadji Abrek,' which a monthly magazine published without his authorization. He began a novel, *Princess Ligovskaya,* in which he recounted his love experiences, and a drama, *The Masquerade,* the publication of which was banned by the censors 'because of the violence of passions and characters represented in this play.'

His messmates and his boon companions of the St. Petersburg salons did not approve of this outburst of literary activity. 'Drop it,' one of his friends advised him. 'If the Emperor ever learns that an officer in the Hussars is writing poetry, there will be hell to pay.'

But Lermontov was looking for trouble. In his poem, 'A Sail,' he evokes the vision of a white and lonely sail shimmering through the bluish haze as it rides over the foam. It is not seeking joy or happiness:

> Beneath, the azure current churns,
> Above, the aureate Sunlight glows,
> Yet for a Storm the rebel yearns—
> As though in storms one found repose!

The scandal provoked by his poem on Pushkin's death in 1837 and his consequent exile provided him with a salutary, though enforced, change.

The adventures and dangers of the irregular warfare in which his regiment was engaged against the rebellious native tribes, the grandeur of the scenery, the weird beauty of Caucasian legends and folklore, the absence of tiresome social obligations, the hardships of a soldier's life— all these seemed to soothe his restlessness. Between marches and skirmishes he managed to find time for writing. The work produced in 1838 shows an increased maturity in both craftsmanship and substance. During this period he wrote his beautiful Caucasian poems, as well as epic songs inspired by the Napoleonic invasion of Russia, such as *Borodino,* and by the reign of Ivan the Terrible, such as *The Lay of Kalashnikov the Merchant.* Both of these are imbued with a strong patriotic feeling; and in the latter poem he used and successfully integrated into modern rhythms certain elements of Russian balladry. He began his only important novel, *A Hero of Our Times,* and one of his best romantic poems, the monologue of a young Caucasian novice who escapes from the monastery in his search of freedom preferring death to the futility of a cloistered existence (*Mtsyri*).

These literary achievements could not, however, change Lermontov's somber mood. He had gloomy forebodings about his future. A young woman laughed at him when he mentioned his 'unusual destiny,' and he answered her in his poem 'Laugh not at my Prophetic Grief,' which contains the astounding though not entirely correct prediction: 'I will not find fame, glory or happiness. The fatal hour shall strike: I shall fall covered with blood, and envious enmity will blast my genius in its bud, and I shall perish, leaving never a trace of my hopes and torments.'

In 1839 Lermontov was granted a pardon; he was transferred to a unit in central Russia and later reinstated in his former rank and permitted to rejoin his Hussar regiment. Upon his return to the capital he plunged into social life again. He had become all the rage. The doors of the most exclusive salons were thrown open to the young officer-poet, victim of political persecution and veteran of the Caucasian campaign. He wrote to a female cousin of his: 'Your poor old Michael is now a lion, yet you never even saw that he had a mane.' The literati belonging to the old nobility were also greatly interested in Lermontov: he became a frequent guest at the homes of the Princes Vyazemsky, Odoevsky, and Sollogub. His works were published in the *Notes of the Fatherland,* the best monthly review of the time, and he was invited to join the Circle of 16, a secret society in which political and social problems were discussed with the utmost frankness.

At first Lermontov seemed to enjoy his success and his varied activities, but it soon became clear to him, as well as to his friends, that nothing was able to lift the burden of melancholy and discontent which he could hardly conceal even at public gatherings. Ivan Turgenev saw him in 1839 at a ball given by Princess Shakhovskaya.

There was something fatal and tragic about Lermontov [he tells us]. His tanned face and dark eyes evinced grim and evil force, passion, pensiveness, and disdain. His fixed and oppressive gaze was in discord with the tender, almost childish shape of his full mouth. His stocky torso, his cavalry legs and big head set on stooping shoulders did not create a pleasant impression. But it was impossible not to feel the force, even the might, of this man.

Turgenev saw him again on the eve of 1840 at a masquerade: slowly turning his head amid the brilliantly masked and flirting women, Lermontov fixed each of them with the oppressive gaze of his sad eyes; from time to time he would utter a few words with a wry smile. At that very moment he was probably planning his sardonic poem, 'After the Ball,' in which he revealed his desire to throw in the face of the smart set his 'verse of steel, of bitterness and scorn.'

In 1840 Lermontov was often seen in the company of Princess Marie Shcherbatova, one of the loveliest and most intelligent women in St. Petersburg society, to whom he dedicated some of his most exquisite lyrics. One evening the son of Baron Barantes, the French Ambassador to Russia, who was also paying much attention to the Princess, exchanged some sharp words with Lermontov and challenged him. Both escaped unharmed from the duel, but news of the incident spread rapidly. Lermontov was arrested, and, by Imperial order, was again exiled to the Caucasus to serve at the front, in the infantry. The blow came just at the moment when Lermontov's prose and poetry were gaining recognition and when his literary future seemed assured.

The severity of his punishment was puzzling. Had it been dictated by the Emperor himself, who had some special reason to hate Lermontov? Some modern biographers contend that the ire of the Court was fomented by a Grand Duchess who had regarded the poet with a tender eye, but had been mercilessly ridiculed by the insolent young officer.

After a farewell party at Karamzin's home, the meeting place of writers, musicians, and painters (such as Glinka, Dargomyzhsky and Briullov), Lermontov left St. Petersburg for his exile. Two days later his *Hero of our Times* was published and, within eight weeks, permission to print his first collection of poems was finally granted by the censors. But the author was too far away to watch the growing success of his books: he was fighting on the border of the turbulent regions of the Caucasus, or resting, during his furloughs, at the Caucasian resort of Piatigorsk. Only in the winter of 1841 was he permitted to come to St. Petersburg on a short leave, during which he wrote such masterpieces as 'The Dream,' 'The Argument,' 'The Oak Leaf,' 'The Rock,' 'The Prophet,' and 'Lonely I walk upon the Road,'—some of the highest achievements of his poetic genius. For the first time in his life he began making plans: he wanted to quit the army, found a review, and devote his life to letters.

Critics and writers acclaimed his works. His name became widely known. Young aristocrats and titled ladies sought his friendship. The Imperial Court and the secret police, however, were none too happy with his artistic and worldly conquests. Forgetting that he was in disgrace, the young lieutenant talked too freely and behaved too boldly. He defied the conventions and pushed his impudence so far as to appear —he, a simple infantry officer—at a ball where members of the Imperial family were present and where, consequently, only the Guards were admitted. He was a trouble-maker and a dangerous liberal, and the authorities ordered him to leave the capital in forty-eight hours. Again there was a farewell party for the exile—this time at Countess Rostoptchina's—but the witty hostess could not win a smile from Lermontov: he was gloomy and kept talking about his imminent death. In the carriage that took him away he wrote: 'Farewell, unwashed Russia, land of slaves, of slavemasters, of blue uniforms and of the people whom they rule. I hope that the mountains of the Caucasus will hide me from your pashas with their all-seeing eyes and their all-hearing ears.'

Two months later, in July 1841, during his furlough in Piatigorsk, Lermontov quarreled with his friend Martynov over a young girl, Katya Byhovetz, to whom both had tried to pay court. In her memoirs, published in the 'sixties she writes that Lermontov had told her she reminded him of Varenka Lopukhina—apparently the reason for his liking her.

The offended Martynov insisted on a duel. It took place on the slopes of Mashuk Mountain, toward sunset, and Lermontov was killed at the first shot. His corpse was transported to Piatigorsk during a terrific thunderstorm which washed out all the roads. The secret history of this strange duel is still not known, for Martynov may have served as a tool in the hands of some more powerful foe of the poet.

III   The news of Lermontov's tragic death aroused conflicting reactions. There is a report that Nicholas I received it with the words, 'A dog's death befits a dog.' One dignitary wrote: 'Martynov has killed this scoundrel Lermontov'; another declared: 'Why do they talk so much about him—after all, he was only a fop, a poor soldier, and a miserable scribbler.'

But there were many others who saw in Lermontov's death an enormous loss to Russian culture. 'As soon as a man of genius appears among the Russians, the low-browed scions of triviality persecute him to death,' remarked Herzen. Belinsky proclaimed Lermontov Russia's greatest poet after Pushkin. In a few years this bold statement became a commonplace. As early as the 'sixties Lermontov was a classic and his poems were included in all text books. The glory he had sought in vain during his brief life was his after his death. His influence is comparable only to that of Pushkin; or as Merezhkovsky puts it, while Pushkin was 'the day luminary of Russian poetry, Lermontov was its night luminary.'

Lermontov was undoubtedly the most powerful representative of Russian Romanticism. However, he did not err in stressing the fundamental difference between Byron and himself. Many of Lermontov's mental attitudes were certainly affectations, springing from his desire to 'play a role'—this was the extent of his Byronism. But while the English poet brought his artificiality and insincerity even to his poems, Lermontov was utterly sincere in his work. He never regarded poetry as a stage: he enjoyed performing romantic parts in real life—and his torments were real enough—but he was never stilted in his lyrics. His poems were an exact transcript of his thoughts and emotions. At the age of fifteen, in 'The Angel,' he revealed one of his main themes: the discord between reality and imagination, the gap between the world he was destined to inhabit and the vision of perfection that haunted his dreams. An angel is singing while carrying a soul about to be born. The sounds remain in the young soul, and all the dull songs of earth can never replace the echo of that angel's heavenly melody. The image of the demon is the second leitmotiv of Lermontov's poetry. 'An Exile from Paradise' symbolizes the negation of accepted values, the rebellion against 'the prison of Being.' Many critics have felt that of the two guardians of Lermontov's poetry, the Demon was stronger that the Angel.

All Russian literature [writes Merezhkovsky] is busy teaching us humility. Every Russian writer who began by revolt promptly subsided and repented: Pushkin wrote his 'Ode to Liberty'—and subsided; Gogol wrote Part I of his *Dead Souls*—and then burned the manuscript of Part II, thus tacitly submitting to the principle of serfdom; Dostoevsky revolted, went to Siberia—and returned as a preacher of humility; Tolstoy revolted—and wound up with nonresistance to evil. . . There is but one man in Russian literature who never gave up and, to his last breath, never submitted—Lermontov.

He remained in open conflict with society and the universe, maintaining (to use his own expression) 'his proud enmity against God.' It was the philosopher Solovyov who therefore called him 'the diabolic superman, the Cain of Russian letters.'

But it is obvious that Lermontov's rebellion is not as infernal and sinister as some critics would like to think. Even his Demon, *The Great Exile,* is a 'melancholy spirit.' Lermontov uses many Romantic images: bandits, corsairs, primitive men of passion and lust crowd his poems, but melancholy accompanies their outbursts. Lermontov is always aware of the 'tears of things' (*lacrimae rerum*) and they pain his mortal heart. His melancholy takes on the character of a national trait: he emphasizes it in the Russian landscape, in the Russian folk songs, in the Russian temperament. He himself is a 'melancholy rebel'—and the combination of revolt and melancholy forms one of the main features of his best pieces.

It would be presumptuous to try to explain Lermontov through any one of the themes of his poetry. His duality involved various unresolved contradictions in his nature and his work. The charm of his poetry lies in the alternation of light and shadow, in the changing colors of his moods. Lermontov, never having attained harmony within himself, stresses in his poetry discord and struggle as primary forces of the universe. He said that 'only in man can the sacred and the sinful unite' and saw in that union the cause of all human woes. It should be added that he was attracted equally by heavenly melodies and by demoniac war songs. In his autobiographical stanzas, 'June 11th, 1831,' written when he was seventeen, he gave an excellent definition of himself and his work: 'From my childhood on I have been longing for wonder. I loved all the enchantments of the world, but not the world itself, in which I dwelt but for infrequent moments.' Byron may have inspired some of his similes, such as 'The soul withered under the burning sun of being,' but his weariness and restlessness, his search for happiness, his awareness of the force of evil, and his grief over the 'errors of Creation' were all perfectly genuine.

Even in his early writings, Lermontov was one of the first Russian writers to deal with the problem of evil. He was well acquainted (more by intuition than through personal experience) with the 'darkness' of life and the 'nocturnal side' of human nature. There is a link connecting Lermontov with the tormented heroes of Dostoevsky. The pathological, warped, and pathetic world of suffering, of inner conflicts, and of 'accursed problems' of God, truth, immortality, morality, and cruelty, which startled the Western readers of *Crime and Punishment* and *The Brothers Karamazov* some forty years later, was already present in the works of Lermontov. Lermontov, however, was a poet, and consequently infinitely harder to translate than Dostoevsky.

It is also significant that unlike Byron the author of 'The Demon' was strangely affected by a 'state of bliss,' by 'glimpses of perfection'— as though the stormy clouds over his head had been suddenly riven to show an ineffable glow in the skies. His use of the adjective 'blue' is amazingly revealing; and he exalts the 'wonderful ecstasy of rebellion' or the intensity of wild freedom ('this passion . . . has ruled my spirit, fired my blood,' says the Caucasian youth) as he does moments of peace and lowly beauty. Particularly in his later work, a year before his death, he is shedding the old rhetorical Romanticism. In the 'Prayer,' 'Lonely I walk upon the Road,' and other poems, he seems to have reached a wisdom and a reconciliation with nature that are found but rarely in his earlier lyrics.

It can be said that, beyond all his individualistic ideas, there was in Lermontov a constant quest for moral justification. His refusal to accept man, society, and the universal order was determined by his search for a higher finality, and this gives to his poetry a dynamic quality and a brilliance that enliven almost every line. This search for moral truth is even more manifest in his semi-autobiographical prose narrative, *A Hero of Our Times*. In it Lermontov relates the adventures of a young officer, Pechorin, an egotistic and wilful individual who, by his early twenties, has experienced—or so he believes—all that life has to offer. He is disillusioned and disgusted with everything. Nothing can delight his

thoughts or fix his emotions. He believes in neither God nor Devil, and
what others call 'ideals' or 'aims of life' are, to his cynical mind, nothing
but childish illusions. Pechorin does not hesitate to sacrifice the love of
women or the affection of men for the sake of amusement or a mere
whim. He plunges into dangerous adventures, elopes with a Caucasian
girl who is later killed by her betrothed, stakes his life on a trifle, ruins
the women who adore him, and still does not succeed in overcoming his
boredom and awareness of the futility of all human endeavor. At the
same time he is capable of genuine feeling; he is courageous and endowed with a strong will. His main trouble is that he is continually
wasting his exceptional energy and his rich potentialities. His life has no
purpose, no central theme. On the eve of a stupid duel with one of his
former friends, Pechorin asks himself:

Why was I born? What was the aim of my life? There must have
been an aim, a high destiny, inasmuch as I feel enormous forces in my
soul. . . I did not grasp my purpose; I let myself be attracted by the
lure of empty and vile passions—and I lost the fire of noble aspirations.

Lermontov does not defend his hero. He regards him with an
amazing objectivity and does not attempt to hide his vanity, his worth-
lessness, or the other negative traits of his character. The title of the
novel, however, contains, if not a justification, at least an explanation
of Pechorin. Pechorin, like Chatsky, and Oneghin, is socially worthless;
he is one of the many 'superfluous men' described by great Russian
writers of the nineteenth century (especially by Turgenev and Chekhov).
Many critics interpreted not only Pechorin, but his creator as well, in
terms of social categories. In their opinion Pechorin's Byronism and
Lermontov's pessimistic approach to man and the universe could be
explained through the analysis of political and social conditions under
Nicholas I. The reactionary atmosphere of the police state stifled the
bright young men and thwarted their energies. Belinsky pointed out
that Lermontov was the child of his century, whose work reflected the
anxieties and doubts of the 'forties, and the general dissatisfaction of
cultured Russians with 'reality.' He has a morose and merciless irony,
but at the same time is sympathetic about the failures of his contemporaries. A living echo of the ideas of his time, he proclaimed its evils
and its lofty flights. 'He lived in a period of oppression,' said Belinsky,
'in a country which was like a military barracks, whereas his main
aspiration was liberty.'

It can be hardly contested that the social and political environment
was largely responsible for Lermontov's pessimism and his feeling of
futility, and that his Pechorin was the product of his times. However,

the poet and his hero were more than that. One cannot reproach Pechorin with the verbal sentimentality of a Chatsky or the indolent superficiality of an Oneghin. He has a strong character and he loves action. Unlike Oneghin, the dandy who depends on other people's opinions, Pechorin defies all social conventions; he is 'anarchically free,' beyond good and evil. As Dostoevsky's Raskolnikov or Ivan Karamazov later on, he discards the accepted moral values and looks for his own truth. He is actually a new hero, and Lermontov, in creating Pechorin, initiated a new literary type. Dostoevsky believed that Russian literature was mainly concerned with the 'humble man,' yet he himself painted magnificent portraits of 'proud men' who all bear a resemblance to their archetype, Pechorin.

At the same time Pechorin is by no means a 'demoniac' hero. Lermontov refuses to employ the exaggerations and pompous artificialities of the Romantic school. His characterization of Pechorin is realistic and sober. Moreover, despite the autobiographical flavor of the novel, the writer does not identify himself with his creation. This objectivity in portraying his hero is extremely significant in a writer such as Lermontov.

Even more astounding is Lermontov's treatment of minor characters. Pechorin's rival in the 'Princess Mary' chapter is Grushnitsky, a young officer, who is a caustic caricature of the affectations and pretensions of a would-be Byronic hero. In depicting Grushnitsky the author was aiming at, and actually scored a hit against, pseudo-Romanticism, the sham Byronism of Russian society and literature. Sketches of other minor characters of the book are also vigorous, deft, and realistic.

A thoroughly subjective writer, Lermontov possessed at the same time the rare gift for perfectly realistic characterization and epic narrative. He proved it in prose as well as in a series of long poems, some of which represent historical events, such as *Borodino,* the story of the famous battle against Napoleon as told by an old veteran, or *Valerik,* a vivid tale of the fighting in the Caucasus, interspersed with bitter remarks against wars and man's inhumanity (not unlike Byron's in *Don Juan*); or *The Lay of Kalashnikov the Merchant,* one of the most striking examples of the integration of folklore rhythms into modern poetic form. That this realistic and objective trend, combined with a strong patriotic element, would have ultimately triumphed in Lermontov's work (as some critics contend) had he not died at the age of twenty-six, is hypothetical. It is certain, however, that Lermontov's art was rapidly maturing and, just before his untimely death, his work reached an unsurpassed verbal beauty and metric and musical richness.

Although Lermontov's poetry followed the path broken by Pushkin and his disciples, and although his verse is not striking for any prosodic innovations, it has great stylistic originality and presents very unusual classical features.

Pushkin achieves perfection in simplicity, and his lyrics are smooth and polished. Lermontov's verse is nervous and somewhat rugged; he intensifies his dramatic, dynamic quality by constantly carrying over the meaning from line to line (enjambement)—which breaks the sentence and gives the impression of an intermittent rhythm (*saccadé*)—by the abundance of masculine rhymes, by the frequent change of intonations, by the recurrence of coruscating, often hyperbolic images, and by contrasts, in semantics as well as in the tonality of sentences. Pushkin's poetry is light, harmonious, transparent. His best poems have the shimmering beauty of precious stones. Lermontov is sometimes almost obscure: his lines hide as much as they reveal; they have the disturbing instability of submarine depths. Lermontov wrote that 'there are words whose sense is obscure or trivial—yet one cannot listen to them without tremor.' This holds true of many of his poems. They have the magic of music and spontaneous movement. The Russian symbolists at the turn of the century pointed out the irrational elements in Lermontov's poems and the strange admixture of the demoniac, idealism, despondency, and moral anxiety which assured them a unique place even in such a variegated literature as the Russian.

On the eve of the Revolution of 1917, Alexander Blok, the last great poet of old Russia, paid a tribute to Lermontov and to his profound influence on modern poetry. He spoke of his 'prophetic grief,' his wise sorrow, his estrangement from his own class and environment, his contradictions, his sense of reality combined with the yearning for celestial perfection, and his ruthless lucidity which enabled him to judge himself objectively. He also stressed the significance of Lermontov as a national poet. In his poem, 'My Native Land,' Lermontov spoke of his 'strange love' for his country. Her glory, her past, and her power left him indifferent, but he was greatly moved by the cold silence of her steppes, the swaying of her endless forests, her poor villages, and the songs and dances of her peasants.

This nobleman who suffered from the political oppression of his times, this idealist who was shocked by the triviality and futility of earthly existence, this poet who absorbed and transformed European Romantic influences, remained fundamentally Russian and reflected in his works many national traits. His wistfulness and his revolt, his quest for freedom and his refusal to accept reality, corresponded to identical features of the cultured Russian society of his period. These features remained intact through many generations, and even today in the Soviet

Union, where pessimistic ideas are banned and many of the feelings expressed by Lermontov are officially frowned upon, the poet is loved, widely read, and acclaimed one of the greatest and most original representatives of the true 'Russian spirit' in native literature.

6

DREAMERS AND PHILOSOPHERS

I   THE FAILURE of the Decembrist
uprising marked the beginning of a long period of political reaction.
Frightened by the sudden threat to his throne the new Czar, Nicholas I,
decided to eradicate liberalism and adopted an aggressive policy for
the consolidation of the autocratic regime. The nobility, the Army, and
the high bureaucracy fully supported his program, which proclaimed
autocracy, the orthodox religion, and national traditions as the firm
foundations of the Empire. The official ideology formulated along these
lines found a few literary exponents, such as Count Serghei Uvarov
(1786-1855), the Minister of Education and President of the Academy
of Sciences, Nicholas Grech (1787-1867), the journalist; and Faddei
Bulgarin (1789-1859), the writer and editor. Bulgarin, connected with
the secret police, became a target for the epigrams of liberal poets, led
by Pushkin. In 1843 Count Uvarov wrote a memorandum to the Czar
in which he contrasted Russia, with her military might and sound
political regime, to the corrupt West, undermined by revolutionary ideas,
the decline of religion, and social instability. Taking up this line Grech,
Bulgarin, and their followers launched an aggressive campaign in their
daily, *The Northern Bee,* and in their review, *The Son of the Fatherland,*
proclaiming that Russia's greatness lay in the inviolability of the
autocracy, its alliance with the Church, and the maintenance of national
traditions such as 'paternalistic serfdom,' the leading role of the nobility
in affairs of state, the obedience of the lower classes, and the popular
customs of patriarchal life. For three decades this philosophy dominated
the political life of the country.

Nicholas I, as well as his ideologists, was convinced that the 'revolutionary venom' was of foreign origin and that the subversive elements

in Russia were nurtured by propaganda from abroad. He therefore attempted to extend his doctrine to other countries, in order to stamp out the 'Red Menace' in Europe and to 'maintain monarchic stability' in the West. This, according to the Czar and his friends, constituted Russia's mission in the world, and the Empire assumed the role of the *gendarme* of Europe. Her military might and financial power, the latter augmented after the monetary reforms of Kankrin, the head of the Treasury, enabled Nicholas to exert pressure on several European states. In 1830, when the revolution broke out in France and Belgium, Nicholas planned an armed intervention in these countries but had to give it up because of the Polish insurrection at home, which occupied him for over two years. In 1833 Russia signed a treaty of alliance with Prussia and Austria and made a solemn pledge 'to support the established authorities wherever they exist, to re-enforce them where they are undermined, and to defend them where they are openly attacked.' In 1847, when the national movement of liberation became widespread, Nicholas offered financial and military assistance to the Viennese government against Piedmont. Two years later he sent troops to combat the revolution in Hungary. Russian Cossacks protected the crown of the Hapsburgs and the integrity of Roman Catholicism.

Nicholas' domestic policy was no less reactionary. He concentrated his attention on the Army, where the rigidly inhuman discipline of the kind introduced by Mad Paul was revived with many horrible variations. The recruits from the underprivileged classes served for twenty-five years, while the sons of former soldiers had to serve for life. Barracks with tongue-tied, underfed, and terrified soldiers were not the only symbol of Nicholas' policies: The Bureau of Red Tape was next door to the barracks. The petty officials were almost as numerous as the military men. Bureaucracy ruled highhandedly over millions of Russians, who had to produce identification papers at every turn and to sign dozens of forms for every legal or commercial transaction. The government clerks, particularly in the provinces, were ignorant, greedy, bureaucratic, and completely indifferent to the general welfare. Gogol had described them in *The Inspector General* and *Dead Souls;* many portrayals of the bureaucrats under Nicholas I are also to be found in the works of Pisemsky, Saltykov, Ostrovsky, and Leskov. Administrative abuses could be mitigated only by bribes; graft and corruption prevailed at every administrative level, including the courts, where Justice was dilatory, cruel, and anything but blindfolded. Common criminals were branded with hot irons on cheek and forehead, floggings were generously dealt out to all who had not the good fortune to belong to the privileged classes. The highly centralized regime was ruthless and wilful. On the slightest suspicion people were imprisoned, beaten, exiled. The schismatic sects were persecuted unmercifully, and the sectarians fled in droves not only into the Siberian forests and the Ural mountains, but even as far as China and Canada. The various nationalities were oppressed, the Ukrainian cultural societies were dissolved, and Tarass Shevchenko (1814-61), the great poet and painter of the Ukraine, the author of *The Blind Lute-Player* (1840), who wrote with fine sarcasm: 'Russia is so happy, she is so well off, that she has become completely speechless,' was exiled with many of his friends. Poles, Jews, Caucasians, Latvians all were mistreated.

Serfdom was firmly embedded. The Czar himself declared that its abolition would wreck the foundations of the autocratic regime. The peasants slaved in the villages; men and women were sold or mortgaged; millions of white slaves depended on the whims of their masters. Any protest was suppressed by force; troops were always at hand if any landowner wanted to 'teach a lesson' to his troublesome serfs. And this lesson was usually taught by means of fire, flogging, and summary executions.

To maintain this system and to insure the subordination of all walks of society, the government had to rely on a tremendous police force. The highest body of this force was represented by the notorious Section III of His Majesty's Private Chancellery. The secret police was in charge of the suppression of 'un-Russian activities' and 'anti-national ideas' by means of spies, denunciations, surveillance, investigations, and administrative measures such as imprisonment and exile. The superior officers of Section III controlled, with the aid of a special body of censors, practically all the political life of the country. Two Imperial ukases (1826 and 1828) granted extensive powers to the censorship. 'Censors were unleashed on Russian literature like a pack of bloodhounds,' states a contemporary. Some of them, in their eagerness to uncover subversive propaganda, made asinine decisions. The annals of censorship under Nicholas I read like a collection of schoolboy boners. In a textbook on physics the expression 'forces of nature' was banned as atheistic, while in a cook book the sentence, 'free air is necessary for cookies,' was suppressed because of its symbolic meaning. A poet who confessed that he cherished his beloved 'above everything in the world' was severely reprimanded by the censor: 'No law-abiding citizen ought to put anything above God and the Emperor.' An ethnographer was not allowed to write that sleighs were drawn by dogs in the extreme north of Russia, because this fact had not been confirmed by the Police Department. Another cautious censor took a different line in banning a book that described certain faulty administrative practices: 'The very danger of this work lies in its truthfulness.' Quite often the censors were concerned about the moral implications of novels and short stories, especially if the ending did not specifically mete out reward for virtue and punishment for vice. Dahl's story of a mysterious gang of horse thieves was banned 'lest the readers have any doubts about the ultimate punishment of criminals by the lawful authorities.' About 1840 the censorship became slightly more rational, but after the 1848 revolution it underwent a change for the worse.

The writers of the period became experts in literary subterfuge: they used most ingenious dodges and circumlocutions in order to disguise their ideas. Readers also became trained in the game, easily grasping all the hints and allusions in novels, poems, and articles. Thus was created the 'Aesopic Language,' as the intellectuals called it—to all intents and purposes a code for the initiated. At the same time many works were being circulated in manuscript copies, adding to the already imposing body of Russian clandestine literature.

Education fared hardly better than literature. In his letter to Shishkov the Czar stressed the 'evil effects of gymnasiums and institutions of higher learning on sons of serfs and peasants.' The lesser landowners and the lower middle class had to be satisfied with parochial schools; county elementary schools were intended for the children of merchants, petty officials, and noncommissioned officers, while gymnasiums and universities were reserved for the nobility, the upper bureaucracy, the higher clergy, and the better bourgeoisie. Nicholas I had always considered the universities as hotbeds of liberal ideas and suspected the students and professors of anti-governmental tendencies. After 1848 all missions for study abroad were suspended, the chairs of European constitutional law and philosophy were suppressed, and the teaching of such dubious subjects as logic and psychology was entrusted to theologians. All the instructors of physics, chemistry, physiology, and other sciences had to watch their step because high dignitaries and cabinet ministers regarded the natural sciences as 'sources of atheism'; the social sciences were blamed for 'propagating the revolutionary plague.' All schools were organized on a military pattern, and the students subjected to rigid discipline, regular uniforms, and formal marching wondered whether they were attending institutions of learning or living in army barracks.

For thirty years the Russians were compelled to breathe this deadly atmosphere of reaction, hypocrisy, and stupidity. As one writer put it, Russia during Nicholas' reign resembled an immense dark wilderness, the silence of which was but infrequently broken by forced huzzahs or shouts for help.

II   To the outside world the Empire
revealed only its monolithic appearance of a military police state. But
behind this façade there existed intense artistic and intellectual activity.
Oddly enough, the most reactionary period of modern Russian history
coincided with the beginning of the Golden Age of its literature and
philosophy. It may be that all the energy of Russian intellectuals who
had been denied social and political initiative found compensation in
study and creativity. Alexander Herzen, the most brilliant critic of his
times, has summed up the matter: 'We devoted ourselves to science,
philosophy, love, military art, mysticism, in order to forget the monstrous shallowness about us.'

Literary productivity flourished despite the fact that the writers had
no freedom of expression and were subjected to the most odious and
annoying pressures. Never before—and never afterward—had so many
outstanding literary artists lived and worked together in Russia. In the
'thirties the great masters of the end of the eighteenth century—
Zhukovsky, Karamzin, Krylov—were still alive and active. A galaxy of
young poets had gathered around Pushkin, sharing with him the brunt
of the struggle against Classicism, sentimentalism, or ill-conceived tra-
ditionalism. They often styled themselves Romantics. Some of them
were Pushkin's schoolmates, such as the clumsy, utterly honest, and
serious Wilhelm Kuechelbecker (1797-1846), whose Romanticism had
a slightly mystical bent, or Anton Delvig (1798-1831), connoisseur of
Hellenic-Roman poetry, lover of sweet melodies and theoretical discussions, and editor of *The Literary Gazette* (the name of which was later
revived by the Union of Soviet writers for their official weekly).

Two other members of this group, Baratynsky and Yazykov, stood
out as the most talented representatives of their generation. Eugene
Baratynsky (1800-1844) attracted some attention in the 'twenties by
his poems on Finland, where he had spent four years as a private in
the Russian forces of occupation. His long narratives in verse ('Eda'—
a story of the unhappy loves of a Finnish girl and a Russian officer—
'The Feasts,' 'The Ball,' 'The Concubine') brought little that was new
into Russian poetry; but his lyrics, as Pushkin justly observed, marked
him as one of the most original poets of the period. He himself has given
quite a just estimate of his work: 'My Muse is no raving beauty, she
will never draw a throng of eager lovers after her, yet now and then
men will be struck by the uncommon expression of her face and by the
calm simplicity of her speech.' This 'uncommon expression' was determined by the intellectual character of Baratynsky's poems, which often
have broad themes of an idealistic philosophy. Reality had for him but
a transient appearance, and he regarded with sorrow the foolish game

of human endeavor. Shut within himself, constantly checking his emotions in the light of reflection, he suffered from the impossibility of reconciling the contradictions of life and he complained of the conflict between thought and feeling. Man, to Baratynsky, was but the slave of his passions and a toy of fate, and nothing could save his work from the universal law of destruction. Mortals were given only 'the freedom of evil and stupidity'; history was one long succession of errors, and complete degeneration awaited corrupt humanity—his apocalyptic vision of its end is in his grim and forbidding poem, 'The Last Death.' Baratynsky's despondency was evident in all his elegies, whether he was describing the barrenness of an autumnal landscape or meditating on the monotonous recurrence of events and things. Like his friends in the group of the Lovers of Wisdom he considered artistic creation the only means of escape from reality. One of his most renowned poems, 'On Goethe's Death,' presents the image of a sage whose sufferings and conflicts find a harmonious solution in rhythmic songs. He interpreted poetry as some kind of inner catharsis, although he remained utterly skeptical about its significance for the common man. Modern man, that 'rational thrall,' is more and more involved in practical utilitarian purposes; industrial civilization will ultimately kill 'the childish dreams of poetry' ('The Last Poet').

Baratynsky died in Naples at the age of forty-four. He himself said that his heart and mind were done with long before the hour of physical death: 'In vain didst thou rush, oh mad, seething soul, trying to speed thy course: thou didst exhaust thyself before the body did.'

Poet of philosophical analysis and intellectual quest, Baratynsky wrote in a dry and slightly didactic style in which he used symbolic images and often fused the spiritual and sensual levels. The idealistic and pessimistic trend represented by Baratynsky was closely connected with the influence exerted in Russia by the German Romantic philosophers (mainly Schelling). Sixty years after his death the symbolists, particularly Briussov, saw in him one of their forerunners and highly praised the formal beauty and the intellectual profundity of his work. Baratynsky's influence can be found in the works of Karolina Pavlova (1807-93), a brilliant poetess of the 'forties, who, though lacking Baratynsky's intellectual power, displayed excellent craftsmanship and a thoroughly modern diversity of rhymes and rhythms, and passionately defended the 'inutility of poetry' as its patent of nobility. He also influenced such men as Vladimir Odoevsky (1803-69), writer of short stories and *Russian Nights,* a philosophical novel (1844); Dimitri Venevitinov (1805-27), a gifted and highly emotional poet; and Fedor

Glinka (1786-1880), author of the successful *Letters of a Russian Officer* (1808-16) and writer of obscure 'spiritual' verse.

While Baratynsky reflected indirectly the plight of a generation oppressed by political and spiritual bondage, the hidden forces of that same generation were being noisily celebrated by Nicholas Yazykov (1803-46), the tempestuous and magnificent poet of youth. Yazykov began as a bacchic bard of freedom and intoxication. He delighted in exuberance and sensuality, and his songs, written in a turbulent and rapid tempo, resounded at the gatherings of Russian students for a hundred years. This 'minstrel of wine and the pranks of immodest love' had something Scythian about him. He also derived from Derzhavin: his poems were thunderous and he loved to show his control of sonorous, metallic words, and galloping rhythms. The best pieces of Yazykov are strong and challenging, loud and passionate, revealing his joy of living.

At the beginning of his career, in the 'twenties, while still a student at the universities of Moscow and Dorpat, Yazykov defined himself as a 'thinking student,' a liberal, and a reveler. Later, this rioting Bohemian, undermined by ill health, personal disillusion, and the oppressive atmosphere of his land, turned into an exemplary, peaceful landowner who went to Mass regularly and joined the Slavophiles. Toward the very end of his life, however, he became one of the most belligerent poets of his group. Some critics accused Yazykov of 'a dirty imagination and indecency,' but he escaped persecution.

In this he was more lucky than his young contemporary Alexander Polezhaev (1805-38), who aroused governmental ire with his 'Sashka,' a poem about the escapades of a Moscow libertine. Polezhaev was reduced to the ranks as a private and exiled to the Caucasus, where the hardships of military service, alcohol, and illness overcame him. He left his regiment without authorization, was cruelly flogged, and a few months later died of consumption. His loneliness and dejection were reflected in thoroughly realistic and despairing stanzas which challenged the Romantic songs of the more fortunate sons of nobility. The fate of Polezhaev was that of a typical victim of the police state, and his bitter poems are often quoted as an illustration of the conditions prevailing in the Russia of Nicholas I.

All the poets of Pushkin's constellation belonged to the nobility. Among other prominent poets only two came from other social strata: Benediktov and Koltzov. Vladimir Benediktov (1807-73), the son of a small provincial official and himself a clerk in some governmental office, gained wide popularity in 1835-42 through his poems, which were uneven, artificial, occasionally brilliant and loudly Romantic in form, but deficient in ideas or strong feelings. Alexei Koltzov (1809-42), the son of a cattle dealer, was self-taught. He did not know any grammar or orthography, but his poems had the ingenuousness and beauty of wild flowers. They dealt with the joys, loves, and sorrows of poor peasant lads and lasses, and described in a naive and touching way their yearning for freedom and happiness. Koltzov's poetry was a transcription of the popular songs of central Russia. In the 'thirties Koltzov came into contact with the literati, who helped him to bring out a collection of his poems in 1835. These created something of a furore among the intellectuals: here was a true poet of the people. His fresh, unsophisticated poetry revealed the wealth of popular poetic feeling. The Romantic era was highly interested in folklore; Pushkin's folk tales had prepared the public to appreciate popular rhythms and subjects, and now Koltzov was presenting them in a new form. Between 1830 and 1850 the best Russian reviews opened their pages to the 'poets of the people,' such as the highly talented Koltzov and his less successful but extremely typical contemporaries, Slepushkin, Alipanov, and Sukhanov.

The poetic Renaissance of the reign of Nicholas I was truly resplendent. Next to Pushkin, the central figure of the period, was Lermontov; then Baratynsky, Yazykov, Tiutchev, as well as scores of minor but excellent poets, such as Ivan Kozlov (1779-1840)—the blind translator of Byron—Ogarev, Vyazemsky, and others. The wide range of poetic creativeness, the diversity of forms, rhythms, and trends, the wide public, the interest of critics, and the influence of writers—all these lent an especial glamor to poetry. Its self-affirmation had a scope and strength felt for many decades to come. The peak of its development was reached in the 'thirties and early 'forties, when the general interest was focused on prose—a process in which Russia followed a little behind European Romanticism.

While in poetry the Romantic elements persisted, in prose they were rapidly transformed or supplanted by Realism. In the 'forties Realism became the leading literary ideal. Its supremacy was easily attained, since it had almost no rivals to overcome. There were few authentically Romantic novels and these were by highly popular but second-rate writers like Ossip Senkovsky (1800-1858), author of *The Fantastic Travels of Baron Brambaeus* (1833), or Nestor Kukolnik (1809-68), the bombastic playwright. The historical novels, initiated by Michael Zagoskin (1789-1852) and greatly influenced by Walter Scott (the melodramatic *Yuri-Miloslavsky, or the Russians in 1612* by Zagoskin), gained a wide success in the 'thirties. They were soon replaced, however, by the more solid works of Ivan Lazhechnikov (1792-1869), whose descriptions of the eighteenth century in Russia (*The House of Ice, The Last Novik*) were historically accurate and more true to life.

Pushkin's stories and Lermontov's novel, *A Hero of Our Times,* were permeated with a realistic spirit. There were even earlier forerunners of Realism. A. Izmailov (1779-1831), a fabulist, has prose descriptions of plebeian heroes, whom he called 'men of the 15th rank,' of topers, catchpoles, and sluts against a background of pothouses, barracks, and slums; he certainly deserved to be known as the Russian Teniers. Still more significant is Vassily Narezhny (1780-1825), who can be considered a predecessor of Gogol. He wrote the picaresque novel, *The Russian Gil Blas, or the Adventures of Prince Chistiakov,* and exposed the evils of the society of his time in *Bursak* and, especially, in the *Two Ivans, or the Mania for Litigation,* a naturalistic picture of provincial pettiness, much in Fonvizin's satirical vein. Novels of strange adventure, which may have influenced Dostoevsky's choice of melodramatic plots, were brought out in the 'thirties by the archaeologist Alexander Weltman (1800-1870), whose *The Wanderer, Deathless Kashchei,* and the more realistic although ironically grotesque *Adventures Dredged from the Sea of Life* (published serially, 1848-63), hold a place of their own in the prose of the period.

The 'thirties and 'forties saw the rise of Russia's greatest novelists, with Gogol in the lead. The creator of *Dead Souls* was the central figure of his times, which were dominated by his works and are often spoken of as the 'Gogol period' of Russian literature. Although it is extremely difficult to label Gogol either a Romantic or a Realist, there is no doubt that the Realistic school won general recognition during the 'forties and 'fifties, when his influence prevailed. It was the time of the literary beginnings of Turgenev, Dostoevsky, and Tolstoy, and of the activity of Goncharov and a number of minor Realistic storytellers. As Russian poetry had attained national recognition with Pushkin and his friends, Russian prose won national recognition with Gogol.

Parallel to the growth of literature were the activities in other arts. Painters, musicians, actors were breaking away from academic patterns and searching for new forms of expression. The first Russian painter to acquire international fame was Konstantin Briullov (1799-1852). His enormous canvas *The Last Days of Pompeii,* exhibited in 1833, created a sensation not only in Russia but in Italy and France. Briullov appeared as a leader of Romanticism in painting. Although his style was rhetorical and exaggerated, his grandiose manner appealed to the imagination and he had a strong influence. The deep religious feeling of Gogol's friend, Alexander Ivanov (1806-58), presented another less popular aspect of Romanticism. His remarkable work, *Christ's Coming to the People,* filled with mystical emotions, was not sufficiently appreciated during his life time. Briullov, Ivanov, and the brilliant portrait painter and designer, Orest Kiprensky (1783-1836), represented the Romantic trend, while the pictures of peasant life by Alexis Venezianov (1780-1847) and the genre scenes drawn from life by the delightful Pavel Fedotov (1815-52) indicated the growth of realistic tendencies.

The same process took place in sculpture with Theodore Tolstoy (1783-1873), Boris Orlovsky (1793-1838) and others. Russian architecture carried on its glorious traditions of the turn of the century. The Neoclassical style of Alexander's period was magnificently expressed in the great official buildings of the capital, such as the colossal Admiralty Buildings, with a frontage of 575 feet, built by Zakharov, or the Kazan Cathedral with its 144 columns, created by Voronikhin, or the St. Petersburg Stock Exchange by De Tomon. The Russian 'Empire' style combined the Western influence with the traditions of ancient Russian architecture, and this mixture was to be evident in monumental structures as well as in mansions where the more intimate aspect of the style was given charming expression. The 'thirties and 'forties saw a great development of the Russian 'Empire' style in the provinces and especially on the estates of the noblemen. Less successful were the attempts of Nicholas I to create a pseudo-Russian style in the new official buildings. Although not lacking grandeur, they are rather cold and pompous, as is the Church of Christ the Savior, by Constantine Ton, one of the architects most favored at Court.

Great changes took place in music as well. Michael Glinka (1804-57) was the truly great composer of the period. He traveled a long way from the sentimental ballads of Titov and Aliabiev, the Romantic opera of Alexis Verstovsky (1799-1862), *Askold's Grave* (based on Zagoskin's novel), and the imitative works by non-Russians, such as Field and Cavos, who lived and composed in St. Petersburg. Glinka, greatly influenced by Pushkin, his friend and favorite poet, based his scores on folk songs and church music. With his songs and operas, such as *Ivan Sussanin* (its title was changed to *One's Life for the Czar* by the order of Nicholas I, and was not restored until after the Revolution) and *Russlan and Liudmila* (1842), based on Pushkin's poem, he launched the national school of music destined to have such a glorious career. The slightly pedestrian realism of Alexander Dargomyzhsky (1813-69), in his popular works (particularly the *Water Nixie* opera) stemmed from the development in Russian music started by Glinka. Music in general played a large role in the cultural life of the 'forties and 'fifties. There was a permanent Italian opera company in St. Petersburg, and Rossini, Bellini, and, later, Verdi, were highly appreciated.

The Philharmonic Society, founded in 1802, organized a number of concerts and invited guest artists from the West, including Berlioz and Liszt. The quality of Russian choirs and orchestras was a surprise to the foreign visitors. Rich noblemen had excellent private orchestras in their St. Petersburg and Moscow homes or on their provincial estates. Vocal and chamber music was an obligatory part of public or private entertainments.

Theatrical activity was also intense. The government subsidized State theaters in St. Petersburg and Moscow, while a number of public and private theatrical institutions were operating in smaller towns. Most of the plays were translations from the French and German—occasionally from English and Italian—but comedies by Russian writers, such as Fonvizin, Griboyedov, Gogol, and minor playwrights, were frequently given. Great actors, such as Mochalov and Shchepkin, were leading the Realistic school of acting, and their influence determined the future development of the Russian stage. The ballet and its training schools, also supported by the government, developed magnificently.

In general Russian music, theater, and ballet of the '30s and 40s acquired the character of a national art, with peculiar traits and original features all their own. The arts had found themselves even as had literature done, and as the intellectuals had tried.

III   One of the most typical features of this period was the spread of all sorts of private groups and circles. They were active throughout the land but particularly in Moscow, where the young noblemen met with a few representatives of the lower estates.

The accepted hero of the previous generation had been the aristocratic youth, usually an officer in the army. Longing for political action, he had played a dangerous game and, on 14 December 1825, he had lost. His successor was the young country squire, a university student, who was fond of discussing lofty philosophical problems with his idealistic friends.

The abstract and theoretical trend of the intelligentsia was determined by many factors. The most important was certainly the pressure of the autocratic regime, which barred any normal political activity and forced the youth into sophistication to escape what Belinsky described as 'the disgusting reality.' Vagaries of thought were the only area not invaded by governmental regulations. The intellectuals, who felt themselves prisoners in the gigantic jail of Nicholas I, enjoyed absolute liberty in their theoretical speculations. They repeated with delight the lines of Schiller—one of the poets most beloved by the Russian Romantics—'Thought is my infinite kingdom, and the Word is my winged steed.' They paid exaggerated tribute to both metaphysics and eloquence. These 'Knights of Talk,' whom Turgenev, not without a melancholy sympathy, described and exposed in *Rudin* and several novelettes, passed through a short period of Byronism in the late 'twenties and subsequently fell under the spell of German philosophy. The doctrines of Herder, Kant, Schelling, Fichte, and Hegel, the esthetics of Schiller, became gospel to Russian university students. The authorities looked with suspicion at these theories imported from Germany, and, at one point, they simply abolished the departments of philosophy. College professors had to resort to all sorts of subterfuge in order to satisfy the demands of their pupils for philosophy. In Moscow, for instance, Schelling was assigned to Professor Pavlov, who officially held the chair of agriculture. Professors of literature, art, and history also lectured on philosophy, and there were innumerable discussions in homes, among people organized into friendly circles.

One of the most influential and typical groups of young idealists was led by Nicholas Stankevich (1813-40), whose mind was as vigorous as his health was poor. The flame of his philosophical quest, the purity of his personality, and the magic of his speech explain the influence he exerted on all who came in contact with him. Convinced as he was that only poetry and philosophy would reveal the essence of things, Stankevich identified the search for abstract truth with the aims of individual life. Philosophy, in his opinion, was the only practical guide for all who wanted to overcome the animal in man. And this point of view was not exclusively his. Members of various circles which had never heard of one another would spend whole nights discussing some difficult passage in Hegel or the second part of Goethe's *Faust*. They did this as intensely as if it were a matter of life and death. They could dispute for weeks over the conflicting interpretations of Schelling's concept of nature, or be overcome with gloom after reading a page of Fichte, yet they were not simply cranks. They did not merely study philosophy; they lived it; they meditated with passion. A theory or doctrine was not absorbed through a logical mental process; it aroused a gamut of emotions, it was experienced.

This is one of the characteristics of Russian intellectuals: ideas are approached on an emotional as well as a rational level. Moreover, the Russians seek the immediate application of any theory to life. They never miss drawing practical conclusions from any doctrine they accept as truth. This trait is probably the basis of what is so often and erroneously called Russian mysticism. It may even be contended that the Russians have never considered philosophy, or any other kind of theoretical knowledge, as self-sufficient, and this explains the difference between them and, let us say, the Germans, who indulge in intellectual abstract brooding for its own sake, without ever seeking its practical implications. The Russians of the 'forties admired Schelling or Hegel as teachers of life. Philosophy was supposed to supply a program of earthly existence, and the Muscovite students were in deadly earnest about the problems of sensory perception, of rational or intuitive perception of reality, of the meaning of human history, and so on, because they made their daily behavior directly dependent on the solutions. When the pantheistic trends of the German Romantic philosophy became popular among the intellectuals, young men and girls (as Herzen reports) never went for a walk in the country without seeing in it a 'manifestation of a union with nature.' One sentence, fished out of some excerpts from Hegel, 'All that exists has a reason for existing,' convinced quite a number of Russian Romantics that they had to bow to Czarism, serfdom, and censorship.

All this may seem ridiculous now, yet it was typical then of the attitude of the intelligentsia. Besides, this sense of close relationship between philosophical doctrines and their socio-political and personal implications determined the whole character of Russian liberalism. Its main principles were formulated in the 'forties after a thorough process of research and rather conflicting phases of development. The best example of this evolution is given by Belinsky: his own ideas, in their perpetual dialectical changes, reflected the theoretical and practical transformations of educated society.

Vissarion Belinsky, the son of a provincial physician, born in Finland in 1811, had an unhappy childhood and a dreary youth. Although extremely gifted and widely read, he had not been able to finish his studies in a provincial gymnasium and was a failure in college. After three years at Moscow University he was turned out because of 'the insufficiency of his academic record.' Poverty-stricken and in ill health, lonely and impractical, he had a hard time earning his living by doing translations and journalistic odd jobs. In 1834 his essay, 'Literary Dreams,' the first comprehensive survey of contemporary literature, attracted general attention. Belinsky joined the Stankevich circle, became friendly with the outstanding writers of his times, and proved himself one of the most passionate exponents of idealistic philosophy, following for the most part Fichte and Schelling. At this time he and his friends were contending that ideal values, as a manifestation of the eternal spirit of a supreme essence, reign triumphantly over all the contingencies of the world.

This conception permitted Belinsky and his numerous followers to escape reality by proclaiming the supremacy of spiritual values over the material. This meant, in practice, that Belinsky and the dreamers of the 'thirties were more interested in a poem, a sonata, or a philosophical argument than in any problem of serfdom, social reform, or political freedom. Were not all these coarse transitory issues mere trifles in comparison with the endless glow of the spirit?

These idealistic ecstasies were genuine enough. It actually did not matter to these philosophers whether they lived in a miserable garret and on stale crusts, as Belinsky did, or dwelt on magnificent estates provided with every luxury and staffed with hosts of servants, as did Bakunin, Herzen, and Turgenev: their true home was on the heights of idealistic speculation, and they looked down with compassion upon the triviality and meanness of average mortals.

This vale of tears was, however, at times far too noisy and odious not to be heeded. Even the loftiest flights of imagination could not hide some simple facts: reaction was stifling and oppressive, the police stupid and unbearable, the abuses atrocious, the conditions of life of the underprivileged shameful and horrible. The earth's moans, screams, and curses were poisoning the pure atmosphere of alpine dreams. Despite all attempts to maintain a philosophical serenity, the young intellectuals could not help being shocked and morally hurt by their environment.

It was at this time (1835) that the ideas of Hegel began to gain popularity among the members of various Moscow circles. Michael Bakunin, one of the most brilliant members of these coteries, a superb dialectician, and the future apostle of revolution and anarchism, interpreted part of the Hegelian philosophy as a direct answer to the pressing moral problems. According to Hegel, the history of mankind is but one more manifestation of the universal spirit in its progressive movement toward freedom and full self-assertion. Whatever we see around us as contemporary reality, contended Bakunin, is therefore a necessary phase of the inevitable evolution. Things and events are logical and perfectly justified. Whatever is real is reasonable from the philosophical standpoint. If everything is but the embodiment of various phases of the self-developing spiritual principle, then we have to accept what may at present appear as a revolting evil.

Both Bakunin and Belinsky drew practical conclusions from these abstract premises. In his article, 'The Anniversary of the Battle of Borodino,' Belinsky declared that all existing forms of social and political life were justified and should be looked upon as inevitable links in the glorious chain of Divine Reason. Implicitly he admitted the necessity of autocracy, serfdom, and reaction against which he was morally protesting. A vehement dispute was aroused by Bakunin's thesis, and shortly afterwards Belinsky himself started to re-examine his own theory.

He felt an irreconcilable conflict between its logical finality and his emotional self. He hated autocracy, slavery, reaction; yet he was obligated to say that they were 'reasonable and justified.' This inner struggle made him quite ill. But after a painful crisis Belinsky rejected Bakunin's interpretation of Hegel. In his new articles he proclaimed that the interests of living human beings ought to constitute the point of departure for all practical philosophy. Liberty, individual or collective, is the prerequisite of any spiritual development.

What is it to me if the whole is prospering, when the individual is suffering? What is it to me if genius dwells on celestial heights when the mob sprawls in the mire? What is the world of ideas in art, religion, history to me when I cannot share it with all my fellowmen?

Logical abstractions do not correspond to historic realities. Man himself creates values, which serve as touchstones in his scrutiny of reality. Beauty, justice, and truth should not remain superior to life; we must change life itself in order to make it truthful, just, and beautiful. This is the true purpose of individual and collective existence, and all of us must fight to attain the goal.

Thus, the formal disciple of Schelling and Hegel affirmed his conversion to ideas of humanitarian socialism. In the 'forties, and particularly toward the end of his life, in 1848, Belinsky's philosophy was strongly influenced by positivistic tendencies. The right solution of social and economic problems became for him 'the main end of any intelligent individual.' With his usual passion he felt 'a fervent, fanatical love of freedom and human independence, which are possible only in a society based on truth and virtue.' Later, he explained that such a society would put human dignity above everything else and would attain the socialistic ideal. Belinsky's socialism had a strong moral tinge. When he says 'The State should not be in the hands of capitalists,' he adds 'Woe to the State which is in the hands of capitalists, since they are men devoid of patriotism or any lofty feelings.' He dreamt of the day when all men would be brothers, when there would be no more senseless conventions and no capital punishment, when there would be neither kings nor subjects, neither rich nor poor. As far as Russia was concerned, Belinsky saw her salvation in reforms, in enlightenment, and in the progress of civilization and humanity.

Belinsky's evolution was identical with the development of the great majority of Russia's idealistic dreamers. Sooner or later almost all of them came to the same conclusions or, at least, became interested chiefly in historical and social issues. Abstract philosophy for its own sake did not last, even as a fashion, for more than a decade. In 1848, when

Belinsky died, Herzen was helping the French to bring about the end of the July Monarchy; Bakunin was directing the fight at the barricades of Dresden; and Dostoevsky was attending the meetings of a secret socialist society in St. Petersburg.

Belinsky's philosophy determined his approach to literature. He started a tradition of literary criticism based on a system of general ideas, and this school, of which he certainly remained the unchallenged leader, left a deep mark in Russian artistic and intellectual life. His influence on contemporary writers and his role in Russian letters were tremendous. Ten years after the great critic's death Ivan Aksakov reported: 'During my wide travels throughout the country I found that every man with any intellectual interests is familiar with the name of Belinsky. There is not a teacher in the provincial capitals who does not know by heart Belinsky's *Letter to Gogol*.'

Literary criticism hardly existed in Russia before Belinsky. In 1800 Karamzin claimed that critics were a by-product of artistic wealth and, since Russian letters, in his opinion, were far from being rich, he considered literary criticism a useless luxury. In the 'twenties, however, during the battles between the Romantics and Traditionalists, book reviews and critical essays were used as political weapons, by Pushkin, Prince Peter Vyazemsky, Nicholas Nadezhdin, and especially by Nicholas Polevoy (1796-1846), the most important of Belinsky's predecessors. Polevoy was a self-taught merchant's son, editor of the *Moscow Telegraph,* and the author of a remarkable *History of the Russian People* in six volumes. Unfortunately this brilliant journalist who started out as a defender of new tendencies, ended by joining the political and literary reactionaries. Nicholas Nadezhdin (1804-56), a professor and the editor of *The Telescope,* also played a prominent part in advancing the critical essay as an art form.

Belinsky was the first to broaden the scope of criticism and to forge it into a powerful factor of intellectual life. His essays in the Moscow papers and later, after he had moved in 1839, in the St. Petersburg reviews, always aroused passionate discussions and stirred public opinion. At the beginning of his career Belinsky had followed the trend of esthetic criticism; subsequently he adopted the method of historical analysis without sacrificing his philosophical approach. The purpose of a true critic, according to Belinsky, was to uncover the basic idea of each work of art, to establish its relationship with the environment in which it was conceived and, finally, to examine how the main idea had been expressed esthetically.

Belinsky had always wanted to write a history of Russian literature, and his essays, embracing its past as well as his times, are valid even today. He assigned their rightful positions in Russian culture to Lomonossov, Derzhavin, Karamzin, Zhukovsky, and others. His interpretations of the work of his contemporaries and particularly his essays on Pushkin, Lermontov, Gogol, Dostoevsky, and Goncharov were also a part of his all-embracing visions. After his anti-Hegelian revolt he emphasized the necessity of a sociological approach, insisting on the fact that each individual writer reflects the society in which he lives. In the 'forties all his writings stressed two main points: he developed his theory of art as an expression of national spirit and he declared himself a partisan of 'naturalness in literature,' thus paving the way from Romanticism to Realism. 'Truly national literature,' said Belinsky, 'always becomes universal, and there is no universal literature unless it is national.' He rejected shallow imitations of foreign patterns, while warning against chauvinism and pseudo-nationalism. 'One who loves his country ardently wishes her to fulfil the ideals of mankind; otherwise patriotism degenerates into isolationism, which loves national things only because they are native, and hates all foreign ones simply because they are foreign.' A nation reveals itself in the way it 'approaches and understands reality, and a truly national writer reflects the fundamental traits of his own people.' Belinsky writes in his essay on Gogol:

As an instance, take a Russian poet. He is born in a land where the sky is gray, the snow deep, the frost crackling, the blizzards raging, the summers torrid, and the soil vast and fertile. All these factors leave an impress upon him. In his childhood he heard tales of mighty men, of brave warriors, of lovely princesses, evil wizards and terrifying ghosts; his ear has been trained since early childhood to the slow, mournful songs of his country; later on he reads books dealing with her history which does not resemble the history of any other land; his youth is spent in a society which, again, is unlike any other; he belongs to a people that does not yet enjoy the fullness of life yet whose present is already interesting as a step, as an advance, toward a beautiful future; yes, this future is only in the bud, yet it is rich in hopes. . . A real poet would sympathize with his country, share its hopes, suffer because of its ills, and rejoice in her joys.

In his last essay, 'A Survey of Literature in 1847,' Belinsky reaffirmed his concept of the social significance of art:

Art for art's sake has never really existed. . . An art of pure detachment revolving in its own sphere and having no connection with any other manifestations of life is only an abstract dream. Art re-creates reality in its most typical and truthful aspects; thus literature is always a reflection of society. He who deprives art of its rights to serve social interests debases the reader instead of elevating him, for such art exhausts its own vital force—i.e. thought—and makes itself an object of sybaritic enjoyment, a toy for dilettante idlers. . . The poet chooses not that which is particular and accidental but the typical and general, which reveal the meaning of his times. . . Today art and literature are more than ever the expression of social problems, and that is the direction in which the Russian Natural school is moving.

The Natural school he defined as 'the sense and soul of Russian literature.'

The critic consecrated the last years of his life to the interpretation and promotion of this new trend, the great representative of which, in his opinion, was Gogol.

Belinsky made writers and readers aware of the national significance of literature and of its impact on the life of their country. His patriotism, however, was totally devoid of any aggressiveness. A liberal and a socialist, Belinsky led a campaign against national complacency, attacked the official doctrine of autocracy, Orthodoxy, and national customs, laughed at narrow-minded Slavophiles, and satirized those who considered long beards, old-fashioned clothes, and bread-cider insignia of nationality. Widely read in European and American literature (he wrote a eulogistic article on Fenimore Cooper), he declared himself a Westernizer and pleaded for permanent co-operation with Europe. He believed that Russia ought to rebuild her institutions on foundations of the European principles of human dignity, freedom, and political and social democracy. In his *Letter to Gogol,* which made a tremendous impression on the intellectuals, he wrote:

Russia sees its salvation not in mysticism, not in asceticism, not in pietism, but in the successes of civilization, of enlightenment, of humanity. It is not preachments that Russia needs (she has heard them aplenty!), nor prayers (she has said them over and over aplenty!) but an awakening among her common folk of a sense of human dignity (for so many ages lost amid the mire and manure) and rights and laws, conforming not with the teaching of the Church but with common sense and justice, and as strict a fulfillment of them as is possible. . .[1]

The great critic maintained and developed the radical tradition of the intelligentsia. He led the fight against despotism, serfdom, hypocrisy, narrow-mindedness, and reaction, and only his premature death saved him from prison or exile.

The prodigious influence of Belinsky was not founded on his ideas alone, he had a most striking personality. This thin, slightly built man whose nervous face bore the stigma of tuberculosis, yet who had the

[1] Quoted, by permission of the publishers, from B. G. Gurney: *A Treasury of Russian Literature,* copyright 1943 by Vanguard Press, N. Y.

stamina of a born fighter, was reticent, shy, almost insignificant in the company of strangers. 'Belinsky's frail body held the burning temperament of a gladiator,' Herzen tells us. When in a discussion some of his cherished ideas were challenged, he would reveal himself a powerful debater, putting so much passion and force into his speech that often at the end of a heated controversy he would have a throat hemorrhage, compelling him to stop abruptly, a handkerchief pressed to his mouth, his eyes still glowing with excitement.

He put the same fiery temperament into his writings. They carried the readers away by their torrential flow of thoughts, by the emotional qualities of his style. 'My power,' Belinsky himself said, 'lies not in my talent but in my passion, in the subjective character of my nature. My articles and my inner self are inseparable.' This was true, although he underrated his unusual literary gifts. The great critic, as Turgenev has remarked in his *Memoirs,* possessed an infallible esthetic sense; he was able to grasp immediately the essence of each work of art, to judge in a flash the individual traits of each writer. His response to poetic beauty was quick and spontaneous; his evaluations, expressed with warmth and strength, were keen, challenging, and sincere.

'Frenzied Vissarion,' as his friends nicknamed him, lost himself completely in his work. His personal life was unhappy; he led the existence of a pauper and was burdened with debts, material worries, and poor health, but nothing could ever lower his spirits. Even the terrible political pressure that doomed all his generation could not shatter his faith: 'We live in frightful times,' he wrote, 'but we have to suffer in order to make life easier for our successors.'

This son of a middle-class family was a professional writer—something of a novelty in the society of nobles among whom he moved. But Belinsky, far from acquiring an inferiority complex, derived a certain pride from his social status. 'I am a man of letters—I say this with poignant joy and pride. Russian literature is my blood, my life.' The great respect in which the Russians hold writers comes partly from the ideas spread by Belinsky and the pathetic example of his life.

7

WESTERNIZERS AND SLAVOPHILES

I THE DREAMERS and philosophers of the 'thirties moved from a search for abstract truth toward social awareness. This was the general trend of the epoch. In the 'forties the generation of Belinsky was already much more concerned with problems of history and politics than with metaphysics and esthetics. Their attention was focused in particular upon Russia's future. Belinsky had held that literature should be national. But what were the basic features of Russian national character? Of Russia's past? And of her present?

The study of German philosophers made these questions of immediate importance. The young Russians knew the speeches of Fichte, in which the German idealist exalted the virtues of his people and called for a revival of national feeling. They also knew that Schelling and Hegel considered various civilizations, such as those of Greece and Rome and of the Anglo-Saxon world, as incarnations of universal designs. Hegel contended that the Germans, for instance, were destined to fulfil an 'orderly freedom' as one of the final stages in the incarnation of 'absolute spirit' in history. His philosophical schemes assigned to each European nation a special role to be performed in strict accordance with a divine blueprint. But however infatuated the Moscow noblemen might have been with the German masters of philosophy, they could not help noticing that the Slavs in general and the Russians in particular were altogether excluded from this prearranged order. Russia fell into the category of 'non-historical nations' (as Hegel superciliously called them), which in the dialectical process of human achievements played but a negative part.

Other factors contributed to the interest in the problem of Russia's historic role: Slavonic studies undertaken by prominent scholars in

Russia, Bohemia, and other countries; the general awakening of national consciousness throughout Europe after the Napoleonic wars; and finally, the expansion of the Russian Empire, whose military strength and diplomatic influence raised the issues of the direction and meaning of her policy. After all, what was Russia's place on the world's stage, and in what did her contribution to humanity consist? Discussions on these subjects were suddenly galvanized by a literary event, that according to Herzen, had the effect of 'a flare shooting through the darkness.'

In 1836 *The Telescope,* a Moscow review, published 'A Philosophical Letter' by Peter Chaadaiev (1794-1856), a former officer in the Guards, a wealthy aristocrat, and a brilliant and highly original man who had traveled extensively abroad and come under the influence of mystical Catholicism. A friend of Pushkin's and of the Decembrists, in the 'thirties he became a hermit, shutting himself up in his great mansion and devoting his leisure to religious and philosophical studies. Disappointed in humanity, embittered by loneliness, and revolted by the regime of his country, he developed a purely negative attitude toward Russia. In his letter Chaadaiev said Russia's past was empty, her present was unbearable, and she had no future. Russian history was a terrible lesson for other peoples: it showed what slavery and isolation could lead to. Russia had always lacked the historical, religious, and cultural unity of the West, which was based largely on Roman law, Christian ethics, and the Catholic Church. Belonging to none of the great families of mankind, she was neither of the West nor of the East, for she was devoid of the traditions of either. From sheer barbarism she had passed to crass ignorance, and then had fallen under the yoke of a brutal foreign invader who left his impress on all aspects of the Muscovite State. An outsider in the universal race for progress, Russia had not contributed a single idea, a single work of intellect or art to the rest of humanity. During the exciting periods of European upheaval when the whole world was aroused, searching for new ways of life (the Renaissance, the French Revolution, and so on), Russia had continued to vegetate in her wooden, straw-thatched huts. A deaf-and-mute bystander, she had become resigned to the fact that the destinies of mankind were decided without her. Even Peter the Great had been unable to change this tragic situation: while forcing his subjects to don European garments and manners, he could not destroy the 'dead wall' between Russia and the West. The only salvation for Russia lay in absorbing the Western civilization and setting foot upon the high road of the Roman Catholic world. Until she did so everything would continue in its hopeless state—with the upper classes corrupted by serfdom, servility, and indifference to truth; the people driven by ignorance and brutality;

and coarseness of manners, coupled with general amorality, reigning in all walks of society.

One can easily imagine the effect of such pronunciamentos in a period of obligatory optimism, which Count Benckendorff had summed up by declaring that Russia's past was glorious, her present magnificent, and her future surpassing all expectations. The publication of *The Telescope* was immediately suspended (a hard blow to its chief contributor, Belinsky). The censor, who had passed the article while playing cards, was dismissed and cut off from any other job, and Nadezhdin, the editor, had to go into exile. As for the main culprit, Chaadaiev was declared by Nicholas I to be a madman. Confined at home, he was ordered to submit to a weekly inspection by a police surgeon. Thus one of the most intelligent and original of Russian thinkers was officially labeled insane.

Subsequently, however, Chaadaiev became less pessimistic about Russia's fate, with the hope that she would be able to contribute to the religious renovation of mankind, which, in his opinion, formed one of the inevitable phases of history as directed by Divine Will. Chaadaiev's religious concepts influenced many Russian thinkers and mystics—particularly Vladimir Solovyov. But during his lifetime his ideas served principally to raise the problem of Russia's destiny. His criticism of the state of affairs in his day appealed to the majority of the intellectuals in Moscow and St. Petersburg, but his sharp comparison of the progressive cultural entity of the West with the retrograde Empire of the Czars, and his claim that Russia should submissively follow the Western pattern, provoked wide controversy. It helped to crystallize the arguments of two divergent groups, the Westernizers and the Slavophiles, who represented the two fundamental trends of Russian thought.

From the 'thirties to the 'fifties the two factions fought against each other, and their struggle brought about rifts and schisms among the intelligentsia. Their main difference persisted throughout the nineteenth and twentieth centuries and even today there are traces of the old dispute, under new disguises, in the Soviet ideologies, and there are Westernizers and Slavophiles in the ranks of the Communist party. In literature these factions determined the attitudes of almost every prominent writer.

Before the great schism in the 'forties, the Slavophiles and the Westernizers were mostly members of the nobility, belonging to the same circles, reading the same books, and having a common philosophical background. Many of the opposing leaders were attached to one another by family ties and personal friendships. By the middle of the 'forties, however, the difference of opinion had led to alienation, and the breach became complete.

Although the beliefs of Slavophile leaders varied according to their philosophical and religious backgrounds or their personal leanings and literary activities, there were a few fundamentals accepted by all. They were formulated by Alexis Khomiakov (1804-60), a rich landowner, poet, publicist, and theologian, a man of phenomenal erudition and memory, and the author of remarkable treatises on Greek Orthodox dogma; by Ivan Kireyevsky (1806-56), philosopher, journalist, and editor; by his younger brother, Peter Kireyevsky (1808-56), an outstanding linguist who knew seven languages and whose collection of 15,000 items of Russian folklore, ballads, and songs made an important contribution to scholarship; Konstantin Aksakov (1817-60), talented poet, critic, and historian; his brother Ivan Aksakov (1823-86), publicist and social worker, who carried on the traditions of the 'forties for almost half a century.

All these writers agreed that the reforms of Peter the Great had disrupted the organic unity of the Russian people. Before his reign the nation had harmoniously developed and maintained its religious integrity and a secular originality of customs and manners. 'The unity and liberty of the Orthodox religion and its principles of spiritual love were embodied in the people of the Muscovite State,' declared Khomiakov. Peter had destroyed this unity by introducing ideas and trends borrowed from the Anglo-Saxon world (Protestantism) or the Roman (Catholicism). Foreign to Russian mentality, they had created continuous discord. With the establishment of the new capital on the banks of the Neva, Russian history had entered its artificial and obnoxious St. Petersburg period. That capital's kowtowing to Western culture and the formal bureaucratic institutions were a betrayal of the national spirit. Despotic autocracy, militarism, materialism, atheism were all of foreign origin—direct importations from Europe. The folk saying that what was a Russian's meat was a German's poison held real wisdom, for European civilization was, on the whole, opposed to the essence of Russian culture. The West was based on formal discrimination (Roman Law), on a will for domination, and consequently, on violence, greed, and competition. Catholicism, with the Papal struggle for power, had degenerated into a secular institution, and Protestant rationalism had dried up the living springs of faith. The West was marching toward its undoing, since truth and love, the foundations of any growing human organization, had forsaken the Old World. Europe, having accomplished its centuries-long mission and now nearing the end of its cultural cycle, must yield to the civilization of the Russians and other Slavic peoples.

This Russian or Slavic civilization was basically religious. While the nations of the West have a cult of law and form, the Russians possess the sense of mercy, of fraternal love and spiritual eagerness; a true Russian does not attach great importance to earthly goods, material gains, or political advantages—including formal liberty. He values his spiritual freedom above all, rather than the theoretical rights of some written constitution. Ivan Aksakov went even so far as to affirm that the Russian people were humble, apolitical, and alien to any idea of conquest, domination, or power. The people entrusted the administration of their worldly affairs to the Czars, and this 'delegation' of temporal power gave its real meaning to the Russian monarchy. It was a people's monarchy which granted to the vast masses of the population what they cherished most: spiritual and religious independence, simplicity of life, and the practice of Christian virtues, remote from political passions or diplomatic quarrels. Western man was following the path of individualism, which can lead only to loneliness and despair, whereas the Russians had a communal sense stemming from the traditions of early Christianity. The collective cultivation of land in the form of a *mir* as well as other forms of co-operative labor were the best examples of his spirit of solidarity.

The Slavophiles reached a conclusion completely opposed to that of Chaadaiev: the salvation of Russia lay in the preservation of her national originality, in the peculiarities of her culture, and in eradicating the futile imitation of the doomed West. They were also irritated by Europe's condescension: the West looked down upon Russia, calling it a semi-barbarian state. The Slavophiles were extremely sensitive and refused to accept the idea of Europe's cultural supremacy. They reverted in their writings to the vision of the Third Rome revived; and most of them proudly emphasized that Russia was the rightful heir of the Byzantine Empire.

Some Slavophiles even refused to wear European garments and appeared in the Russian attire of the seventeenth century, with long beards in true Muscovite fashion. But such eccentricities were rather rare; as a rule the Slavophiles did not extend their anti-Westernizing attitude to European art, science, or literature. In this they differed from the conservative wing of the movement, which was led by Professor Stepan Shevyrev, with Michael Pogodin serving as a connecting link between the Slavophiles and the government's 'official nationalism.' Shevyrev contended that if any of the three foundations of Russian life—absolutism, Orthodox religion, and popular nationalism—were shattered, the whole fabric of Russia would collapse. He advocated a merciless fight against European liberalism, 'this revolutionary, ra-

tionalistic, atheistic, and disintegrating poison.' Pogodin considered that
Europe was afflicted by a mortally contagious disease, and he spoke of
the 'contaminated breath of the West.'

However, such reactionary views were not shared by the leading
Slavophiles. The Aksakovs and their friends criticized the autocratic
regime for not having fulfilled its mission. In their opinion it was its
duty to grant the people the 'full freedom of life and spirit,' including
the 'freedom of opinion and speech,' and to abolish serfdom. Only after
the re-establishment of 'Orthodox popular democracy' could Russia
assume the leadership among all the Slavs and set an example to the
decadent West. Many of the Slavophiles emphasized the future role
of Panslavism. Their activity was directed toward the 'reunion of all
rivers and streams in the great Slavic sea'; they tried to establish permanent relations with the intellectuals of Bohemia, Slovakia, Serbia,
Bulgaria, and other Slavic countries, and they worked on the Russian-
Polish rapprochement. The Westernizers often reproached them with
playing the game of the St. Petersburg government, whose protective
attitude toward other Slavic nations was determined by power politics.

There is no doubt that the Westernizers were stronger in their
criticism of Russia's political regime than were the Slavophiles, who
never questioned the fundamental validity of the monarchy. Pushkin
echoed Chaadaiev when he wrote: 'It is true that our social life is dreary.
This lack of public opinion, this aloofness as regards duty, justice, and
truth, this cynical contempt for the mind and human individuality are
indeed hopeless.' But the promises and conclusions of the Westernizers
were quite different from those of Chaadaiev. On the one hand, Belinsky,
Ogarev, and Herzen, and on the other, Turgenev, Granovsky, and
Kavelin did not agree in their political and social views; yet they considered themselves a homogeneous group because they all shared certain
fundamental principles and were ready to oppose the Slavophiles. They
contended that Russia was a part of Europe, and therefore belonged
to Western civilization. Her development had been delayed by the
struggle to defend the West against Asiatic invasions, and consequently
her backwardness was actually the ransom she had had to pay. She
must now catch up with the Occident, absorb the best elements of
Western culture, and become a full-fledged member of the European
community of nations.

Peter's reforms, they maintained, had been not only right but also
inevitable. They had pointed out the only possible way for Russia to
develop, and the continuation of Europeanization became a historical
necessity. The drawbacks of the St. Petersburg period did not lie in its
break with the outdated Muscovite tradition, but in its reluctance to

accept all the corollaries of Peter's innovations: the Czars and their 'inner circles' were wary of parliamentarism and liberal institutions.

Nicholas I [wrote Herzen] follows the traditions of Peter the Great in his foreign policy, but suppresses them at home. Which means that while the territory and the international importance of the Empire increase, its public life is reduced to less than nothing. Everything is done for the throne, nothing for the people. The Emperor is no more than a military man, and all the attempts at education and culture initiated by Peter are simply thwarted. The Western ideas of human dignity, freedom, and justice must be applied to Russian life; serfdom must be abolished, the whole regime transformed into a constitutional, liberal and democratic monarchy or republic. All the talk about Russian humility and Orthodoxy is merely helping the reaction; the future of the country lies not in the resurrection of Byzantine prejudices or pseudo-national smugness, but in free thought, science, individual and collective liberty, and the transformation of the social and economic order.

Such was the program of the Westernizers. It is quite obvious that it avoided the problem of religion and was based on purely secular grounds. The Westernizers were either indifferent to religion or wholly atheistic, like Bakunin, who compared the concept of 'God in heaven' to that of a 'tyrant on earth.' Belinsky and Herzen shared the doctrines of Western positivism.

Like the Slavophiles, the Westernizers also had their left wing, led by Belinsky and Herzen. Their right wing was best represented by Timothy Granovsky (1813-50), a professor of history who was carrying on the traditions of Nikita Muraviev and other moderate Decembrists. His ideas on law, parliamentary regime, and constitutional guarantees, as well as his conception of Russian history as part of an all-European development, were incorporated into the doctrine of Russian middle-of-the-road liberalism in the nineteenth and twentieth centuries and were taken up by its last leader, Pavel Miliukov (1859-1943). Belinsky, and particularly Herzen, resumed the traditions of Pestel and the radical Decembrists; they were the forerunners of the socialistic movement.

II   At the time of Belinsky's coming to St. Petersburg and proclaiming his readiness to 'contend against our revolting reality in the name of human dignity, individuality, and socialism,' some of his friends were studying the materialistic philosophy of Ludwig Feuerbach, whose *The Essence of Christianity* had found many followers among the Westernizers. They had also fallen under the spell of the French Utopian socialists, such as Cabet, Blanc, Fourier, and George Sand, whose humanitarian dreams appealed to their imagination. This radical trend, both political and philosophical, was most brilliantly interpreted by one of the outstanding writers of this period, Alexander Herzen (1812-70).

The illegitimate son of Ivan Yakovlev, a wealthy Moscow aristocrat, and of a humble German governess, Herzen had a very happy childhood and was surrounded by love and attention (his father gave him the pet name of Herzen from the German word *Herz*—the heart). He had an excellent education, was widely read, and in 1829 entered the University of Moscow as a student of science. There he found many young men who, like himself, were ardent admirers of the Decembrists, loved Schiller, talked about idealism or universal justice, and made secret pledges 'to serve humanity.' Herzen, his bosom friend Ogarev, and their followers were chiefly interested in political problems, particularly after the 1830 revolution in France and the unsuccessful Polish insurrection (1831). The works of Saint-Simon and his humanitarian ideas of collectivism charmed the members of this group. They also read the 'forbidden verses' of Russian poets. Although their ideas were somewhat vague and general, their feelings were definitely against 'any oppression, coercion, or despotism' and for 'the principles of the French Revolution.'

In 1833 Herzen received his doctorate in philosophy and a year later he was arrested together with Ogarev and other 'young enthusiasts' and exiled to the northern provinces. The romantic admirer of Schiller, the lover of beauty and science, was compelled to endure for five years the primitive life of one of the most backward regions of Russia. This experience cured him of all his illusions. After a short sojourn in St. Petersburg, where he was planning to live with his young wife Nathalie, he was exiled again in 1839 as 'a dangerous and passionate freethinker.' It took him almost three years to be permitted to settle in Moscow. By this time Herzen was thirty and he summed up his life experience in the following terms: 'twelve years of childhood, four of school, six of adolescence, and eight of exile, persecutions, and reprisals.'

Herzen had a keen analytical mind with a strong ironical bent and he pitilessly criticized the vagueness of the Moscow idealists and their reluctance to face reality. Brilliant and witty as a writer, Herzen created his own style of journalism: his articles, essays, pamphlets, and letters sparkled with humor, bold images and amusing *bon mots,* while they combined erudition with skepticism, logical realism with a real desire for higher values, objective observation with creative imagination. Between 1842 and 1847 Herzen published under the pen name of Iskander (Alexander) several philosophical essays—'Dilettantism in Science,' 'Letters on Studies of Nature,' and so on; the short satirical story, 'Doctor Krupov,' whose hero epitomized human history as a bedlam; 'The Magpie,' a story of the tragic fate of a serf actress; and *Whose Fault?*, a dramatic novel of love, whose hero, Beltov, belongs to the series of 'superfluous men.' The novel treated the problems of family and of woman's social standing and also vividly depicted the life of the provincial gentry. This utterly realistic work became widely popular and received high praise from Belinsky. 'You have an enormous amount of intelligence,' the critic wrote to Herzen; 'I do not know why one man should have so much brain power, yet at the same time your intelligence is animated by and warmed with the hearty humanity of your nature.'

Herzen soon became one of the leading figures of the Russian intelligentsia and, together with his friends Belinsky, Granovsky, and Annenkov, headed the Moscow Westernizers in their fight against the Slavophiles. In comparison with the idealism of the 'thirties Herzen represented a new trend. Rejecting the 'dreams of childhood' he came out as an apostle of critical positivism. He affirmed that experience formed the only test of human knowledge, and that only experimental and rational methods could lead to any real achievement in the natural as well as the social sciences or in history. An enemy of dogmatism or 'closed systems of thought,' he rejected the 'specter of Absolute Truth' and refused to attribute a religious meaning to collective or individual life. Life's purpose was life, said Herzen; the goal of human existence was not God, or the Hegelian self-developing Spirit, or the Kantian Idea, but the fullness of being. To be was the supreme goal, and this includes for the individual all the manifestations of life. Development and realization of all his potentialities was man's natural objective. This assertion did not imply an acceptance of egotism or hedonism; according to Herzen the fullness of life meant suffering as well as joy, intellectual as well as sensual experience, and, above all, activity, struggle, self-expression, and creativity, for these were the primary forces of human nature. The unfolding of individual potentialities was, however, hindered by numerous obstacles. Prejudices of caste and class, moral and social conventions, and economic and political conditions turned the individual into a slave, a brute, or a worthless creature. How could one speak of 'harmonious development' to a serf, to a pauper, or to a victim of an absolutist state? How could the ideal of 'fullness of life' be attained under a despotic regime which distorted the soul, imprisoned the mind, and corrupted the body?

A cursory analysis of the main factors of human enslavement and unhappiness led Herzen to condemn the economic and political structure of the society of his time. Modern civilization was based on capitalist exploitation, which was only another form of cannibalism, obdurate political oppression, and moral hypocrisy. Only when the rule of the upper classes was replaced by a regime of political and social democracy based on solidarity, free labor, science, and socialism, would conditions for the normal development of the human individual finally be achieved.

These ideas of Herzen's, expressed with his usual forcefulness, definitely marked the end of Romantic idealism and the development of the moral and individualistic approach to social problems that had prevailed for so many generations among the Russian intelligentsia.

Herzen's popularity was at its height when, in 1847, he decided to go abroad with his family. After the death of his father he found himself in possession of a large fortune and could afford to do whatever he pleased. In Italy and France he took an active part in the political events on the eve of the Revolution of 1848. Revolutionaries of all nations gathered in his Paris salon, on the Avenue Marigny. His witty speeches, delivered in French, German, Italian, or English, charmed and surprised his cosmopolitan guests. Although the outcome of the Revolution of 1848 disillusioned Herzen and his life on the Continent did not meet all his expectations, he decided not to return home, but to disregard the summons of the authorities in St. Petersburg, who were concerned about the activities of one of the Czar's most prominent subjects.

Revulsion and premonition do not allow me to cross the Russian border. . . No, I will not, I cannot cross this border of the kingdom of darkness, of arbitrariness, of silent agony, of solitary death, of gagged suffering. . . I can foresee the inevitable ruin of the old Europe. . . Everything I love on this earth is persecuted, everything I respect pilloried. . . Yet why do I remain here? I remain because it is *here* that the battle is being waged. . . Social problems are being solved here. . . The oppression is great, yet the protest is loud; the combatants are often sent to the galleys in chains, but they go with their chins up, uttering the free word. And when the word is alive, the deed is not yet dead. For months I hesitated and weighed everything, but finally decided to sacrifice everything for the sake of human dignity and free speech. I will be your uncensored word here, your free press, your unofficial representative.

Herzen became more than that. This great *émigré* soon became the ambassador of the unofficial, revolutionary Russia at the court of Europe's democratic peoples. After many wanderings and a series of personal tragedies, culminating in his wife's premature death and the loss of his mother and son at sea, Herzen settled down in London in 1852 and established the Russian Free Press. His house again became a center for the exiles of all countries; and he resumed his literary activity and wrote his best work—the seven volumes of his memoirs, *My Past and My Thoughts,* one of the most significant books in Russian literature. He started the publication of an annual, *The Polar Star,* which bore on its cover the portraits of the five Decembrists executed by Nicholas I. Thus did Herzen affirm the continuity of the Russian liberal and revolutionary tradition.

In 1856 his best friend, Nicholas Ogarev (1813-77), a poet of delicate lyrical qualities and great civic feeling, joined him in London and Herzen began the publication of his periodical, *The Bell.* This journal had an extraordinary career. The first uncensored publication in the Russian language, it was devoted to his country's internal affairs, exposing 'all that was ridiculous or criminal, evil or ignorant in Russia,' and fought for 'free speech, the abolition of serfdom, of censorship, and administrative abuse.' Smuggled into Russia through all sorts of channels, *The Bell* was avidly read by the intellectuals as well as by the bureaucrats. Legend tells that prime ministers, and even the Czar himself, often found copies of *The Bell* on their desks. Secret contributors supplied Herzen with firsthand information on matters in Russia, and many officials trembled lest their chicanery be brought to light by *The Bell's* ruthless editor. Herzen's articles were discussed everywhere. For almost ten years *The Bell* was the accepted mouthpiece of Russian public opinion, and nobody saw anything paradoxical in the fact that it came from London and a group of *émigrés.*

After the Polish insurrection of 1863 and the rise of the Nihilistic movement, Herzen's political program lost its appeal and he was attacked by the liberals as well as by the younger radicals. The gap between the *émigrés* and the generation of the 'sixties widened, and *The Bell* went into a gradual decline. In 1865 Herzen transferred the paper to Geneva, and then to Paris, where its publication was suspended in 1867.

Although Herzen played a very important role as a founder of the Russian free press and as an exponent of the liberal movement of the 'fifties, his significance lies in his doctrine of Russian socialism that he gradually formulated during his stay abroad. In some ways it represented a synthesis of the Slavophile and Westernizing tendencies.

Herzen went to Europe an uncompromising opponent of the Slavophiles. The events he witnessed in France and Italy during the Revolution of 1848 and the ensuing reaction shattered his faith in the Occident. He felt a strong aversion to contemporary European life, which was based on smugness, material security, and property and was teeming with survivals of feudalism. The West seemed to him a world completely rotten in its social fabric and about to collapse. As a socialist and a revolutionary he predicted the failure of all attempts at reform: 'The world in which we live is dying, and no remedies can help its hopelessly diseased organs; it ought to be buried, in order that its successors may be free to breathe—yet there are some who still hope to cure the patient and put off the end.' The weaknesses of the revolutionary parties of Europe, according to Herzen, were plainly evident, and all their attempts at overthrowing the existing order were either abortive or inefficient.

In the same way as the aristocracy, which has degenerated into a group of diseased morons, shallow Europe will finish its shallow existence in a twilight of stupidity, in sluggish sensuality without convictions, without any arts or vigorous poetry. . . Europe is foundering like a wrecked ship. . . It is approaching a terrific cataclysm. The world of the Middle Ages has collapsed; the feudal world is at its end. Political and religious revolutions . . . have destroyed all faith in thrones and altars but they have not realized freedom. They enflamed desires they are unable to fulfil. Parliamentarism, Protestantism were mere reprieves; their time has gone by. Since 1849 we have come to understand that neither the petrified Roman Law, nor sophisticated casuistry, nor the meager theistic philosophy, nor ruthless religious rationalism, can stave off the accomplishment of social destiny.

This destiny, in his opinion, led inevitably to the destruction of the 'anthropophagic economic system, founded on the exploitation of man by man.' In his remarkable book *From the Other Shore* (1850) one of the most original, inspired, and prophetic works of nineteenth-century political literature, he comes to the conclusion that the Old World is doomed:

It can be saved neither by martial law nor a republican form of government, neither by executions nor charity—not even by the division of land. . . In different countries men can be more or less free, more or less equal, but as long as this regime, this civilization, exists, men can nowhere be truly free and equal.

Yet in the midst of his disappointment his faith in Russia's future was stronger than ever: 'In the chaos of this agony, in the labors of new birth, in this world which is falling apart, our eyes turn toward the East,' wrote Herzen in 1851. History was an improvisation, the flood of history would make its way through thousands of gates, and it may well be that the gates would be the gates of the Baltic and Russia would inundate Europe. Herzen affirmed his belief in the great social destiny of Russia with the same fervor with which he had exposed the exhaustion and pettiness of European bourgeoisie. In numerous articles and pamphlets, particularly in his letters to Michelet, the famous French historian, and to his other friends, and especially in *The Russian People and Socialism,* Herzen outlined his new doctrine. The peculiarity of Russia's past justified a belief in her 'particular path of development.' Russia was not bound to repeat all the phases of European development, as so many Westernizers had insisted; she had no need of copying the ways of Occidental democracy, bourgeois revolutions, and parliamentarism.

Why should we shed our blood to get those half-measures and half-decisions reached by Europe? There are other horizons and possibilities. . . The future of Russia does not depend on her alone; it is bound up with the future of Europe. Who can foretell the fate of the Slav world if reaction and absolutism finally triumph over revolutionary forces? Perhaps Russia will perish. But in that case Europe, too, will perish. And progress will pass on to America.

Russia would never be a country to do things by halves; she was not going to undertake a revolution merely for the sake of replacing Czar Nicholas by a lot of little Czars—members of parliament, judges, and gendarmes. The Russian people were interested in social change because their life was based on socialistic principles: the *mir,* or rural commune, and the *artels,* or co-operatives of artisans, were the two main socialistic foundations of the Russian land. In acknowledging the importance of the *mir* and the *artel* Herzen was following the Slavophiles, but with this essential difference: where the Slavophiles saw them as bulwarks of tradition, conservatism, and stability, Herzen discovered an instinctive communism in them. At the same time he did not deny the role of the West: Europe had formulated ideas of collectivism, freedom, and human dignity, of which Socialism was but the ultimate expression. Europe, however, lacked force and a natural disposition toward Socialism; while Russia possessed a primitive but forceful element—her Socialism was inherent in her working classes. Russia, therefore, able to escape the evils of Europe, would be the country of social revolution. The problem of the relation between Russia and the West was very simple: either the Russian revolution would awaken Europe and lend it new forces, or the Old World would be faced with ruin. 'There are only two interesting problems,' Herzen wrote in 1854: 'The social problem and the Russian problem. Basically they are two facets of the same problem.'

Russia was going to offer her solution of the crisis by a revolution in which European ideas or socialism would merge with the Russian practice of common cultivation of land and co-operative labor. The social problem in Russia could be solved only in the spirit of socialism. Herzen never defined how this revolution would take place (he also called it the 'funeral march of the old world, and the induction of the Slavs into universal history'), but he often intimated that the social upheaval would come in connection with a war when 'the people would cross their borders, and awaken in the midst of blood, battles, fire, and devastation.'

Herzen used to say that the Slavophiles and Westernizers reminded him of the ambivalent Janus whose two faces looked in opposite directions, and who yet had but one heart. He never doubted that the two opposing factions had the same love for Russia in their efforts to solve the problem of her future. The solution he offered combined the Slavophiles' belief in Russia's great destiny, in her 'peculiar way of development,' with the Westernizers' radicalism, socialism, and high evaluation of Occidental ideas of progress, freedom, and individual dignity. Thus Herzen formulated the principles of 'Russian socialism' with its messianic character, its idealization of the peasant's way of life, and its reluctance to follow in Europe's path. Under the name of *Narodnichestvo* (or Populism) it became one of the most important currents of Russian political thought and practice.

To what extent Herzen may be called a forerunner of certain modern trends in Communism is open to discussion. Although Lenin contended that Populism was merely wishful thinking and 'did not contain an ounce of Socialism,' he recognized the 'great role played by Herzen in the preparation of the Russian revolution.' The inner drama of Herzen, with his violent disillusionment and fervent affirmations, his varied activities and final solitude, was the reflection of a period

when the revolutionary spirit of the bourgeois democracy in Europe was *already* dying, while the revolutionary spirit of the socialist proletariat was *still* not ripe. . . This explains the lack of solid ground under Herzen's feet, his pessimism, and his many returns to liberalism, which he himself so often denied and cursed.

The revolutionary messianism of Herzen took a more violent turn in Michael Bakunin (1814-76), the founder of international anarchism, who likewise believed that the emancipation of mankind would come from Russia and the Slavic world. In Bakunin, who claimed that the destruction of the Russian and Austro-Hungarian Empires would start a new era for all of Europe, the ideal of revolutionary Panslavism was much stronger than it was in Herzen. Bakunin dreamed of a United States of the Slavs, and was very active in revolutionary propaganda among Czechs, Serbs, Croatians, Poles, and other Slavic peoples. His struggle against Marx in the First International was the first clash between the European and Russian concepts of revolutionary action.

The contribution made by Herzen to Russian thought and political activity was so spectacular that it overshadowed his importance as a writer. His works, not allowed in Russia until 1905, were circulated only in surreptitious editions which were zealously hunted down by the police. Nevertheless, Herzen was an extraordinarily powerful writer. Tolstoy, in his letter to the painter Gay, wrote in 1888: 'What an astonishing writer. If his works were not forbidden to the young, our whole life of the last twenty years would have been different.' Herzen raised the journalistic essay to the stature of a work of art, and utilized in all his articles and pamphlets the qualities he displayed so lavishly in his best book, *My Past and My Thoughts*. These memoirs present a great variety of material: an unsurpassed description of Russian society under Nicholas I, a panorama of political and ideological currents in the 'thirties and 'forties, including a brilliant characterization of the Westernizers and the Slavophiles, a sweeping picture of Europe in 1848 and after, and a unique series of sketches of what was called at that time Young Europe—the *émigrés* and radicals of a half dozen European countries. One part of the book Herzen had withheld from publication until fifty years after his death—the story of his wife's love affair, which wrecked his family life—a sort of confession 'written with tears and blood, a work that burns and glows,' as Turgenev put it; 'Herzen was the only Russian who could write that way.'

Herzen was a realist, who esteemed Gogol highly, and his own writings, especially in their richness of anecdote and fullness of detail, belong to the great Realistic current of the nineteenth century. But they also have a most unusual combination of passion and irony, reflecting the fundamental duality of Herzen's personality: he possessed a strong analytical mind made keen by scientific and philosophical training—many great men of Europe admired his vast erudition and his sense of history—yet at the same time he was a man of powerful emotional drives and genuine revolutionary feeling.

His writings all shine with wit and irony and move from profound general statements and definitions to colorful images and vivid epithets. A thinker first and then an artist, Herzen had a unique gift for dynamic sentences full of striking contrasts and for numerous digressions which were always *à propos*. With the daring of a pioneer he made free with all the accepted rules of good writing, coined new words or unusual turns of speech, and mixed scientific terminology with poetic language. 'His style, madly irregular, fills me with delight: it is like living flesh,' Turgenev said of him. Master of characterization, he has left memorable portraits of his contemporaries, whimsically blending facts, outbursts of civic indignation, humor, and theoretical discussions. He himself remarked that this apparent disorder was held in check by the co-ordination of two or three pairs of reins. And this writer, who had so often yielded to the restless demon of hatred or indignation, who was so sensitive to pain and passion, had a singleness of purpose that puzzles and charms the modern reader.

It may be added that despite his twenty-five years of life abroad, Herzen is one of the most genuinely Russian stylists. No knowledge of Russian literature can be complete without Herzen, and it is not too much to say that no true understanding of Russian mentality and history is at all possible without a study of his memoirs and his journalistic writings.

8

GOGOL

I   IT IS unanimously agreed by critics
and readers that Gogol is the initiator of Russian realistic prose—
much as Pushkin is declared the greatest master of the new Russian
poetry. But Pushkin, however the interpretations of his work may vary,
has expressed himself with the utmost clarity and there is nothing perplexing in his artistic aims and achievements, whereas Gogol presents
a most vexing literary enigma. His restless and warped personality, his
erratic and pathological life, his tragic inner conflict, which drove him
almost to madness, the strange destiny of his greatest book, *Dead Souls,*
which was left unfinished, the peculiar quality of his genius—all open
the way to the endless controversy over the source and meaning of his
creativeness, as well as over his place among the Russian classics. It is
true that to us he seems more complicated and puzzling than he did to
his contemporaries. In the 'forties and 'fifties his tales and comedies
were hailed as the highest examples of straightforward realism, and
there was uniformity in their interpretation. Nowadays we consider them
from a different angle.

The son of a small Ukrainian landowner who was descended from
Cossacks, who loved the theater and wrote verse and comedies in
Ukrainian, Nicholas Vassilievich Gogol-Yanovsky was born in 1809
in the county of Mirgorod, in the province of Poltava. He spent his
childhood on his parents' small estate, and part of his adolescence in
the provincial town of Nezhin, where he attended the newly established
Lyceum. His background was typically Ukrainian, and he was very
close to the soil of southern Russia, with its heroic traditions, songs,
folk dances, and the droll humor of its easygoing people. Peasants,
Ukrainian Cossacks, the provincial gentry, and petty officialdom sur-

rounded him during his formative years. The monotonous drabness of provincial life filled him with horror; he did not want to become one of those narrow and smug 'little folk' he encountered in Nezhin. 'I am terrified,' wrote Gogol, 'when I consider that fate may cast me into this wilderness and assign to me the dreary quarters of anonymity.'

At the age of seventeen he had a vague vision of a 'happy sunny life' that would enable man to live up to his high destiny and prevent him from being simply 'a transient and insignificant guest on this earth.' He was wildly enthusiastic about the theater and literature and, like Dickens, was a most successful amateur actor and excellent at reading in public. He was also attracted by the idea of becoming 'a useful citizen and serving the State.' His plans, however, were nebulous; he lived in his dreams much more than in actuality. Unlike his contemporaries, he did not devote his time to amorous adventures: as a matter of fact there were no women in his adolescence. Nor were there any in his later life.

In 1828 Gogol went to St. Petersburg, where his attempts to become a professional actor failed. Forced to look for work, he finally secured a post in a governmental department, where he became fully acquainted with petty clerks and pompous bureaucrats.

His friends at Nezhin advised him to take to poetry and to renounce prose, in which, according to them, he made but a poor showing and gave vent to vulgar humor. He followed this advice, and his first work to appear, in *The Son of the Fatherland* (a St. Petersburg daily), was an anonymous poem, praising the blessed soil of Italy. He next published at his own expense and under the pen name of V. Alov, a long-winded and highly romantic Idyl in Pictures, *Hans Kuechelgarten,* written in the tradition of Zhukovsky and the German Idealists. The one book reviewer who happened to spot the small book wrote so jeering a criticism that Gogol burned all the copies of this unfortunate work he could get back from the bookshops.

He continued to write, however, but from then on only in prose. He studied painting, associated with artists, and became enthusiastic about scores of projects. One of his *Dikanka* stories, published in a review, led to his meeting Zhukovsky and Pushkin. It is quite possible that his contact with the latter contributed to Gogol's decision to drop all his scattered activities and concentrate on literature. In 1831 he published the first (the second appeared a year later) volume of his *Evenings on a Croft near Dikanka,* which brought him immediate recognition. Pushkin was delighted by their 'genuine gaiety, devoid of affectation or starchiness,' and by the 'poetic sensitiveness' of the book. The naive and shrewd humor of the garrulous bee-keeper Rudy Panko, whom Gogol made the imaginary narrator of his tales, captivated an extensive public.

The *Evenings* were based on Ukrainian folklore and presented a mixture of legends or fairy tales with the vivid products of Gogol's own imagination. The chief hero of these fresh and amusing stories was the Devil, and the plot usually hinged on his attempts to get the robust and carefree Cossack peasants into his clutches and raise havoc in their lives, particularly in their love affairs. Naturally, the Devil did not always fare well. The finicky minor demon who put the moon in his pocket on Christmas Eve did succeed in breeding confusion among the swains courting the buxom Solokha, who happened to be his own leman, but was overcome in the end by the young blacksmith Vakula, who availed himself of the fiend's help in winning the heart of a proud village belle. Often the intrigues of the Devil are frustrated by the intervention of benign spirits, as in 'May Night, or the Drowned Girl,' in which father and son are rivals in a highly complicated love affair full of grotesque situations. The ghost of a girl who had drowned herself because of her stepmother, a cruel witch, finally helps the young man to marry the young woman he loves. In the other stories, however, the Devil either mocks mortals, as in 'The Bewitched Spot,' where dung is substituted for a buried treasure, or he brings them to utter ruin, as in 'St. John's Eve,' in which a young man sells his soul to the Devil to get the money he needs to marry a pretty girl and binds himself to commit certain horrible crimes. Horror also predominates in 'A Terrible Revenge,' a highly fantastic tale of incest and murder. The most powerful of Gogol's horror stories is 'Viy,' the legend of the monstrous king of gnomes, whose iron eyelids droop to the very ground. When those eyelids are raised for him, Viy's glance kills—and it is thus that Thoma, a young seminarist, is killed, for having aroused the love of a fascinating young witch and then bringing about her death.

Devils, spooks, evil spirits, sorcery, and witchcraft are presented for the most part by Gogol in a curious blend with comic adventure. Supernatural and humorous elements are so intertwined in the *Dikanka* stories, and also in *Mirgorod,* their sequel, that this becomes a characteristic device. It reveals the usual Romantic pattern: Romanticists were fond of contrasts and therefore often alternated horror with humor. In Gogol, however, these traits were indicative of an odd point of view: he felt strongly the intimate connection between the laugh-provoking triviality of life and the horrifying shallowness of existence as created by the Arch Foe.

This tendency became more pronounced with time. In 1831 and 1832 Gogol was still evincing his natural gaiety, his irresistible comic vein; his laughter was hearty and spontaneous. All his descriptions of village life were genuinely realistic, yet it is doubtful that his highly idealized Cossacks ever existed as he depicted them. In general, even in this early work, Gogol, under the mask of a smug and naively superstitious story teller, employed a deliberate interplay of fantasy and realism. The same may be said of his style: partly Romantic with hyperbolic images and metaphors, pages of poetic descriptions in a vibrant, sweeping manner, and rhythmic sentences of rather involved construction; and partly Realistic, with its strongly vernacular dialogue. But Romantic or Realistic, Gogol was always verbose, and his language was full of superlatives, sonorities, drolleries, phonetic twists, and an astonishing variety of intonations. It is an exclamatory (and declamatory) language, rich in texture and color and very different from the northern sobriety of Pushkin's elegantly balanced prose or the muscular dynamism of Lermontov.

Fully in the Romantic tradition, *Tarass Bulba,* a short historical novel, was published in 1835, in the *Mirgorod* collection. Bulba, a man of strong passions and primitive virtues, while warring against the Poles and Tartars, avenges the execution of his son, Ostap, who had been captured by the enemy, and with his own hands kills his younger son, Andrii, who, bewitched by a beautiful Polish girl, had turned traitor to his own people. The Romantics, headed by Walter Scott (whom Gogol greatly admired), were eager to 'reconstruct' the heroic past and national traditions. From this point of view *Tarass Bulba* is a specimen of literature that flourished throughout Europe in the 'thirties and 'forties. It is a bold work in the tradition of tales of high chivalry. Contrasting descriptions of heroic deeds and comic adventures are interspersed with scenes of war, slaughter, mass movements, and pathetic situations. Presenting a rather idealized pictu.e of Ukraine's past, with stock figures instead of living characters, it often lapses into pomposity and artificiality. What saves this story from oblivion is Gogol's adroit use of humor: the opening scene, where Tarass, immediately after greeting his sons upon their homecoming from school, launches into fisticuffs with them to test their strength; the description of the undisciplined Cossack camp on an island in the Dnieper; and several sketches of minor characters, all truly delightful. Some descriptions of nature are in the authentic Grand Style, and there is genuine pathos in the narration.

Evidently Gogol was seeking, through the exaggeration of the heroic epic, a remedy against triviality and the machinations of the lesser demons. He was carried away by the vision of Men of Might, and Tarass Bulba appealed to him not only as a protagonist of Ukrainian folklore, but also as an exemplar of those who fulfilled his ideal of man's high destiny. This attitude determined all his studies of the past. A great lover of history, he thought at one time of becoming a teacher and in 1834 gave a course on the Middle Ages at the University of St. Petersburg; but after an inspired and brilliant introductory lecture the course proved to be an utter fiasco.

Elements of Romanticism became less obvious as Gogol progressed as a writer. Even in the sequel to the *Dikanka* stories there is one that does not resemble the other legends, fairy tales, and anecdotes: 'Fedor Ivanovich Shponka and His Aunt' is an unfinished sketch of a petty squire with a timid soul, thrust by his determined and domineering aunt into a matrimonial adventure. The realism with which his drab existence is pictured is coupled with a strong sense of the grotesque. The comic caricaturing of the odd characters transforms them into monsters, into all sorts of 'pig snouts'; they are droll and, at the same time, frightening.

In the *Mirgorod* series, there are two stories in the manner introduced in 'Shponka and his Aunt': the idyllic 'Old-Fashioned Landowners' and the outrageously funny 'How Ivan Ivanovich Quarelled with Ivan Nikiphorovich.' One might easily mistake the first tale for an approving portrayal of a loving couple, a Darby and Joan mezzotint: that of Athanasii Ivanovich and Pulcheria Ivanovna, whose serene days glide away peacefully and uneventfully. They live in the low-ceilinged, stuffy little rooms of their small estate, spend their time and energy in canning, preserving, salting, and pickling, and have no other cares than household ones, particularly those of the kitchen. Yet under the surface of this general picture, so full of savory and comic details, there lurks Gogol's usual dread of insignificance and triviality.

This dread also forms the background of the story of how the two Ivans quarreled, which is as humorous as that of the elderly couple is pathetic and is told with all the ludicrous detail of a caricature. The story deals with two friends who lead the jog-trot existence of Mirgorod's inhabitants: they eat and sleep and make much ado about nothing. For Ivan Ivanovich the eating of a ripe melon is a memorable event: he collects the seeds of each melon and puts them in a paper bag, which he labels 'This melon has been eaten on such date.' The names of any guests partaking of a melon are duly inscribed: 'Messrs. so and so also participated.' Ivan Ivanovich and Ivan Nikiphorovich are physically very much alike, the main difference being that the head of the former resembles a turnip, tail down, while the head of the latter is the same turnip, but with its tail up. They are neighbors and the best friends in the world. Their friendship, however, comes to an end at the moment when Ivan Nikiphorovich in a fit of temper over nothing at

all calls Ivan Ivanovich an old goose. The offended squire starts a lawsuit, the offender parries with a counter-suit, and an endless petty feud
fills their lives and consumes their energies. Despite the artificial excitement of attempts at reconciliation, new complications, court rulings, and
judicial pleas, the two former friends continue to lead a dull vegetative
existence, barely enlivened by their picayune intrigues. And then the
story ends abruptly with the author's unexpected remark: 'Life in this
world is a bore, gentlemen!'

In the first stage of his development as man and writer Gogol was
amused by the silly human bipeds who quarrel over trifles and attach
vast importance to all sorts of rubbish. Later the drabness of their
existence, their pettiness and shoddiness, irked and saddened him. He
felt that such heroic men as Bulba belonged to an idealized past which
could never be revived. Life was a Mirgorod, and he was bored by its
shallowness, horrified at its vulgarity. This gay young Ukrainian, who
told Pushkin, Pogodin, Pletnev, and other illustrious men of letters
stories so funny that they rolled with laughter, used to stop in the
middle of his most uproarious yarn and look at his friends with a
peculiarly searching look in his half-frightened, half-melancholic eye.

This same blending of humor and melancholy, of a strong satirical
vein, through which stupidity, vanity, and pettiness were made the
target of mirth, with a morbid fear of emptiness, a sort of *horror vacui,*
is more and more in evidence in his *Arabesques,* or *Tales of St. Petersburg* (1835). Here the writer, at twenty-six, manifested beyond all
doubt an 'extraordinary, powerful, and high talent which entitles him to
a leading position in Russian literature,' as Belinsky enthusiastically
remarked in his review of the book. The *Arabesques* are far removed
from the naïve gaiety or horrors of the *Dikanka* stories. Gogol's anxieties, his strange visions, his feminine and uncanny intuition, his
capacity of shifting from a concrete, visible plane to an imaginary or
altogether mystical reality, are fully evident in 'Nevsky Prospect,' 'The
Portrait,' 'The Memoirs of a Madman'—just as they later appear in
'The Nose' and 'The Overcoat.' Some of them fit perfectly into the
structural pattern of the Romantic movement and are akin to the tales
of T. A. Hoffmann, that stupendous and ambiguous storyteller and
author of the *Serapion Brethren.*[1] Like Hoffmann, Gogol intermingles
reality with the supernatural, but where the German writer resorts to
intricate plots, the Russian master prefers the incidents of everyday life.

In this respect 'Nevsky Prospect' is most significant. Its hero, a
young painter by the name of Piskarev, glimpses a woman of heavenly

---

[1] Gogol and Poe make a fascinating subject for comparison. Both show how man is
beset by evil—whether he is morbid (as in Poe) or stupid (as in Gogol).

beauty amid the throngs of passers-by on the great Nevsky thoroughfare. Encouraged by his easygoing friend, Lieutenant Pirogov, the painter follows his 'Madonna,' and the enchantress leads him straight to a brothel. Horrified by this sudden dénouement Piskarev flees, but he cannot forget the pure and lovely features of the young girl. He dreams about her; her image is ever before him in his garret, but when he tries to see her again he finds only a filthy den of prostitutes, she being merely one of them. Unable to bear this discord between his vision and reality, Piskarev commits suicide. The contrast is heightened by the comic adventures of Lieutenant Pirogov, who does not look for any Madonnas but seeks merely the earthly favors of a buxom German *Frau* and is beaten up by her jealous husband, a baker, and his fellow tradesmen. The triviality of Pirogov's love affair and its stupid and vulgar ending is set off sharply against the dreams, torments, and self-destruction of Piskarev.

The nonsensical platitude dealt with in the story borders on the fantastic, and the devil, the mean little devil of Gogol's stories, does not dwell in the darkness of some Walpurgis Night but lurks just around the corner. The evil, the extraordinary, the supernatural are parts of the commonplace. The smug and scurvy Major Kovalev in 'The Nose' loses his self-esteem by the inexplicable disappearance of his nose. The police do not seem to be overexcited by this misfortune and use routine methods to investigate the matter. After many mysterious incidents the nose finally resumes its place between the plump cheeks of Major Kovalev, and life goes on as usual. This symbolic and whimsical story has attracted the attention of Freudian commentators, who identified the loss of the nose with Gogol's supposed sexual impotence. Whether or not this clinical explanation is true, it is obvious that the story tackles again one of Gogol's favorite themes: triviality assuming the form of the supernatural. The petty, stupid, and self-sufficient Kovalev is the hero of most extraordinary events without ever being aware of what is happening to him. His own emptiness and mediocrity are the hotbed for evil. From this allusion Gogol goes even farther: perhaps stupidity, triviality and insignificance are evil itself, are the devil, the reflection of a menacing, distorted world of ugliness, confusion, cruelty, and horror, wherein Madonnas become prostitutes and Viy changes into an awful foreboding of reality. The borderline between the *usual* and the *extraordinary* is purely imaginary, and it is extremely difficult to distinguish mirage from truth.

Visions and dreams acquire for Gogol the palpable tensions of reality; compared to them the words and deeds of everyday life fall to pieces, resolve themselves into dust. Dreams also serve as gratifications for those who cannot find a place in life. The petty official in 'The Memoirs of a Madman,' mistreated by the higher officials and secretly in love with his chief's daughter, leads a life of humiliation and misery until he goes out of his mind and imagines he is the King of Spain. Thereupon he wins all he was denied in the world of sanity—freedom, love, power, responsibility, a purpose in life. He goes out of his mind because he could not win a place for himself in society. His fight against obscurity and his longing for a 'high destiny' end in a lunatic asylum, where the doctors drench his head with ice-cold water.

The tragic fate of the underdog who has neither the strength nor the opportunity to escape the yoke of poverty and social inferiority, 'whom nobody loves, whom nobody defends, whom nobody is interested in,' is one of Gogol's main themes. It was later taken up and developed by Dostoevsky, just as Gogol's horror of triviality and pettiness found an echo in Chekhov. It is also the theme of 'The Overcoat,' one of the most significant of Gogol's stories, which belongs to the group of St. Petersburg tales, even though written much later (1842).

Akakii Akakiievich, the hero of 'The Overcoat,' is likewise a petty official. He is meek and uneducated, victim of all sorts of humiliation, shabby in appearance, short of stature, balding, and, of course, exceedingly poor. His life is so drab and devoid of any distractions that in his free hours Akakii Akakiievich copies governmental papers by way of diversion. But his 'dreary quarters of anonymity' are suddenly illuminated by a great change: Akakii Akakiievich determines, out of absolute necessity, to order a new overcoat. After unbelievable tragic-comic sacrifices and privations he finally fulfils his dream and is the owner of a splendid overcoat, which serves as a means of his becoming a human being again. His joy, however, is short-lived; as he is walking home through the wintry night, after a celebration given by one of his superiors, in honor of this acquisition, Akakii Akakiievich is held up and robbed of his overcoat. The unfortunate victim complains unavailingly to the police and finally seeks the intervention of a certain Important Person, who loses his temper at the sight of the humble, wretched petitioner, and orders him to be thrown out. Akakii Akakiievich is broken and crushed; there is nothing else left for him to do but die. But, after his death, a ghost that looks very much like a poor clerk without an overcoat begins to haunt the frosty streets of St. Petersburg. One night the Important Person who had mistreated Akakii Akakiievich is suddenly overtaken in his carriage by the ghost: 'Your overcoat is just the one I need!' he is told, 'You didn't put yourself out any about mine and, on top of that, hauled me over the coals—so now let me have yours!' After that memorable night, the spirit of poor Akakii Akakiievich never appeared again in the twilight darkness of St. Petersburg nights.

The tragic-comic misadventures of his hapless hero were interpreted as a symbol of the millions of underprivileged, and this interpretation gave a profound significance to 'The Overcoat.' Herzen called it 'a colossal work,' while Dostoevsky, speaking of Russian writers, affirmed that 'we have all emerged from "The Overcoat." ' The representation of the 'average man,' the down-trodden victim of social injustice, the 'humiliated and wronged,' has become one of the main trends of Russian prose, and Turgenev, Dostoevsky, Pisemsky, Uspensky, Garshin, Korolenko, Chekhov, Gorky, and a host of minor writers have followed in the wake of Gogol, without, however, attaining his unique combination of realistic and supernatural elements.

II   The humanitarian implications of 'The Overcoat' were obvious to Gogol's contemporaries, who sometimes compared him with Dickens. By this time they were prepared to accept the definition of Gogol's literary manner he himself formulated a few years later: 'Laughter through tears.' This interpretation, however, applies to only a part of his work. Nobody would deny that compassion for the poor and a melancholic attitude toward life underlie Gogol's humor. But what Gogol called 'tears' is above compassion or pathos and differs from them. Gogol also had a genuine feeling of 'another reality,' a sense of something that was beyond the reach of concrete investigation and that made all the adventures of human actors, comic or pathetic, appear as mere shadows. Life was all the time dissolving itself into non-being, into a phantasmagoria of hundreds of grotesque, sniggering faces. In the St. Petersburg tales this feeling is given through descriptions of the city, or, more exactly, of its eerie atmosphere, which serves as a symbol of the other world. St. Petersburg, as a living subject of poetry, had already been used in Pushkin's poems, particularly in 'The Bronze Horseman.' In Gogol the city becomes indistinct, almost shapeless: the atmosphere of the capital is like a mist in which all real objects and human forms lose their firmness and their contours and are transformed into vague phantoms. The writer who was called the head of the Realistic school and who possessed inimitable talents of observation and characterization, displays in this instance also a fantastic, warped, and almost morbid spirit.

Strange as it may seem. Gogol himself was hardly aware of what he was doing. His work was mainly intuitive, almost unconscious, at least as far as some of its implications went. He always paid great attention to the wording of his tales and comedies, rewriting some of them as many as eight times in order to polish the style, to change scenes, or to add fine strokes of characterization. His first draft, however, was always 'somnambulistic'; many of his metaphors, jests, sometimes whole scenes, and certainly quite a few of his minor characters came about merely through simple associations of sounds and words; Gogol played with words, tossed them about, amused himself with their droll combinations—and seemed surprised and enchanted when they produced comic or lyric effects. Frequently he was like a child who does not expect his soap bubbles to display such brilliant and swiftly changing colors. One thing is certain: Gogol was never fully aware of the social implications of his early works. Nor was he aware of it even when he had written the play that created as great a political stir as it did a literary sensation—*The Inspector General.*

The germ of the play's story was imparted to Gogol by Pushkin. It may be pointed out that most of the plots of Gogol's tales and plays were based on incidents taken from life. This side of Gogol's creativeness is completely disregarded by some over-sophisticated critics who deny his realism and contend that he created everything out of thin air—or, at best, out of pure imagination.

Gogol had always wanted to write for the stage, and his minor plays (*The Gamblers, The Lawsuit, A Busy Man's Morning,* and especially the delightfully funny *The Marriage*) attest his quality as a playwright. He believed that the stage could establish that contact between the writer and his audience that he sometimes felt lacking upon the publication of his books.

Only to think [says Gogol] that a gathering of several thousand individuals, who differ so much if you take them one by one, can suddenly be stirred by the same emotion, shed the same tears, roar with the same laughter. The stage is a cathedra from which one can tell the world a lot of good things.

The Inspector General was first heard at a reading in 1836, at a literary party at Zhukovsky's home. Pushkin was among the guests and laughed uproariously. The censors, however, frightened by the comedy's daring, refused to pass it, but Zhukovsky arranged for it to be read at the Imperial Court. The Czar liked the play and authorized its production. It was first given 19 April 1836 at the Alexandrian Theater in St. Petersburg. The new play was so extraordinary that the audience was stunned and actually forgot to applaud. When the curtain was rung down, the whole house rose in uproar.

'It is a calumny, a silly farce, dangerous propaganda,' screamed the conservatives. 'No, it is magnificent, it is true to life,' countered the liberals. The controversy raged in the press, and polemics concerning *The Inspector General* divided all educated society into two uncompromising factions. 'All the young people,' V. Stassov, a contemporary who was to become an art critic, tells in his *Memoirs,* 'were most enthusiastic about the comedy. We had to defend it against the attacks of the outraged older generation. The discussions were vehement, filled with rancor and scorn.'

Gogol was taken back by the violence of public opinion and particularly by the attacks from 'respectable' quarters. His aim in writing *The Inspector General* was, as he himself has stated, 'to pile up all the vile things in Russia and to laugh at them.' He could not understand why this work of his should have unleashed such passions. 'Everybody is against me,' he exclaimed in grief and surprise; 'Not merely individuals but whole groups: functionaries, merchants, the police.' The controversy upset and depressed him to such an extent that his health, always precarious, was impaired, and the physicians advised him to go abroad for a cure. Later he wrote all sorts of afterpieces to *The Inspector General,* trying to justify himself and his good intentions. These writings are typical of Gogol's psychology, but hardly add anything to the work itself.

The action of the comedy takes place in a small provincial town, ruled by a coarse and harsh Mayor, one Skvoznik-Dmuhanovsky, and a gang of ignorant, corrupt, and complacent officials. This little world of knaves and morons is roused by the rumor that an Inspector General has been sent from the capital to investigate the town's administration. While discussing this unpleasant news with his officials, the Mayor is told that a mysterious stranger by the name of Khlestakov has put up at the best hotel, where he is behaving in a most perplexing manner. Everybody is convinced this is the Inspector General traveling incognito in order to take the administration by surprise. Giving him a splendid reception at his house, the Mayor tries to bribe Khlestakov, and he is even about to throw his daughter into the arms of the talkative and flirtatious young man. As the important guest, his pockets filled with gifts and money, is finally taking his leave, the prying Postmaster rushes in with a letter he has just opened. It is written by Khlestakov and describes his extraordinary adventures to a friend in St. Petersburg, laughing at the dupes who had mistaken him for an Inspector General, calling all the officials scandalous names, and boasting of having cheated them all. The Mayor and his assistants have scarcely any time to protest: the arrival of the real Inspector General is suddenly announced to the petrified group of city fathers.

The *Inspector General* has a folk saying for its epigraph: 'Don't

blame the mirror if it's your own mug that's crooked.' The administrative incompetence, the coarseness and ignorance of bureaucracy, the
graft and brutality of the police, the conscienceless oppression of the
lower classes—victims of poor education, poor justice, poor economics,
the low moral and intellectual level of the average citizen—all these
reflected, as in a mirror, the actual conditions of Russian life. Thus,
Gogol claimed that he had given an objective picture of provincial
Russia. The comedy was surely conceived as a grotesque, but the caricatures were none too far from reality. All of them, including the sharply
etched minor ones, were types everybody could easily recognize.

This searing social satire did not spare the representatives of St.
Petersburg society. Khlestakov, the bogus Inspector General, is a flighty
young man who loves to boast and show off. He talks of himself as an
Important Person, a general, a great writer; he gets drunk as much on
his own eloquence as on wine; there are no limits to his tall tales, since
he is truly amoral. Nothing really matters to Khlestakov, and he himself
is utterly shallow—a symbol of that light, vulgar, ingenuous, and horrible emptiness that inspired Gogol with a mystical dread of death, of a
universal void. Gogol himself acknowledged that he regarded Khlestakov
as essentially a type. 'All men are Khlestakov—for at least a few
minutes, or a moment only. It is so hard not to become Khlestakov,
even if but once. A sleek officer in the Guards, a statesman, or even
we sinful writers, turn into Khlestakovs now and then.' For many
generations *khlestakovshchina* was used in Russia as a synonym for
gasconade or braggadocio. But Khlestakov is more than a mere strut-
ting petty adventurer, and the actors and directors of the twentieth
century, notably Michael Chekhov and Vsevolod Meyerhold, tried to
give greater depth to the interpretation of *The Inspector General*.

Khlestakov is changeable and elusive; lacking personality, he becomes the symbol of non-existence, the incarnation of that trivial and
horrible vacuum from which stem grimacing ghosts, the lesser demons,
and sniggering monster-faces. And was not Khlestakov himself one of
those despicable demons who, without using any diabolical tricks or
witchcraft, contaminate life with their small talk, their drawled banality?

As this futile, irresponsible, flighty man is utterly ridiculous, so, of
course, is the audience who listens to him with mouths agape, ready
to swallow all the pretentious piffle he is tossing to them. As is usually
the case with Gogol, something almost frightening is peeping out from
behind these comic appearances—and the author seems to wonder
whether anybody's life could stand the test of a general inspection.
Did Gogol have in mind a vision of a Higher Inspector General? Had
Gogol a full understanding of the symbolism and social implications

of his comedy when he made the Mayor turn on his subordinates with the tirade: 'What are you laughing at? You're laughing at your own selves!'—a speech which is now usually directed at the audience, and cutting their laughter short.

Whatever the interpretation and its symbolism, *The Inspector General* is a great comedy. It stands up well even if no attempt is made to look beneath the obvious. And the obvious is a social satire in which, as in all other works of Gogol, the grotesque is a means of representing reality. Gogol was certainly dealing with material from actual life, and his contemporaries regarded *The Inspector General* as a caustic exposé of the evils of their times. Here was a new achievement in the satirical tendency represented by Fonvizin and Griboyedov, but without the didactic pompousness of the former or the idealistic and ironic verse of the latter. It was Russia as everybody knew it or was afraid to know it, portrayed through a series of characters and situations familiar to all. The names of the comedy's protagonists immediately became nicknames, tags to be given to so many real mayors, judges, postmasters, gossipy landowners, and so forth, who went around without suspecting that they had been classified and pinned down forever by Gogol's 'anger, salt, and laughter'—his own epithet for one of his unfinished comedies, which preceded *The Inspector General*.

As Belinsky pointed out, the comedy was an example of the 'Natural' school: the creative impulse had come from everyday life, which had supplied the plot and characters; the author had reflected the contemporary scene realistically, without being hindered by rhetoric, foreign patterns, or Court influence. Moreover, this realistic representation did not limit itself to being a factual report or even an objective narrative; it was a masterpiece of critical realism. The author had clearly stated his attitude toward the material from life he had used in his picture.

These remarks of Belinsky determined the attitude of all succeeding critics: Gogol was always evaluated as the initiator of Russian critical realism. When European and American critics talked at the end of the nineteenth century of the Russian school, what they generally meant was the school of critical realism founded by Gogol.

Belinsky was also aware of the extraordinary literary values of this comedy in which a trivial anecdote grew into a vast social picture subordinated to the rule of psychological and logical unity. The conduct and the speech of every character in the play necessarily stem from that character's personality, and therefore each action and word are convincing and real. The events in the plot follow a closely knit sequence, and the play is so constructed that every person appearing on the stage is directly or indirectly involved in the general action (there are no side issues or subplots). The plot and its solution are clean-cut, and the ending is in the spirit of the whole.

Gogol's contemporaries felt that in this ending he went against the accepted rules: instead of the usual punishment of vice and reward for virtue, he let Khlestakov go scot-free, and virtue has no opportunity to triumph. His other knaves and rogues, though momentarily petrified by the arrival of the real Inspector General, are left to their own fate, which need not be so very harsh: who knows whether they may not be able to extricate themselves from the mess by new bribes and trickery? Their sole punishment consists of the laughter of the spectators—'laughter, that only honest and noble personage of the comedy.' The sparkling and funny dialogue, the rendering of the moral defects and speech peculiarities of each character, the accumulation of ridiculous but credible incidents made *The Inspector General* a highly enjoyable performance.

The play still is a favorite in the theater not only in Soviet Russia but elsewhere.

The unexpected impact of and the discussions created by *The Inspector General* brought perplexity and torment to its author. He seriously questioned his art and, in particular, his right to portray and laugh at 'the contemptible and insignificant things in life.' In an *Afterpiece* to the comedy he tried to defend himself by pointing out that laughter brings purification and carries with it 'sparks of eternal, mighty love. . . He who has often shed copious tears is, perhaps, laughing more than any other.' The problem of the relation between the artist and his work was continually on his mind: he attempted to solve it in the rewriting of 'The Portrait,' an uncanny tale published in *Arabesques* (1835). The new version of the story (finished probably at the beginning of 1841) is most revealing from an autobiographical point of view and throws light on Gogol's main inner conflict.

If we look beneath the surface of the romantic plot of 'The Portrait' and its multiple symbolism (the connection between evil and money, between wordly success and moral degradation, and so on), we come to the conclusion that Gogol was seriously tormented by the problem of the representation of evil in art. He feared that the artist might become the unwitting channel through which evil flows into the world. This can happen if he copies nature and faithfully reproduces ugliness, triviality, or cruelty without revealing his own attitude toward the 'contemptible, obnoxious, and insignificant' facets of reality, which would make of his work a source of evil. Stark realism is therefore morally dangerous. Gogol believed that at a certain point laughter turns to cynicism, and that the artist who laughs at ugliness comes at last to enjoy it. And it is thus that mirth destroys the storyteller, who becomes mesmerized, as it were, by the world's grimacing masks.

Six weeks after the first performance of *The Inspector General* Gogol sailed for a German port. He was ill, melancholy, and uneasy. On the eve of his departure he read to Pushkin the initial chapters of a new work he had begun: *Dead Souls,* the germ of which had come from Pushkin just as had that of *The Inspector General.* Pushkin laughed heartily at first, but then he became serious and finally uttered his famous *mot:* 'Lord, how sad is our Russia!'

Gogol called *Dead Souls* a poem (in the epic sense) to indicate its lyrical unity and special form, but he was rather uncertain about the scope and probable length of his new work until he found himself abroad. After Germany he visited Switzerland, from where he wrote to Zhukovsky, on date of 13 November 1836: 'I have changed all I have written of *Dead Souls,* have worked out a new plan, and am now writing in accordance therewith. If I carry it through the way it ought to be, what enormous and original subject matter there will be, dumping in a single heap all that is vile in Russia!' He kept on with this ambitious project in Paris, where he received the news of Pushkin's death. He was terribly shaken: 'My life, my highest joy, are dead with him. . . I never undertook anything, never wrote anything without his advice. All that is good in me I owe to him. And *Dead Souls,* my present work, is also of his creation.' So profound was his grief that he could not work and decided to leave France for Italy.

For the next three years in Rome, *Dead Souls* progressed by fits and starts. His desire to write this 'colossal poem in three parts,' as he now envisioned it, was frequently diminished by his growing interest in religious and mystical subjects, which was nurtured by his platonic friend, Princess Volkonskaya, and several Polish Roman Catholic priests. His health was also handicapping him; he was susceptible to fits of depression and anguish, which sometimes took the form of a real mental and physical affliction. He resumed writing the first part of *Dead Souls* upon his return home in 1839, but, unable to finish it, he went back to his beloved Rome in a state of mental agony. In 1841 the first part of *Dead Souls* was finished, and Gogol hurried back to Moscow, where he made numerous corrections and additions. After a wearisome struggle with the censors, who regarded the work with fear and suspicion,[2] *Dead Souls* was finally published in May 1842, and created a sensation.

[2] One objection was that the soul, being immortal, cannot be dead. That a 'soul' in the sense of 'serf,' could be bought, sold, or mortgaged, did not seem to strike them as incongruous.

Belinsky summed up the general impression of this poem:

This is a purely Russian national work. It derives from the depths of popular life; it is as truthful as it is merciless and patriotic; it strips the veils from reality; it is inspired by a passionate love of the true essence of the Russian world. It is a work infinitely artistic in its conception and fulfilment, in its characterization and details of Russian everyday existence—and at the same time it is full of social and historical implications.

The hero of the poem, Chichikov, a former customs official, arrives in a provincial town and begins a round of visits among the local landowners in order to acquire dead 'souls,' or serfs, from them. Nobody understands why the affable, good-mannered, and round-cheeked Chichikov wants to buy such unusual merchandise, but as long as his purchase liberates the owners from having to pay taxes for their deceased chattels and as long as a fair price is offered (ranging from a few kopecks to a couple of rubles each, occasionally given him outright), the landowners, who regarded their serf-souls, alive or dead, as mere property, readily agree to the transaction. Chichikov's aim is to mortgage these souls (legally, since they were still regarded as valuable until the next census) and through this swindle to build up for himself a respectable social standing that might lead to a prosperous marriage. Russians under Nicholas I did not ask: 'How much is So-and-So worth?' but rather 'How many souls does he own?' And Chichikov could boast of being the happy owner of thousands of souls, without making clear whether they walked the earth or were lying beneath it. He is no villain, but merely a man possessed by a passion for acquisition. In his pursuit of wealth he has no scruples. Yet this plump, affable man, with ingratiating manners and *savoir faire,* is a paragon of respectability. He looks like an Important Person; everybody, including the Governor, invites him to their houses and he conquers all hearts, particularly those of the fair sex. And his success is due to his utter banality. He does not know what the soul is: so that he is able to deal in dead souls with an imposing matter-of-fact attitude as if they were just another kind of farm produce. Like all the lesser demons who spring out of nothingness, he is pleasant, unobtrusive, noncommittal— the supreme expression of the commonplace.

Chichikov travels about a great deal (in keeping with the picaresque framework so prevalent in European literature of the early nineteenth century), and his wanderings bring him in contact with all sorts of provincial squires. Though of the privileged class and practically the rulers of Russia, they are no better than Chichikov. The obliging and mawkish

Manilov seemed a fine, kindly sort when met for the first time, but in the long run he is as boring and cloying as a marshmallow. The sluggishness of his ideas is comparable only to the inanity of his dreams. He has no interests, no real desires, no strong urges, his plans are like smoke, and his existence has no pattern.

Korobochka, the owner of only eighty souls, who complains of being a poor widow-woman, is actually as hard as nails. This sanctimonious, superstitious old egotist, who lives in her shell and looks upon everybody with suspicion, also belongs to the race of acquirers and is doing rather well. She is miserly, but not to the extent that Pliushkin, that Harpagon of the steppes, is. Unlike the Molière character, Pliushkin is truly horrifying. He has sacrificed everything to the demon of acquisition, and all human feelings have gradually withered in him. A victim of his own ravening covetousness, he looks like a beggar and his greedy eye is ever on the alert for anything he can scavenge: a nail, a rag, a piece of string—'you never know; even a piece of string can come in handy.' His moral degradation has gone so far that he has lost all decency or pretension: here is evil in all its appalling starkness.

The heavy, clumsy Sobakevich, the great eater who cannot forgive the doctors for having invented such nonsense as diet, is a different type of acquirer. He is coarse and sleek, an aggressive and cynical *koulak,* a backbiter who slanders all his friends and squeezes all his slaves in his bear-like paws.

Next to the acquirers stands the wastrel, Nozdrev, the good fellow, a liar and braggart, the hero of taverns and county fairs, ready for anything, and spending his days and nights on cards, horses, drink, and brawling. Nozdrev's life is noisy and disorderly; his estate is run down and his peasants suffer because of the folly of their master. He wastes energy, time, and money, and all his boisterous outbursts end in nothingness—as do Pliushkin's avarice, Korobochka's meanness, Manilov's shoddy daydreams, and Sobakevich's coarseness.

The swindler who is buying up dead souls meets living dead souls everywhere. He is surrounded by them in town as well as in the country: the governor who embroiders on tulle, the chief of police who organizes a buffet feast (levied from the shopkeepers) for Chichikov, the petty officials in the court house, the gossiping ladies, the bribe-taking functionaries—not one of them is spiritually alive. All of this provincial Russia with its small talk, drivel, rubbish, ignorance, greed, and triviality seems a fantastic and pointless jest.

This gallery of grimacing portraits forms the substance of the book, which otherwise has little plot or exciting action. As usual in Gogol, all his descriptions, unmistakably realistic in the precision of details and

characterization, are imbued with the grotesque. The whole style of
Dead Souls is a blending of realistic presentation and fantastic features.
Hundreds of ridiculous names and witticisms whirl in a riot of mirth;
down-to-earth details such as the eighty-six varieties of food mentioned
in the book swell into hyperbolic similes (the roast of beef that resembles a boot marinated in bread-cider, for instance). The drollery of
situation and character is enhanced by coined words and witty phrases,
by intentional slips and odd repetitions. There is a quirk, a hint, and a
wink in each sentence of Gogol's. Each one effervesces, is iridescent, is
changeable in its rhythm, with sudden transitions from mirth to lyricism,
from tittering to the rise and fall of declamation—and then reverting to
an ingratiating whisper, a chuckle, an uproarious laugh, and the brittle
humor relapses into a quaint phonetic pattern of words and sounds, like
a series of fireworks. The swing of Gogol's prose and its lyrical qualities
reach their height in this poem, which made the symbolist Andrei Bely
say: 'Nietzsche and Gogol are perhaps the greatest stylists of European
prose, if style is taken to reflect in form the life and rhythm of the soul.'

The structure of *Dead Souls* is very complex, based on several
superimposed planes which are not apparent at first glance. At times,
in reading the novel, one has the same illusion as on stepping into a
room without suspecting that another room is beyond the first, and a
third beyond the second; you enter with the assumption that you will
find only walls and no other doors, while in reality you are walking
through a whole enfilade. The multifold meanings of the novel-poem
become deeper the more you read it. One of its levels reveals Gogol's
metaphysical wistfulness: 'If men are what they are, then some grave
error must have been committed in their creation. Can it be possible
that mortals were really created in the image of God?' It is easy to grasp
that at this point Gogol's laughter acquires ambiguous and tragic
accents.

In no other work of Gogol's is the narration so often interrupted
by lyrical digressions or meditative passages. Occasionally they are in
a hilarious vein, like the pseudo-earnest disquisitions about the fat and
the slim, or about those gentlemen 'who are called the fair to middling
sort,' or about popular sayings: it is these passages that are responsible
for the superficial resemblance to *The Pickwick Papers*. But most of
them are really serious, ranging from indignation (as in the concluding
lines on Pliushkin's fate) to profound and grave thoughts on Russia.
Despite the variety in mood these passages form the undercurrent of
the poem, its symbolic plane.

In the distinctly symphonic structure, the theme of Russia's destiny—that fundamental problem of the 'forties—serves as a leitmotif,

recurring with all its sad musicality in many variations. The britzka, Chichikov's light carriage on springs, in which he first appears, recurs in the last chapter of Part I, transformed into a troika, as a symbol of Russia. And the author, who gives such an awesome image of his country, lets himself be carried away by his lyrical flight, and exults:

And art not thou, my Russia, soaring along even like a spirited, never-to-be-outdistanced troika? . . . What signifies this onrush that inspires terror? And what unknown power is contained in these steeds, whose like is not known in this world? Ah, these steeds, these steeds, what steeds they are! Are there whirlwinds perched upon your manes? . . . Whither art thou soaring away to, then, Russia? Give me thy answer! But Russia gives none. With a wondrous ring does the jingle-bell trill; the air, rent to shreds, thunders and turns to wind; all things on earth fly past and, eying it askance, all the other peoples and nations stand aside and give it the right of way.[3]

A vision of emptiness and apathy stands out against such lyrical passages: the unsparing revelation of Russia's vacuum is counter-balanced by Gogol's faith in the vast sweep of Russia's future. He thus endeared himself both to the Slavophiles, who were delighted by his 'apotheosis of the national character,' and to the Westernizers, who hailed his exposé of social and moral backwardness. *Dead Souls* was an artistic condemnation of that 'revolting reality' that the intellectuals of the 'forties rejected on rational grounds. Annenkov, the friend, biographer, and critic of great writers of his period, read Gogol's poetic novel and wrote to Belinsky: 'Why do such loathsome people exist in Russia, why do such incredible things take place in our homeland, how can such opinions, attitudes, utterances come into being without evoking horror?'

Gogol expressed the negative attitude of a generation that sensed its tragic conflict with its environment and tried to solve the problem of national consciousness—the same problem that Gogol, without being fully aware of the impact of his work, raised by his portrayal of Russian mentality and its distortions. Not interested in philosophy, science, or world literature, he had but a dim comprehension of social problems (one would look in vain for any indictment of serfdom in *Dead Souls* or elsewhere in his work) and shared the ideas of neither the Slavo-philes nor the Westernizers. But he had, as the critic Ovsianiko-Kulikovsky has pointed out, the psychological or psychopathological equivalent of their *Weltanschauung*. He communicated with the

[3] *Chichikov's Journeys (Dead Souls)*, Readers Club, New York, 1942. Quoted by the kind permission of the publisher.

world through his special artistic antennae, his sensitivity or receptivity providing him with a certain sixth sense. 'His organism is of a different make,' Aksakov has stated. He was not good at rationalization or abstract thinking, and all his attempts to formulate ideas ended in miserable failure. As Leo Tolstoy said, Gogol 'had an enormous talent, a beautiful heart, and a small, timid, fearful mind': but his intuition and emotions were daring and unerring. As he said himself, he felt 'the frightful, shocking mire of trifles, and all the significance of banal, isolated characters.'

Sensitive, morbid, unbalanced, enclosed in his world, he was deprived of love, of women, of the simple and natural joys of existence. He was absorbed by the 'workings of his soul,' by his ill health, by his longing for contemplation and a saintly life. The sensational reception of *Dead Souls* upset and frightened him. In 1842, upon his return to Rome, he decided to withdraw from society and devote himself to religious meditation.

He was in an appalling physical and psychical state. This frail man with his long nose, pointed chin, hollow cheeks, and unhealthy complexion, his thin body supported by short and crooked legs, his jerky movements, and the high-pitched voice of a eunuch, looked like a clown or a martyr. ('Charlatan or martyr,' Aksakov called him; 'What a shrewd, sickly, and weird creature,' said Turgenev.) He was still able to tell funny stories and to laugh, but his laughter was constantly interrupted by tears and fits of depression, and his chuckles often turned into moans. At any rate, he could hardly restrain his laughter; it was inseparable from his melancholy. 'I laughed to fight off my anguish,' he confessed. 'To entertain myself I imagined all sorts of funny things.' 'My character was rather melancholic and inclined to meditation,' he wrote to Zhukovsky. But the laughter always overcame him; he could not resist this irrepressible desire for drawing caricatures. Like Victor Hugo's *L'Homme qui rit,* the more he tried to seem serious the larger his grin appeared. This was his tragedy; it gnawed at him day and night, because he simply could not bear the world he himself had brought to life. That world, as Valery Briussov has remarked, resembles the horrible throng of repulsive masks in Poe's 'The Masque of the Red Death.'

He was surrounded by an unbearable void, from which rose nightmarish visions of God's wrath and an agonizing dread of death. Was he not a great sinner? Had he not laughed at everything, had he not represented all sorts of horrible and contemptible things, even as the painter in his 'The Portrait' had done?

He did not want to be a mirror for the reflection of distorted monster faces. Gogol had a lofty idea of his poetic mission; he wanted to serve

God through his writings, to give his readers edifying examples of goodness. These ideals determined the general outline of Part II of *Dead Souls*. For more than three years, amidst seizures of illness, the horror of death, mystical exaltation and spiritual prostration, Gogol wrote and rewrote the further adventures of Chichikov. He created a new gallery of portraits and sketches of the provincial gentry. Some of them, such as those of the glutton Pietukh or the blustering, guffawing General Petrishchev, are in the old line of grotesque, but others deal with a type of landowner not fully treated before, such as Khlobuev and, in particular, Tentetnikov. The latter is intelligent, well educated, kind-hearted, but lazy and sluggish. He is an idler and a drifter, one of those lonely souls of the 'forties who belonged to the long series of 'superfluous men'—or rather, noblemen. In his way he is a precursor of Goncharov's Oblomov and he also serves as a span from Gogolian monsters to more positive types. Tentetnikov longs to accomplish things but never succeeds in overcoming his impotence; while real things are accomplished by aggressive men, such as Murazov the tax-farmer and the gentleman-farmer Kostanzhoglo (also called, in some texts, Skuldvonzhoglo.) The latter, according to Gogol's plan, was intended to be a combination of all the moral virtues and practicality: it was such men as he who were to promote Russia's material progress. Yet while the negative or ridiculous characters of Part II are alive and vivid, the positive protagonists, such as Kostanzhoglo-Skudvonzhoglo, Murazov, and the princely administrator, all prove to be bloodless and unconvincing.

The plot of Part II, much more involved than that of Part I, fails to convince. Gogol had planned to describe the collapse of Chichikov's scheme, his arrest and repentance, the intervention of the gold-hearted millionaire, and finally the hero's release and his moral crisis, which was to hold forth a promise of reform and ultimate salvation. But Gogol did not succeed in making his religious ideas triumph through artistic exposition, and he knew that he had failed. Disgusted with himself, exhausted by the constant inner conflict between the artist attracted by laughter, triviality, and the ludicrous, and the anchorite who believed in divine retribution, moral preachments, and Christian humility, in 1845 Gogol burned a preliminary draft of Part II of his novel during one of his fits of hypochondria.

His next move was to try to fulfil his duty as a writer by simply telling his beliefs in journalistic form. Between bouts of illness, mystical visitations, and paroxysms of despair, he compiled and issued in 1847 a new book: *Select Passages from Correspondence with Friends*. While it did contain many interesting thoughts, especially those dealing with

180   THE EPIC OF RUSSIAN LITERATURE

literature and the theater, the central idea of the book shocked even the pinkest of liberals: in his religious zeal Gogol attempted to accept and to justify all the vile things he had so efficiently (if unwillingly) exposed in his previous work. He hailed despotism and blind obedience to the Church and asserted that literacy was harmful to the people, that serfdom was a wholesome patriarchal institution, that capital and corporal punishments were excellent, that fear was the best foundation for family life, that no reforms in the administration of justice were necessary, and so on. The whole spirit of the book exuded unbounded submissiveness, coupled with conservative obscurantism. Tolstoy's characterization of Gogol can be fully applied to the book: 'As soon as he attempts to write on religious-moral subjects, or to attach a morally religious and edifying aspect to the artistic works he has already written, he creates horribly revolting rubbish.'

Belinsky's indignant review of the *Selections* deeply affected Gogol, and he wrote to his former friend. Belinsky's reply could not be published, but it attained an enormous underground circulation. The police did their utmost to hunt down copies of this masterpiece, which was to become the credo of Russian radicalism, and those found in possession of the *Letter* were thrown in jail or exiled.

Belinsky's *Letter,* as well as the indignant reaction of many of his friends, dealt another blow to Gogol. The failure of the *Selections* was one of the factors that impelled him to return to literature. He affirmed now that his duty consisted of making peace with life through art. 'It is true,' he wrote to Zhukovsky after the completion of his *Confessions of An Author* (1847), which constituted his apologia for having written the *Selections,* 'that it is not my task to edify others with sermons. My task is to talk in living images. I ought to show the face of life and not to argue about it.'

In 1848 he resumed work on Part II of *Dead Souls.* His physical condition and his mental state were, however, extremely poor. He went on a pilgrimage to Palestine, but the whole journey passed in a sort of haze and brought him no spiritual help. After endless traveling and suffering he returned to Russia, where his life was one prolonged agony. He had no money, his health was declining so rapidly that he had to stay in bed for months, he had hallucinations and was often haunted by the thought that, as a writer, he had sold his soul to the devil, and he longed to atone for his great sins. In his rare moments of calm he wrote and corrected Part II of *Dead Souls.* It progressed slowly, but the few chapters he read to his friends aroused their enthusiasm: here was the true Gogol, brilliant, keen, and witty.

But it was these qualities of his work that tormented him: his main purpose was to lead his readers toward truth, light, God—toward 'man's high destiny'—yet no sooner did he sit down at his desk than his pen, as if possessed, began to depict the contemptible and vile. Instead of godlike images he created demons, swinish snouts, eccentrics, monsters. Whatever he touched became shallow, nonsensical, hideous, or droll; everything turned to derision, and that derisive laughter, that destructive demoniacal laughter, resounded in his ears. Was he not the prey of the Fiend?

Such was the opinion of his father confessor, the morose and ignorant monk Matthew, who assailed his writings and frightened him with the torments of Hell if he did not renounce his art. Father Matthew pressed him to repudiate Pushkin, 'a sinner and a heathen,' and to renounce that 'snare of the Devil,' literature. Shattered by visions of the horrors of Hell, exhausted by fasting and prayer, Gogol made the supreme act of penitence: weeping bitterly, he burned the manuscript of Part II of *Dead Souls,* the fruit of four years of effort, pain, and joy.[4] This sacrifice, however, brought his complete collapse, and twelve days later (21 February 1852) Gogol died. Thousands of people followed him to his grave. A peasant woman looked at the crowd and asked:

'Who's dead? Are all these people his relatives?'

'His name is Gogol,' someone answered her, 'and all Russians are his relatives.'

---

[4] Some excerpts of Part II of *Dead Souls* were found in the initial drafts Gogol had forgotten to destroy. They give only an approximate and incomplete idea of the text he had thrown into the flames.

9

CRITICAL REALISM: GONCHAROV AND OSTROVSKY

I   GOGOL'S contemporaries did not pay much attention to his personal tragedy. They admired his work mainly as an exposé of the black injustice of Russian life. For them he was the greatest critical Realist; his laughter was interpreted as a crushing blow to the affectations of the Romantics; his representations of everyday life and of banal, everyday characters were counter to the craze for the unusual and for the saturnine, black-caped hero; while Gogol's language and his informal, homely style were considered efficient weapons for the Natural school. Gogol had achieved the same reform in prose that Pushkin had accomplished in verse, and this facet of his work carried greater weight than his lyricism or his mysterious symbolic passages. Naturalness in approach and style, observation as method, critical analysis of life material as artistic principle: those were the slogans of the period associated with Gogol's name. Between the publication of *Dead Souls* (1842) and the death of its author (1852), the Realistic school affirmed itself through such works as Nekrassov's anthologies, *The Physiology of St. Petersburg* and *St. Petersburg* (the latter, published in January 1846, included Dostoevsky's 'Poor Folk'); tales of peasant life (*The Village* in 1846 and *Anton Goremyka* in 1847) by Dimitri Grigorovich (1822-99), a highly popular sentimental realist; *Polinka Sachs* (1846), a novel by Alexander Druzhinin (1825-64), storyteller, critic, and connoisseur of English literature; Turgenev's *Hunting Sketches;* short stories and novelettes about common folk by Lugansky the Cossack, who, under his real name of Vladimir Dahl (1801-72), compiled the valuable and fascinating *Dictionary of the Living Great Russian Tongue* and made a monumental collection of Russian proverbs; tales by Count Vladimir Sollogub (1814-82), author of the well-known novelette, *The Coach,* and by Jacob Butkov (1815-56); the first plays by Ostrovsky; and, last but not least, *A Common Story* by Goncharov, who was destined to be so important in the final triumph of the Realistic movement.

Ivan Alexandrovich Goncharov, born in 1812, in Simbirsk, a small town on the Volga, belonged to a family of grain merchants who had made their way into the nobility. Three main influences helped to form his character and his opinions: the patriarchal and torpid atmosphere in which he spent his childhood and which was responsible for his indolence, for the leisurely pace of his orderly existence, and for his very appearance—that of an unhurried, well-fed gentleman; the University of Moscow, where he spent three years acquiring certain vaguely idealistic tendencies; and, finally, his connection with the St. Petersburg bureaucracy, which began in 1834 and lasted for over thirty years. Stout, heavy, impassive, and pensive, with rather somnolent eyes, he looked a typical governmental official—and was. His rise was slow but steady: in 1856 he was appointed censor to the Ministry of Education and subsequently held various posts until his retirement in 1867. The routine of his career was monotonous and irksome, but the remuneration was a matter of necessity to him. His personal life was singularly uneventful and devoid of excitement. Having been disappointed in love, he became a confirmed bachelor and found his only compensation in writing. He wrote slowly and painfully, his literary projects usually undergoing a long maturing process: it took him ten years to write *Oblomov* (1849-59) and the same length of time to complete *The Precipice* (1859-69), although the ideas for these works had been gestating in his mind for over twenty years.

The publication of *A Common Story* (1847), when he was thirty-five, had been preceded by a long training which included poetry, short stories, and translations. It was acclaimed by the critics and the public. Partly autobiographical, it dealt with a provincial young man, Alexander Aduev, who comes to St. Petersburg to win fame, love, and friendship. Alexander writes sentimental poems, talks about Greatness and Beauty, shuns work, which he finds dull, and spends his time in idealistic day-dreaming or emotional outbursts. However, this romantic youth is taught a harsh lesson by his Uncle Peter, a successful bureaucrat, the owner of glass and porcelain works, and a man of action, culture, and rational positivism. Their endless discussions gradually destroy Alexander's illusions. Younger men, claims Uncle Peter, ought to throw overboard all their lofty concepts of poetry and glory: what they really need is science, business, work. To his edifying sermons Uncle Peter adds certain concrete measures: he papers the walls of a room with his nephew's poems while the poet himself is made to translate French and German articles on agriculture. Alexander does his best to catch up with sober reality. He gets a start as a government clerk and in ten or twelve years is a new man—without the author explaining, however, how the change has actually come about. He has shed his hair together with his illusions and acquired a little paunch instead; he is about to marry a girl with a dowry of 500 serfs and 300,000 rubles in cash. The soaring Romantic has turned into a solid citizen, a good second-rate bureaucrat—hence the title of *A Common Story.*[1]

Goncharov's sympathies are definitely with Uncle Peter, who stands for the triumph of the city over the backwoods. The author intimates that bureaucrats of the new order are different from the Gogolian monsters, that they represent the material progress of Russia.

Belinsky called *A Common Story* a 'blow to Romanticism, daydreaming, sentimentality, provincialism,' and proclaimed it an example of critical Realism. The reading public enjoyed the spirit of the book as well as its simple construction, its easy although somewhat bookish dialogue, the fullness of its details, the abundant flow of the narrative, and its many social implications. Social realism and literary realism were happily mated in this work, which may seem somewhat schematic to us now but, in 1847, represented intense realism.

Goncharov was trying to portray representative types of Russian society, and this was the aim of *Oblomov,* his best and most popular novel, brought out in 1859. In this monumental work, which in bulk and construction resembles the Victorian three-decker novel, Goncharov intensified and enlarged his critical analysis of provincial Romanticism. But his indictment, now directed against the whole way of life based on serfdom, here took on a broader scope.

Ilya Oblomov, the hero of the novel, had been raised in Oblomovka, an estate on the Volga river, a thousand miles from Moscow, where the patriarchal mode of life was ordained by lethargy and tradition. Wrapped in cotton-wool, pampered, and spoiled, little Ilya is helped in everything by the many serfs whose sole purpose in life is to catch the least word or glance of their masters. No work is ever expected of him. Hundreds of serfs toil and moil for Ilya—and for all the other Ilyas of Russia, big and little. In a chapter entitled 'Oblomov's Dream' (published separately, with great success, in 1849) Goncharov gives Oblomov's recollections of Oblomovka, that slumbrous Land of Cockaigne, with its sweet pastries, endless tea drinking, thick feather beds, and insidious indolence.

---

[1] It would be interesting to compare it with Balzac's *Lost Illusions* and Flaubert's *Sentimental Education.*

Ilya's childhood ends when 'ominous rumors began to spread even in Oblomovka that mere literacy no longer sufficed: those of the nobility had now to learn all sorts of unheard-of sciences.' Young Oblomov is sent to school and later enters a university. But education can change neither his temperament nor the habits he has acquired during his tender years; he is lazy and immature. But he is not a bad man—actually he is kindhearted, intelligent and amiable. Like his literary predecessor, Gogol's Tentetnikov, he manages to learn a great deal at the university and, although his knowledge is sketchy and he lacks the sacred flame of the men of the 'forties, he has an idealistic bent and his intentions are excellent. In his early youth he has even talked of being of service to his country. But all his projects are nipped in the bud by his inability to act. After an unsuccessful stretch in the Civil Service, Oblomov retires before he is thirty. Now he can lounge all day on his sofa, contemplating the vague contours of his reveries and bickering with his morose valet Zakhar. There is an indestructible bond between master and servant: one can not live without the other; both are the end-products of the same way of life.

Oblomov has no material worries and can glide along peacefully from one day to the next. He drops his friends one by one, shrinks from social obligations, hardly reads, puts off the writing of a letter for weeks—he is simply happy being lazy. Living is a burden, and Oblomov shies away from it. He even tries to tell Zakhar that daydreaming is as important as any other 'activity.' Sometimes he explains his attitude by saying: 'I know, I understand everything, but I have no will power.' On another occasion he justifies himself by advancing the claim that, since he is a gentleman, he was not born to work. When Zakhar sets other people up as examples for him, Oblomov is offended: he belongs among those privileged ones who, thank God, have no need of rushing about, who have plenty to eat and are well off. This conscientious idler seeks to escape from life into the protective warmth of his carefree childhood, and his friends invent a name for his attitude: *oblomovshchina* or *oblomovism*. He objects to this terminology and, although not an intellectual, he tries to rationalize his behavior. It is man's nature to aspire to tranquility. Even those who work and worry (or 'torment themselves,' as he puts it) have security, retirement, and rest as their ultimate goals. Fame is 'an honorable leisure in which one enjoys recognition and well-deserved peace.'

This almost Buddhistic concept is upset when Oblomov falls in love with Olga—a resolute foe of oblomovism—a delectably feminine young girl endowed with brains and a desire for action. 'Love and life are the same for me,' she declares to Oblomov. 'And life is duty, responsi-

bility—and so is love.' Of course, she is bent on 'saving' Oblomov and
sees herself as a physician confronted by a difficult case. Her strong
personality, charm, and moral integrity act as a powerful tonic on him.
At one moment he seems ready to overcome his sluggishness: he runs
Olga's errands, pays calls, takes long walks, resumes reading, and
formulates ambitious plans. But this transformation is no more than a
fire of straw: his love for Olga requires too much exertion. In the final
struggle between his desire for tranquility and his love for Olga inertia
is the victor.

The collapse of their love affair is painful for both. Olga falls ill and
goes abroad, where she meets Stolz, a man of action, whom she eventually marries. However, she is too active and independent to be satisfied
with the bourgeois happiness Stolz offers her; she is constantly afraid of
oblomovism. Oblomov, after a brain fever, relapses into his routine of
endless siestas. Now he is done for. He settles down as a roomer in the
suburban house of Agatha Matveyevna, an ignorant, prosaic, but kindhearted widow who gives him the illusion of having happily returned to
Oblomovka and his boyhood. To Agatha Matveyevna he is a gentleman,
and she serves him as a slave, attends to his whims, pawns her pearls
to feed him better, shares his opinion that idleness is a mark of nobility,
seeks happiness in food, sleep, and indolence. Oblomov marries her and
on her ample bosom finds his 'undisturbed peace of life,' his modest and
sloppy nirvana.

In the person of his hero, Goncharov condemned the whole way of
life of the patriarchal and conservative petty nobility. On the other hand,
he intimated that Oblomov's horror of activity might be a national
trait. Dobroliubov, the young critic whose famous essay, *What is
Oblomovism?*, set a pattern for the interpretation of the novel, contended
that the superfluous noblemen portrayed in Russian literature of the
'thirties and 'forties—Pushkin's Oneghin, Lermontov's Pechorin, Herzen's Beltov, Turgenev's Rudin, and, in particular, Gogol's Manilov and
Tentetnikov—had been more or less infected with the virus of oblomovism. All these characters shared a common disposition for day-
dreaming, rationalizing, and passivity. Their humanitarian longings had
no relation to their everyday lives. They varied in temperament and
personality, of course, but they were equally inefficient and socially
worthless. What made Oblomov different was that, not belonging to the
intelligentsia, he did not share its liberal aspirations, he was a supporter
of serfdom, and his utterances were similar to those of Gogol in his
Selections. Oblomovism, as a result of slave labor and a patriarchal way
of life, infected the bureaucracy and the middle class as well as the petty
nobility. It was therefore a typically Russian defect.

Later on Lenin expanded Dobroliubov's formula: 'The Oblomovs are not only the landowners but also the peasants, intellectuals, workmen, and communists. The old Oblomov still lives, and we must wash and scrub and shake and push him around to make him sensible and useful.' Dobroliubov considered that 'oblomovism was the key to many a riddle of Russian life,' and that Goncharov had made an enormous contribution to literature by describing this important phenomenon. At the beginning of the twentieth century some Russian critics also enlarged Dobroliubov's interpretation. According to them oblomovism was not only psychological conservatism, an escape from reality, and a complex of immaturity with the subsequent idealization of infantilism, but it was also a sign of Oriental fatalism: Oblomov does not want to be an agent in the process of history; he reflects the attitude of so many Russians who believe that individual intervention in current events is useless and that a perfect *laissez-faire* inactivity is the highest expression of wisdom.

Whatever the subsequent generalizations on oblomovism may have been, at the time of its publication Goncharov's novel struck its readers by its peculiar tone. The former 'superfluous heroes' of Russian literature all had had a slight Romantic tinge. Oblomov had none; he was mercilessly revealed: he was not put up on any polished pedestal but was made to sprawl on an old sofa. His condemnation was stressed by the portrayal of Stolz, the antithetic figure of the novel, whose half-German origin emphasized the truly Russian nature of oblomovism. Stolz, Oblomov's schoolmate and friend, is a student of life, widely traveled, an excellent businessman, and an enlightened capitalist. This paragon of work and activity believed that initiative, practicality, and a spirit of enterprise would revive Russia and promote the material progress the country needed so badly. He is a typical representative of the late 'fifties and early 'sixties, when the bourgeois way of life was about to replace serfdom, and the advent of a down-to-earth rationalism was welcomed by a large segment of public opinion. This new bourgeois is not an obscurantist like Gogol's Kostanzhoglo; Stolz does not merely dream of railroads, ports, and plants; he also wants schools, good books, education, a free press, and justice based on law. Naturally, Stolz also stands for psychological change. Oblomov thrives on his imagination—Stolz relies on experience and facts; Oblomov is an idler and a gentleman—Stolz is a builder and a businessman; Oblomov dreams—Stolz acts; Oblomov is superstitious, inclined to vague mysticism—Stolz is rational and reasonable. This energetic and optimistic positivist knows where he is going, and his strong will power is well controlled and regulated. Stolz gets everything he goes after: he marries Olga, becomes the manager of the Oblomovka estate, and undertakes the education of Oblomov and Agatha's son.

Goncharov placed all his hopes for Russia's future in people such as the uncle in *A Common Story* and Stolz. Their creator could not realize that all these businessmen and bureaucrats had no program of social or political reform, that they were practical without being constructive and without understanding all the issues of Russia's complex make-up. Dobroliubov hinted at this by saying that 'Stolz has not yet risen to the level of a socially minded citizen.'

It might be added that Stolz is hardly convincing artistically. The author talks a great deal about him but hardly ever shows him in action. As a character he is pale and abstract, an *a priori* creature used as a contrast necessary for affirmation to Oblomov. Stolz certainly lacks the completeness and sharpness of all the other characterizations in the novel.

Goncharov, on the whole, had little success with his positivist heroes, as was shown again in his third novel, *The Precipice* (1869). Despite long years of germination and writing, *The Precipice,* a highly popular work, is definitely inferior to *Oblomov* and glaringly displays all of Goncharov's weaknesses as a writer. The setting of the novel is again Russia on the eve of the abolition of serfdom, but its hero, Raisky, is an awakened Oblomov. A man of talent, impressionable and emotional, Raisky shifts from music to painting, from painting to writing, and from writing to sculpture. The idealistic tendencies of the 'forties in his case take the form of estheticism. Though not afflicted by Oblomov's laziness, he is nevertheless still incapable of systematic effort. He lacks patience, endurance, earnestness; his life is as irregular and frivolous as his character. After having failed as an officer and as a civil servant, he wants to be an artist; yet there is no place for a professional artist in aristocratic society, and Raisky comes to the conclusion that all fields of activity are closed to him. He substitutes art for life (which makes him highly revealing as autobiography) and his painting and writing are forms of self-compensation. He has overcome Oblomov's passivity, but not to the extent of becoming a useful member of society.

He works by fits and starts, has attacks of ennui, and needs a change of scene or some new passion to keep his interest alive. All his ardors, whether for pretty women or alluring projects, die down as quickly as they flare up. In Malinovka, his hereditary estate, to which he returns after an unsuccessful attempt to awaken passion in a frigid St. Petersburg lady, Raisky meets two cousins of his: the naive, buxom Marfinka, the embodiment of health and all domestic virtues, and the proud, wilful, and independent Vera. Raisky falls madly in love with Vera and commits many indiscretions and follies, only to discover that she is attracted by Mark Volokhov, a ne'er-do-well and a political exile under police surveillance. He is a cynical materialist with exaggerated manners, ready to rob any orchard of respectability or to borrow money he never intends to repay. His contempt of routine, his disregard of convention, and his advocation of free love appeal to Vera's imagination. Partly hoping to reform this black sheep, partly swept away by passion, she gives herself to Volokhov under highly dramatic circumstances. But their love has no future; Vera's madness is short-lived and as devastating as a thunderstorm. Volokhov decamps, and Vera realizes that she was wrong in rebelling against her environment. Her Grandmother Berezhkova was right: the simple, patriarchal, and time-honored life is far superior to the illusions of pride and sophistication. And as Raisky, who has become her friend, goes abroad, Vera waits for time to heal her wounds and make her responsive to the love of Tushin, an upright, honest landowner and businessman.

Although Tushin is a lumber king, the author avoids making him a second Stolz. During the ten years that separate *Oblomov* from *The Precipice,* Goncharov's hopes in the salutary role of the bourgeoisie had undergone some changes. The danger of the revolutionary radicalism of the 'sixties had prompted him to idealize Oblomovka and to seek salvation in patriarchal conservatism. Grandmother Berezhkova, a magnificent character, represents the common sense, the human warmth, and the wisdom of a woman who is faithful to Russian traditions and has remained whole and harmonious, even in her defects—her quick temper, her benevolent despotism, her superstitions and snobbishness. She personifies Russia, as does Tushin, a simple man, yet 'our true party of action,' as Goncharov introduces him. Tushin has sprung from Russian soil, lives in the wild forest region beyond the Volga, looks like a bear, and is endowed with physical strength matched only by his moral probity. Vera's adherence to both him and her grandmother has a profound symbolic and social significance.

Goncharov was against the Oblomovs and hoped that they would be replaced by the Stolzes. However, when the younger generation of the 'sixties rallied to socialism and radicalism, evincing no desire to become businessmen, Goncharov grew sentimental over 'good old Russia' and contrasted it with the 'folly of nihilistic reformers.' This attitude explains many of the novel's faults: the exaggerated and highly ridiculous, almost absurd, portrayal of Volokhov, who is so much of a villain that he seems unwilling to do even the simplest things in an ordinary way; the wan and unreal figure of Tushin, whose main virtues have to be imagined; the lack of verisimilitude in the most dramatic episodes of Vera's love affair; and a downright lack of taste or artistic restraint in several passages in which the author insists on explaining the meaning of his story. At the same time Raisky, although overdone and slightly boring, Marfinka, Berezhkova, and certain incidental figures do come to life and are done in the best manner of the Realistic epic novel. Less convincing is Vera, although dozens of Russian critics claim that Vera, as well as Olga, initiated a succession of new and attractive feminine types in Russian literature. At any rate, the psychological validity of her return to the 'old truth' after her experience with Volokhov and of her desire to make this experience known to others is highly debatable. Here, as usual, Goncharov's artistic mastery is impaired by his striving to point a moral. Whenever he attempts to rationalize or generalize, he is at his worst: Raisky's disquisitions on passion are dull; the conservative opinions of Tushin and Grandmother Berezhkova are as vague and vapid as Volokhov's revolutionary pronouncements. Whenever Goncharov talks about morality he is as narrow-minded and irritating as any second-rate Victorian novelist. Goncharov's main defect is that he intrudes like a *raisonneur* in a French comedy; also he is guilty of a senseless lengthiness and a certain laxity in the handling of his material. These latter drawbacks were, however, inherent in the very spirit of his writings. He represented with the copiousness of a Flemish painter the minute details of reality. Poet of indoors, lover of the domestic scene, he is at his best in still life, in the rendering of the simple rites of existence.

In 1852-5 he made a trip around the world as the secretary of an expedition sponsored by the government, and he wrote a lengthy description of this one and only adventure of his life. But from the two volumes of his *Frigate Pallas* (1856), still in many ways an excellent book of travel, we learn that he had no feeling for exotic countries. His descriptions of nature are rather scanty; what interested him, whether in Japan, India, or China, was the way people walked, dressed, and ate. This is indicative of his artistic method. His placid, moderately witty style resembles, as a Russian critic put it, 'a room with easy chairs, heavy drapes, and soft carpets, where footsteps are muffled and the discordant notes of passion are muted.'

Goncharov is in no such hurry as Gogol, whose cascading and changeable style reflects the inner restlessness of the author; Goncharov ambles along, like a man who has plenty of time on his hands and assumes that his reader is in the same position. Patiently, precisely, without missing any detail, he describes the preparation of food in Oblomovka or Malinovka, the thoughts of Oblomov or his conversations with Zakhar, or the crockery in Agatha's pantry. Utensils, clothes, objects, play an important part in his novels, and often they become highly significant: Zakhar's jacket, torn at the armpits; the swing of the pendulum in Agatha's clock, the singing of her canary, or the sound of her coffee-mill. Even his similes have a substantial, earthy savor (China is for him 'a chest filled with old lumber').

The same method is applied to the portrayal of the characters: each one is shown from every angle, analyzed minutely, explained thoroughly. The thoroughness, the insight, the plastic relief of representation, the artful distribution of light and shade, and the whole system of images that form the backbone in the skeletal structure of his novels, all are truly admirable, even though they may occasionally provoke a feeling of satiety and leave little to the imagination.

Goncharov possessed all the qualities that made the Russian novel such a revelation to the West. He discarded complicated plots, adventurous or surprising incidents, and the long arm of coincidence—in short, all the tricks of the shilling shocker and the penny dreadful. The only thrill to be found in his works—as in the works of all great Russian Realists—lay in the illusion of life, the faithful reproduction of its flow, the penetrating portrayal of every character. The whole fabric of Goncharov's novels is made up of the solid material of life. It is for this reason that the element of time plays such a prominent role: while unrolling his panorama the writer conveys a feeling of the 'march of life'—the narrative flows on like a river, and we follow all its twists and turns. In Goncharov this river-like quality, which brings him close to Tolstoy, has a majestic pace and a simple stateliness, which command respect.

Dobroliubov has pointed out that Goncharov paid equal attention to all the details of his narrative: the same even, well-regulated light illuminates his lengthy descriptions and his frequently repetitious dialogues. The action unfolds slowly and usually runs along two parallel lines: Oblomov's love for Olga has a counterpart in Stolz's love for her; Raisky's passion for Vera is balanced by Vera's feelings for Volokhov, and so on. This device is enhanced by the antithesis of contrasting characters: Oblomov and Stolz, Marfinka and Vera, Olga and Agatha Matveyevna, Volokhov and Tushin, Alexander Aduev and his uncle. Even in his most dramatic passages, such as those in *The Precipice,* the voice of the narrator is seldom stirred by emotion: it maintains its even tone and balance. However, this tranquility, this indulgent humor and common sense, combined with a sort of reasonable down-to-earth quality, do not imply that Goncharov's art barred personal evaluation, as preached by the Naturalists. His novels undoubtedly reflect his own life; in fact, it would be rather difficult to talk about his objectivity, since he shows so clearly his preferences and opinions, his likes and dislikes. He constantly takes his stand and never misses a chance to inform his reader what he thinks about his own heroes, and the sententious way he judges them adds a peculiar flavor to his writings. Chekhov disliked it so much that he excluded Goncharov from his list of literary demigods, to which the creator of Oblomov clearly belongs.

That Goncharov's opinions are occasionally flat and their expression pedestrian is due not only to his way of being moralistic and rational; despite his placid exterior he was a man of many contradictions and unsettled drives. He had the ideas of a Stolz, the temperament of an Oblomov, and the yearnings of a Raisky. At heart he leaned toward simplicity, a patriarchal way of living, art for art's sake. It was for these reasons that he depicted his Marfinkas and Berezhkovas with such love. His positive types were more the products of his head than of his heart. Born a realist, he became a Critical Realist because he wanted to respond to the social demands of his times. However, too much weight should not be attached to his declarations that his three novels reflected three decades of Russian life. It would be more appropriate to call them three variations on the same theme, and that theme was Oblomov. He explored and described this type thoroughly—and therein lies his chief merit. An ethical problem underlies all his reproductions of reality, and this trait is as typical of the Russian Realistic current as of the whole pattern of Russian literature. Goncharov felt obliged to conform to the general trend and to be something more than an artist—a preacher.

After the 'sixties Goncharov produced nothing save a few sketches, recollections, and articles—of which 'A Million Torments,' about Griboyedov, was remarkably well done. With advancing old age he grew pathologically nervous, suffered from a persecution mania, and wrote slanderous pamphlets against his chief rival, Turgenev, accusing him of plagiarism and of having given to Flaubert and Auerbach some of his plots and ideas. For many years he was one of the few surviving representatives of the Gogol period in Russian literature, and the only really great one among them. He died in 1891, surrounded by that respectful indifference usually accorded to old artists who have outlived themselves.

II   The Patrician Writers of the 'fifties, living on their country estates or in their Moscow mansions, hardly ever gave a thought to the fact that just across the Moscow River there was a whole district of the city populated with peculiar people who looked and acted as if they had come from some other planet. There were bearded merchants, firmly convinced that the earth rested on the backs of three whales, Old Believers (or Schismatics) who would never commit the sin of making the sign of the cross with three fingers, sleek shopkeepers who, in their households, adhered to the traditions of the seventeenth century.

This world of grain dealers, shopkeepers, middlemen, swindlers, shysters, matchmakers, and topers was discovered and introduced into Russian literature by Alexander Ostrovsky (1823-86). He knew them well, for he was born and lived among them. The son of a poor government clerk, Alexander had spent his childhood in the sedate streets of the 'Across-the-River' quarter, where the clumsily but solidly built houses were surrounded by truck patches and neglected gardens characteristic of their owners. Later on he attended the Law School at the University of Moscow, but did not graduate, and wound up as a clerk in the Court of Equity and the Court of Commerce. In both places he found ample opportunities to study the peculiar Russian breed of merchants and middle-class folk, whose private lives erupted in lawsuits and feuds. At this time his father had resigned from office and had begun practicing as a pettifogger—and from his clients Ostrovsky added to his wealth of observations. In this manner he gathered an enormous amount of material and gained a deep insight into the manners and mentality of a whole class of people that until then, as he claimed, had been 'veiled in the night of ignorance.' In 1856 he undertook a long journey in the Volga region which also enriched his fund of facts, stories, types, and incidents.

As far back as 1847 Ostrovsky had begun to describe the folk 'Across-the-River' in scenes that were later incorporated in his comedy, *It's All in the Family*. The first draft of this play, entitled *The Bankrupt,* had been frequently read aloud in the literary salons of Moscow, at one of which Gogol had heard and liked the piece. Although the play won acclaim, it offended the Moscow merchants and exasperated the authorities. In 1850 Ostrovsky was forced to resign from his position and was put under police surveillance. Until 1861 the censors refused to pass the comedy for stage production either in Moscow or St. Petersburg. Between 1850 and 1861, however, Ostrovsky wrote and produced eleven other plays (among them such masterpieces as *Poverty No Disgrace, The Poor Bride, The Thunderstorm*) which assured his success. In the 'sixties he dominated the theater as the creator of a truly national repertoire.

Despite the opposition of influential noblemen, who complained that his plays 'had the fusty smell of the sheepskin coats of peasants and tradesmen,' Ostrovsky won immediate recognition. It was mainly owing to the subject matter and the realism of his plays. He did in the theater what Gogol and Goncharov had accomplished in fiction: instead of the melodramas and lewd farces (mostly translations) that crowded the stage at that time, he offered dramas and comedies whose characters and plots were part of life in Russia, solidly rooted in native soil and genuinely national. The novelty of his subject matter bordered on revelation. The merchants from 'Across-the-River' described by this literary Columbus were not merely illustrative of one class; their psychology and manners belonged to various strata of Russian society.

It was a peculiar world in which crass ignorance was blended with superstition, and the authoritarian pattern of family relation, a rapacious attitude toward property, and mistreatment of the helpless were regarded as perfectly normal. Education hardly crossed the threshold of the stuffy households of Ostrovsky's characters. Some of them, such as the frivolous Lipochka in *It's All in the Family,* were convinced that the highest manifestations of culture consisted of fashionable dress and a parrot-like repetition of two or three phrases in French. His provincial characters did not go even as far as that. In *The Thunderstorm* the merchants of Kalinov, a small town on the Volga and completely cut off from the world, believe any nonsense told them by pilgrims and wandering nuns—that there are dog-headed men living overseas, that the whole world, with the exception of Russia, is divided between two sultans, the Turkish and the Persian, and so on. Dikoi (Wild Man), the tycoon of the town, becomes quite wroth when he hears that thunderstorms are caused by electricity and that lightning can be neutralized by conducting rods. 'What foolishness!' he shouts. 'A thunderstorm is sent us as a visitation, and yet, the Lord forgive me, you want to defend yourself with rods and poles. What are you, a heathen?'

The moral standards had all the rigidity of the Middle Ages. Wives, children, shop clerks, and servants owed absolute obedience to the master. As head of the family and of his business he had unlimited rights and unchallenged authority. The whip hanging on the wall of an 'Across-the-River' bedroom, no mere symbol of masculine authority, was a frequently used instrument of punishment and persuasion. If you beat your wife, ran the proverb, the soup will taste better.

When Bolshov, in *It's All in the Family,* decides to marry off his daughter, he dismisses all the objections of Podkhalyuzin, whom he has chosen as his son-in-law, with: 'Isn't she my daughter? I made her, and I can do whatever I please with her.' The head of the family is convinced that the pattern of divine and social order consists of God in Heaven, the Czar on earth, the father at home, and the master at the shop. And this atmosphere of unlimited authority bred the *samodur,* or petty tyrant. In his comedy, *A Hangover from Other Folks' Wine,* Ostrovsky gives a definition of the *samodur:*

He's a man who won't listen to anybody or anything; you can split your guts trying to argue with him, but he'll always stick to his point. When he stamps his foot the whole household has to get down on their knees—or may God save us all! He's a wild, wilful man with a heart of stone.

Nor is he only a wilful person (and quite often a blockhead as well); he is given to moods, wants his whims to be taken as law, delights in inspiring fear, and is apt to make most contradictory and absurd decisions. In one of Ostrovsky's comedies the husband keeps thumping the table with his huge fist until his wife is all jittery, whereupon he laughs: 'It's nothing—I merely wanted to be sure and put fear into you. Now, what about some tea?'

The *samodur* enjoys humiliating those under him and usually brags about his money. Dikoi in *The Thunderstorm* boasts of being a Very Important Person, for he has plenty of money: 'You ought to know you're a worm,' he tells Kuligin, a poor inventor. 'I can spare you or crush you, just as I please.' For the sake of money he is ready to cheat and to commit all sorts of base actions, inasmuch as all *samodurs* realize that riches are the basis of authority. Considering property the only sign of achievement or success, they discard any moral or religious scruples when it comes to getting it. Bolshov, in *It's All in the Family,* stages a false bankruptcy to defraud his creditors, but is betrayed by his sneaky accomplice Podkhalyuzin. Korshunov, in *Poverty No Disgrace,* ruins his friend Lyubim, while Lyubim is thrown out into the street by his own brother. Old codgers or whippersnappers—both are equally birds of prey and no pity is shown by either in the ruthless game of acquisition.

The main conflicts in this 'reign of darkness' revolve around money and marriage. Fathers choose mates for their sons and daughters, often with the help of professional matchmakers. The problem of dowry is of primary importance: a poor girl, especially if she is pretty, is doomed to become a victim of lust and depravity, like Larissa, in *Dowerless,* one of Ostrovsky's best plays. In *Poverty No Disgrace* the rich merchant Tortsov suddenly decides that his daughter Lyubov is to marry Korshunov, a shady businessman who has driven his first wife to death by his cruel jealousy. And Lyubov, although she is in love with Mitya, a poor clerk, says to her father: 'I dare not disobey your command.' Everyone is perfectly aware that marrying Korshunov would be her ruin, yet no one voices a protest. Her mother knows of nothing better than to weep, and when Mitya proposes elopement Lyubov answers: 'I must submit to my father's will—such is a maiden's lot, and it must be right, since it has been so ordained from of old.' Fortunately her Uncle Luybim, an old drunkard, comes in just when the bridal feast is under way, accuses Korshunov of being a swindler and a criminal, and tries to awaken the better feelings of the girl's father.

In *The Thunderstorm* Katerina, married to Tikhon, suffers deeply from the prevalent hypocrisy and sanctimoniousness and from the domineering of her mother-in-law, the ruthless Kabanova. This female *samodur* is a despot who believes only in the observance of church ritual and in traditions: 'What will happen when we old folks die? How the world will remain in being I don't know!' For her the patriarchal past is the only fount of wisdom and decency. A similar attachment to the past assumes refined forms in such 'nests of gentlefolk' as Berezhkova's, but unfolds in all its crudeness and ugliness in the case of primitive and ignorant people such as Dikoi or Kabanova. Katerina, a sensitive, poetic nature with a profound longing for beauty and freedom, simply cannot comply with the rigid rules of Kabanova. She transgresses the moral code of her environment and, during the absence of her husband, yields to her love for Boris, a somewhat educated young man from Moscow, who is mistreated by his Uncle Dikoi. She pays dearly for her moment of passion and liberty. When Tikhon returns, Katerina cannot pretend and hide what she considers a mortal sin. During a thunderstorm she makes a public confession, and retaliation is swift in coming. Boris is packed off to a place on the Siberian border, without daring to protest. Tikhon, obeying his mother's instructions, suppresses his pity for his unfaithful wife and mistreats her, while Kabanova makes Katerina's life so miserable that finally she throws herself into the Volga.

Katerina, Boris, and the self-taught inventor Kulighin are all above their oppressive environment. 'We have hard ways in our town,' says Kulighin. 'You'll find nothing but coarseness and stark poverty here. Honest labor will never get you more than your daily bread. And whoever has money tries to enslave the poor, so as to get still more.' Boris, the best educated of the three, is too weak and dependent on others. And Kulighin, the *raisonneur* who dreams of solar clocks and lightning conductors, has but a vague hope that education and science will some day cure the ills of his native town.

Despite its tragic end, *The Thunderstorm* showed that there was a 'sunbeam in the realm of darkness,' the title of Dobroliubov's long article on the drama in 1860. Something had gone wrong in the authoritarian system of the Dikois and Kabanovas, those representatives of a new bourgeoisie, whose grasping domination had come to replace the old paternalism of the nobility. They ruled through fear, money, and aggressiveness, but Katerina, Boris, and Kulighin were so many threats to their power.

In addition to being a social drama, *The Thunderstorm* was a drama of tragic love, of a romantic soul whom the stone walls and bars of her domestic prison could not keep from passion. The interplay of realism and symbolic allusions, the drama of action and contrasting characters, the re-creation of a tense atmosphere of love and fate make this play Ostrovsky's best work. It shows the constant inner growth of its author.

In the early 'fifties Ostrovsky associated himself with the group of young Slavophiles connected with *The Muscovite*, a monthly, who acclaimed him as a 'painter of true Russian customs.' As a matter of fact, although Ostrovsky exposed the 'realm of darkness' in several of his first comedies (*It's All in the Family, The Poor Bride*), he also displayed a great deal of sympathy toward the old traditions. This was particularly true in *Know Your Place* (1855), whose heroes, Russakov and Borodkin, might be taken for paragons of the domestic virtues, and in *Poverty No Disgrace*, the very setting of which included the celebration of the Russian Christmas, with its songs, dances, mummers, and old customs. The scapegrace Lyubim Tortsov, who exposes Korshunov, awakens the conscience of his brother, and brings about a happy ending for the two young lovers, was interpreted by the Slavophiles as the embodiment of the 'Russian soul'—expansive, irrational, kind, human even in the slough of drunkenness—while Korshunov, an Anglophile and outwardly a Westernizer, symbolized the corrosive effect of kowtowing to foreigners. Lyubim's speech as he is shown the door: 'Lyubim Tortsov may be a drunkard but he's a better man than you—make way, Lyubim Tortsov is going!' never failed to bring down the house. Tortsov's brother is forever arguing with his wife, who upbraids him for no longer caring for any of 'our Russian ways.' He hires a butler in cotton gloves instead of a youth in a Russian smock or a peasant girl, because he wants to be 'in the swim,' for the same reason that Lipochka, in *It's All in the Family*, wants to learn French. 'Your fashionable falderols,' his wife assures him, 'change from day to day, while our Russian ways have lasted from time immemorial. Folks in the old days were just as smart as we are.'

The class of merchants Ostrovsky depicted was too close to the patriarchal peasantry from which it had sprung to forget the old traditions, some of which went back to the seventeenth century. The men and women of this class reflected the ways of life and characteristics typical of the agricultural population of the Russian steppes—lack of moderation, animal spirits, physical strength, wilfulness combined with

Byzantine formalism, a strict code of morals blended with wild impulses. In depicting characters that remained fundamentally Russian even to their eccentricities, Ostrovsky was accomplishing a profoundly national task. This was one of the reasons for his popularity among the Slavophiles. But his association with the *Muscovite* group soon came to an end. He could never be dogmatic and, for the sake of an abstract idea, 'arrange' the facts he had observed. The national traits in his heroes, such as Russakov, Borodkin, or Krasnov, or the idealization of a Lyubim Tortsov could not hide the despotism, ignorance, and other evils of the 'realm of darkness.'

Besides, the political events and the whole social atmosphere of the period contributed to the sharpening of his critical tendency. The disastrous outcome of the Crimean War proved the inefficiency of a regime based on serfdom, a corrupt bureaucracy, and a hierarchy of *samodurs,* great and small. The Slavophiles, boasting of Old Russia's integrity as opposed to the declining West, sounded none too convincing after the victory of decadent Europe over saintly Russia, and Ostrovsky definitely stressed the exposure and criticism in his plays. He became a regular contributor to *The Contemporary* and other reviews of the Westernizers. The liberals, as well as the radicals, saw in him one of their own, even though Ostrovsky never took any political stand and maintained friendly relations with many conservatives.

In 1856 he published *A Profitable Business,* the hero of which, Zhadov, refuses to follow the example of avaricious bureaucrats. An exposé of the latter forms the bulk of the comedy. It was followed, in 1859, by *The Mistress' Pet,* a caustic indictment of rural despotism and, in 1860, by *The Thunderstorm.*

As a writer of increasing reputation who refused to commit himself to any of the existing political or literary groups—except for his allegiance, in a broad sense of the term, to the Realistic movement—Ostrovsky was constantly expanding the range of his plays and turning to new topics that led him far from the world of the merchants. He portrayed the declining nobility in the comedy of *Wild Money,* devoted a series of excellent plays to the life of provincial actors (*The Forest* and *Talents and Suitors* are the best of these), tried his hand at historical dramas, which were the fashion in the late 'seventies, and even wrote a fantastic drama, *The Snow Maiden,* which was to inspire Tchaikovsky and Rimsky-Korsakov.

Not content with his literary activity, this industrious playwright devoted a great deal of his time and energy to the improvement of the situation of actors and writers. The theater in Russia was a State monopoly, and no private theatrical enterprises were allowed in Moscow or St. Petersburg until 1881. Some playwrights offered their plays without any payment in order to have them produced in Moscow and St. Petersburg, since production there amounted to permission to put them on in the provinces. The actors were either treated by the administrators as hirelings of the government, or, in the small towns, considered by the public on a level with mountebanks and prostitutes. Ostrovsky fought for the reform of all legislation dealing with the theater. He also attempted to cultivate in the public a respect for the actor and a higher appreciation of his work. He knew from bitter experience the difficulties of any career connected with the stage: despite his popularity, he made but little money and was always on the verge of poverty. The Administration of the Imperial Theaters, although compelled to produce his plays, disliked these homespun wares which looked so crude next to the graceful French comedies, and put many obstacles in Ostrovsky's way. He succeeded, however, in founding various mutual-aid theatrical associations and, in 1874, he established the Society of Russian Playwrights and Opera Composers for the protection of their rights. This Society functioned all over the country until 1917, and then served as a model for the similar Soviet organization.

In 1886 Ostrovsky was appointed Director of the Moscow Theatrical School and of the repertoire for the Moscow theaters. But this official recognition came too late: the playwright died a few months later.

When his literary heritage is studied in its entirety it reveals, despite the variety of topics, an amazing unity of purpose. Most of his plays pictured the conflict between the wilful and the submissive, the rich and the poor, old age and youth. The warmth and comprehension with which he portrays all the oppressed or ruined victims of the *samodurs* forms the main background of his plays and creates their atmosphere. Ostrovsky's is that famous 'pity' that Europe discovered in Russian Realism, that sympathy for the downtrodden. In Ostrovsky, who avoided lapsing into sentimentality (except for a few 'happy endings,' often tacked on at the insistence of the censors), the pity is enhanced by the pathos of the struggle of the individual for his freedom and dignity. In *The Forest,* Neschastlivtsev (Unlucky), a minor actor, defends his profession before a group of the gentry:

Mountebanks? *No,* you are the side show performers, we are the noble actors. We love earnestly and, if we dislike somebody, we quarrel and fight, but when we want to help we do not spare our last coppers. But what about you?

Ostrovsky may appear repetitious and elementary. Several critics, particularly some early in the twentieth century, deprecated him as a limited painter of manners, who confined himself to one historical milieu. It is understandable, they claimed, that he would appeal to his contemporaries, but only twenty years after his death he had dwindled to the rank of a regional and outdated playwright. The lack of interest shown by the West to translations of his work proved, in their opinion, his limitations: his characters failed to rise to the universal significance of truly great works of art, because Ostrovsky used a superficial or wrong psychology, and lacked any central, unifying idea.

The validity of this criticism was constantly challenged by facts. Instead of declining, Ostrovsky's popularity in his country was constantly increasing. During the theatrical season of 1870 his plays were given daily in four or five theaters; in 1912 in seven or eight; and in 1940 twenty-eight Ostrovsky plays were produced daily in the U.S.S.R. alone. In the previous year the total number of their performances topped 10,000. Tolstoy's prediction of 1886 had come true: Ostrovsky had become a national playwright. No changes in political weather could affect him, and today, more than 125 years after his birth, he is the most widely read and most frequently performed playwright of the Soviet Union.

What is the reason for such popularity? It cannot be explained by the scarcity of good Russian plays or by the fact that in contemporary Russia playwriting is lagging behind other highly developed theater arts. Ostrovsky has a steady appeal because he had the knack of portraying Russian characters in a matter-of-fact, realistic way. There is no mysticism, pathology, or complication in his plays, even though he presents despots or cranks. His characters have the Russian exuberance, but not in terms of frenzy or morbid exaggeration, as in the writings of Dostoevsky. They are not exceptional, romantic types, but average, simple men and women, and even their crimes, follies, or depravities have nothing mysterious or unacceptable about them. No wonder that for many Europeans and Americans who seek the 'thrill' of the 'Slav Soul' Ostrovsky is not spicy enough. In a country of extremes, struggle, and various forms of political dictatorship, the conflict between the individual and his environment is always of immediate interest, and this conflict, familial or social, is Ostrovsky's central theme.

Another reason for his appeal lies in the fact that he is not only a sound writer but also wholesomely optimistic. According to a prejudice widely prevalent outside of Russia in Europe and in America, Russian literature is exceedingly morbid. Facts disprove this superficial and faulty conclusion. Pushkin, Goncharov, and Tolstoy, express a vigorous affirmation of human values, a faith in life, and an acceptance of the universe. Ostrovsky has the same positive spirit, and in that sense he is typically Russian.

The very flavor of Ostrovsky is conveyed to his audience by his language. He belongs to the auditory type of writer, for whom the sound of the word, the sonority of a sentence, the intonations of a speech hold first importance. His dialogue is of the highest stage value because it reproduces living colloquial speech, interspersed with lively remarks, amusing slips of the tongue or distortions, with a generous use of slang, local expressions, and changes of tonality. Most of his middle-class protagonists speak an idiom that is either the Moscow speech of the period or the unadulterated vernacular of the peasants. Ostrovsky's language is hardly ever marred by bookish or foreign expressions. It is the country itself, with its steppes, its villages, and provincial towns, that we hear in Ostrovsky's dramas and comedies and that makes them so difficult to translate. Even their titles sound odd, since most of them are nothing but old saws: *Even the Wise Stumble; Sin and Sorrow Are the Common Lot; It's All in the Family—We'll Settle It Ourselves; Even a Cat Has Lean Times,* and so on.

The construction of Ostrovsky's plays is simple. His plots are logically consistent and avoid surprises, except at the very end, which is occasionally quite abrupt. The solution is often presented in the form of a catastrophe, or a change of mind in one of the main characters. The dramatic intensity, however, never exceeds naturalness. Ostrovsky himself made a distinction between theatrical Realism and 'copying reality.' When the Meiningen theatrical troupe, famous for its stage Naturalism, came to Russia in 1880, Ostrovsky, at first enthusiastic, came finally to the conclusion that 'the triumph of the property man and the stagehand has nothing to do with Realistic methods.' Like most Russian Realists, he understood that truth never means imitation, and that the Realistic approach in art must be accompanied by interpretation and an organization of material. This conviction directed his artistic creativeness and is partly responsible for his abiding popularity. It also accounts for his historical importance. Fonvizin, Griboyedov, and Gogol were great playwrights, but they all left only a few plays. There was no national repertoire before Ostrovsky, and many people despaired that there ever would be one. Ostrovsky proved it was perfectly possible; he himself has left a legacy of forty-seven original plays—comedies, dramas, historical chronicles, fantasies, several plays in collaboration, and translations from Cervantes, Goldoni, and Shakespeare (*The Taming of the Shrew*)—thus laying the foundations for an authentically Russian theater. This fact in itself had a revolutionizing effect. Moreover, he founded a whole school, which brought about a revival and a renewal of Russian literature.

All these facts entitle Ostrovsky to a unique place in Russian art: both his admirers and his detractors recognize his merits as the founder of the modern national theater in Russia.

10

The Critics and the Nihilists

I   THE REIGN of Nicholas I ended with
the collapse of an illusion. The Crimean War (1853-6) revealed the
weakness of the government based on serfdom, backwardness, and
reaction. It is true that Russian soldiers and sailors had shown heroism
and an utter disdain of death, particularly during the eleven months of
the siege of Sebastopol (immortalized by Leo Tolstoy in his *Tales of
Sebastopol*). But technically, politically, and economically, Russia had
not been able to contend with the coalition of Great Britain, France, and
Turkey. Her military equipment was outdated, her arms were obsolete
or poor, the bureaucratic leadership, undermined by graft and ignorance, had made criminal blunders: the troops in the Crimea lacked
everything, from rations to field maps. The formal discipline and military rigidity practiced by the Czar's generals proved to be of little use
under conditions of actual war. Russia's defeat in the unfortunate
Crimean campaign was the defeat of a system. The Empire lost her
international prestige and her position in the Middle East. National
pride received a body blow, and the Slavophiles resented it as much as
did the opponents of intransigent absolutism.

Alexander II, Nicholas' successor, understood the necessity of reform. A pupil of Zhukovsky, intelligent and kind, he seemed the right
man to carry them out. Unfortunately, despite his moderately liberal
tendencies, he lacked firmness of character and made no attempt to
break away from the isolation of his sumptuous Court. Old bureaucrats
were entrusted by the Czar with the task of revivifying his regime, and
they went about it reluctantly, trying not to yield an inch more than
was absolutely necessary.

The main problem of course, was serfdom. Russian economic life could not progress so long as it was based on slave labor. Besides, the fact that half of the population lacked the simplest human rights was always a potential source of trouble. The number of peasant uprisings and of slain slave-owners increased steadily: more than 720 such uprisings had taken place during the reign of Nicholas I. In 1856 Alexander II informed the Moscow gentry: 'The existing order of chattel-slavery cannot remain unchanged. It is much better to abolish serfdom from above than to wait until it is done away with from below.' In 1857 special governmental commissions set to work on this problem in collaboration with the representatives of nobility, who were for the most part such Slavophiles as Samarin and Prince Cherkassky.

In the higher social circles, which were profoundly stirred by the Crimean defeat and the promises of a new order, the Slavophiles and Westernizers, the moderates and radicals, all joined in denouncing serfdom and in demanding reforms. Everyone spoke of Ivan Aksakov's poem, proclaiming that Russia was stigmatized by the shameful brand of slavery and decadent with servility, laziness, and injustice. Herzen addressed an open letter to Alexander, advocating liberation: 'I am ashamed to confess to you how little would make us contented.' Even the strict censorship could not prevent the crusade against serfdom. 'The plague of Russian life' was attacked in articles and works of fiction; literature played a great role in the abolitionist movement. Turgenev's *Hunting Sketches* (the first of which appeared in 1847, and which were published in book form in 1852), Grigorovich's tales of peasant life, and dozens of minor works left a deep impression on their numerous readers and were responsible to a great extent for the united front presented by the intellectuals against serfdom. The sweep and range of the movement was unlike anything else in the history of the intelligentsia, and its intensity, as well as its extent, surprised and even alarmed the government.

In 1861, after a long struggle (and preceding Lincoln's Emancipation Proclamation), serfdom was abolished and the white slaves, whose numbers equaled the then population of North America, became legally free. Over twenty-one million men were set free and allotted land; the women were merely emancipated. The conditions of the emancipation were rather complicated, the allotments of land were small, and the peasants were faced with redemption payments for the next forty-nine years. These payments (made to the government, which in its turn paid the landowners) with accruals of interest, in addition to the head-tax, weighed heavily upon the former serf: by 1905 the peasants had paid over two billion rubles (or about a billion gold dollars) to the Imperial Treasury. Another important feature of the reform, owing to the pressure of the Slavophiles, was the retention of the *mir,* or rural community—as a matter of fact, practically all the land allotments were assigned to these primitive self-governing bodies, which in their turn distributed them for cultivation among the individual members.

Until the new policy of Prime Minister Stolypin in 1906, this was the salient factor in Russia, highly approved by the Slavophiles and by the Narodniki (or Populists). On the other hand, since the land allotments had been small, the peasants were not satisfied with the land reforms and were suspicious of their former masters, who had retained large tracts of arable lands. The 'land thirst' of the peasants and their resentment of having been let down in 1861 were persisting causes of agrarian unrest. This unsatisfactory rural situation had certain immediate results; there was a considerable number of peasant uprisings, which the government crushed with unnecessary harshness. The suppression, in 1862, of the uprising in the village of Bezdna, in which the troops killed a hundred peasants, was typical and naturally aroused the indignation of the intelligentsia.

The collapse of serfdom necessitated other readjustments in the structure of the state, and, in the years that followed, Alexander II promulgated a series of further reforms. In 1864 the *zemstvos* were established: self-governing bodies in each country, district, and region (and, subsequently, each city), which were granted control over roads, schools, and medical aid. Despite the undemocratic manner of election to these bodies, they were effective and were culturally very important. No less substantial were the judicial reforms: improvement of court proceedings, introduction of trial by jury, organization of lawyers into a formal bar, public hearings, amendment of the criminal and civil codes, and so forth. Yet these reforms, though progressive and liberal, reflected the government's reluctance to go the whole way. Thus, while it was announced that corporal punishment was abolished, it was nevertheless retained for Siberian exiles and for peasants under certain communal adjudications. Likewise, the introduction in 1874 of universal military training, which meant an enormous alleviation for the peasants and a step toward equality of treatment for all citizens, was accompanied by special exemptions for noblemen and university graduates.

But whatever their shortcomings the great reform marked the end of the old era pictured by Gogol and others. A new social order came into being in Russia after the emancipation, and until 1905 Russia remained within its framework. Nevertheless it was a most discriminatory order, and only the classes privileged by birth (the nobility), function (the clergy), wealth (Merchants of the First Guild, landed proprietors), or education (university graduates) fully enjoyed the civic rights granted them by the Emperor. The large masses of the people, the peasants, the lower middle class, the artisans, the workers, were still treated as second-class citizens, subject to oppression and exploitation by the authorities. Even the *zemstvos* were managed by governors appointed from St. Petersburg, and their decisions could be vetoed by police functionaries. Moreover, there had been no constitutional changes in the method of government: the regime remained autocratic, the police omnipotent; freedom of conscience or the press depended on the pleasure of petty officials; censorship, although somewhat abated, still held the whip hand over literature.

The reforms of the 'sixties were undoubtedly the most important advance in Russian history since the time of Peter the Great. But Russian absolutism was still like a gigantic dam holding back the pressure of turbulent waters. The dam had not been destroyed, the free flow of the waters was still restrained; yet the dam had been breached here and there, permitting at least some outlet.

II   The years between 1854 and 1866 were distinctly an epoch of rising spirits and great public activity. The energies dormant under Nicholas I, or channeled into metaphysics, now sought to manifest themselves. The sons of the dreamers and philosophers, ashamed of the inefficiency of their fathers, turned resolutely toward the new gods—practicality and action. The men of the 'sixties idolized Action as their sires had worshiped Ideas in the 'thirties. Everyone was eager to do something: the businessmen to trade, the engineers to build, the young men and women to learn, and the revolutionists to get on with a revolution. Even the bureaucrats were infected with the new spirit: they were refurbishing the old façade of Russian monarchism.

Science and education were particularly active. A group of educators, headed by Pirogov, the famous surgeon, and the pedagogue Ushinsky, started a new humanistic trend in the schools. In 1863 academic autonomy was granted to the universities, and the following year the gymnasia were reorganized and divided into the Classical (teaching Greek and Latin) and Real (with mathematical and scientific courses predominant). In the 'sixties such scientists as the chemist Dimitri Mendeleyev (1834-1907), author of the *Periodic Law of Elements;* the physiologist, Ivan Sechenov (1829-1905), the embryologist, Karl von Baer (1792-1876), and many others were doing notable work, while the traditions of Nicholas Lobachevsky (1793-1856), the great mathematician and the founder of non-Euclidean geometry, were carried on by Sophia Kovalevskaya (1850-91). In the humanities young scholars continued historical research under the leadership of Serghei Solovyov

(1820-79), whose 29 volumes of *A History of Russia* covered the history through the end of the seventeenth century. Studies in folklore and ancient literature made great strides under eminent scholars, such as Alexander Veselovsky (1838-1906) and Alexander Pypin (1833-1904).

The assertion of Realism in art provoked disputes and schisms. A group of fourteen painters forsook the Academy of Art and inaugurated what was later to become widely known as Itinerant Exhibitions. The Itinerants formed a new movement which became very popular, practically dominating painting and sculpture until the end of the century, and which was revived under the Soviet regime. Their works were not only Realistic but also had political and social tendencies, mostly Populist. The superb painter Ivan Kramskoy (1837-87), who did *Christ in the Desert;* Vassily Perov (1833-82), painter of peasant life and portraitist of Dostoevsky, Ostrovsky, and Turgenev; Nicholas Gay, that mild Christian; Nicholas Yaroshenko, the radical who painted the portraits of Saltykov and Mendeleyev; Marc Antokolsky, the sculptor— all these with their numerous friends and disciples formed a united front against art for art's sake. The last and the greatest of the Itinerants was Ilya Repin (1844-1930), the founder of a Russian school of Realistic painting, who has left such masterpieces as *Volga Bargemen, Dnieper Cossacks Answering the Soldan of Turkey, Ivan the Awesome Mourning the Son He Slew*.

Realism made headway in music as well. The 'Mighty Handful'— Milii Balakiriev (1836-1910), Caesar Kuy (1835-1918), who was also Professor of Fortification, Alexander Borodin (1834-87), who was also a chemist, Nicholas Rimsky-Korsakov (1844-1908), and Modest Mussorgsky (1839-81)—supported by such critics as Vladimir Stassov, Herman Laroche, and Alexander Serov, a composer in his own right, definitely shaped the Russian national school of music founded by Glinka and made its fame world-wide. In the 'sixties Tchaikovsky also began his career, and the brothers Anton and Nicholas Rubinstein, equally famous as composers and pianists, founded conservatories in Moscow and St. Petersburg, which became the centers of a flourishing musical culture.

On the stage Realism triumphed with such geniuses as Michael Shchepkin (1788-1863),[1] Prov Sadovsky (1818-72),[2] and many other

---

[1] Shchepkin was born a serf. Among his foremost roles were the Mayor in the *Inspector General,* Harpagon, and Shylock. He raised the Russian theater to unbelievable heights, and it is still influenced by his traditions.

[2] Sadovsky was a superbly talented comic, and the foremost delineator of Ostrovsky's types.

excellent performers. A number of road companies brought plays by Gogol and Ostrovsky to the most distant regions of the Empire.

And, to complete this picture of cultural expansion, it should be added that many museums and art galleries were founded in the 'sixties. Among them was the famous collection in a State gallery of the Moscow Croesuses Paul and Serghei Tretiakov.

This eruption of energy which started in the early 'sixties, led to an intensification of all political, moral, and psychological conflicts among the intellectual strata of Russian society and to constant clashes of groups and opinions. New schisms were added to the old ones and they cut deeply into the codes of public opinion formed in the 'forties. The official Nationalists seemed the least affected: they stuck to their formula of Fatherland and Throne, accepted the reforms as the Czar's 'gift' to the people, supported all the reactionary measures of the government, and tended toward rigid conservatism. Michael Katkov (1818-87), a former admirer of the Magna Charta and the editor of *The Russian Messenger* monthly, became the theoretician of the group and the leader of reactionary journalism. The Slavophiles felt heavily the impact of this period of change and transition; and, faithful to their slogan 'authority to the Czar, freedom of life and spirit to the people,' they joined the opposition and fought against serfdom. In 1855 K. Aksakov, in his memorandum to Alexander II, declared that the country presented a picture of inner discord under the sugar-coating of unscrupulous lies. Slavophile papers and magazines openly criticized the outdated institutions of the regime and were attacked by the censors. However, the influence of the main group of Slavophiles declined after the abolition of serfdom and the disappearance of the old leaders. The young Slavophiles rallied around the Muscovite and later the monthlies *Time* and *Epoch,* which had been founded by Dostoevsky. They revised the negative attitude of their fathers toward Europe and emphasized their own love for the people, claiming to stand 'on native soil' and to be the true exponents of popular tradition. They wavered, however, between fear of revolution and visions of humanitarian universalism *à la* Dostoevsky. The intensification of the revolutionary movement at the end of the 'sixties thrust them to the right, deepening the breach between them and the Populists, with whom they had had many points in common.

The differences among the Westernizers were of a wider range. Their moderate wing included broad-minded landowners, workers in the *zemstvos,* and a considerable number among the aristocracy, high bureaucracy, and the liberal professions. They aspired to a constitutional monarchy modeled after the British, expected a great deal from

capitalism and the economic growth of Russia, favored foreign invest-
ments in native industry, and preached 'reasonable' practicality. At
certain times the positions they took seemed to coincide with those of
Herzen. The alliance of Herzen with the moderate liberals was, however,
of short duration. The stubbornness with which Alexander's government stuck to the prerogatives of absolutism, the reprisals against the
radicals, and the reactionary course taken by domestic policy after 1863
destroyed all of Herzen's illusions if he ever had any: he reverted to
bitter attacks against the regime and threatened it with revolution.
Another reason for the split between the *émigrés* and the moderate
Westernizers was the outbreak of the Polish insurrection in 1863, which
was mercilessly crushed: fifteen hundred rebels were executed, thirty
thousand perished in battle, and many thousands more were exiled to
Siberia (Joseph Conrad's father being of the number). One of the
results of this insurrection and of other unrest in the Western regions
of the Empire was the intensification of restrictive measures. At the
same time events in Poland had caused a rise of nationalistic feelings
in Russian society, even among the liberals. Herzen, who had fully
supported the Poles, was accused of a lack of patriotism, of being more
Polish than Russian, and so forth; the split over the Polish question
marked the decline of Herzen's influence within Russia and led to his
final rupture with the liberals.

The liberal Westernizers were divided into two main groups: the
Gradualists, who believed in a slow evolution of the regime, and the
radicals, who were of a socialistic trend and more or less inclined toward
a revolutionary solution. However, there was a variety of shades between these two extreme groups. The Gradualists, such as Botkin, Turgenev, and Druzhinin, tried not to idealize the people and their traditions or institutions, and demanded a complete Westernization of the
country.

But in addition to this vertical division there was a horizontal one,
which cut into the Slavophiles and Westernizers and into liberals and
radicals alike. This division came from the differences between two
generations, the quarrel between fathers and sons, which became particularly acute in the 'sixties. This horizontal division caused a rift
between the two main social and psychological groups among the intellectuals—the Aristocrats and the *Raznochintsi* (a Russian term embracing the scions of various lower classes).

The new men who came to the fore in the 'sixties and fought resolutely against oblomovism, their main enemy, bore all the stigmata of
their social background: they were the sons of country priests, emancipated serfs, small merchants, petty civil servants, or impoverished

squires; they were used to hard work and the harsh facts of life. They simply refused to obey the old leaders, showed a rather critical attitude toward governmental reforms, and rapidly acquired a strong influence over the intelligentsia. The number of Raznochintsi was being steadily increased by teachers, members of the bar, journalists, physicians, and university students—particularly those who had got their education the hard way. Most of them professed radical opinions. Here again there was a division between those grouped around Chernyshevsky and Dobroliubov, and the followers of Pisarev. There were also other minor groups, but all of them were 'sons,' and representing the mentality of the younger generation, regardless of their political opinions.

III   The most typical and influential representative of the new spirit was certainly Nicholas Chernyshevsky, economist, historian, novelist, philosopher, and critic. The son of a well-to-do priest, he was born in 1828 in Saratov, on the Volga River. He attended a theological seminary and, at the age of eighteen, was a student at the University of St. Petersburg. In 1848 he came in contact with the group that later was to be called the 'circle of Petrashevsky.' Most of its members were Utopian Socialists and ardent admirers of Robert Owen, George Sand, Saint-Simon, and Fourier. Chernyshevsky shared their tendencies; but while the young men who gathered in the evenings at the house of Petrashevsky were such idealists and enthusiasts as Dostoevsky or Pleshcheyev (who subsequently became well known as a poet), he defined himself as Realist and Rationalist. Petrashevsky and his friends were arrested, tried, and subjected to the torture of a mock capital execution in 1849; but Chernyshevsky, fortunately escaped arrest. Four years later he made his literary debut and soon became one of the editors of *The Contemporary,* the influential organ of liberal Westernizers and radicals, published by Nekrassov. Almost immediately he was recognized as the leader of the young generation, and his authority remained unchallenged for more than two decades.

Widely read in Feuerbach, the German materialists, and the French socialists, Chernyshevsky had laid a firm foundation for his philosophical and historical materialism. Metaphysics were for him the 'prehistory' of science, and he refused to admit any source of knowledge outside of experience. A firm believer in the unity of mind and body, Chernyshevsky defined pleasure and interest as the main determinants of human behavior. Man has all sorts of needs, ranging from such primary ones as breathing, eating and drinking, to secondary ones of an emotional and intellectual nature. Happiness implies the satisfaction of most human needs and ought to be the goal of any well-organized society. As long as human beings are the agents of progress it is of the utmost importance to have a clear idea of historical events and of contemporary social, economic, and political issues. Any individual who wants to help progress along must have a definite program of potential improvements. Social rationalism is a prerequisite of any public action.

This analysis of contemporary life led Chernyshevsky to the conclusion that the causes of poverty, injustice, oppression, calamities, and deviations from that which is right were mainly economic. Class struggle, social inequality, the competition of groups and governments, the unequal distribution of capital and land, were all deeply rooted in economics and could be eradicated only if the whole structure of society was transformed. According to Chernyshevsky, this could be brought about only under Socialism, which he defined as a government of co-operation, solidarity, and popular ownership of capital, land, and factories.

In his famous *Comments on the Political Economy of John Stuart Mill* he made a penetrating analysis of contemporary economic theories and formulated his conviction of the inevitability of Socialism as a result of social development. In this, as well as in his recognition of the progressive role of capitalism in its early stages, he came very close to Marxism—both Marx and Engels valued him highly. His position, however, was between Marxism and Populism (or Russian Socialism). Chernyshevsky criticized Herzen's 'utopias' and scouted all talk of Russia's 'mission' and the collapse of Europe. This staunch Westernizer and positivist admitted, however, that the *mir,* or rural commune, that 'relic of the past doomed in the long run to disappear,' could render invaluable service in the transition to Socialism. He was, on the whole, of the opinion that Russian agriculture would not follow the European pattern of concentration of capital, and he studied carefully 'the particularities' of Russia's social structure. Without raising the problem of moral or political superiority, he recognized that Europe and America had their own courses of development, while Russia, owing to her traditions and her own ways of life, would reach the same objectives in a different manner. This attitude made Chernyshevsky equally opposed to the Slavophiles and to the revolutionary messianism of Herzen and Bakunin.

A foe of historic fatalism, Chernyshevsky shared the faith of Herzen and the Populists that the 'human will, guided by reason,' could intervene in current history; despite his positivism he asserted that progress could be ultimately explained by the superiority of human intelligence. 'Everything in human life can be reduced to moral issues,' he wrote to his son in 1877. This moral approach formed a link between Chernyshevsky and his forerunners, such as Belinsky and Herzen, although his socialism was distinctly more realistic and economic. His political diagnoses were based upon hard facts, and his surveys show a sober, clear intelligence coupled with an acute perception of political realities. In 1862, when even Herzen doubted the victory of the North in the American Civil War, Chernyshevsky was calmly confident and predicted correctly the general course of events.

For many years Chernyshevsky led a campaign against serfdom. He believed in a peasant revolution following the emancipation, and wanted the Russian youth to be prepared for a great upheaval. Of course, the censorship prevented him from fully expressing his belief, but his readers understood all his allusions and were never mistaken in regard to his radical opinions.

Chernyshevsky's influence as a literary critic was no less important than his role as an ideological leader; moreover, his articles on contemporary writers advanced many points of his political and social doctrines. Two of his books, *Essays on the Gogol Period in Russian Literature* (1855), and the dissertation for his doctorate in philosophy, *The Esthetic Relationship between Art and Reality* (1853-5) became classics of sociological criticism and later provided the philosophical foundations for Marxist literary criticism in the Soviet era. Rejecting idealistic esthetics, Chernyshevsky proclaimed the supremacy of life over art. His point of departure was reality, and this materialistic concept determined all his conclusions. Real life in nature and society finds representation in art. Not infrequently such representation—which is the fundamental goal of art—assumes the character of interpretation or indictment of various phenomena; in that case we have critical Realism, as in Russian literature during and after the time of Gogol. The theory of art for art's sake is nonsense; the concept of abstract beauty is as preposterous as the illusion of objectivity in history. Each historian, from Tacitus to Macaulay, not only reports facts but also evaluates them according to his political and social opinions. Writers in general are also not dispassionate: Hobbes was an Absolutist, Milton a Republican, and Rousseau a Revolutionary Democrat. Whenever an artist represents Beauty with a capital 'B' he really reflects the feeling of a social group or class.

Each century, according to Chernyshevsky, had its historic mission. 'The life and glory of our times are two drives: humanism, and the endeavor to improve the conditions of human life.' This forms the content of contemporary art, from which everything useless should be banned: art must be socially significant. 'Literature and criticism have for us Russians an enormous importance such as they surely have nowhere else.'

In 1862 Chernyshevsky was arrested, in connection with the unrest among university students, and thrown into the Fortress of SS. Peter and Paul. There he wrote his novel *What Is To Be Done?*, which was to become a gospel to the young generation. This didactic work, poor in characterization, structure, and language, happened to have a tremendous public appeal. Its main theme is feminine emancipation, which is discussed at some length by the heroine, Vera Pavlovna, with her first husband, the medical student Lopukhov, whom she marries to escape the sordid environment of her family. Subsequently she debates the same question with her second husband, Kirsanov, who is also a physician. Vera Pavlovna symbolized the New Woman, whose primary concern is not with her good looks but with equality and economic independence. An active, practical person, she organizes a co-operative dressmaking shop. When Lopukhov realizes that she no longer loves him he stages a pretended suicide and goes to America to leave the field clear for his friend and rival Kirsanov.

These three characters represented the young generation with all its typical traits—and it was the pleasure of recognition that made the novel so popular. Another reason for its success were the allusions to the radical and revolutionary ideas of the time. In one of her dreams, Vera Pavlovna not only sees the stages of the progress of feminism but also has a vision of an ideal society, based on reason, science, freedom, and social service. The most appealing pages of the novel, however, are those devoted to Rakhmetov—a young nobleman who turns Spartan, renouncing woman, wine, and pleasure of any kind (except smoking!) in order to dedicate himself completely to The Cause. Although his mysterious activities are never explained in the novel, its readers then understood very well that the strong, unemotional, highly rationalistic Rakhmetov was a revolutionary. Chernyshevsky wrote with admiration that Rakhmetov 'did not spend a quarter of an hour a month on relaxation or rest.'

This perfectly self-controlled and never-erring hero subordinated all his acts to the supreme goal he had set for himself—the triumph of revolution and Socialism. As a contrast to all the superfluous men of Russian literature he was truly a new hero—and as such fired the imagination of young people throughout Russia. It is extremely revealing that this schematic image of action, logic, and virtue could mean so much to Chernyshevsky's contemporaries. The first revolutionary socialist in Russian fiction appeared as an intransigent extremist, ready for renunciation and sacrifice and resembling in his monastic austerity religious fanatics. The radicals aspired to serve as soldiers of the revolution and brothers of a socialistic order: for many years to come Rakhmetov remained their ideal, and the students sang of 'the man who wrote *What Is To Be Done?*' Officially the name of Chernyshevsky had been banned from the press. In 1863, a year after his arrest, he was branded a political criminal and deprived of all civil rights. Although no specific charge was brought against him and despite the absence of any evidence, Chernyshevsky was accused of 'pernicious influence on the young' and sentenced to penal servitude. He spent twenty-one years in mines and prisons as an exile in Siberia.

These ordeals did not, however, impair his moral integrity, his absolute devotion to science and Socialist ideals, and his puritanical attitude toward duty and work. But they did ruin him as a writer and as a scholar; after 1864 his scattered articles and essays never equaled the writings he had published at the peak of his career. He was not allowed to return to Russia until 1883, and died six years later, in 1889, in his native town of Saratov.

IV   Chernyshevsky's ideas were popularized in literary criticism by his most talented disciple, Nicholas Alexandrovich Dobroliubov (1836-61). This young man, who died of tuberculosis at the age of twenty-five, and whose literary activity lasted only five years, was the most influential Russian critic after Belinsky.

Born into the family of a humble priest at Nizhni Novgorod (now Gorky), Dobroliubov, like Chernyshevsky, studied in a theological seminary, and later attended the Teachers' College in St. Petersburg. In 1856 he published his first article in *The Contemporary,* and the next year was appointed editor of its critical and bibliographical sections.

This stern-looking, bespectacled, prematurely aged young man, with a long face framed in side whiskers, had a powerful mind, a phenomenal memory, and a capacity for working at all hours of the day and night. The Patrician Writers felt uncomfortable in his presence: they were slightly awed by this 'democratic peasant,' who was unbending in his revolutionary faith and puritanical in his moral judgments. Here was the true representative of the young socialist and radical, so uncompromising, rigid, and vehement that he made even Herzen thoughtful and uneasy.

Dobroliubov's articles on Turgenev, Goncharov, Ostrovsky, Saltykov and others assured his reputation. They were generally lengthy essays, the springboard for which was provided by some novel, play, or tale. Dobroliubov was interested in art as a form of social communication and argued fiercely against the art-for-art's-sake theory, so prevalent among the liberal gentry. When discussing a writer or a book he always considered to what extent they expressed the natural yearnings of a period and of a people. Art had the duty, declared Dobroliubov, of dealing with social phenomena and, if it did not reflect them truthfully, completely, and profoundly it was undesirable and should be discarded. The critic's task was to help the reader to comprehend the social and artistic meaning of a book: 'Real criticism deals with works of art in the same manner as with the facts of life.' His articles did not analyze merely *Oblomov,* or *On the Eve,* or *The Thunderstorm,* but also the segment of Russian life each work portrayed and the social ideas it touched upon. Dobroliubov was a sociological critic, for whom literature represented a part of the broader unity of life and at the same time was an implement for transforming life. Like Chernyshevsky, he associated literature and revolution, and demanded from writers a conscientious service to society.

He was an excellent writer, and his articles were brilliant with civic indignation, sarcasm, wit, and pathos. No less successful were his satirical poems against the moderates, Slavophiles, or pseudo-liberals, which he regularly published in the *Whistle* (a supplement to *The Contemporary*) and in the *Spark* (a satirical magazine directed by Vassily Kurochkin, the poet, whose masterly translations of Béranger made the latter extremely popular with the Russian readers). The tradition of satirical periodicals, dating back to Catherine's reign, was resumed and revived in the 'sixties, and Dobroliubov, Nekrassov, Kurochkin, and a number of others were successful in this genre. For fourteen years *The Spark* (banned by the censors in 1873) served as a mouthpiece for the democratic revolutionary movement and was highly influential in educated society.

Chernyshevsky and Dobroliubov determined the tendency and the tone of literary criticism for generations to come. Their ideas were accepted as a sort of obligatory credo by the radical intelligentsia. Thus, sixty years before the Revolution the two writers had established the foundations of what today determines the literary policy of the Communist party and of the Soviet critics.

Chernyshevsky and Dobroliubov represented the 'revolutionary democracy' of the 'sixties. It was another critic, Dimitry Ivanovich Pisarev (1840-68), who gained acclaim and an enthusiastic following as the exponent of Nihilism.

By an odd coincidence Pisarev's life was almost as short as Dobroliubov's: he drowned at twenty-eight, while swimming in the Baltic Sea. Unlike his two great contemporaries, he belonged to a rich and noble family, received excellent education in the gymnasia and the University of St. Petersburg, spoke several foreign languages fluently, and was destined by his family to have a diplomatic career. He turned to writing instead, and proved to be an indefatigable worker during the nine years of his literary activity. After Dobroliubov's death and Chernyshevsky's exile he occupied the first place in Russian journalism, although he was badly handicapped by political persecutions. In 1862 he was arrested and put in solitary confinement, and most of his sensational articles were written in a prison cell. They were published in *The Russian Word,* a monthly review founded in 1860 and second in influence only to *The Contemporary.*

Pisarev, a consistent materialist, shared the revolutionary bent of *The Contemporary* group but, while Dobroliubov and Chernyshevsky were mainly concerned in social issues on a large scale, Pisarev devoted his attention to the problems of the individual. Pisarev believed that natural sciences offered the only 'safe ground for a truly rational and wide outlook on nature, man, and society.' For the sake of complete independence and freedom of thought, Pisarev, who had a strong critical sense, denied all authority in morality, society, or literature. His ideal man was a 'thinking realist' who would accept only what was within the bounds of reason, logic, and utility. Pisarev's attitude toward life and art was strictly utilitarian. In his challenging articles 'The Realists' and 'The Destruction of Esthetics' he discarded sentimentalism, platonic love, romanticism, idealism, mysticism, and poetry as 'sheerest drivel.' Novels, poems, and paintings were, in his opinion, far too often mere conglomerations of words or colors. 'Thinking realists' had no time to play with such rubbish. 'We are poverty-stricken and stupid,' declared Pisarev, 'and whatever distracts us from our main tasks—education, scientific development, material and social progress—is useless and therefore obnoxious.' Money spent for ballets, theaters, or books of poetry should be used for building railroads and factories. A pair of boots was of more importance than a tragedy of Shakespeare's, and a shoemaker was superior to Raphael, since the work of the former had a practical purpose. Pisarev attacked Pushkin's poetry as something that merely helped the drones to kill time.

He undoubtedly enjoyed making such controversial statements and, feeling himself an *enfant terrible,* deliberately made them in a coarse and crude manner. But his witty, vigorous, and caustic articles were not merely challenging or exaggerated; they expressed the feelings of the generation that admired the Rakhmetovs and did not want to waste their time reading love poems or waxing rapturous over the purple hues of a sunset. As Bazarov in Turgenev's *Fathers and Sons* said: 'Nature is not a temple but a workshop, where man should stick to his job.' Pisarev declared that Bazarov was a 'thinking realist,' and that the younger generation, instead of reviling him, ought to adopt Turgenev's term and call themselves 'Nihilists.'

The Nihilism of Pisarev and of the thousands upon thousands of his followers was not the outright revolutionary doctrine that in Europe and America it is generally assumed to be. The vast movement of the 'sixties, of which Nihilism was but one facet, was in the main a revolt of the individual against any restrictions—moral, political, or personal— and against any authority—of the State, the Church, or the family. It was a kind of intellectual terrorism, which was to be replaced ten years later by a political one. The Nihilist was fundamentally a materialist and an atheist. For him experimental science took the place of God. 'Everyone of us,' wrote Bartholomew Zaitzev (1842-82), journalist and one of the leaders of the movement, 'was ready to be hanged for Moleschott or Darwin.'

A Nihilist who respected himself had to repudiate any connection with the idealism and estheticism of the preceding generation. A university student who discussed the problem of the immortality of the soul committed a grave sin in the eyes of his comrades. The Nihilists were intransigent and dogmatic, as so many iconoclasts are. Together with Pisarev they were overthrowing all the idols in such a frenzy that their supposed freedom of thought, for them, became a more powerful idol.

In the beginning the Nihilists were aware of social conditions, without being expressly socialistic. Pisarev himself, for instance, did not believe in the masses: he called the toilers the passive material, the nebula of history, incapable of struggle for a better life. He considered only the members of the intelligentsia, composed of thinking realists, as a driving force in human progress. The Nihilists' claims of equal rights for both sexes, their high talk of free love and the economic independence of women, and their criticism of marriage as merely another form of sale and purchase provoked more stir in society than the most daring political utterances of the radicals. The Nihilists loved to stress their contempt of good manners and all the 'useless frippery' of the leisure classes. The men affected Russian blouses and spoke loudly, using coarse expressions. The girls smoked, cut their hair short, and, to the horror of their parents, stayed till dawn in the quarters of their male companions. It was difficult to convince the shocked fathers and mothers that this highly suspicious behavior only involved orgies of talk: the Nihilists, despite all their posing, were rather puritanical and ascetic in matters of sex. Whatever their blunders and exaggerations, however, they greatly contributed to the movement of feminine emancipation, which was one of the most significant trends of the period. As a result of a vigorous campaign in the press and in society women gained admission to the institutions of higher learning, and universities for women were founded in Russia.

Nihilism was just a growing pain, according to Mikhailovsky, the great sociologist: under the disguise of youthful fanaticism, rudeness, and exaggeration there was a real and very reasonable desire for work and practical action. After the emancipation of the serfs, the younger generation believed that an unlimited field of activity had opened to them. As Katherine Breshko-Breshkovskaya described it in her *Memoirs,* her contemporaries went into all sorts of professions and positions; they established schools and model farms, taught technical sciences in towns and the *a-b-c's* in villages, invaded governmental offices and the *zemstvos;* the women as well as the men became physicians, engineers, teachers, lawyers. Some of the Nihilists regarded their activities from a purely practical side, emphasizing that they were free from 'altruism, sentimentalism, and other rubbish of the past,' but the majority dreamed of serving the people.

At the beginning the Nihilists attempted to act in a perfectly legal and normal way. These attempts seemed, however, highly suspicious to the authorities, and all sorts of regulations and restrictions thwarted the efforts of thousands of well-intentioned young men and women. The government feared their enthusiasm and energy and had no desire to 'crown the reforms' by a transformation of the monarchy. Reactionary measures followed the abolition of serfdom; as far back as 1862 students were beaten up by the police for demonstrations for academic freedom. The arrests of leaders such as Chernyshevsky and Pisarev added to the discontent of the younger generation, pushing it towards radicalism—and toward Socialism, since in Russia the Socialists were the vanguard of public opinion. This agitation, which manifested itself in proclamations, student strikes, and demonstrations, and in the activities of numerous secret circles, reached its peak by 1866, when Karakozov, a student, fired at the Czar as he was riding through the capital. Karakozov was hanged, and, although his attempt was an individual action without accomplices, innumerable arrests were made throughout the country. To be found in possession of a photograph of Chernyshevsky was enough to send a man to prison. The government reverted to an openly reactionary policy. The Socialist-Populists in their turn adopted revolutionary and terroristic tactics, which made the 'seventies a period of desperate underground activity.

'Russia is being thrust toward a catastrophe,' wrote Alexander Herzen: 'my heart bleeds at this sad spectacle.'

11

LITERARY TRENDS OF THE 'SIXTIES

I   IN NO other field was the activity of
the 'sixties as intense as in literature. In this era of transition, dissension,
and struggle, literature more than ever before served as an outlet for
ideas and energies—a substitute for the pulpit and the parliamentary
rostrum. It was a tremendous force—a fact everybody had to acknowledge. The echo aroused by each separate book reverberated in the
articles of the 'leaders of thought': literary criticism gained such an
influence because it had become practically the most popular form of
political and philosophical writing. Discussions on literary matters
always ended with an examination of all contemporary issues. Here
again we are confronted by a phenomenon that hardly has any parallel
in the West. Literature was regarded and respected in Russia as something highly important—and important it was as it assumed a manifold
role in shaping opinions, formulating ideals, and stimulating action.
'Literature in Russia,' wrote Chernyshevsky, 'constitutes almost the
sum-total of its intellectual life.'

Its impact grew in the 'sixties for purely material reasons as well.
The reading public had become numerically three times as large as
that of the 'forties, and it was increasing daily. The growth of towns
and of means of transportation contributed greatly to the rapid distribution of books in the provinces, while the Raznochintsi had brought
with them thousands upon thousands of new readers from various social
strata, particularly from the middle class. The reform of the educational
system at the end of the era—the opening of the gymnasia, the elementary schools, the *zemstvos,* and other institutions of learning—was also
of great service in the development of literature. Commercial publishers,
taking advantage of this situation, concentrated their efforts on enlarging

the number of prospective book buyers; in fact, many publishing enterprises were established in the 'sixties in the twin capitals, as well as
in provincial towns. More than a thousand new books were published
yearly. Periodicals doubled and tripled their circulation. Things were
different from the times of Pushkin: now writers could be professionals
and earn their living by their pens. The number of men of letters increased to such an extent that Pisarev talked of them as forming a
large part of the 'thinking proletariat.' Next to the great masters of the
period there were scores of minor writers, most of whom were not
without a distinct artistic value. A simple list of prominent novels of
the period would probably surprise those European critics who confined
Russian Realism to the 'miraculous emergence of the Giants,' such as
the authors of *Fathers and Sons, Crime and Punishment,* and *War and
Peace*—all three of which were published during the 'sixties.

The decade following the Crimean War marked a definite separation
between the New Russia and the Old. The character of the cleavage,
the duality, and the contradictions are self-explanatory. The flourishing
cultural movement of the 'forties was resumed, continued, and increased
during the era of great reforms, but it was diverted into numerous
channels. The conflict of currents within the Realistic school, the clash
between the patrician writers and the Raznochintsi, among the radicals,
liberals, and conservatives, between the Westernizers and the 'Writers
of the Soil,' the attacks of the Nihilists and the revolt of the esthetes,
the rift between the new generation and the men of the 'forties—all
these make the picture extremely complex.

The definite victory of Realism, which followed the pattern shaped
by the 'forties and the 'fifties, coincided with the dominance of prose
over poetry. The previous generation of writers had, on the whole,
consisted of poets and dreamers, whereas the present was one of prose
writers and practical men. In the 'sixties the novel, the tale, and the
short story were the favorite forms, and drama and comedy also made
considerable headway. The Russian Realistic novel reached its zenith in
these years. Before the close of the 'sixties Turgenev had written *Rudin,
A Nest of Gentlefolk, On the Eve, Fathers and Sons,* and *Smoke;*
Dostoevsky had published *The Humiliated and the Wronged, The Gambler, Crime and Punishment,* and *The Idiot;* Tolstoy, *The Cossacks* and
War and Peace; Goncharov, *Oblomov* and *The Precipice;* Pisemsky,
A Thousand Souls; Saltykov, *The History of a Town.* What an extraordinary harvest within a decade!

The Realistic tradition took many paths, and not infrequently the
same writer would follow several of them. Most novelists attempted to
sum up the past, feeling it their duty to capture the failing light of a

disappearing society. Goncharov, Turgenev, and Pisemsky were the leading representatives of this tendency: Turgenev described the good old times with nostalgia, Goncharov with a regret tempered by an indulgent smile, and Pisemsky with simple pleasure and healthy mirth. Most of the writers of this group could not help sympathizing with the delicate poetry, the patriarchal way of life, and the simple virtues of pre-reform Russia, even though they were quite aware of its evils. Often no mention whatsoever was made of these evils, and there would result something that was almost apotheosis. *War and Peace* was such a book—the most harmonious and complete monument erected in the 'sixties to Old Russia by its greatest writer.

Serghei Aksakov (1791-1859), author of *Family Chronicles* and *The Childhood Years of Bagrov's Grandson* belongs to the same category, although his case presents certain peculiarities. The father of Konstantin and Ivan, the two founders of Slavophilism, he published his *Chronicles* when he was sixty-five and his *Recollections* a year before his death. These memoirs of a man who in his youth had sided with the literary reactionary Shishkov and the old die-hards were acclaimed by Dobroliubov and the younger generation; before his death Aksakov learned that his work was a classic. It is hardly enough to say that his descriptions of family life on an estate near Ufa, in Eastern Russia, were realistic. Aksakov, who had not been too keen on Pushkin but was enthusiastic about his friend Gogol, was a realist *sui generis*. Almost photographic in his portrayal of Bagrov, an irascible old gentleman of the eighteenth century, in his vignettes of country meals, excursions, and family intrigues, or in the recollections of his school days in Kazan, Aksakov focused his attention on fidelity to fact, on scrupulously exact images. There is nothing critical about his limpid prose, which lacks the ethical note that seemed obligatory in his times. He follows no particular style and has no social implication or any other purpose in his writings. He wrote for the pure joy of recollection, because he loved the life and the people he described—and he tried merely to be faithful to the memory of his senses. Mirsky has called him an 'ocular realist.'

Aksakov was attached to everything purely Russian; he was close to Mother Earth, and his readers could smell the fields and forests and see the rivers and steppes of their land from his descriptions—in a beautiful racy idiom. And these descriptions, on the whole poetic without being sentimental, had a distinctly idyllic quality. In this Aksakov was close to the mood of most of the Patrician Writers who, regardless of their political opinions, felt nostalgic about the doomed nests of the gentlefolk.

The Critical Realists, who claimed to be following the Gogolian tradition, also described the past, but only in order to point out its ills. Much as they admired the even flow of Aksakov's prose and his objective portrayals, they never imitated his detachment and impartiality. On the contrary, they were biased, and there was always a moral note in their works, as in the cases of Saltykov-Shchedrin the master satirist (*Satires in Prose,* 1862; *Letters from the Provinces,* 1868; *The History of a Town,* 1870), of Dostoevsky in *The Village of Stepanchikovo,* or in many of Ostrovsky's plays. The trend of realistic disclosures was particularly strong in the theater, which was dominated by the figures of Ostrovsky and Gogol.

While Ostrovsky had but minor disciples—Count V. Sollogub, with his comedy of *The Official,* N. Lvov, and A. Potekhin, who was a professional playwright and a faithful follower of his master—the grotesquerie of Gogol found an outstanding representative in Alexander Sukhovo-Kobylin (1817-1903). His dramatic and adventurous life still attracts biographers and raises all sorts of insoluble problems. Accused of having murdered his French mistress, he underwent prison, trial, acquittal, retrial, a special investigation, appeals to high courts, and so on. Like so much of Russian literature, *Krechinsky's Wedding,* his best comedy, was written in jail. It has the *brio* and the swift pace of French comedies, but the portrayal of Krechinsky, a Slavic Raffles who bears some resemblance to Nozdrev and Khlestakov, and, in particular, of his factotum Raspluyev are first-rate characterizations in the style of the Russian Realistic-grotesque. *The Case* (1862), a dramatic sequel to the comedy, was a violent exposé of graft and bureaucratic corruption, which the author knew of through bitter experience.

Later, in 1869, he completed his trilogy with *Tarelkin's Death,* a symbolic farce of macabre inspiration. Raspluyev recurs in all three plays, which are full of violent irony and outright pessimism. These 'tragedies without catharsis' belong among the masterpieces of the Russian theater.

Sukhovo-Kobylin is another of those remarkable Russian writers whose very names are hardly known to the West; however, *Krechinsky's Wedding* was produced in Paris in 1902, at the Théâtre Renaissance, with Gémier in the title role. The trilogy also attracted many producers after the Russian Revolution: remarkable revivals of Sukhovo-Kobylin's plays were produced at the Moscow Art Theater by Meyerhold and Vakhtangov.

The satirical trend so stressed by Sukhovo-Kobylin also found expression in humorous periodicals and in political or literary parody. The apogee of parody was reached in Kosma Prutkov, who was created by Count Alexis Tolstoy and two other talented poets, Alexis and

Vladimir Zhemchuzhnikov. Like many another literary creation, Prutkov kept growing, and in time his creators provided him not only with portraits but a biography. The insufferably smug, narcissistic Kosma Petrovich Prutkov, poet and 'Director of the Assay Bureau,' started as a playwright under the pen-name of Y and Z (an aegis for Alexis Tolstoy and Alexis Zhemchuzhnikov), but began to publish under his own name in 1854. From then on he became a whiplash in the hands of his creators for the castigation of literary and political pretentiousness, snobbery, and stupidity. In the 'sixties Kosma's seemingly inane yet delightful fables, allegories, aphorisms, and poems appearing in *The Whistle* were part and parcel of the satirical trend of the progressive groups. One of the most trenchant of Prutkov's satires was his 'Memorandum for the Establishment of Uniformity of Thought in Russia,' suggesting daily governmental bulletins on what the citizens were to think of current affairs.

Among the educated, Prutkov enjoyed a well-deserved popularity. Many of his pseudo-profound dicta found their way into the journalistic idiom or have become actual folk proverbs: 'Flip the mare's nose and she'll wag her tail,' 'If you want to be handsome, join the hussars,' 'No one can encompass the unencompassable!', 'Look at the Root!', 'The Volga flows into the Caspian Sea,' and so on and on. All these, together with his military maxims in rhyme, made him the delight of Russian readers for half a century, and even now he has a wide audience, while his very name has become a synonym for smugness, triteness, stale sententiousness—and fun.

In the 'eighties his creators completed his *Autobiography* and added new material to his Collected Works, but they stressed his nonsensical character at the expense of his status as a political satirist.

II   Although the stylistic differences between the objective manner of Aksakov and the grotesquerie of Sukhovo-Kobylin are perfectly obvious, they were nevertheless both ranked as Realists. Of course, the writers of exposés felt more closely drawn to one another than to Aksakov. They had a common bond: all of them, whether seriously or humorously, were reproducing and interpreting the current social trends. In the first decades of the nineteenth century the main efforts of Russian writers were directed toward the creation of a national literature and were concentrated on fashioning a common language in prose, poetry, and drama. This task, completed in 1820-40, had gone hand in hand with the search for a national awareness, so revealingly expressed by the Decembrists, Slavophiles, and Westerners. During the decade of 1850-60 the center of activity

shifted from national to social awareness, and literature concentrated
more on problems of social structure or social transformation than on
issues of national destiny. The positive nationalism of the Slavophiles
or the negative nationalism of the Westernizers held less meaning for
the men of the 'sixties than did the doctrines of Socialism, Liberalism,
or Conservatism. Most writers—even those who dealt with the past—
reflected all the disputes, aspirations, and struggles of their contemporaries. Feminism or Nihilism, for instance, was described not only by
Chernyshevsky and Turgenev but also by dozens of minor writers, who
were labeled the Men of the 'Sixties.

Thus Realism as a whole was impelled toward the social novel, and
the division among the writers derived not so much from stylistic dis-
tinctions as from ideological ones. The compact group of socially aware
Realists, with progressive, liberal, or radical leanings, was probably the
most influential one during this period. Their ideas were attacked by
their conservative opponents—but these, too, were writing social novels.
Whether the 'message' was one of Feminism and democratic revolution,
as with Chernyshevsky, or one of anti-Nihilism, as with Leskov, or of
anti-Feminism, as with many reactionary writers of the time, their works
followed the same Realistic pattern in the representation of life. The
bitterest foes of the radicals in practice agreed with Chernyshevsky that
a writer should reflect his times and they tried to achieve this in keeping
with their particular philosophies. In short, the social novel predomi-
nated regardless of its content or its ideas, thus demonstrating the delusions of those who accuse the 'radicals' of having 'contaminated' the
Russian novel with tendentiousness and 'social significance.'

By the 'sixties social awareness was a general characteristic of all
Russian literature, whether radical or conservative. Of course, some
supporters of 'pure art' questioned the efficacy of such literature from
a more fundamental point of view. They discussed the problem of the
meaning and purpose of fiction, and at times succeeded in provoking
serious rifts and quarrels, for conflicting interpretations of art divided
the writers no less than did political ideologies. As a rule the conservatives stood for pure art, while the democrats and radicals backed art
laden with social significance. But here again this separation was not
inflexible. Dostoevsky and Tolstoy, both anti-radicals, were resolutely
opposed to the theory of art for art's sake. Turgenev wrote social novels,
while he waged war against the 'destroyers of esthetics'; and the poets
of the 'esthetic tradition' often wrote political poems.

The clash of groups and parties was complicated by the changes in
the social structure of the intelligentsia, and the advent of the Raznochintsi had also made its impact on literature. A whole class of writers,

coming from the people and maintaining connections with their original backgrounds, described their life experiences in a starkly realistic manner. They usually pictured poverty, ignorance, drunkenness, and misery; their descriptions were rough and crude. Despite their deficiency of form, the factual material of these forerunners of Naturalism attracted general attention; in addition to their subject matter they introduced a milieu that was not to be found in the works of the Patrician Writers and that revealed some of the darkest corners of Russian life.

Bursary School Sketches by Nicholas Pomialovsky (1835-63), the son of a poor deacon, exposed the mores of theological seminaries administered by sadistic and ignorant teachers who indulged in flogging their pupils, and made them kiss the scourge, or applied salt to their bloody backs. Pomialovsky, having spent fourteen years in these grim institutions and having been flogged no less than four hundred times, also described the terrible physical conditions of the bursary schools, the moral degradation of their students, the complete disregard for their intellectual development, and the system of education based on coarseness, violence, and mechanical memorizing. The picture of this disciplinarian orgy induced Pisarev to compare the fate of its students with that of Russian convicts, as recorded by Dostoevsky in his *Notes from the House of the Dead* (1861), that great and terrifying human document about his experiences among the outcasts in Siberia.

Nicholas Uspensky (1837-89), another Realist, also came from the provincial clergy and had passed through the inferno of a theological seminary. Lack of funds prevented him from studying medicine, so he turned to writing stories, which, for the most part, dealt with peasants, village priests, petty officials, and innkeepers. He did not idealize the people but brutally exposed the coarseness, ignorance, and alcoholism of the underdog. These stories might have succeeded in the 'sixties, when crude Realism was a fashionable novelty and when all the shortcomings of the poor were explained by the existence of serfdom; but in the 'seventies, when sentimental idealization of the peasants and workmen had become prevalent, Uspensky's objectivity seemed out of place. Frustrated and embittered, he led the life of a pauper, ruining himself by excessive drinking and finally committing suicide.

Under the Soviets his name was often mentioned as that of a forerunner of proletarian literature and was generally coupled with the name of Fedor Reshetnikov (1841-91). Son of a priest and at one time a student at a theological seminary, Reshetnikov published his *The People of Podlipnoye* in 1864, a novel that gave an appalling picture of peasant life in the extreme north of Russia. Reshetnikov's natives are incredibly ignorant: they cannot count above five, they worship wooden idols in secret, they are decimated by epidemics and starvation and exploited by the clergy and officials, and, on the whole, fare no better than animals. In other tales Reshetnikov described the life of factory hands through an equally crude but impressive accumulation of shocking details. His works are primitive and crude—traits common to many writers among the Raznochintsi. *The Notes of a Soldier* by Alexander Pogossky (1816-74), published in 1855, was written in a lively, humorous style and was probably the least crude of the works produced by the writers of this group.

The most important representative of the Raznochintsi in poetry was assuredly Ivan Nikitin (1824-61), the son of a small shopkeeper and himself the proprietor of a tavern patronized mostly by cab drivers. His life was a succession of hardships and he died of tuberculosis, leaving a few poignant songs in a melancholic strain. One of them, 'The Grave is Dug Deep,' acquired great popularity. In his descriptive poems he represented the dreary life of peasants and burghers, in a tone as gloomy and heartbreaking as that of his lyrics. This self-made, uneducated poet was akin to the peasant-poets who had preceded him in the 'forties. His choice of rhythms was limited and monotonous, but he handled them rather skilfully and his deep melancholy was genuine.

The Raznochintsi wanted to present facts, 'the sober truth of life.' They did so in a crude and unattractive manner, but their 'factology' became a trend and had strong populist leanings. They described the lower classes, even to the derelicts, and they took their heroes from the people. In this they coincided—on literary, not on political grounds— with the writers of the 'organic trend,' which was obviously under the influence of the Slavophiles. To Turgenev and the other highly cultured Westernizers, who worshiped the grace and vigor of Pushkin's 'pellucid prose,' Reshetnikov, Pomialovsky, and Uspensky were uncouth Scythians hardly worthy to be called writers. However, the Westernizers felt much the same about certain novelists of noble descent, whose manners and style, although infinitely superior, nevertheless betrayed a rebellious primitiveness.

A case in point is that of Alexis Pisemsky (1820-81), an impoverished nobleman who, after graduating from the University of Moscow, spent many years as a civil servant in his native province of Kostroma, where he acquired an excellent knowledge of its peasants and burghers. His first tales, published in the *Muscovite* in the 'fifties, won critical acclaim for their simple and sound humor, the realism of their characters, and the vigor of their presentation. When three years later the author moved to St. Petersburg the literary set decided that he was an eccentric. This frank and outspoken man with his Kostroma accent and provincial manners would not accept the current slogans; he showed a hearty dislike of foreigners and a growing skepticism toward civilization, and shocked the liberals by his old-fashioned pronouncements. His originality, his practical and rather shrewd mind, and his attachment to peasant food and expressions appeared alien to all the things the educated society of the capital loved and cherished. He seemed to have emerged from some distant past, his thoughts and attitudes were those of a boyar or a scribe of the seventeenth century, and he talked like an old, shrewd plowman. 'He smelled of the wildwood, of the black loam, of what the French call the *parfum de terroir*,' Annenkov declared. This gentleman *muzhik* was, nevertheless, both sensitive and nervous. Later in life he suffered from all sorts of phobias and, after the suicide of his son, became a hypochondriac. His last years were afflicted by fits of a real mental disease.

In the Russian Realistic school Pisemsky ranks immediately after the great masters, and some critics contend that he ought to be placed side by side with them. Pisemsky evinced his power and dramatic qualities even in his first novel, *Boyarshchina* (1845), which presents a gloomy picture of decaying provincial gentry in the story of a sensitive married woman ruined by an unhappy love affair. But it was his *A Thousand Souls* (1858) that won him a place among the best writers of the period. This realistic picture of pre-reform Russia combined the excellent characterization of major and minor protagonists with an interesting and rather involved plot. This was a novelty, since the Russian realists before Dostoevsky had never paid much attention to the story element of their novels. Pisemsky broke with this tradition, and his next novel, *The Stormy Sea* (1863), was practically a thriller, including crime, embezzlement, rich villains, courtesans, wicked Jews, and eccentric revolutionaries. Although *The Stormy Sea* had a *succès de scandale,* it is far inferior to his other novels, such as *Men of the 'Forties* (1869), *In the Whirlpool,* and even *The Freemasons,* a heavy historical tale of the eighteenth century.

Pisemsky also wrote a series of plays. One of them, *A Hard Lot* (1860), the story of a peasant who kills the child his wife had begotten by their master, made its audiences sit on the edge of their seats with its tragic realism and the inexorable development of its plot. For a long time it remained one of the best 'popular tragedies' in the Russian repertoire. Also excellent are his *Sketches of Peasant Life* and various short stories in which peasants, traders, artisans, and petty officials are portrayed without the least trace of the sentimental mawkishness that infected so many tales of the period. There is nothing kind about Pisemsky's treatment of his characters; at times his realism is harsh and almost implacable. It was thus that he depicted Kalinovich, the hero of *A Thousand Souls,* a young climber who wants to get on in life and marries a crippled heiress, although he is in love with Nastenka, a most charming mistress. Kalinovich acts like a scoundrel while having no illusions about it, and though he undergoes painful inner struggles, he has enough will power and ambition not to change his plans or deviate from the path he has chosen. Once at the top of the bureaucratic hierarchy he starts 'cleaning house,' fights against graft and corruption, jails the chief villain of the town—a princely crook—and, in general, behaves like a 'positive' hero. (Pisemsky claimed he had the right to show the good as well as the evil sides of Kalinovich.) At any rate Kalinovich, the intelligent and unscrupulous lover of comfort, pursuer of wealth, and irreproachable civil servant, has a definite place in the gallery of types drawn by Gogol, Goncharov, and Turgenev.

All Pisemsky's characterizations are vivid and convincing. Nastenka's father, Peter Godnev, a school principal, is a 'simple heart'—one of those beloved characters of Russian fiction the list of which extends from Ivan Kuzmich in *The Captain's Daughter* of Pushkin, through Maxim Maximovich (in Lermontov's *Hero of Our Times*) to Prince Myshkin in Dostoevsky's *The Idiot.*

The breadth and action of Pisemsky's novels were not, however, their only remarkable features. His racy, full-blooded style, the richness of his vocabulary, the truly Russian turn of his speech always enchanted his admirers. He too was a Scythian, and his literary lineage is to be found among such men as Arch-presbyter Avvacum and Narezhny. His humor and his love for farcical situations and the grotesque show, of course, how much he owes to Gogol. He represents the anti-Westernizing, native tradition, which is usually associated either with the Populists or with the Raznochintsi, although he belonged to neither group.

Pisemsky's originality and importance were obscured by the campaign launched against him by the radicals, who had been profoundly offended by the satirical and angry parts of *The Stormy Sea.* They lumped him together with other anti-radical writers of the so called 'Reactionary' group, such as the sensational writer Vsevolod Krestovsky (1840-95) or the anti-Nihilist Victor Kliushnikov (1841-92), whose novel *Mirage* appeared in 1864 at the same time as Leskov's *No Way Out,* which was also construed as a sarcastic attack on radicalism. Dostoevsky's *The Possessed,* although of a different caliber, is likewise an example of this trend, which aimed at describing radicals, and even liberals, in a most derogatory way. Of course this controversy was of a political nature. Pisemsky or Leskov or Kliushnikov did not question the validity of social realism or of critical realism; they fully accepted it as a literary method. Nevertheless their novels were anti-radical, whereas those of their adversaries approved of the new political trends and even sympathized with the growing revolutionary movement. Incidentally, the number of novels openly siding with the socialistically inclined young generation was very small in the 'sixties; it increased considerably in the following decade. This was one of the reasons for the extraordinary success of Chernyshevsky's *What Is To Be Done?*— it had a unique function at a time when a counterpoise to the anti-revolutionary novel was badly needed. As a matter of fact, the best writers of the period were not revolutionaries: they were generally mild liberals, or even conservatives. Among the masters only Nekrassov and Saltykov could be classified as genuine representatives of socialist radicalism. It was the numerous minor writers and journalists who formed the rank and file of radicalism, and the radicals had a large and responsive audience.

Although the Patrician Writers had ceased to play the leading role in literature after the abolition of serfdom, becoming more and more identified with the intelligentsia—that classless conglomeration of educated individuals from all walks of society—a sizable group of aristocrats still strove to put back the clock. They rose up in revolt against the spirit of the Raznochintsi—particularly against tendentiousness—and attempted to bring literature closer to the idealism of the 'forties.

The supporters of 'pure art' prevailed more in poetry than in prose; it also had a few exponents in literary criticism. Some of the latter, such as that phlegmatic dandy Alexander Druzhinin (1824-64), Pavel Annenkov (1812-87), an excellent memorist, or Stepan Dudyshkin (1820-66), had neither the temperament nor the stature to compete with Chernyshevsky, Dobroliubov, and Pisarev. The only serious rival to these three was Apollon Grigoriev (1822-64), a vivid writer and, as a poet of passion, akin to Yazykov.

Grigoriev got his fill of Idealism and Romanticism during his student years at the University of Moscow, of which city he was a native. He translated *King Lear* and published a volume of poetry in 1846. An intellectual and sentimental bohemian, Grigoriev shifted from mysticism to atheism, from Schelling to the Utopian Socialists, from political radicalism to violent anti-liberalism. He came to the defense of Gogol's *Selections* and challenged all the progressive democrats of his period. The victim of an unhappy love affair, he described his torments in highly subjective lyrics. Their scope was narrow, their mood often borrowed from Lermontov, yet this autobiographical poetry, although of no great timbre, occasionally had a striking sincerity. 'His poems,' said Blok, 'express his fate with such completeness that they reflect all the main trends of his life boldly and vividly.' This last of the Romantics, who felt in himself the soul of a Hamlet, could never solve the tragic conflict between himself and his environment: his impressionistic, sickly poetry constantly set his inner self against hostile reality.

The Symbolists published his collected poems in 1916, and pointed out that many of them were adaptations of Russian gypsy songs. Some of Grigoriev's lyrics (such as 'Two Guitars') are still sung in night clubs all over the world and are a 'must' at Russian parties, although hardly anyone knows him as the author. Forgotten as a poet, Grigoriev survived as a writer of ballads, some of which, to the accompaniment of a guitar, sound like vehement complaints or confessions recited by some ardent but ill-starred lover.

The climax of Grigoriev's active life came in the 'fifties, when he associated himself with the *Muscovite* and tried to infuse new life into the Slavophilism of Shevyrev and Pogodin. Tired of his many revolts and spiritual pilgrimages, he now defended the 'wisdom of the soil,' grass-root virtues, and the stability of existing institutions. Unspoiled Russian traditions, claimed Grigoriev, were preserved not only in the peasantry but in the middle class as well—among the merchants, to be precise. He therefore welcomed Ostrovsky as a genius poet of the patriarchal way of life.

His critical articles, scattered in various reviews, created considerable stir. A disciple of Schelling, he defined poetry as an intuitive, irrational activity and put the qualities of subjective receptivity and sincerity far above conformity to reality. He thought that it was wrong to assume that the aim of literature is to describe society, and thus that the criticism of Dobroliubov missed the essence of art. Criticism should be organic, treating a work of art as a whole, and subject to its own laws, which have nothing to do with real life.

Since his ideas ran counter to the general trend, he had but few followers and never achieved any material success. He led a strange and irregular life, full of passionate love affairs, catastrophes, and desperate rebirths. He taught literature in Orenburg, where he translated Byron's *Childe Harold,* then came back to Moscow, contributed to various magazines, quarreled with everybody—with Slavophiles as well as liberals—drank hard, gambled, was constantly penniless, wound up in a debtor's prison, and died in 1864. Today we can appreciate the fine spirit and the esthetic intuition of Grigoriev as a critic, but during his lifetime he was apparently the defender of a lost cause, waging war against those very things—tendentiousness and Realism—that were then destined to triumph in literature, as well as in all other fields of art.

12

NEKRASSOV, TIUTCHEV, AND THE MINOR POETS

I   WHEN THE news of Lermontov's
tragic death reached St. Petersburg in the summer of 1841 it deeply
affected a certain young man of twenty, emaciated, ill, and underfed.
His name was Nicholas Nekrassov. His constant dream was to become
a great poet and he had been writing verse since early childhood. He
admired and imitated Lermontov and had even brought out a pamphlet
of poetry called *Dreams and Sounds,* which sold not a single copy.
Poetry was Nekrassov's secret passion, and he devoted his nights to it;
during the day he tried to earn a few coppers by writing squibs for
almanacs, rhymed advertisements, articles on beehives and tobacco, or
potboiler farcical skits.

He was born in 1821, in a family of upper Volga noblemen, running
mostly to gamblers, hunters, and profligates. His early years were spent
among his father's serf-concubines, huntsmen, and village lads. He worshiped his mother, a kind and handsome woman of Polish descent, but
could not get along with his father, who mistreated his wife, drank
heavily, and was forever boasting of his noble birth and hunting dogs.

Young Nekrassov made a poor showing as a student at the gymnasium in Yaroslavl, and in 1838 his father, extremely displeased, sent
him to St. Petersburg to enter the Army. But the seventeen-year-old boy
disobeyed him; he wanted to become a university student, not a commissioned officer. To bring his offspring to his senses the father cut off
his allowance, and Nekrassov found himself literally without a kopeck
on the streets of St. Petersburg, where for three years he existed as a
homeless derelict. His face, puffy from sleepless nights, was swathed
in a ragged red muffler, his wrists, crimson from the cold, stuck out
from the short sleeves of a tattered violet-hued frock coat. As he con-

fessed later, he 'was famished every day for three years.' To earn enough
for a piece of bread and a slice of sausage he resorted to all sorts of
shifts and stratagems: by hanging around lodging-houses he made a
few kopecks writing letters or filling out legal forms; he did odd jobs
in the St. Petersburg slums and felt very fortunate when he was entrusted with making up the posters for a waxworks museum.

This sordid struggle could not, however, break his determination to
become a man of letters. Doggedly he plodded on toward his goal, trying
his hand at every possible genre—comedies, essays, criticism, and—
whenever he found leisure—sentimental and flowery poems. Even the
abysmal failure of *Dreams and Sounds* did not discourage the young
author: 'I vowed to myself,' Nekrassov writes in his *Memoirs,* 'that I
would not die in a garret, that I would win through, and become successful at any cost.'

The year of Lermontov's death marked a turn of good fortune in
his situation. His skits and farces were accepted by a theatrical manager,
and Panaev, a rich patrician writer, introduced him to Belinsky. This
meeting had a lasting influence on the young poet. In Belinsky's circle
he learned of the idealistic strivings and dreams of the 'forties. The
discussions on socialism, emancipation, democratic equality, and human
progress shaped his convictions and determined his radical inclinations.
He was quite different, however, from Turgenev, Annenkov, Botkin,
Panaev, and other wealthy gentlemen, who loved talking about metaphysics, European civilization, and esthetics; he cut a strange figure
in the literary salons, this day laborer, this hired hand of literature, who
had worked in the slums and had mixed with all sort of ragamuffins.
He admired and loved his idealistic friends, particularly Belinsky, whom
he adored, but he showed himself cynical and even unscrupulous in
practical matters, never hesitating to exploit the writers he met.

At any rate, this attitude did help him in his undertakings and personal affairs. Shifting from one literary enterprise to another, he soon
emerged as a successful publisher, made money, became co-editor of
the important monthly, *The Contemporary,* in 1846, and even won the
woman he had loved for years with tormented passion and who had
inspired many of his best lyrics. Avdotia Panaeva, the pretty wife of
Nekrassov's friend and the one-time owner of *The Contemporary,* had
been practically deserted by her frivolous husband when she finally
yielded to the poet. Dostoevsky, who had fallen in love with her at first
sight, found her intelligent, comely, affable, and extraordinarily forth-
right. For sixteen years she remained Nekrassov's muse, mistress, wife,
friend, and literary assistant. She wrote novels with him, she helped him
with the monthly, she seconded him in all his artistic and political

battles. The most important men of the 'sixties frequented her salon. She counted among her guests Turgenev, Goncharov, Tolstoy, Dostoevsky, Ostrovsky, and many others. 'If the roof of her living-room had collapsed on one of her Monday evenings,' said Chukovsky, the critic, 'Russian literature would have perished.'

By 1848 Nekrassov had realized one of the dreams of his undernourished youth: he had made money, rode about in carriages, and spent large sums gambling, drinking, and later, after his break with Panaeva in 1863, keeping French mistresses, in addition to home-grown ones. His paternal heredity had got the best of him; a sensual man, he loved comfort, good food, old wine, young women, great hunting parties. His life of dissipation did not interfere with his business, however; extremely clever, aggressive, full of initiative, he showed himself somewhat rapacious as a businessman, ready to battle or compromise to get what he wanted. These qualities, added to his capacity for work, endurance, and strong will power, were to prove invaluable in his difficult position as the editor of the magazine that had become the symbol as well as the organ of the radical intelligentsia. He succeeded in attracting the contributions of the greatest writers of the period, so that each issue of the monthly was a genuine literary event. His acute critical sense enabled him to evaluate manuscripts by unknown authors; he discovered and published without hesitation the novel *Childhood* by an unknown young man named Leo Tolstoy.

Nekrassov worked like a galley slave, writing poems, novels, and satires for his monthly, reading proofs, corresponding with hundreds of people, and examining piles of manuscripts (for the first issue of 1850 he read, at a fair estimate, 3,840,000 words). His struggles against censorship were unceasing, especially during the seven years of darkest reaction (1848-55), when over a million words were denied publication: nevertheless he stubbornly adhered to the radical tone of *The Contemporary* and made it the organ of Chernyshevsky and Dobroliubov, withstanding even the opposition of his own friends. In 1860 Turgenev and a whole group of liberal writers, irritated by the positivistic and revolutionary trends of the monthly, decided to break with it; yet Nekrassov, despite the pain caused him by this public rupture with his friends, preferred to side with the new generation.

This blow was followed by a succession of other trials: Dobroliubov died in 1861, Chernyshevsky was imprisoned, Panaev passed away, *The Contemporary* was suspended for eight months. Panic-stricken Nekrassov tried to win the good graces of the government. After Karakozov's attempt to kill the Czar in 1866, he wrote a poem about the man who

had saved the Emperor's life, and hailed Muraviev, who had so in-
humanly suppressed the Polish rebellion. Nevertheless this flirtation with
reaction had no effect on the fate of his monthly: *The Contemporary*
was definitely banned, while Nekrassov was made the target of indignant
attacks from the left. He could not remain without a periodical, however: taking over the wobbly *Notes of the Fatherland,* he transformed
it into a success by making it the sounding board of the Narodniki
(radical Populists). For many years, as editor and promoter of periodicals, he practically shaped a whole body of public opinion. The left
wing acclaimed him as their leader and as a representative of the
revolutionary trend. But his most important role, of course, was that
of a poet—and here again the picture is rather complex, reflecting the
fundamental duality and the inner drama of Nekrassov the man.

His contemporaries regarded him as primarily 'the poet of the
people' and, more precisely, the poet of the people's 'grief and sufferings'—and so he is regarded even today. Both before and after the
Emancipation he portrayed a good many peasant types: some idyllic,
like Grandfather Mazai, but for the most part tragic, like old Vlas,
a rapacious man who repents after a sudden illness and goes around as
a pilgrim, collecting money for building churches; or Orina, the poor
mother whose stalwart son is ruined and done to death by the rigors
of military service; or Daria, the comely widow who is frozen to death,
and the heroine of his epic poem 'Jack Frost,' with its wonderful description of the Russian winter. In several poems he pictured the fate of
peasant women, crushed by slavery, hard work, the cruelty of their
masters, and the coarseness of their own mates. Shorter poems, such as
'The Unreaped Row,' 'The Forgotten Village,' 'The Funeral,' and many
others are expressive in their melancholy, almost despondent mood.
But the height of pathos and his humane sympathy for the misery and
grief of millions of his countrymen is attained in a few lyrical pieces.
In his famous 'Reflections Before a Mansion Doorway' he wrote lines
which were memorized afterwards by generations of reflective Russians:

> Point out to me but one dwelling
> (Such a corner to me is unknown)
> Where your sower, your savior-provider—
> The peasant—is not heard to moan?
> He moans in the fields and on highroads;
> He moans in prisons, in chains;
> In mines; 'neath cornkilns and hayricks;
> Under carts as he sleeps on the plains.
> He moans in his own wretched hovel—
> God's sunlight to him is but pain;

> He moans in each hole of a town
> As he pleads before judges in vain.
> Go thou to the Volga. Whose moan
> Far over the great river floats?
> That moan among us a song is:
> Tis the haulers, who tow the great boats.
> Volga, Volga! When, in the springtime,
> Your waters the fields overflow,
> They flood not the land as 'tis flooded
> With its people's unfathomed woe—
> Where the people are, the moan is. . .
> What means, then, your moan never-ending?
> Will you waken once more in power,
> Or, having made but a song like a moan,
> Have wasted your destiny's dower—
> And your soul forever will slumber?

After the abolition of serfdom Nekrassov asked: 'The people are freed—but are they happy?'—and his answer in the negative expressed the feelings of educated society. Never before, in the history of Russian literature had the cause of the peasants found such an impassioned pleader. He assumed the role of spokesman for these illiterate multitudes, and his poems have the genuine quality of folk songs, as, for example, 'Who Finds Life Good in Russia?' (1870-74). This treasury of popular life is an unrhymed epic, dealing with the adventures of seven peasants who meet with all sorts of people—merchants, priests, artisans, farmers—while trying to find out who lives in happiness, peace, honor, and prosperity in 'wretched and abundant, oppressed and powerful, weak and mighty Mother Russia.'

Nekrassov's peasant poems were as popular as his other short and long pieces, which reflected the yearning for freedom and the fighting spirit of the radical youth. They appealed to the imagination and aroused people to action like martial music, often formulating the aspirations of educated society:

> Lord, set your chosen followers free,
> Release them from their ancient bands,
> Entrust the flag of liberty
> At last to Russian hands [1]

or expressing admiration for those who had fought and suffered in the past. 'Russian Women' (1873) deals with the Princess Trubetskaya and Volkonskaya, who had followed their Decembrist husbands

[1] *Poems from the Russian,* translated by Frances Cornford and Esther Salaman, Faber & Faber Ltd., London, 1948.

into Siberian exile. The same exaltation of courage and idealism runs through 'The Bear-Hunt,' in which the admirable portrait of Belinsky, as the Teacher, is a blending of pathos and delicacy.

Nekrassov's poetry covered many topics but it was in the main devoted to eulogizing those who had given their lives for their people and for liberty. 'Nothing comes free,' he said. 'Fate demands expiatory victims. The cause of Freedom can be firm only if cemented with blood.' He refused to sing of 'the beauty of valleys, skies, and sea, or of the caresses of the beloved, in these days of woe.' The word 'woe' was often used by Nekrassov to indicate social slavery and political oppression— and the censors, as well as the readers, did not mistake the real meaning of his melancholic stanzas.

Long before the Marxists he declared that poetry ought to have a message and that artists ought to be aware of social conditions. 'You may not be a poet, but you must be a citizen'—this slogan, taken for granted in the 'sixties and 'seventies, expressed his personal feelings. As a poet-citizen Nekrassov had his own symbolism from which he drew his strength and which furnished the themes of his poetry. One aspect of it was the Fatherland and the 'wide, clear road' that lay ahead of it. This faith in Russia was closely related to the symbol of the people, who represented the country, the soil, the virtues of simplicity and patience, and the sources of native greatness. Both themes merged in an apotheosis of radical nationalism. Unlike many of the poets of his own times, Apollon Maikov, Nicholas Shcherbina, et al., who looked for inspiration to Greece, Rome, or the Renaissance, or who dealt with abstract concepts, Nekrassov was an eminently national poet, intent on portraying and interpreting the domestic scene, the Russian landscape, and Russian men and women. His message went straight to the heart of his generation: the success of his poems was tremendous. The first edition of his collected poetic works, published in 1856, ran out of print in a month's time. No re-issue, however, was allowed by the authorities, who were disturbed by the growing influence of this exponent of radical dreams. This, however, prevented neither Nekrassov from publishing his poems in various periodicals nor his numerous admirers from memorizing them and spreading them throughout the country by word of mouth or in manuscript copies.

Nevertheless this poet, who claimed to have chosen to sing 'thy sufferings, O people of astonishing patience,' this bard of his people's sorrows, was a nobleman and an intellectual. The day he dreamt of, when the peasant would be buying the works of Belinsky and Gogol at country fairs, had not yet come; and the poems of Nekrassov were read and admired by educated society, mostly by men and women who were well off and who therefore felt the same moral obligations toward the underprivileged as did Nekrassov himself. There was a contradiction between Nekrassov's life and his work, between the shrewd businessman and the sensitive, bitterly despondent, suffering poet. Ashamed of his wealth and influence, of the many things he possessed and loved, he was perpetually conscience-stricken. He was not a man for sacrifice, not a fighter like Chernyshevsky or Dobroliubov; he was not able to live up to his ideals like a Rakhmetov; and he felt repentant and contrite whenever he pictured to himself the average radical student, who usually had to pay with prison or Siberian exile for his faithfulness to ideas Nekrassov was sharing and propagating.

Caught between the regime that threatened his publications, his work, his position, his influence, and his fortune, and the high moral standards of the intelligentsia, who wanted him to be a Knight *sans peur et sans reproche,* Nekrassov always proclaimed his guilt and was ready to wear sackcloth and ashes. Hence his inner torment and his repentance during the visitations of conscience, hence his public confessions, his cry of *Peccavi!* in so many verses, his constant self-accusations, invariably followed by a pathetic self-defense. Whether this was a myth or a situation of real life, this theme of guilt, remorse, and self-redemption constituted one of the most striking trends in his poetry.

In one of his last poems he again tried to explain the main contradiction of his existence:

Soon I shall die, leaving thee but a poor heritage, O my country! A fatal yoke oppressed my childhood, a painful struggle marred my youth. If brief, a tempest strengthens us; if long, it makes the soul accustomed to taciturnity. . . I did not offer my lyre for sale, yet there were times when its notes jarred. . . O Fatherland, forgive me all for the drop of blood I had in common with my people.

In another poem he makes the confession: 'The fight kept me from being a poet; the poems kept me from being a fighter.'

In spite of his self-contradiction, repentance is one of the main themes of Nekrassov's poetry, to which it bestows a distinctly moral character. His restlessness and penance are expressed in a pathetic manner, with grief and sincerity. Ibsen's definition of artistic creation as a perpetual trial of one's own self may be fully applied to Nekrassov. He acted both as prosecutor and defender, and he himself described his muse in aphoristic sentences, which were repeated by critics and readers: 'Muse of vengeance and of sorrow. . . This wan Muse, flogged and covered with blood; none but a Russian could behold her with love.'

His love lyrics also are stamped with despondency and contrition. Some of them are unforgettably melancholy, as is his classic 'If I Drive at Night through the Dark Street,' or they are highly emotional: 'I like not your irony: leave it to those who have outlived themselves, or have not lived at all.' After Pushkin and Lermontov only Nekrassov ever rose to such intensity of feeling, to such directness of self-expression.

This atheistic and materialistic man, enamored of reality, was a hypochondriac: all his poetry sounds like a requiem. He mourns over the sufferings of others as well as his own; this constituted his main aim in poetry. According to some critics, in this he struck a truly national note: the melancholy of the Russian landscape, the grief of generations who slaved, suffered, and died in the immensity of the Russian land correspond to the *andante lacrimoso* of his songs. 'He wept more effectively and beautifully than any other Russian poet,' remarked Chukovsky; he sobbed over the sad fate of the peasants and over his own 'broken life,' over his mother, over Belinsky, over the wives of the Decembrists. His mellifluous verse, drawling with dactylic endings and prolonged vowels, sounds like a solo in a choir—a slow, mournful voice repeating his complaint, which other voices pick up in a collective moan. It is not chamber poetry or a stage recitation; in its oratoric sweep it has a definite aim: to move and stir the audience, and to make the individual join in the chorus and feel a part of a whole. In addition to the fact that many of Nekrassov's poems have the people rather than an individual as their hero, their choral, collective aspect is obvious and has a strong social impact. Their appeal, however, is to a limited group, not to the multitude and this again makes them different from both Derzhavin and Mayakovsky.

The problems confronting Nekrassov are always of a moral nature. In Lermontov, man faces God and Nature; his own passions have roots in the hostile elements of the universe. In Nekrassov man faces men, and his emotions derive from the activity of humanity in the aggregate —society, state, party. Lermontov is concerned with the individual acting in a world of solitude, evil, and pride. Nekrassov is concerned over man's behavior in the world of his fellow men, all conditioned by their work, social environment, or political struggles. Where Lermontov expressed himself in Romantic terms of rebellion, challenge, and abstract ideas, Nekrassov tried to bring his poetry down to earth and used a simple, almost pedestrian form. He dealt with concrete, contemporary material, such as railroads, banks, prisons, the sweat of peasants, lack of money, or shabby clothes. The reunion of poetry and life proclaimed by Pushkin becomes in Nekrassov the reunion of poetry and actuality— in both content and style. Consequently he seemed vulgar, graceless, and journalistic to those of his contemporaries who felt horrified by this invasion of *muzhiks,* rustic shouts, city slang, and newspaper lingo, into the sanctuary of Apollo.

The social and political purpose of his poems offended the esthetes to the same extent as his style shocked all the lovers of sweet melodies and poetic smoothness. They did not understand that Nekrassov was a Realist—mainly a peasant Realist—and that his advent, anticipated by Koltzov and the group of peasant poets of the 'forties, corresponded to the entire trend of native Russian literature. A product of his times, he carried through the same reform in poetry that Gogol was supposed to have accomplished in prose: the triumph of realistic understatement over the stilted and inflated Romanticism. This Realism was combined with an affirmation of the popular tradition. Drawing upon peasant songs, using formalistic preambles, deliberate repetitions, parallels, negative similes, and other devices of folklore, Nekrassov built all his poetry on the rhythms and structural peculiarities of the ballads—the recitative and oral heritage of Central Russia.

It is true that Nekrassov is extremely uneven. Writing was for him like a fever, tormenting and exhausting. He was afraid of moments of inspiration and tried to avoid them. Whatever he wrote, yielding to this 'sacred illness,' was genuine and beautiful; when he simply used his ability as a versifier his poems sounded like the work of a scribbler. Some of them—dealing with railroads, engineers, moneylenders, censorship, and other modern topics—are simply editorials in rhyme. Of course, they had their value in counteracting the so-called 'esthetic poetry' and they were an instructive novelty to his readers. Resuming the traditions of Radishchev, Ryleyev, and Pushkin, he broadened and perfected Russian civic poetry. He thus became the forerunner and master of all the poets of political struggle, popular feelings, and revolution, who flourished until the end of the century. He did create an actual school, but his influence went beyond the limitations of any group: not only social awareness but also the civic aspiration and the moral anxiety of a repentant nobleman helped to form Nekrassov's legacy to his successors.

This warped and twisted man came to an atrocious end: he suffered from cancer of the rectum, and his agony lasted two years. He died in 1877, his last poem dealing with the old theme of repentance and justification:

O Muse, I am at Death's door. Even if I am guilty of much, even if the malice of men will exaggerate a hundredfold my faults—pray, weep thou not. Our lot is an enviable one—for long wilt thou maintain the living blood-tie between myself and honest hearts.

No poet provoked such violent discussions, and probably no poet with the single exception of Pushkin, was so admired and revered as Nekrassov. In the 'seventies and 'eighties he was the bard of the Populists and the radical intellectuals. Revolutionaries adopted his lines as slogans, liberals quoted them in newspapers—and this tradition has continued uninterrupted until the present. In the Soviet Union he is officially recognized as 'a democratic poet with revolutionary tendencies' and an example of 'civic poetry of social utility.' Today Nekrassov's dream has been fulfilled; he has become the poet of large popular masses, the herald of the agrarian revolution.

Even in his time he was strongly attacked by the representatives of 'pure poetry.' They reproached him for the coarseness of his images, the 'low level' of his poems, the prosaic ring of his lines, his heavily specific subject matter. Turgenev rejected his poetry with revulsion. Many contemporaries criticized his use of dissonances, his rhetoric, exaggeration, love of melodrama. Nekrassov himself qualified his verse as uncouth and rugged, and had many doubts about the value of his own work. Of course, the supporters of civic poetry praised him extravagantly, while a few writers, such as Dostoevsky, valued him highly. In his speech at the poet's funeral Dostoevsky declared that Nekrassov was second only to Pushkin and Lermontov.

It is curious that it was the Symbolists, the disciples of art for art's sake, who pointed out in the 'nineties the true nature of Nekrassov's style. They claimed that all his poetry was that of the folk song occasionally interrupted by 'conversational verses.' Most of Nekrassov's poems are narratives with a definite topic, occasionally with a plot; yet these tales in verse cannot be spoken—they must be sung. His long poems are distinctly operatic, his diction is that of a ballad-singer, and the sobbing melody, which is the main motif of Nekrassov's poetry, has the genuine ring of popular music, of couplets sung at village reunions, of the *lento* of work-songs, of the sentimental ballads chanted by peasant girls. Much later Blok remarked that Nekrassov expressed the very essence of Russian character through his 'triumphantly sad tunes, borne by a blizzard.' As an evidence of this truly national character of his poetry the amazing fate of some of his songs is usually cited: they were taken over by the people and were adopted in villages and factories, where the name of their author was unknown. 'The Peddlers' (a dramatic ballad of love and crime) or the lyric 'There Goes, There Drones the Green Noise, the Noise of Spring' have become favorites, as have his 'Lullabies' and other incisive poems, which form an indispensable part of the entertainment wherever and whenever Russian youth foregathers.

The representatives of Nekrassov's school were minor poets. Jacob Polonsky (1819-98), friend of Turgenev and many Westernizers, hailed progress, democratic virtues, and freedom of speech in civic verse. He also gained fame as a delicate lyricist, and his graceful and humorous poem, 'The Grasshopper Musician,' has become an anthology piece. Alexis Pleshcheyev (1825-93), of noble descent, was a member of the Petrashevsky circle and a victim of government repressions. He published sentimental civic poetry of semi-social and semi-Christian inspiration, and also won renown as an excellent translator of European poets, especially Barbier and Heine. Another masterly translator of Heine, Mikhail Mikhailov (1826-65), died in Siberia as a political exile; some of his poems were exceedingly popular with the radical youth. A wider range of literary activity was attained by Vassily Kurochkin (1831-75), a poet who sang of the revolutionary spirit. He was also the editor of *The Spark,* which formed the nucleus of a group of poets: Peter Weinberg (1830-1908), translator of German poets and chairman of literary organizations; Dimitri Minaev (1835-89), translator of Byron and Shelley; Nicholas Loman (1830-92); Vassily Bogdanov (1838-86); and others.

II   Those who opposed Nekrassov's poetics and themes during his lifetime claimed to be carrying on in the true Pushkin tradition. They differed from the poet of the people's sufferings not only in their political leanings but in their subject matter and language as well. Some of them tried to avoid the pressure of contemporary reality by an escape into the past, others limited themselves to the description of beauty, while a few identified their poetry with philosophic reflection. A common bond linked the representatives of all these currents: they had all revolted against Nekrassov in the name of pure art, and sometimes even in the name of art for art's sake, even though most of them also wrote civic poetry. An important group of poets resumed the classical trend of Batiushkov and Gnedich. The Greek and Roman civilizations had always held an appeal for Russian writers—perhaps because of the lack of a Renaissance in their own country. At any rate, a true Hellenistic school came to the fore in the 'sixties, in opposition to the realistic and civic trends of the era. Apollon Maikov (1821-97), the son of an academic painter and brought up in a highly artistic environment, defined his poetic activity as a 'search for beauty.' He found the 'realm of eternal youth and harmony' in visions of Rome and Athens, and his poems on antiquity, full of mythological references, have a fluidity of image, a relief in description, a visual preciseness, and a certain emotional detachment that recall the objective perfection of the French Parnassians. Some of the best of Maikov's poems are 'poetic landscapes,' and here again his verse is elegant and direct, with a distinct pictorial quality. Maikov was not satisfied with these achievements, however; he wanted to express ideals, sometimes of a lofty philosophic nature, as in his famous poem of 'The Three Deaths,' which describes the different attitudes toward life and annihilation of the stoic Seneca, the poet Lucanus, and the Epicurean Lucius, all of whom had been doomed by Nero. He also portrayed the clash between ancient and Christian ethics in his vast descriptive epic, *Two Worlds*.

After a brief friendship with the liberals, including Belinsky and Petrashevsky, Maikov joined the Slavophiles and wound up among the reactionary nationalists. As an exponent of the monarchical credo he praised the patriarchal way of life and fought against the 'subversive trends of society,' particularly against Nihilism, which he attempted to ridicule in his long poem, *The Princess* (1877). The heroine of this poem, the illegitimate daughter of a saintly princess, turns to Nihilism and practically kills her mother.

When Nekrassov called upon writers to 'serve the great aims of the age,' Maikov objected that poets ought not to accept such a false slogan. Only the ignorant mob can be interested in present-day cares; a poet should escape from the noise and bustle of triviality into the sanctuary of the Muses. 'The poet is alien to all, he dwells on a mountain top, while the multitude toils in the valley.'

For Nicholas Shcherbina (1821-69) the road to the mountain top led through the study of Hellenistic culture. A nobleman from the Black Sea area—the only region of Russia where remnants of Greek colonists were still being found by archeologists—Shcherbina tried to convey in his well-balanced, polished verse the pantheistic spirit and the sensual beauty of ancient Greece. While in the civil service in St. Petersburg, he joined the circle of those literati who opposed the 'ugly Populism and the journalistic lingo' of Nekrassov and wrote caustic epigrams against his literary adversaries.

Leo Mey (1822-62) also believed that the poet should look for inspiration to the past; instead of Athens, however, he explored and idealized the ancient history of Russia. His blank-verse dramas, *The Czar's Bride* (1849) and *The Woman of Pskov* (1860), were adapted as popular operas. Mey wrote in the same vivid and imagistic manner as Maikov and, although a minor poet, he had considerable merit in having advanced the historical narrative poem. He was also an excellent translator.

Of much greater calibre was the poet whose popularity firmly established during his lifetime, has lasted even to this day. Count Alexis Constantinovich Tolstoy (1817-75) was a prolific writer, and his works had both wide and diversified appeal. Young (and even not so young) readers still enjoy *Kniaz Serebriany* (*The Silver Knight*), a novel of sixteenth-century Russia, written in the Walter Scott manner. Theatergoers still praise his *Death of Ioann the Terrible, Czar Fedor,* and *Czar Boris,* a poetic trilogy wherein he portrays the three Czars in the tragic light of their moral conflicts and against an engrossing background of dramatic events. Lovers of pure lyrics admire and memorize Tolstoy's melodious and romantic poems. He wrote humorous verse and parody in the epigrams of Kozma Prutkov and in droll ballads, such as the one about the revolt of the eunuchs in the Vatican or the dream of Popov the pettifogger. In the Russian genre there are his heroic ballads of ancient Russia, such as 'Vassily Shibanov,' or 'Prince Michael Repnin,' classics that every Russian schoolboy had to know by heart. Many of Tolstoy's lilting lyrics are familiar, even to those who may never have opened his books; for numerous Russian composers used his 'drawing room ballads' (so different from Grigoriev's gypsy songs, or Nekrassov's peasant ones): 'In the Midst of a Noisy Ball,' 'The Birch is Wounded by a Sharp Axe,' 'Do Not Ask, Do Not Pry,' are in the repertoire of concert artists and amateur singers abroad as well as throughout his native land.

This extremely versatile poet became a man of the 'forties under the strong influence of Schelling and the German Romantics. He believed that art forms the bridge between earthly existence and the other worlds, and that the poet, a priest of the goddess Beauty, is but an instrument of the higher spheres. In his rare moments of inspiration, between sleep and waking, he obeys the command of mysterious forces: 'In vain, O poet, do you pretend to be the true creator of your songs,' Tolstoy proclaims. The poet is but the mouthpiece of Eros, of that divine and universal principle of love that, according to Dante, *move il sole e l'altre stelle*. These Romantic moods contributed to the wistfulness of his lyrics, which revealed the influence of Zhukovsky and Lermontov. They also determined his position in the 'sixties, when he deliberately set himself 'against the current'—a phrase used as the title of his most challenging polemic poem. The theory of utilitarian art became the particular target of his furious attacks. Thanks to his temperament, his sensitiveness, and facile pen, he played a prominent part in the literary struggles of his era. The defenders of civic poetry and tendentious literature saw in him one of the leaders of the noble aesthetes; nevertheless he remained for some time closely associated

244   THE EPIC OF RUSSIAN LITERATURE

with *The Contemporary,* in which he published his parodies and other
Kozma Prutkov material.

Tolstoy contended that humor, satire, and parody had the right to
be tendentious and to have a practical aim; in his opinion, however,
they had to be kept apart from the higher forms of art. This return
to the old hierarchy of genres, which had been done away with by
Pushkin, was somewhat unexpected in poets who claimed to be following in Pushkin's steps. Tolstoy, Maikov, Mey, Shcherbina, and other
minor writers wrote in light, easy meter and used the style, the technical
devices, and even the rhyme schemes of the great poet, so that as far
as the language and the general tone of their poetry went, they were
carrying on his tradition. Of course, Nekrassov could claim that his
poems merely expanded the range of Pushkin's colloquialisms and
strode on in the direction indicated by the author of 'Russlan and
Liudmila,' or others of his pieces of creative folklore. But Alexis Tolstoy
and his friends accused Nekrassov of betraying the very principle of
Pushkin's poetry, which was to create an esthetic feeling through harmony, balance, and musicality. Neither the purpose nor the melodramatic and rugged form of Nekrassov's verse could satisfy his adversaries. He served the heathen gods of strife, hatred, and triviality, while
they served the sun-like Apollo.

In this great schism of the intellectuals Tolstoy managed to preserve an independent attitude. He broke with the liberals, attacked
radicalism and socialism, and ridiculed progressive trends in 'Potok,
the Man of Might,' a comic ballad that simply delighted the conservatives. The Court circles, however, to which he belonged as a com-
panion of the future Czar Alexander II and later as a diplomat and
high dignitary, were eyeing him askance. In his letter to the Italian
scholar Angelo de Gubernatis Tolstoy states that he felt repelled
equally by the abuses of the regime and by the pseudo-liberals. He
belonged to the large group of aristocratic opposition, not so much by
birth as through his romanticism. The brutality and rigidity of the
Czarist administration offended his esthetic feelings, and he preferred
the feudal independence of the past to the uniform despotism of St.
Petersburg. He also praised the republics of antiquity and the city-
republics of the Renaissance. Novgorod and Florence merged in his
dreams: Tolstoy contrived to reconcile a peculiar kind of Slavophilism
with a passionate love for Italy, an enlightened vision of liberty with
an attachment to the traditions of his native soil.

All this created a rather unique situation: the satires by this friend
of the Emperor were enthusiastically received by the radicals he fought
so energetically in his other works. As a matter of fact, Tolstoy's

Russian History before Gostomysl, with its series of hardly flattering characterizations of the Czars, or *Popov's Dream,* poking fun at high bureaucrats, were completely in the spirit of the anti-governmental mood of the intelligentsia. On the whole, the works of the writer who for many years symbolized to his contemporaries art for art's sake, had a most paradoxical fate: those that avoided the formula of 'pure art' and contained some political idea or moral bent proved to be less affected by the passing of time. Such was the case with his ballads and the dramatic trilogy in which Tolstoy's psychological approach to history and his excellent characterizations, as well as the whole action, hinge on the main theme: Evil can generate only evil. Of course, Tolstoy could claim that for him beauty was complemented by goodness, in the same way as pagan sensualism could be complemented by Christian sentiments; or, on another level, his love of Western culture was inseparable from his endeavors to resuscitate the Russian style.

Sensitive to the influence of Populism, which he fought on political grounds, Tolstoy imitated the superficials of national originality, occasionally even lapsing into sentimentality or falsity. What saved him from worse lapses was his happy, overflowing sense of life, his capacity for enjoyment, his virility and straightforwardness, which give an air of sincerity and nobility to all his works. Even his adversaries respected him, and the humanity of this aristocratic poet gained him recognition among a wide democratic audience.

III   While Nekrassov's opponents were attempting to challenge his dominant position in literature, there was another poet who was being compared with Pushkin and Lermontov. Fedor Tiutchev (1803-73) seemed more of a diplomat and a man of the world than a poet. Goncharov called him a dilettante, and his friends claimed that he hardly knew the pains or the joys of artistic creation but simply jotted down rhymed lines on the spur of the moment. Tiutchev did not like to talk about his poetry; he seemed to look down upon it as one of those gentlemanly hobbies that are excusable but utterly unimportant. This attitude, however, was a pretense: in a moment of frankness Tiutchev wrote: 'I love poetry and my country above all else in this world.'

The son of a rich landowner, Tiutchev received an excellent education, graduated from the University of Moscow, and entered the diplomatic service in 1822. He spent twenty-two years in embassies abroad, mostly in Germany, coming back to Russia only on short leaves. Externally he was a typical Westernizer, versed in all fields of European culture, expert in international politics, speaking French like a Parisian, the friend of the leading men of Europe, including Heine and Schelling, and was married twice, in each case to a woman of foreign descent. His life abroad, however, far from making him a cosmopolitan, intensified his nationalistic feeling and Slavophile sympathies.

In 1844 his diplomatic career was interrupted, and he settled down in St. Petersburg, where he held high posts in the Foreign Office (in the late 'fifties he was Chairman of Foreign Censorship). Upon his return he became a welcome guest at the Imperial Court, and in aristocratic salons as well as in literary circles: this Russian-European was a brilliant and witty conversationalist, whose *bons mots* were repeated everywhere in St. Petersburg. The poems he showed to some writers also aroused enthusiasm. Although Tiutchev had been writing verse since the age of twelve, his work was hardly known: the twenty-four lyrics signed with the initials F.T. and published by Pushkin in *The Contemporary* in 1836, had not evoked a single critical comment. Until 1850 the name of Tiutchev did not appear in the press. Only in that year did Nekrassov write an eulogistic article, calling his talent first-rate. Four years later, under the urging of Turgenev, Tiutchev published about a hundred poems in *The Contemporary:* they were soon issued in book form, together with his earlier work. This slender volume, according to the poet A. Fet, contained better poetry than did many bulky tomes, and this opinion was shared by Nekrassov and Turgenev, the latter assigning him first place among contemporary poets.

But for many years Tiutchev remained the poet of the literati, of a narrow circle of select readers. This situation hardly changed until the late 'nineties, when the Symbolists, who studied and admired Tiutchev, launched a revival and he was introduced to large audiences through anthologies and text books. In the twentieth century he was definitely recognized as one of the major poets and was widely read, although the peculiar character of his work hardly favored great popularity. His influence was always considerable and is still felt by many contemporary lyricists.

The 400 short poems (including translations) left by Tiutchev present an amazing compactness and unity. Written with the utmost elegance and simplicity, although in a highly literary and somewhat archaic style, they present a consistent view of the universe. The depth of their philosophic meaning and the emotional intensity with which the abstract concepts are transmuted into art are unique not only in Russia but perhaps in world lyricism. Other great poets, such as Goethe or Shelley, for example, have written philosophical poems, but they usually expressed their ideas in long epics or symbolic dramas, such as *Faust* or *Prometheus Unbound*. Tiutchev's poems rarely run to more

than twenty lines; they are precise, epigrammatic, almost aphoristic—
and their significance is revealed in a lyric flash, brief, swift, and
dynamic.

Tiutchev possessed in the highest degree what may be called cosmic
consciousness. A landscape, a human emotion, the rites of everyday
life, were each made to relate to the wider universe or they symboli-
cally reminded him of some hidden truth. Like the Manichean sectarians, he imagined this world as an island in the sea of Chaos. The
initial Chaos is for Tiutchev the very essence of the universe; everything derives from the 'old native chaos,' and the gentle phenomena
of nature resemble a golden pall thrown over a nameless precipice.
Chaos 'moves amid the terrors of night, amid the terrible songs of the
wind,' the orgy of 'that angry sovereign, Fire,' the 'hollow wails of time,
breaking in on the universal silence of darkness,' the storm and lightning, the 'refractory flame of life.' Sometimes it is visible in air polluted
with contagion. In 'Malaria,' which he wrote in Italy, Tiutchev exclaims: 'I love this wrath of God, this mysterious ensconced Evil poured
over flowers, over the crystal-clear spring, amid the iridescent sunbeams,
under the very sky of Rome.'

Chaos underlies man's existence; it lurks in his dreams: 'Life is
surrounded by dreams, even as the earth by the ocean, and the waves
of the elements beat noisily upon the shore.' Its voice sounds in human
recollections: 'Oh, wake not the tempests from their sleep; beneath
them Chaos is stirring in the night.' The eternal pair—Death and Sleep
—as well as our passions are all part of Chaos. When, in 1830, Tiutchev learned of the revolution in Paris, he wrote the lines that were to
be remembered and quoted a century later, during the Russian upheaval: 'Fortunate is he who has been on this earth in its fateful
moments: the gods themselves have asked him to their feast.'

Like wars, uprisings, and madness, love is also descended from
Chaos: it shatters and ruins, it is not an idyll but a contention of
hearts, and the result of the struggle is always fatal. Tiutchev constantly
repeats these epithets, pointing out that we wreck what we love
and that the joy of destruction is inherent in man, just as is his attraction for evil and annihilation: love and suicide both lure him on.
(Dostoevsky found in Tiutchev's poems many of his own ideas, and
referred to him as 'the first poet-philosopher.')

The heritage of Chaos makes mortals the victims of discord. Their
souls 'dwell in two worlds'—the world of night, which breeds forebodings, revelations, and dreams, and that of daylight, with its palpable
clarity. 'Oh my prophetic soul, oh my anxious heart, how you quiver on
the threshold of a well-nigh double existence'—these are the opening

lines of one of Tiutchev's most revealing poems. This duality is caused
not only by the heart's capacity to grasp the speech of the wind and
the storm, of night and passion, and of the irresistible call of Chaos,
but also by the mind's reluctance to submit to the laws of nature. Man
disrupts the universal order by his complaints and the rebelliousness
of his thought. This thinking reed does not join in the chorus of waves,
in the harmonious melody of the universe; he is the only one to murmur
in protest and to sing his own song. Stormy Fate tosses him about,
yet he refuses to face the fact that our life is less substantial than a
wisp of smoke—than even the shadow of a wisp of smoke. A shelter-
less orphan doomed to solitude, man nevertheless rebels against his
fate—which is that of a block of ice driven out to sea, where it is
destined to melt. Our ego is but a lure of our mind, and that ego must
dissolve in the 'all-engulfing, all-pacifying abyss of the Cosmos.' Leo
Tolstoy could not listen without tears to Tiutchev's pantheistic lines:
'All things are within me, I am in all things; let me partake of annihilation, let me be diffused in the slumbering Universe.' Nature is no hostile
force to Tiutchev. This Great Mother, whose visage is resplendent with
immortality, is alive: 'She has soul and freedom, love and speech.' Her
enchantment is like pure fire; she breathes in the miraculous beauty in
flowers of the springtime, in the 'fading smile' of autumnal leaves, in
the bliss of being amid all the charm of earthly joys.

His descriptions of nature, exalting the beauty of life, are also
symbolic pictures paralleling states of mind. This parallelism is particularly striking in Tiutchev's love lyrics, which have a special place in
his work. When he was forty-seven, happily married for the second
time, and father of grown-up children, he met Elena Denissieva, a
young friend of his daughter, and fell violently in love with her. This
passionate affair lasted until Denissieva's death fifteen years later, when
Tiutchev was over sixty. It inspired his most poignant lyrics, which
describe with tragic force the exultation and despair of this autumnal
love, made 'more tender and uncanny' by his declining years. These
poems, intense, pure, and pathetic, have a place among the highest and
most beautiful specimens of Russian poetry.

Tiutchev remained aloof from the literary quarrels of his time, and
said hardly anything that could be used by the supporters of the civic
poetry or his adversaries. Of course, he believed that 'poetry descends
from the skies upon the sons of the earth, and pours the oil of peace
on the stormy sea,' and his poems had no connection with current
events. On the other hand, however, he has left a whole series of
political poems that, together with his pamphlets (written in French),
reveal his nationalistic convictions. He was always interested in and pre-

occupied by the problem of 'Russia and the West' (the title of his unfinished treatise), contrasting Eastern Europe, 'where Russia at all times was the soul and the driving force,' to Western Europe. Before the Crimean debacle he believed that the autocracy, centered in St. Petersburg, was the best guarantee of stability in a world of social upheavals, and that the Slavs of all countries would unite around the throne of the Czars. The reunion of the Slavs was one of the main themes of his political lyrics.

After 1855 he became rather pessimistic and expected a revolutionary attack from the West against the shattered rock of the Russian Empire. In a curious mixture of conservatism and messianism he wrote a few well-known poems that express his love of his country and predict her great future. Moved by the 'scanty nature, by the poor huts of the ever-patient Russian people,' he affirmed that no one could understand Russia or measure her unusual stature; one could only take Russia on faith. This was another example of the choice Tiutchev had made in the struggle between mind and heart: in the end he relied on intuition and the vague leanings of his 'prophetic soul.'

Individual poems stand out from the works of Tiutchev like fragments of a unique book, or like inscriptions on stones forming the façade of a temple. A pure lyricist, he never used verse for description or narrative, and the oratoric, declamatory swing of his poems resumes the Derzhavin tradition. This impression is enhanced by his deliberate use of archaisms, of Church-Slavonic terms, and of foreign names—mostly taken from mythology, such as Zeus, Atlas, Hebe. Tiutchev writes in a solemn, lofty style, and always resorts to composite words: 'the thunder-seething cup of a spring rain' and similar expressions make his poems oddly old-fashioned.

All these formal traits link Tiutchev more with the poets of the eighteenth century—Lomonossov, Derzhavin—than with Pushkin. His philosophy reflects the romanticism of Schelling and certain trends brought to Europe from India, but his style is an outgrowth of the ancient church traditions of Russian Orthodoxy. A man of the 'forties in upbringing and general and political outlook, this poet of passion, chaos, love, and nature was the last great master of the High Style, who used the Church-Slavonic rhetoric extensively. After Pushkin, with his all-embracing simplicity and harmony; Lermontov, with his rebelliousness and ethical anxiety; Nekrassov, with his love of the people, grief, and repentance, Tiutchev was the fourth great leader of Russian poetry. He was the profound interpreter of cosmic mysteries, who represents the philosophical Romanticism and the pantheistic aspirations of the Russian religious mind.

13

TURGENEV

I   TURGENEV has always been considered the most European of the Russian masters. Just as Herzen had served as the envoy of the Russian Revolution, Turgenev, during the more than thirty years he spent abroad, acted as the ambassador of Russian letters in England, Germany, and France. He was a more familiar figure in Paris than in St. Petersburg, and his friends—Flaubert, Maupassant, Zola, Auerbach, Henry James, and many others— belonged to the élite of European letters. He traveled widely and knew statesmen, artists, and aristocrats, and his works were translated into several languages long before those of any other Russian writer. Although he was a Westernizer in his political and cultural convictions and he loved Europe, Turgenev was hardly influenced by the European literature of his time. On the contrary, it was his work that served as a model and an inspiration to many European and American writers.

For many years Turgenev was the most comprehensive, cultured, and balanced Russian writer, devoid of those extremes of thought and form among the Slav Realists that seemed to shock the West. Many European readers of the second half of the nineteenth century claimed that getting used to the Russians was a painful process. The main objection was the lack of moderation, their going to extremes: they did not sigh but sobbed; they did not laugh but roared; their gaiety lapsed into the burlesque and the grotesque; their unhappiness turned to tragedy; and their realistic novels were epics, running to thousands of pages.

For those who had never heard of Pushkin, Turgenev's lack of exaggeration and his poise in everything, from style to political opinions, came as a surprise. He seemed the first great scion of the Muscovite

Empire to possess a sense of proportion. His writings had the delicacy
of water colors: his novels, never too long, presented an even flow of
narrative; his short stories, well planned, well organized with simple
plots, were charmingly poetic and light. All the traits that were expected, and later were found, in the Scythians—fanatical attachment
to ideas, passionate brutality, moral extremes, physiological exuberance,
emotional intransigence—were apparently completely absent in Turgenev. What, then, made him so Russian?

Turgenev's European and American friends felt very strongly his
national connotations, and not merely because this tall and robust man
seemed to fit so well into the preconceived pattern of a Slav gentleman.
Henry James noted that this cosmopolitan's 'roots have never been
loosened in his native soil,' while Renan, in a speech on the occasion
of Turgenev's body being shipped from Paris for interment in Russia,
said: 'No man has been so much the incarnation of a whole race as
Turgenev; generations of ancestors, lost, speechless, in the sleep of
centuries, have come to life and found utterance through him.'

In the freedom and spontaneity with which he judged things—so
different from Anglo-Saxon conventional standards or French logical
formality—in the humanistic bent of his mind, in his quick emotional
responsiveness, in all the contradictions of his personality, there was
something extremely typical of an intellectual bred under the skies of
Moscow and St. Petersburg. Furthermore, Russia was the core of his
preoccupations, and it was always about it that he wrote. It was, in fact,
his self-appointed task to register all the changes in the mentality of
Russian society and all the shifting ideals of its intellectuals.

This was one of the most important facets of Turgenev's literary
activity. He has come down in history as the chronicler of Russia's
cultural and psychological evolution. In the Soviet Union, as under the
Czars, every schoolboy is taught that one can study the development in
national consciousness that took place between 1840 and 1870 through
such of Turgenev's heroes as Rudin, Lavretsky, and Bazarov.

Turgenev's literary career began in the early 'forties, when the mind
of the rich young nobleman, born in 1818 in Orel, had been formed by
the universities of Moscow, St. Petersburg, and Berlin. In Germany he
studied together with Stankevich and Bakunin; upon his homecoming
in 1841 he formed a friendship with Belinsky. A year later he won his
doctorate in philosophy, and in 1843 made his debut as a poet with
Parasha, a narrative in verse, which was favorably reviewed.

As a true son of the 'forties, Turgenev was attracted equally by
many branches of art and knowledge. For several years he tried to find
himself by writing poems, plays (in which he showed himself a fore-

runner of Chekhov), essays, and book reviews, and finally found the right path in the short story, with 'Khor and Kalinych,' published in 1847 in the first issue of *The Contemporary* under its new editor, Nekrassov. The success of this tale encouraged the writer, then about thirty, to continue with the series of stories that were later collected under the title of *Hunting Sketches*. He wrote most of them abroad, between 1847 and 1852, the year they were brought out in book form, and attained great popularity. Their social impact was comparable to that of *Uncle Tom's Cabin,* but, unlike the American abolitionist, the Russian avoided any save an oblique attack on serfdom and refused to emphasize scenes of abuse, cruelty, or violence. With his usual sense of proportion he simply portrayed various characters among the peasants and landowners he met during his hunting trips.

There was no unity of plot in the twenty-one sketches (twenty-five in the edition of 1880), but a general idea ran through everyone of them. Turgenev's object was to give a realistic picture of the peasants, to show them as human beings endowed with the same feelings of dignity, love, and courage, with the same aspirations that were usually attributed only to the upper classes. His dwarf Kassyan is looking for truth and has an uncanny feeling for nature, which he loves dearly; Yashka Turok, the amateur singer, holds the audience under the spell of his passionate and wistful songs; the paralyzed Lukeria, on her protracted deathbed, shows a saintlike patience, has beautiful dreams, and is still responsive to every manifestation of life around her; the grim and ruthless forester Biryuk (Lone Wolf) finally sets free the starving muzhik he has caught in the act of cutting down his master's timber, and thus solves the conflict between duty and mercy, between human law and divine truth; the peasant boys around a bonfire at night tell folk tales and ghost stories of a highly poetic nature.

Turgenev also represented the victims of serfdom: women whose lives had been ruined by forced marriages and the stupid wilfulness of their masters ('Ermolai and the Miller's Wife'; 'Raspberry Spring'); men assigned to the most fantastic tasks ('Lgov') or crushed by poverty, by injustice, by heartless masters and corrupt stewards ('The Tryst,' 'The Office,' 'The Steward'). Later, in 'Moo-moo,' Turgenev dealt with the same theme, telling the pathetic story of a mute serf whose love for a puppy was brutally crushed by a selfish proprietress.

Turgenev never stressed the evils of serfdom. He simply made the human dignity of the peasants stand out against the background of social injustice. Such a confrontation was in itself an indictment; it was reinforced by the lively and often ironic portraits of landowners. Here again Turgenev did not introduce monsters or ogres; he intimated rather than accused. Penochkin, the aristocratic slave-owner in 'The Steward,' is one of the most cultured squires in the county, his French is faultless, his manners refined, but when at one of his delightful dinners the red wine is not served at the right temperature he merely whispers an order: 'See about Fedor'—which means that the unfortunate flunky is to be thoroughly flogged. Another Turgenev hero, the kind, talkative, and hospitable Stegunov, listens with an angelic smile to the swishing of a whip and jovially imitates the knouting: 'Chuki-chuki-chuk!'

Another group of landowners betrays the economic and moral degradation of the class that enjoyed the privilege of owning souls. Their portrayal aroused the concern of the authorities under Nicholas I: in the secret report on the *Hunting Sketches* their author was charged with 'ridiculing the landowners, presenting them in a light derogatory to their honor, and in general propagating opinions detrimental to the respect due to the nobility from the other classes.' Lvov, the censor who passed the book, was ousted from his post, while Turgenev himself was arrested, jailed, and subsequently confined for more than a year on his estate, under the pretext that he had published an article on Gogol's death 'in disregard of censorship regulations.'

Turgenev, who had become fully familiar with the horrors of serfdom in a childhood spent at Spasskoye, his mother's estate, and whose liberal leanings, strengthened by his friendship with Belinsky, Herzen, Nekrassov, Granovsky, and other idealists, had taken his Hannibal's oath to fight relentlessly against serfdom. His *Hunting Sketches* fulfilled this youthful pledge: they served as an eloquent defense of the oppressed and an objective and efficient plea for their liberation. Their impact was enormous, the social implications being enhanced by the lack of any tendentiousness. Their success was not due merely to their appearance at the right moment, when the best part of educated society was engaged in a crusade against serfdom; it was also a literary novelty in being a sober, realistic description of life, done in a detached, objective manner, without any indications of the author's sympathies or aversions—except for his tone and certain vague intimations—and with no sentimentality or patronizing of the underdog.

Turgenev did not limit himself to the presentation of only positive characters among the peasants: next to the practical and patriarchal Khor he painted the romantically inclined Kalinych, and next to the smug and cruel Sofron, a bailiff who exploits his own fellows, he put the unfortunate Antip. What struck the reader most in the *Sketches* was their combination of scrupulous fidelity to life with high artistic refinement in the light touch of the characterizations, in the sense of balance directing the selection of significant details, in the polished language, and in the splendid descriptions of nature. The landscapes of central Russia, with its unencompassable fields of wheat, its forests and rivers, forming the background of each sketch, not only are appropriate to the structure of the stories but also assume an independent stylistic value.

The plot of each sketch usually consisted of some individual episode, its main interest lying in psychological portraiture and in the pictures of nature which conveyed, in a slightly wistful, delicate manner, the very atmosphere of the Russian land. This was ever more remarkable in that Turgenev's language had nothing of the whimsical exuberance of Gogol, of the epic totality of Goncharov, or of the vernacular rudeness of Ostrovsky or Pisemsky. Turgenev's was a gentle, even style, typical of an educated nobleman who spoke a very cultured, refined Russian and who—roughly half a century after Karamzin—was also writing with grace, elegance, lyricism, and poetic sensitivity.

Turgenev kept to this style in all his novels, and particularly in his short stories, which are the best examples of his extraordinary craftsmanship. With the years it became more diaphanous and subtle, more flexible and shaded, with more emphasis on fluency, gradation, and rhythm. Iambic, dactylic, or choric measures are distinctive in many of his descriptive prose passages with their well-rounded sentences, the pace of which is deliberately slowed down. The prose of Turgenev has a singing, melodious quality; its rhythm is even, precise, and calm— very different from the shifting, nervous rhythms of Gogol or the lengthy but feverish wordiness of Dostoevsky.

Turgenev created a school of writing made up of numerous disciples, among whom the first place belongs to Chekhov. The perfection, the lustrous regularity, and musicality of Turgenev's manner won the admiration and delight of many readers and critics, who found his artistry unequaled; it also caused angry comments by those who—like Dostoevsky or Leo Tolstoy—accused him of affectation, and an exaggerated concern for purely formal achievements. Later on, and down to our own day, the Karamzin-Turgenev high literary tradition was opposed by the 'naturalness of popular parlance': the followers of the 'tradition of the soil' quoted the arch-presbyter Avvacum, Pisemsky, and Leskov as representatives of the 'anti-Turgenev' trend.

II   Even in the *Hunting Sketches* Turgenev had begun the study of the contemporary scene that led him to his social novels. His sketch 'A Prince Hamlet of the Shchigrov District' portrays an erstwhile student of Hegel, whose idealism proved of but little help in the rough-and-tumble of a backwoods environment; he is an eccentric tormented by self-analysis, angry at the world, and distressed by his own superfluity. The chief hero of 'Chertopkhanov and Nedopiuskin' is an impoverished, hare-brained squire whose romantic temperament, mad bravery, and maniacal pride clash constantly with vile reality and finally cause his tragic end in loneliness and despair.

No other writer explored so thoroughly as Turgenev the question why so many gifted, intelligent, and well-intentioned Russians make a mess of their lives and wind up as social and personal failures. The superfluous nobleman haunts the poems and most of the ten plays he wrote before 1852 (*The Hanger-On, A Month in the Country,* and others). For the hero of his short novels he usually chose either some mild, submissive young man who simply cannot cope with life and is therefore doomed to be unhappy (Jacob Pasynkov, Andrei Kolossov, and many others), or a well-bred and sensitive intellectual whose inner riches are wasted because he cannot find any outlet for his energy (*The Diary of A Superfluous Man, Faust*) or because he is unable to carry out his plans (*Asya, Spring Freshets*). These heroes continue in the wake of tradition—Griboyedov's Chatsky, Pushkin's Oneghin, Lermontov's Pechorin, without, however, imitating their predecessors.

In *Rudin* (1856), Turgenev's first novel, the superfluous man appears in a new guise. The son of a petty squire, Rudin studies in Moscow and Germany. A pure product of romantic idealism, he makes inspired speeches in the literary circles of the 'thirties and 'forties, on freedom, beauty, and sacrifice. But this exhorter and propagandist is utterly incapable of achieving any practical aim; he understands neither people nor reality, he is good for nothing, he talks too much, and his wishful thinking makes him take his dreams for accomplishments. Lacking endurance and consistency, he is lazy and weak; the articles he talks so much of writing never materialize.

He also lacks will power: when Nathalie, a charming girl of seventeen, fascinated by his enthusiastic eloquence, offers him her love, Rudin, who loves her in return, hesitates, not daring to make a decision. Evidently he is no better fitted to cope with love than with anything else in life. An unhappy, homeless wanderer, he fails to find a place in his own country and is killed on the barricades of Paris during the Revolution of 1848, an anonymous victim in an alien strife.

His friend Lezhnev points out Rudin's disinterested idealism and his love of truth. Rudin was ready to give up his life for superior values —and his example, his word, were as effective as any practical deed, says Lezhnev. To awake, to stir up, the society of their time—this was the historical task of the Rudins in the 'forties, and they perished in fulfilling it; and Turgenev is ready to render a verdict of 'not guilty' on his superfluous hero. To explain this indulgence some critics offered the hypothesis, duly supported by documentary evidence, that Rudin was modeled after Turgenev's friend Michael Bakunin, the anarchist, that cerebral and imaginative enthusiast with 'a cold heart but flushed cheeks.' It might also be that Rudin was in part a self-portrait, reflecting in a disguised and distorted fashion certain traits in the character of his creator. But there were other reasons for Turgenev's attitude: he loved the idealists of his student years, and he was perfectly conscious of the abnormal social and political environment that bred these superfluous men.

Three years after *Rudin,* in *A Nest of Gentlefolk* (1859), Turgenev introduced a type that was almost an antithesis to the loquacious hero of the 'forties. Fedor Lavretsky, a kind, silent, athletically built landowner, has but one trait in common with Rudin: he also lacks a sense of reality and has had but scanty experience in life. Brought up in an artificial atmosphere created by his father, a free-thinker and Anglomaniac, Lavretsky has been deliberately estranged from his Russian surroundings and is like an alien among his own people. The University of Moscow does little to help him overcome his timidity and sense of insecurity. He falls in love with the first pretty girl he meets, but his marriage with the shallow and unfaithful Barbara ends on the rocks while the newlyweds are living in Paris. This proves a great shock to Lavretsky, whose simple, honest mind is bewildered by feminine wiles. He returns home and, strongly imbued with Slavophile ideas, tries to shake off his European ways and to adapt himself to his native environment.

While this process of purification is under way, he meets Liza Kalitina, the daughter of his neighbors, and learns what true love can mean. Liza's is one of those deeply religious natures that are never made for the harsh realities of this world. Sensitive, poetic, pure, this frail girl has a strict and uncompromising moral code and a strong personality; she is single in her love and in her faith. She loves Lavretsky and is about to marry him when the unexpected return of Barbara, whom everybody, including her husband, had believed dead and buried, puts her in an awkward position. Liza, unable to fight for her happiness, accepts her misfortune as God's punishment for her sinful passion, accuses herself of egotism, and finally decides to renounce the world and take the veil. Barbara departs, and Lavretsky is left alone. He manages his own estate and helps his peasants, but his life is empty. When he looks at the young people who play and laugh around him, he murmurs: 'Welcome, lonely old age; burn out, useless life.'

Of course, one may say that Lavretsky is the victim of an unhappy love and thus reduce his drama to an emotional complex. But there is his submissiveness, his resignation at having drawn a losing number in the lottery of life. It is part of his general passivity. He is a kind, intelligent, and normal man, entitled to a normal life; instead he is doomed to melancholy and unproductivity, and his loneliness is symbolic of his social alienation. Lavretsky and Liza were doomed because they both belonged to a disappearing world of aristocratic estates, those islands in the boundless sea of Russia, whose way of life, uniqueness, and depth were all dying out. Turgenev described this life with a nostalgia, a lyricism, and a delicacy of analysis and description that made the book a melancholy litany of the past. With its undertones and light shadings, *A Nest of Gentlefolk* is undoubtedly the most sentimental of the realistic novels of the period; perhaps it is also the most poetic.

This novel marked the end of the era of superfluous men; the new generation did not waste its time mooning over estates going to rack and ruin or the unhappy love affairs of well-fixed landowners. The air was filled with expectation, and Turgenev, eager to chart the social temperature, tried to detect the symptoms of the imminent fever in a new novel with the purposive title of *On the Eve* (1860).

Although artistically inferior to *A Nest of Gentlefolk,* it provoked more discussion and polemics since, while Turgenev's former novels had been devoted to the past (a very recent one, it is true), *On the Eve* dealt with the present and, instead of depicting superfluous men or self-sacrificing women, it introduced new, energetic characters. Helena is the embodiment of strong-willed womanhood, resolved to live up to her ideals of freedom and activity. Like Goncharov's Olga, Helena heralded the advent of feminine emancipation; the men who surrounded her failed to arouse her feelings. Bersenev was another idealist of the 'forties who prated about Schiller and Schelling; Shubin, the sculptor, was so absorbed in antiquity and Italian art that his Epicurean dreams built a wall between him and Russian reality; while Kurnatovsky, the man whom Helena's family wants her to marry, is merely an honest bureaucrat, lacking vision and temperament. Helena bestows her love on Insarov, a Bulgarian who had devoted himself to the liberation of his native country from the Turkish yoke. With silent passion he concentrates on his work; he may appear narrow-minded, but at least he is not afflicted with introspection—he is inspired with force and decision.

Helena chooses him because he personifies her ideal of manhood and social usefulness. Sacrificing her fortune and social standing, she becomes the wife of this impecunious Bulgarian, leaves her family, follows Insarov abroad, and after his premature death remains in Europe to continue his work. Her refusal to return home is made on the assumption that Russia had not yet produced its own Insarovs: 'Why go home?' she asks: 'What can one accomplish in Russia?' Shubin complains to Helena's uncle, an obese gentleman who merely sits in an armchair and twiddles his thumbs, that instead of real men, all one can find are all sorts of small fry, little Hamlets, nincompoops or timid souls plagued with self-analysis. But the uncle's enigmatic glance seems to be directed toward the future and to reflect some hope. Is he not the symbol of huge, immobile Russia, which will one day stir from its lethargy to reveal all its latent strength? This hope was probably the message of the novel: Dobroliubov, in his famous review of the book, 'When Will the Day Itself Come?' affirmed that 'Russian Insarovs will not fail to appear soon, for we are truly on the eve of a new day.'

Turgenev did not like this review. He could not get along with the representatives of the new generation, for despite his liberal opinions he was shocked by the rudeness of the Raznochintsi and by their anti-esthetic trend. He resented their attempts to tell the artist what to write and, after a succession of minor skirmishes with Nekrassov and Cher-nyshevsky, he broke away from *The Contemporary* group. *On the Eve* was published in the monthly *Russian Messenger*. But as an artist and as a careful observer of moods and trends in Russian society he could not help realizing the importance of the psychological change in the intellectuals. The Raznochintsi were demanding a hero of their own— and therein lay the answer to Shubin's complaint. Taking as his model a young physician he had occasionally met, Turgenev wrote his most discussed and probably greatest novel, *Fathers and Sons* (1862), in which he attempted to depict a type whose characteristics had not yet been defined by any writer. This was the challenge of Turgenev's new work: its hero, Bazarov, summed up various mental and emotional features that were still in the process of formation. As a type he out-distanced reality: His contemporaries recognized themselves in him, but they also felt that the novel mirrored the future as well as the present; they were still only moving toward Bazarov.

The combination of what existed with what was predicted by art in a flash of divination made *Fathers and Sons* particularly controversial and provoked more violent polemics than had been ever aroused by any other work. Was Bazarov a prototype of the young men of the 'sixties or a figure born in the writer's imagination? And, if the latter, did he personify existing trends as Turgenev had represented them? Was this representation flattering or derogatory? Was Bazarov a carica-ture or a true likeness?

In his novel Turgenev introduces Bazarov as a young physician who has just received his diploma and is taken by Arkadii Kirsanov, his friend and admirer, to the latter's estate for a short vacation. Arkadii's father, Nicholas, and his uncle, Paul—both men of the 'forties —are greatly shocked by Bazarov. This grandson of a deacon and son of a poor country surgeon is brusque, cynical, rough; he discards affability and polite manners as useless burdens, does not care for the niceties of life, and is crude and abrupt in his speech. He hates romanticism, pomposity, and rhetoric: 'Please, Arkadii,' he tells his friend, 'don't talk so beautifully.' Opposed to vagueness and idealistic estheticism and convinced that a good chemist is of more value than a poet, Bazarov looks down at the 'fathers'—the charming, weak Nicholas, who is ashamed of his liaison with the daughter of his housekeeper, and the old bachelor Paul, a former officer in the Guards and a beau who, after an unhappy love affair, has retired to the country to lead the life of a squire in the British style. Bazarov clashes with the aristocratic Paul, who has never lifted a finger to do any productive work and who spends his day reading and changing his still-dandified clothes. As a materialist and a down-to-earth fellow Bazarov judges people according to their practical achievements. Now, what had Paul done in his life? He had loved, had been deceived by some rattlebrained female, and then had turned melancholic and spent his years in doing nothing. Away with him!

Bazarov boasts of his own rational, cut-and-dried, heartless attitude and denies the power of sentimentality: reason and will ought to control human behavior. He himself is a hard and intelligent worker, without cant, hypocrisy, or prejudice, and he proves it when he falls in love with the beautiful widow Odintzova for whom comfort, tranquility, and dreams are worth more than passion and excitement. Bazarov overcomes his feelings and conceals his sufferings precisely as he hides his love for his aged, quaint parents. Despite his front of coarseness and cynicism, he is a man of intense emotions—and he inspires either love or hatred.

He knows what he wants and he goes after it resolutely: his main objectives are work and the betterment of life. Both tasks require courage and sacrifice; thus, such men as his friend Arkadii are not fit for them: 'You have neither daring nor anger; that won't do for our job,' he tells Arkadii on taking leave of him.

You aristocrats can never get beyond dignified meekness or dignified outbursts, both of which are bosh. You won't fight, for instance, yet fighting is what we want. . . The dust we raise would hurt your eyes, our grime would soil you; besides, you haven't grown up to us yet, you still admire yourselves, you like to scold yourselves . . . and that sort of thing bores us, since what we want is to scold and break other people. You're a good lad but you're a softy, a mushy liberal, and a gentleman—good day to you, Señor.

Bazarov (like all the other Turgenev heroes) is not given any time to show his capabilities. He wounds and infects a finger during an autopsy and, since there are no antitoxins in the little village where he is staying with his parents, even his father, an old doctor, is unable to save him from dying of blood poisoning.

Bazarov's death assuredly had a symbolic meaning. Did it signify that Russian reality was not yet ripe for him? Or that he was doomed to fall victim to the backwardness of his environment? At any rate Pisarev accepted him as the 'Representative of our young generation; Bazarov sums up all the traits that are scattered in many individuals. Turgenev studied this type, and understood it well.' Pisarev was, however, the only critic to accept *Fathers and Sons* unconditionally. Most of Turgenev's contemporaries accused him for quite different reasons. He is slandering the younger generation, shouted the radicals; he is too lenient toward the horrible Nihilists, contended the conservatives. Turgenev kept receiving congratulations, insults, and even some threats from unexpected quarters: the revolutionaries called him an enemy of the people, while the reactionaries labeled him the obedient flunky of the Nihilists. In vain did he cite his realistic method and emphasize that 'To reproduce truth, the very reality of life, is the highest happiness for the writer, even if that truth does not coincide with his own sympathies.'

Most liberals considered *Fathers and Sons* a political *faux pas,* since the novel was extensively exploited by the reactionaries in their detraction of the progressive movement. The word 'Nihilist' became a sneering label for the exaggerations of radicalism—and this deeply distressed Turgenev. Of course, when the discussion subsided, friends and foes had to acknowledge certain points that they had all missed in the heat of battle.

The novel could not be reduced merely to terms of Nihilism; it had a manifold significance and deserved to be analyzed on different planes. As its title implies, it deals with the eternal conflict between age and youth, each holding to its own truth; it showed the old generation faithful to its traditions and the young eager to make a new start. Their clash—inevitable at all times—is magnificently depicted by Turgenev in many details: the patronizing attitude of Arkadii toward his father; the uneasiness, almost fear, felt by old Bazarov in the presence of his son, his attempt to boast of his own medical lore, and so on.

Bazarov himself is more than merely a man of the 'sixties; he is a national type, as fundamentally Russian as any previous literary hero. He belongs to a social group different from that of the Oblomovs and the Pechorins—and it was this that made him appear extraordinary. For the first time in Russian fiction there had appeared a man who was strong, positive, and—without lapsing into the inhuman rigidity of a Rakhmetov—imbued with a rational approach to life, a matter-of-fact spirit, a moral integrity coupled with strength of character and the desire for work—a desire so passionate that Bazarov's cynicism was transmuted into idealistic aspiration.

To a greater extent than any other literary character Bazarov was the precursor of the heroes of Soviet literature: whoever would understand the mentality of the average Soviet intellectual is bound to study *Fathers and Sons*—a book that survives as one of the most modern of Turgenev's works. His subsequent novels (*Smoke* and *Virgin Soil*) cannot compare with that masterpiece. In no other novel has Turgenev achieved such a blending of intellectual, emotional, and purely descriptive elements. The attention paid to the main character does not detract from the minor ones: Arkadii, his fiancée Katenka, his father and uncle, Fenichka, his father's mistress, Bazarov's parents, Odintzova, all are amazingly lifelike and convincing. Although less poetic than Turgenev's other novels, *Father and Sons* nevertheless contains exceedingly moving passages, such as those dealing with Bazarov's emotions, his death, and the pilgrimage of his grief-stricken parents to his grave in the village cemetery.

III   *Fathers and Sons,* published after Turgenev's break with *The Contemporary,* caused the radicals to attack him bitterly, and the writer, then forty-four, thought that he had alienated the younger generation and lost contact with the main current of national thought. He attributed this to his life abroad, which had permitted him only short visits to Russia, and decided that, having nothing more to say, he ought to give up writing. Yet he could not help thinking and being concerned about his country, which his self-imposed exile had brought still closer to his heart. Henry James was right in asserting that the problem of Russia and of bettering its conditions formed the dramatic core of Turgenev's life.

In 1867, five years after bringing out *Fathers and Sons,* he published a new novel, *Smoke,* whose slender though charming plot served merely as a vehicle for the discussion of various political ideas. Russian reactionaries, revolutionaries, Slavophiles, and Westernizers, coming together at Baden-Baden, give free expression to their opinions of contemporary issues. This time Turgenev had his own mouthpiece,

Potughin, who, loving Europe and believing in its civilization, wishes Russia to adopt the principles and achievements of the West.

Turgenev belonged to that large and influential group of mild liberals, mostly recruited from among the nobility and the intellectuals, that was firmly opposed to the autocratic regime, yet whose aim was a gradual transformation of Russia into a constitutional monarchy modeled on that of Great Britain. They expected the Czar to grant reforms under the pressure of growing public opinion and they disapproved of revolutionary methods and what they called Socialistic Utopias. Turgenev's political opinions were, however, always obscured by his fundamental pessimism: Litvinov, the hero of *Smoke,* feels that life in general and in Russia in particular, is as illusive as smoke, and that all political agitation is just a futile game.

This idea was stressed in *Virgin Soil,* the last of Turgenev's novels, published in *The Messenger of Europe* (1877). It pictures the Populist movement of the 'seventies, during which thousands of revolutionaries went to the villages or factories in order to stay and share the life and work of the common people. They are portrayed from a critical point of view: Nezhdanov, another variant of the superfluous man, is a repentant nobleman who, trying to propagandize the peasants, realizes the falsity of his position, loses faith, and commits suicide; Paklin, Kisliakov, and their revolutionary friends are merely crackpots. The positive idea of the novel is personified in Solomin, the manager of a spinning mill. His simple, practical work is opposed to the generous but fantastic dreams of the Populists. He is merely the average, useful man, without any particular talents or brilliant ideas, ready to do the 'necessary dirty and anonymous work.' In some ways he is related to Goncharov's Stolz, except that he is an educated technician and businessman, a representative of a growing bourgeois middle class. Marianna, a sincere and idealistic girl who longs to alleviate the sufferings of the people and who shares Nezhdanov's life, understands Solomin and follows him. She is the most attractive person in the novel: like Helena in *On the Eve,* Chernyshevsky's Vera Pavlovna, and Goncharov's heroines, she is one of the New Women, who had become a powerful factor of political life in Russia.

Turgenev had met quite a few Populists among the *émigrés* in Paris, and had even subsidized *Forward,* one of their publications, edited by Peter Lavrov. But these casual contacts could not give him a true picture of the Populist movement, and *Virgin Soil,* marred by factual errors and omissions, partly owing to the censorship, showed merely the seamy side of Populism. The Populists, who played such a great role in the 'seventies, disliked the novel; as did the conservatives, who were greatly aroused by the caricatured portrayal of Sipiaghin and Kolomeizev, two characters who were exponents of nationalism and reaction.

Virgin Soil marks the end of Turgenev's activity as a novelist. In the six years between this novel and his death Turgenev wrote a few novelettes (*The Song of Triumphant Love, Clara Milich*), tinged with mysticism, and a collection of remarkable poems in prose, which he called *Senilia*.

IV   Turgenev called himself a Realist, and defined his artistic aim as the truthful and dispassionate portrayal of life. He often pointed out his own objectivity: being a Westernizer did not prevent him from presenting the Westernizer Panshin (in *A Nest of Gentlefolk*) unfavorably and making him come off second-best in the argument with the Slavophile Lavretsky; being an anti-Nihilist did not deter him from bringing out all the good points and even virtues of Bazarov; being an atheist did not affect his sympathetic comprehension of Liza's religious feelings.

Belinsky praised Turgenev's precise observation, his capacity for grasping the essence and the peculiarities of each character, and his superb artistry in revealing the causes and effects of human actions and in describing nature. Although he is justly considered one of the world's greatest storytellers, the story itself never attracted Turgenev: the plots of his novels and tales are so simple as to appear slight, and always hinge on the reversal of a love affair. The main thing for him is to show men and women, their relations and their emotions and ideas, without ever attempting a thorough psychological analysis—he always leaves such an analysis to the reader. The latter, however, it put on the right path by hints, allusions, and the mood created by landscapes and the rhythm of the language. The actual work of psychological penetration is done behind the scenes of the novel, by the highly intelligent author who allows only the ultimate results of his exploration to appear in his writings.

This method is responsible for the kind of psychological impressionism or imagism we always find in Turgenev's novels and stories. Turgenev has stated that he wrote not because certain incidents or adventures had occurred to him, but because he had in mind the representation of a certain person, whom he tried to conceive with factual and psychological completeness (he even wrote, for his own use, preliminary biographies of all his main characters). Or, as Henry James put it:

An idea with him is such and such an individual with such a nose and chin, such and such a hat and waistcoat. . . Abstract possibilities immediately become to his vision concrete situations . . . as we read we are always looking and listening.

This concreteness assumes the form of absolute compactness and economy of words. Turgenev's art is very different from Goncharov's factual thoroughness, Dostoevsky's metaphysical depth, or Tolstoy's universality. Turgenev limited himself in the scope and range of his writings, as well as in his ways of expression. His novels are short; the action unfolds without digressions or parallel plots and usually takes place in a brief span of time; the protagonists are reduced to a minimum; the author does not indulge in any analysis of their feelings or their behavior, always employing the method of indirect allusions and under-statements.

When he wants to clarify a detail, however—to demonstrate Insa-rov's strength, for instance, or Bazarov's skeptical attitude toward ac-cepted authorities—he does not beat around the bush but comes straight to the point. The dialogue—adroitly individualized and functional in psychological portrayal—also serves for the exposition of ideas. His protagonists not only talk, but also discuss facts and abstract concepts. Rudin and Lezhnev deliver long speeches on various subjects; Lav-retsky and his friend Mikhalevich discuss the men and trends of the 'forties; Bazarov and Paul Kirsanov have arguments over love, science, and esthetics; Potughin and Litvinov exchange lengthy opinions on Europe and Russia's destinies. In general, Turgenev's heroes are de-fined more by what they say than by what they do.

It can be said of all his novels that they had the definite purpose of representing the aristocracy and the intelligentsia in their intellectual and social metamorphosis and that they form a gallery of Russian types as they actually existed between 1840 and 1870. His short stories, more concerned with the love episodes in the life of aristocrats, mostly Super-fluous Men, are a sort of poetic accompaniment to the novels, although esthetically they are the best part of his literary bequest. But, if most of Turgenev's writings were social novels, what was their message? And, if there was none, what constituted their central theme, and what did they convey, and continue to convey, to their readers?

Turgenev did not see in life only material for his imagination. He looked for topics and people that corresponded to his personal in-clinations. All the works of this objective realist were highly subjective and unraveled many inner conflicts that had tormented him since his early youth. He possessed a great gift for understanding contradictions, for picturing with an equal persuasiveness an idle aristocrat, a Nihilist, a dreamer, or a practical man. Was it objectivity or ambivalence? It certainly could not be explained, as some critics have attempted to do, only by his insight and tolerance.

There was another reason for Turgenev's noncommittal attitude. A rational atheist, he did not believe in God and showed little enthusiasm for humanity. He kept to the middle of the road in politics, went along with the gradual reformers, was on friendly terms with radicals, but never committed himself to any definite group. In art he defended the objective representation of reality, praised harmony and balance as the main principles of an aimless estheticism, and took pride in the fact (contested by the critics) that his novels, both long and short, neither proved anything nor attempted to do so. He certainly appreciated freedom, human dignity, education, culture, and progress, but he never displayed any ardor in proclaiming those values.

As a matter of fact, there was very little positive affirmation in his work. The friends of his youth, such as Belinsky, Bakunin, and Herzen, had been enthusiastic about philosophy, anarchism, or Socialism; his contemporaries, such as Gogol, Dostoevsky, Tolstoy, struggled for religion, God, or morality—but Turgenev did not identify himself with any doctrine or intense belief. Here, again, he kept to the middle of the road, like an intelligent onlooker who enjoys the show but will never take part in it as an actor. He lacked religiosity, which some people believe to be a Russian national trait, and was hardly interested in the quest of all-embracing, all-absorbing concepts or systems of ideas.

This was probably the hidden cause of Turgenev's curious personal relations: almost all the great writers of the period quarreled with him. Dostoevsky's friendship turned into intense hatred: he despised Turgenev's independence, his fine manners, his wealth, his good looks, his polished style, and poetic elegance, and he accused him of superficiality, hypocrisy, and aloofness. Tolstoy's clash with Turgenev, almost ending in a duel, revealed the profound gulf between Tolstoy's moral intransigence and Turgenev's ethical indifference. Goncharov charged his literary rival with all the mortal sins. Turgenev's relations with Chernyshevsky and Dobroliubov and later Nekrassov were more than strained, and these friends of his thought him too much of an aristocrat and a skeptic. Apparently those who made their lives consistent with their convictions were irritated by his genteel superiority, his interest in all things, his refusal to yield to anything, his polite pessimism veiled with poetic melancholy. And why was he pessimistic, this wealthy patrician who could arrange his life as he pleased and who was favored by fortune—an illustrious writer with leisure enough to chisel every phrase (something Dostoevsky could never forgive him), equally famous at home and abroad, a man of great intelligence, wide culture and striking appearance, a welcome guest in half a dozen world capitals?

Whoever will read several of Turgenev's novels and tales in succession will not fail to notice that they all have unhappy endings. Rudin, Insarov, Bazarov, Nezhdanov, Chertopkhanov, Pasynkov—all meet sudden and, for the most part, violent deaths. Liza dies for the world's sake; Lavretsky continues to vegetate in a sort of deadly atonement. All the love stories also end with failure or death ('Spring Freshets', 'First Love', 'Asya', 'Clara Milich', 'Phantom', 'Faust', and so on). In general, in Turgenev's tales something always happens on the threshold of fulfilment: accidents or catastrophes meet his men and women at the very door of happiness.

This is not accidental. Turgenev, like his hero Litvinov in *Smoke,* felt the vanity of human illusions and the absurdity of life. The idea of eternity terrified him; he speaks of it time and again, like a man who has a long and involved account to settle with it. His *Senilia*—the most complete and frank expression of his true self—repeatedly deals with the fear of death. 'A Conversation,' 'The Dog,' 'The Hag,' 'The End of The World,' and a number of other poems in prose revolve around the one topic—the inevitability of annihilation. The mysterious female vampire Ellis in 'Phantoms' (written in 1863) reflects his own qualms: 'Why do I shudder in such anguish at the mere thought of annihilation?' For merciless and aloof Nature the existence of man is no more important than that of a flea ('Nature'). From the summits of the Alps, for the Jungfrau and the Finsteraarhorn, centuries pass like seconds, and to them the humans in the valley look like ants who will disappear one day, leaving immaculate the white eternity of their snow ('An Alpimalyan Dialogue'). A blind woman of gigantic proportions pushes on a bony, stalwart female who holds the hand of a small, bright-eyed girl, the child struggles in vain, but is driven along—and these three figures are Fate, Force, and Freedom. Men are imprisoned within a circle of fatality—and there is nothing beyond its bounds except 'the clangorous barking from the thousand throats of death,' 'darkness, eternal darkness,' the interminable void of destruction. This fundamental pessimism overshadows not only the tales of Turgenev's old age but his earlier works, such as 'Andrei Kolossov,' 'Faust,' 'A Backwater,' 'Journey to Polessie,'—all written in his thirties.

In one of his letters to Pauline Viardot he writes: 'I cannot stand the empty skies, but I adore life, its reality, its whims, its accidents, its rites, its swiftly passing beauty.' It was not an easy love. He fled from the 'empty skies' into the palpable reality of human affairs, he sought oblivion in the activity of others, in love and illusions. Eternity is madness, death is a nightmare, and Turgenev forgets them only when he meets some spontaneous manifestation of life—in beauty, action, or thought.

The charm of a momentary pleasure moves him to tears, for he always realizes how short and transitory it is bound to be. A green branch on a spring day fills him with tremulous delight: it is the very image of beauty, of the sweet joy of being. In his lecture, 'Hamlet and Don Quixote,' he gave preference to the Knight of La Mancha, since the Spaniard's illusions overcame his fear of death; his love of action liberated him from the burden of reflection, which dissects and kills the spontaneity of existence.

As a friend and disciple of philosophers, Turgenev, of course, was much closer to the Prince of Denmark than to the ecstatic Spanish hidalgo. In picturing the superfluous men he was in part making self-portraits, particularly when he showed how the self-analysis and self-criticism of his heroes destroyed their ability for action. But he admired the Don Quixotes, and he also loved men like Bazarov, Solomin, and Insarov, who were the very antithesis of himself.

Another curious aspect is his interest in political and social struggles. He was always excited by men's most spectacular activity—that of social transformation—because he was a patriot and sincerely loved his country and also because in this activity he found another affirmation of life, another evidence of 'whims and accidents,' which helped him to forget 'the toothless Ancient.' He was not energetic or particularly active by nature, but others' expenditure of energy gave him a sense of security and heartened him, in the way the love of other people inspired him with joy and admiration, not unmixed with melancholy. Beauty was another, though momentary, victory over annihilation; contemplation of it brought a rapture enhanced by the consciousness of its evanescence. His tears of ecstasy were mingled with tears of regret.

Well aware of his inner conflict, he dreamt of harmony and the simple, natural life. In 'Faust,' and in the 'Journey to Polessie,' he came to the conclusion that 'the quiet and slow animation, the unhurried restraint of sensations and impulses, the equilibrium of health in every individual being, are the prerequisites of happiness.' The only lasting happiness lies in the serenity of a somewhat monotonous existence based upon instinct and resignation. The same law applies to art: a good work of art must possess the same equilibrium, the same poise, even when dealing with anxiety or madness. He praised highly 'the tranquility in passion' of the great tragic actress Rachel, citing her as an example of the highest esthetic achievement.

268	THE EPIC OF RUSSIAN LITERATURE

Here again his duality was patent. Although he was denied the romantic vision of happiness, all his heroes aspire to its bliss. This aspiration is an irresistible human need, a manifestation of the life instinct—and it is doomed to failure and annihilation. With incomparable poetry he describes this wistful expectation of soul and flesh, this flowering of desire and love, this hope of triumphing over the ruthless domination of time. The best pages of Turgenev are devoted to this promise of happiness that reaches its height in the awakening of love and in the springtime of nature. In 'Three Encounters' the image of the tense, almost painful, silence of a magnificent summer night filled with scents and susurrations and cravings, with the languor and yearnings of mind and body, with a strange sensation of happiness—a promise and a recollection—is one of the most lyrical passages in the European prose of the nineteenth century; and as a parallel to these pages, there are the chapters describing Liza's love for Lavretzky in *A Nest of Gentlefolk*.

Turgenev never pictured the fulfilment of love, the satisfaction of the senses and of the heart. For him the apex had been reached before—in the highest and most intense moment of a dream that can never come true.

It may be argued that in this as well, Turgenev was being autobiographical. His was a strange love life. As a child he had to endure the tyranny of his mother, a domineering woman frustrated by her late, rather disappointing marriage and made wilful by her great wealth and her power over the serfs. She is described in 'Moo-moo,' 'First Love,' 'Punin and Baburin,' 'A King Lear of the Steppes,' and 'The Office.' She dominated and oppressed her sensitive son; she whipped him for the slightest fault and controlled his every step including his first sexual experience: when he came of age she sent one of her chambermaids to teach the mysteries of love to the young master. Turgenev has told about this in a highly revealing letter to Flaubert, which seems to intimate that after this first experience he ordinarily divorced love from sensual pleasure. At any rate, he could derive physical joy from intercourse with socially inferior women, and for some time lived with a pretty peasant girl who bore him a daughter. Later Turgenev undertook to educate his child in Paris.

In 1843, the year of his first literary success, at the age of twenty-five, he met in Moscow the famous French singer Pauline Viardot Garcia, who had come to Russia on a concert tour. This encounter shaped his entire future. He loved Pauline Viardot with all the strength and passion of which he was capable, and remained faithful to her for the rest of his days, leaving Russia for her sake. For over three decades his life was closely associated with that of the Viardot family (Pauline had a husband and several children.) He died in 1883 on her estate (where he had been living), at Bougival, near Paris.

The whole truth concerning Turgenev's relations with Pauline Viardot is still not known: the existing documents prove that those relations were of a complex nature and brought him a great deal of suffering, humiliation, and discomfort. It is possible that his childhood and the painful experiences of maturity had developed certain feminine traits in his character—his sensitivity, his lyrical mellowness, his delicate melancholy. At any rate, whether or not these are qualified as feminine, we have to acknowledge that he usually depicted weak men and strong women. As a rule, Turgenev admired strong feminine characters, and he gave his heroines all the passion, the will power, the intensity of feeling, and directness of purpose his superfluous males usually lack. His women are either ideal images of pure, passionate, and determined girls at the moment of their first love, or portraits of merciless Amazons intent on dominating their victims (Irina in 'Spring Freshets'; Zenaide in 'First Love,' although she met her master; Odintzova, to some extent, in *Fathers and Sons*). They are more outspoken and resolute in love, often taking the initiative. Nathalie comes to Rudin to tell him she is ready to elope; Asya, whose name serves as the title of a charming tale, confesses her feelings to her lover, who turns pusillanimous and talks nonsense (Chernyshevsky laughed at him in his essay, 'A Russian at an Assignation'—which Turgenev found outrageous); Gemma, in 'Spring Freshets,' is the only one of his heroines to be consumed by a pure flame while her beau falls prey to a mature seductress; the young actress Clara ('Clara Milich') loves so passionately that she commits suicide when she is coldly repulsed, but after her death she takes possession of her reluctant lover.

It is also quite possible that his predominant impulses toward oblivion and for 'the palpable reality of life' influenced his attitude toward women and love. He cherished in them not the allure of sex but the wholeness of nature, the spontaneity and unity of emotion. In his novels the fullness and potency of love is revealed mostly to women. Liza, Helena, Nathalie, Marianna, Gemma, Asya—all of them attain the culmination of their emotions. Love is the highest affirmation of life, and in women its flame burns most intensely. That love also was ultimately an illusion he knew very well, yet he always returns to it as a last refuge, and one of his tales, written in his old age, is entitled 'The Song of Triumphant Love.' Youth, spring, lovely damsels striving for happiness: this is the vision that inspired him. It is always projected against the background of his lyrically interpreted landscapes. There is something fresh, tremulous, hopeful, and pathetic in these still-life paintings which reflect Turgenev's nostalgic feelings for his native land.

Certain severe critics contend that Turgenev's search for beauty often turned into prettiness, while his art became arty. It is true that his softness and gentleness have at times a cloying aftertaste. He makes life and nature appear rather tame, he avoids mentioning the seamy side of reality or plunging too deeply beneath its surface, for fear of encountering the monsters of depravity, hatred, or abnormality. He takes great care not to pain or shock his readers, and his prose is decorous and seemly, suave and well-bred. His voice is never raised or altered; there are no surprises in his narrative, no breaks in his sentences. Whatever one may feel about this kind of literature, its craftsmanship is undeniable: Turgenev was an extraordinary artist.

This refined and intelligent writer whose irony—and there is far more irony in his works than is usually acknowledged—underscored his sadness, this accomplished stylist who believed that 'such a great, mighty, and free language' as Russian must have been given to a great people, this esthete who wrote social novels, this patrician who described the peasants, this democrat who sang requiems over the nobility, this realist who was so elegiac, this poet who was so precise, is one of the most beloved writers in Russia. His popularity, already very great during his lifetime, soared at about 1900, when he was particularly admired by the young and studied in schools as a classic.

A slight change in his popularity took place in the first years after the Revolution of 1917, when some Communist zealots, using Bazarov's language almost verbatim, rejected Turgenev as 'an exponent of the aristocracy, estheticism, love-nonsense, and weakness.' The attitude of Soviet readers, however, made these critics change their tune; between 1918 and 1948 twelve-and-a-half million copies of Turgenev's works were published in the Soviet Union. His novels and tales were, of course, included in the programs of all secondary schools, and they were also widely popular with adult readers.

That most of his novels have already a historic interest and that on the whole he seems somewhat old-fashioned do not affect his status as a literary favorite. *Fathers and Sons* leads his novels in popularity, seconded by *A Nest of Gentlefolk* and his short stories. In a country where earnest, ponderous writers prevail, Turgenev represents something partly approaching the Western concept of light literature: his books are pleasant and vivid, easy to read and to remember, they have a universal appeal; and their form is as neat and meticulous as that of the charming handicrafts of old times. Widely read and enjoyed today, he will probably continue to be one of the most popular writers for many years to come—as long as his languor, his melancholic grief, combined with the exaltation in love and beauty, and his conception of art as an orderly arrangement of emotional values, still stir the poetic and esthetic senses of Russian readers.

14

DOSTOEVSKY

I ONE MAY evening in 1845 Dmitri Grigorovich, a young nobleman, brought a manuscript, written by a friend of his and entitled *Poor Folk,* to Nekrassov, who was about to publish a literary anthology. They read the manuscript aloud. The pathetic story of a humble clerk and his self-sacrficing love made Nekrassov so enthusiastic that he wanted to rush out and make the author's acquaintance forthwith. Grigorovich objected that the author must be asleep at that late hour. 'Who cares?' retorted Nekrassov. 'We'll wake him up. This is more important than sleep.'

And so, at four o'clock in the morning, they were congratulating and embracing a baffled young man named Fedor Dostoevsky. The impression made on the latter by this surprising visit was everlasting. 'This was the most delightful moment of all my life,' he wrote later. Glory itself descended upon him and illuminated his poor lodgings amid the tremulous pallor of a St. Petersburg dawn.

Dostoevsky, like Turgenev, was a man of the 'forties, brought up in an atmosphere of idealistic philosophy and romantic longings. His background, however, was completely different from that of the wealthy patrician. He came from an impoverished family of obscure gentry. His paternal grandfather was a priest; his father, a former army surgeon, who was on the staff of a Moscow Hospital for the poor, had married a merchant's daughter, a kindhearted and meek woman who bore him eight children. Fedor Mikhailovich Dostoevsky, born in 1821, spent a rather gloomy childhood in the hospital yards and in the low-ceiling rooms of the doctor's cottage, filled with religious pictures and icons. His father, an irritable and morose man, ruled his large family with an iron hand: his sons had to ask permission to sit in his presence. The strict discipline, the unyielding paternal authority, the religious devotion, and the whole traditional way of life in the Dostoevsky household were more typical of the merchant class than of the petty nobility, which explains certain features of Fedor's character and what he himself later called his 'lack of form,' of *savoir faire*.

At the age of seventeen he was sent to the Academy of Military Engineering in St. Petersburg, where he found a regime of rigid formality, severe punishments, and strict drilling. He suffered atrociously because of his poverty, his ill-health, and the mockery of his companions, who laughed at the clumsiness and shyness of this silent, nervous, odd-looking youth. His only joy was reading: he was passionately fond of Sir Walter Scott and E. T. A. Hoffmann, knew Schiller by heart, read the French novelists avidly, adored Pushkin, and later, Gogol. He wrote himself—historical tales, dramas, poems in a high-flown style—and was making bold plans for other literary undertakings. A commissioned officer by 1842 and a draughtsman at the engineering section of the War Department by 1843, he nevertheless had very little liking for his position and finally resigned with the intention of devoting himself entirely to literature. The following years he lived in utter destitution, earning a few rubles by translating Balzac, his favorite writer, and the works of several French Romantics, paying frequent visits to the pawnshops, and forced, on cold winter nights, to seek shelter in disreputable dives. On those rare occasions when he came into some money, as when he received his inheritance from his father, he spent it on theater tickets, gay suppers, and gambling. His life was as irregular and unpredictable as his mind: he could pass, with amazing rapidity, from elation to despondency and from wonderful hopes to grim despair. The success of *Poor Folk*, published in 1846 and acclaimed as an example of 'Realistic Humanism,' had not improved his financial status but it did open to him the doors of literary salons, where he lost his heart to the attractive Panaeva and met a number of prominent writers, Turgenev among them. However, his next novel, *The Double*, as well as some of his short stories, did not please the critics—and apparently not the readers either.

In 1846-7 Dostoevsky went through a period of discouragement and inner crisis. His vanity had been hurt by hostile criticism, he was burdened with debts, exhausted by work, exasperated by the bondage of his literary commitments—mostly translations, the main source of his meager income. His health, undermined by bad food, cold and damp lodgings, an irregular, occasionally dissipated life, was also impaired by hypochondria and what he called 'fits of mystical horror.' His irritability, his outbreaks of lust or his passion for gambling, alternating

with repentance and abasement, his pathological sensitivity and the contradictions of his character worried his few friends. But he also enchanted them by imparting to them his fantasies and wonderful dreams.

In 1848 most of these were fervent visions of a regenerated mankind
and an ideal future. Under the influence of Belinsky he became interested in social problems and read Saint-Simon, Cabet, Fourier, Owen,
and other Utopian-Socialists. He joined the circle of Petrashevsky,
moved everybody to tears by his comments on the Christian-Socialist
Lamennais, and made inspired speeches—without ever suspecting that
all his words were being recorded by an agent of the secret police.

In April 1849, all the members of the circle were arrested and
imprisoned in the Fortress of SS. Peter and Paul. The imprisonment
worsened Dostoevsky's physical condition, and it is almost certain he
had his first fit of epilepsy while under solitary confinement. Eight
months later, on 22 December, the prisoners were taken to Semenovsky
Place and lined up before a scaffold surrounded by stakes. Despite the
fierce frost they were stripped to their shirts and, shivering, were compelled to listen to sentence of death for all of them. The first group of
three, sentenced to be shot, wearing white shrouds and blindfolded,
were tied to stakes. Dostoevsky waited for his turn in a second group.
The firing squad pointed its rifles at the victims.

Then, suddenly, the commanding officer waved a white handkerchief: the execution was stopped at the last moment, and a commutation
of the sentence, at the 'Czar's merciful behest,' was proclaimed. The
bonds of the three men were loosed. The hair of one of the three had
turned white; another had gone mad. Dostoevsky, under the new sentence was condemned to four years of hard labor and four years of
military service as a private in Siberia. On Christmas Eve, wearing
chains weighing ten pounds each, his body covered with sores, he was
put into an open sleigh which, through blizzards and storms, was to
take him all the way to Siberia.

The journey lasted two months. In the prison at Omsk he found
himself in the company of murderers whose nostrils had been torn out
by the public executioner, of criminals branded on their foreheads, of
grimacing and blaspheming humanity jangling its chains. For four
years he had to endure the heavy toil, the dirt and darkness of prison
barracks, the inhuman regulations: the prisoners were flogged if they
did not sleep on their right side or moaned too loudly at night. The
only book Dostoevsky was allowed to read was the New Testament, and
all his religious feelings, dormant during his association with Belinsky
and Petrashevsky, emerged with redoubled force.

In the letter to his brother ten days after his term was over (February 1854), Dostoevsky wrote:

> My stomach was ruined. I was repeatedly ill. As a result of my bad nerves I became epileptic. And I have rheumatism in my legs. I shall not tell you—it would take too long—what happened to my soul, my beliefs, my mind and heart, during these years. But the constant concentration on my inner self, to which I escaped from bitter reality, bore its fruit.

By comparison with the penal servitude the life of a private in the garrison at Semipalatinsk, on the border of Siberia and Central Asia, seemed to Dostoevsky a great relief: he could at last correspond with his brothers and friends and could read and write.

In 1855, he started to write the first drafts of works that were to appear later (*The Village of Stepanchikovo, Notes from the House of the Dead, The Humiliated and the Wronged*). He felt attracted, at this period, by Maria Isaeva, an intelligent and sensitive woman of twenty-eight, who sympathized with the former convict and showed an almost maternal affection toward him. After the death of Maria's husband, Dostoevsky proposed to her, but he had to go through many sufferings and difficulties before their marriage in 1857. The jealous Dostoevsky reproached his wife with not responding adequately to his frantic passion, and the marriage proved a failure. By 1859 Dostoevsky's love seemed extinct, while Maria's health (she had tuberculosis) deteriorated rapidly. In the following years he took care of her as he would have of an unhappy and lonely friend.

By 1858 Dostoevsky was at last permitted to return to Russia proper and to publish his writings. Now he was free and, after a break of nine years, could resume the lifework he had begun as a young enthusiast. In his late thirties his past was already extraordinarily oppressive; he looked old and tired, this silent and grim man with a short and stocky body, a big head set on broad shoulders, a nervous tic on his thin, bloodless lips, and with a sunken, yellowish and tormented face.

When, in 1859, Dostoevsky moved to St. Petersburg, the intelligentsia and particularly the youth, stirred by expectations of reforms, warmly greeted the writer who had been a political martyr. They learned soon enough that he was not their man. His devotion to the Church, his Slavophile sympathies, his sharp anti-Nihilist and anti-revolutionary attitude all disappointed the radicals. His popularity as a writer, however, grew steadily. After 'Uncle's Dream,' a short story, and the satirical short novel, *The Village of Stepanchikovo* (1860), his novel *The Humiliated and the Wronged* (1861) was called by Dobroliubov the best book of the year. It was followed by *Notes from the House of the Dead,* which was widely read and highly appreciated by liberal Westernizers as a realistic exposé of prison life and by the Slavophiles for its faith in the Russian people.

By this time Dostoevsky was strongly attracted to journalism. In 1861 he founded, with his brother Mikhail, the review *Time,* wherein he preached 'the reunion of educated society with the people' and prophesied that Russia would save the West.

Unlike Leo Tolstoy and Turgenev, for whom literature never was a profession, Dostoevsky was a professional writer: writing was his daily routine, the very essence of his life, and his only way of earning a living. Like most people of his time, he was convinced that the artist's supreme duty was to assume political and moral leadership, that one should write about life and respond to the calls of contemporary events. He fervently defended these ideas in numerous articles, and they made him popular with the Radicals and Nihilists.

All the ordeals he had gone through could not break his vitality and his tempestuous temperament. As his friend and biographer Strakhov remarked, Dostoevsky *felt* his ideas and expressed them with the same inspired enthusiasm he had displayed years before, at the meetings of the Petrashevsky circle. But now an emotional climax would often be followed by an epileptic seizure: he would stop suddenly in the middle of a sentence, a wild scream would escape from his distorted lips, and he would fall down in convulsions. Each fit made him ill for two or three days, and sometimes these seizures occurred weekly, or even at intervals of a few days. They were preceded by moments of elation and creative energy, during which he wrote his best pages or kept his friends spellbound with his talk. Vladimir Solovyov, the philosopher, said that after two hours of conversation with Dostoevsky one felt as if drugged or in a state of voluptuous torment, of feverish inebriation.

His disease was aggravated by his restless existence, his worries and ceaseless work. *Time* was suspended by the government; publishers who had advanced him money were pressing him hard for copy; he had endless financial and moral troubles; his wife, staying in a provincial town, was dying—and, at the same time, he was desperately in love with Appollinaria Suslova, a beautiful, self-willed, and capricious young woman in her twenties. The story of this love reads like one of Dostoevsky's own novels: the proud Suslova served as a model for the figures of Paulina in *The Gambler,* of Nastasya Philippovna in *The Idiot,* of Lizaveta in *The Possessed,* among others. This incredible affair between the forty-two-year-old epileptic genius and the intransigent, frigid, and sensual young woman unrolled in a highly dramatic sequence, mostly abroad—in France, Italy, and Germany—between 1863 and 1865.

Dostoevsky had been supplanted in Suslova's heart by less interesting but also less demanding and more malleable lovers, and she did not hide this from her former friend, although she consented to accompany him in his travels about Europe. The agony of a dying love was made more painful for him by the humiliating consequences of his gambling madness. An inveterate gambler since early youth, he lost everything in the casinos of Germany and had to beg his distant friends for help. After the death of his wife in 1865 he went abroad again, officially to attend to his health but actually to meet Suslova, who had definitely settled in Paris. The few months of flaring passion, quarrels, ruptures, renewed attraction, short reconciliations coupled with the most humiliating concessions, ended in a final break and a fever of gambling that left him penniless. He returned to St. Petersburg completely exhausted, physically and mentally.

His new venture, the review *Epoch,* had to fold up, and its bankruptcy left Dostoevsky with heavy financial obligations. His brother Mikhail died, and he had to provide for his family as well as to help Maria's boy, his stepson. In this dreadful situation, harassed by creditors and publishers, Dostoevsky published his *Notes from the Underground* (1864), *Crime and Punishment* (1866), proclaimed his masterpiece by stunned critics and deeply impressed readers, and *The Gambler.*

The last, a highly revealing autobiographical work, he had dictated to his young and pretty stenographer, Anna Snitkina, who impressed him by her kindness and simplicity. A month later he proposed to her and they were married in 1867. Anna became a good angel to the man she loved and admired with rare devotion. She gave him the feeling of security he so badly needed and made his life altogether easier and more normal. He fully appreciated her affection and returned it with all the tenderness and love he had.

After the marriage they went abroad to escape the creditors and to work in peace. The first year away was not too bright: they had to live in poverty, almost in destitution; Dostoevsky was as addicted to roulette as ever; and their first child died. But nothing could stop the creative urge: he kept writing *The Idiot* (published in 1868) and made numerous plans for new novels. In 1871-2 *The Possessed,* that violent attack against the revolutionaries and Nihilists, provoked endless polemics and contained what was little more than a caricature of Turgenev— under the name of Karmazinov—a vain and hypocritical literary lion.

The years between 1871 and his death a decade later were the most quiet and normal period of Dostoevsky's life. He led a more or less regular existence under the watchful eye of his wife, who bore him three children. Although the wolf frequently returned to his door, his financial situation improved greatly as the sales of his books kept mounting. In the 'seventies he was celebrated throughout the country as Russia's outstanding writer. He continued to work in his usual, intensive way. In 1876 he began the monthly publication of *A Writer's Diary* —a miscellany, written entirely by himself and consisting of philosophical or literary essays and articles on current events, occasionally interspersed with some short story, such as 'The Boy at Christ's Christmas Tree' or 'The Muzhik Marey.' Despite its special character the *Diary* had fourteen thousand subscribers. Although its political articles alienated the liberals, Dostoevsky's nationalism was of so individual and peculiar a kind that they seemed ready to discuss his ideas without any prejudice. Also in 1876, he published *A Raw Youth* and, by 1879, had finished his most important book, *The Brothers Karamazov*—the result of many years of work.

In 1880 his popularity reached its zenith. His speech at the unveiling of the monument to Pushkin in Moscow, when Dostoevsky expressed his faith in Russia's great destiny and its universal role in the reunion of all nations, won rapturous acclaim. Russian society suddenly realized that Dostoevsky, like Pushkin, was a truly national writer, an artist of titanic stature and, above all political dissensions, the exponent of the unexpressed hopes of many generations. But this success was the last Dostoevsky was to enjoy.

In January 1881, he fell ill and had a pulmonary hemorrhage, followed by frequent losses of consciousness. In a moment of lucidity he asked his wife to open at random the New Testament he had brought back from his Siberian exile. She read aloud: 'Suffer it to be so now: for thus it becometh us to fulfil all righteousness:' [1] 'You see,' said Dostoevsky, 'suffer it to be now—which means I am to die.'

And he closed his eyes in resignation. He passed away on the evening of the same day.

II   Dostoevsky's life is usually divided into three periods, corresponding to the stages of his literary evolution. *Poor Folk* is as typical of Dostoevsky of the 'forties as *Crime and Punishment* is of the ex-convict of the 'sixties, or *The Brothers Karamazov* of the master novelist of the late 'seventies. Dostoevsky as a writer passed through definite stages, yet he maintained through all of them an astounding unity of purpose and theme. As a matter of fact,

[1] St. Matthew, III.15.

even at the beginning of his extraordinary career he formulated all the problems that obsessed him to the day of his death.

Formally, Dostoevsky began as a disciple of Gogol—the Gogol of *The Overcoat,* a story he held in the highest esteem. Makar Devushkin, the hero of *Poor Folk,* is a humble clerk in a government bureau. His next door neighbor is Barbara, an unhappy young girl with whom he is desperately in love and who is as poor as her unfortunate lover. Makar never confesses his feeling but performs the impossible to help her, hiding his own weakness and poverty. Each lives in a shabby tenement, teeming with other individuals mistreated by fate. Makar's sacrificial efforts do not, however, suffice to keep Barbara from cares, illness, and misery, and when he realizes his utter helplessness he seeks oblivion in drink and comes to almost utter ruin.

Much the same is the case of the drunkard Pokrovsky, the literary forebear of Marmeladov in *Crime and Punishment* and the first in the long succession of Dostoevsky's alcoholics and derelicts. But Pokrovsky is capable of great love for his son, an idealistic, ailing student; Makar, in his self-denial, accepts humiliations and privations. All of these characters have 'pure hearts,' as Barbara, for instance, or her servant Fedora, or Gorshkov, a victim of legal injustice, or the other poor folk. The pure-hearted simpleton, a favorite hero in Russian literature, acquires a new psychological and philosophical depth in the novels of Dostoevsky.

His heroes are drifters, pariahs, from the lowest strata of society, yet from the moral point of view they are the salt of the earth. The condemnation of the society that rejects or mistreats them is therefore made on ethical grounds. Makar is good and pure, yet he suffers and rots in his misery. This offends our sense of justice; there is a gap between man's condition and the moral order as expressed in Christianity. This is the precise significance of Dostoevsky's first novel, and it heralds the main theme of all his work. It also reveals the author's almost morbid interest in human suffering, his mastery in portraying pathetic figures and evoking those poignant scenes of destitution and doom that are in all his novels. His contemporaries saw it as evidence of his realistic humanity; in the twentieth century this tendency was attributed to Dostoevsky's sense of Christian compassion—or to his sadistic and masochistic impulses.

There is no place for the characters of *Poor Folk* in this world. They live in the nooks and crannies of the basement of that edifice called civilization. They are helpless, abandoned to their fate, irrevocably lonely.

This feeling of isolation becomes pathological in Golyadkin, also a poor clerk, who is the hero of Dostoevsky's second novel, *The Double* (1846). This book was considered by critics an imitation of certain Gogol tales ('The Memoirs of a Madman' and 'The Nose') or of Hoffmann's 'The Elixir of Satan'. Dostoevsky never conceded the failure of *The Double;* he revised and reprinted it in 1866 under the subtitle of *A St. Petersburg Poem,* and wrote as late as 1877: 'I never expressed in literature an idea more important than that of *The Double.*' While writing it, he confided to his brother Mikhail: 'It will be my masterpiece; Golyadkin is ten times better than *Poor Folk.*'

What was it he cherished so highly in this lengthy, heavy-handed, and fantastic tale, written in the form of a report of a nightmare? *The Double* gives the confession of a poor and humble clerk who, under the pressure of want, humiliation, utter solitude, and his desperate passion for the daughter of his superior, gradually loses his mind and beholds his own wraith. At the beginning this wraith is elusive, poor, and humble, a true double of Golyadkin, but he soon grows bolder, becomes impertinent, pushes Golyadkin aside, accomplishes all that the unfortunate clerk merely dreamed of, is successful in his work, in society, in love, and finally completely eliminates the man of whom he was supposed to be a mere reflection. The furious Golyadkin attempts to kill him and perishes in the unequal fight against his malicious, uncanny double.

The split personality of Golyadkin is presented with the realistic lucidity that Dostoevsky usually displays in his descriptions of madness or pathological disturbances. European psychiatrists, who are in general deeply interested in Dostoevsky, have devoted special studies to *The Double,* which portrays 'with an incomparable clinical exactitude' the case of an erotomaniac and paranoiac afflicted by delusions of persecution. In Freudian terms the tragedy of Golyadkin, this new incarnation of the 'subliminal man,' is the result of the conflict between his Ego and Super-Ego, his double symbolizing all that Golyadkin wished to be. And from the psychological we ascend to a philosophical level: as Golyadkin is an outcast, he has no place in society; neither has he a place in the universe. What if he were the image of man in general— of that strange being who is an alien wherever he dwells in space (earth, nature, society) or in time (life, death, immortality)?

Golyadkin is confused and frightened by reality, he talks about it in the dramatic, incoherent, and feverish way of all Dostoevskian heroes, and he is desperately seeking support. In this search his fantasy creates the double as a means of self-gratification. But visions and ideas become objective reality; they materialize, turning into independent and powerful agents. This is also one of the reasons for Golyadkin's undoing: he is overpowered by the creations of his own mind, as are all Dostoevskian heroes who, like Raskolnikov, Ivan Karamazov, the Nihilists of *The Possessed,* seek a guiding force in themselves instead of turning toward God. Here again we are confronted with one of the main ideas running through all of Dostoevsky's work.

No less important is the concept of the wraith, the double. The problem of split personality and universal duality was to haunt Dostoevsky until his death. So many of his heroes have their doubles (Raskolnikov and Svidrigailov, Ivan Karamazov and Smerdyakov); his protagonists appear as twins and contrasting pairs (Myshkin-Rogozhin, Nastasya Philippovna-Aglaia, Dolgorukii-Versilov, and so on). His universe is a dichotomous one. 'Why do you wonder about our duality?' writes Dostoevsky to his brother. 'It is the commonest of human traits: my duality was throughout my life my great torment and my great delight.' The tragedy of all his heroes lies in this duality. It is not only a part of human nature, but perhaps it is in the nature of things as well. The human soul is a battlefield for the combat between God and Devil; the Antichrist rises against Christ; everywhere the interplay of opposite elements maintains the universe in dynamic instability.

In general, even the least successful of Dostoevsky's short stories written between 1844 and 1848 contain all the characteristics he was to disclose later as a mature writer. The problems of good and evil, of duality in human beings and the universe, of the betterment of society, of the relation between religion and progress, all are included in Dostoevsky's early works.

In his half-lyrical, half-dramatic confessions of the 'forties some of his dreams and ideas are not yet fully expressed. It is revealing that when Dostoevsky resumed his literary activity after years of penal servitude and silence, he started from the point where he had been stopped in 1849.

His short novel, *The Village of Stepanchikovo,* is a satire in the Gogolian tradition. It is also his first attempt at a standard type: its main character, Thoma Opiskin, is an incarnation of hypocrisy and egocentric impulses. The problem of evil in man, of man's pleasure in provoking trouble, inflicting pain, and dominating other people, although treated in lighter vein than previously, reveals the constant preoccupation of the writer's mind. The story is also the most complete expression of Dostoevsky's sarcasm, of the ironic streak found in most of his novels.

In the *Notes from the House of the Dead* the old theme of human duality is stressed in a description of the 'divine spark' in criminals, and it is intertwined with the secondary motive of national psychology, which gradually comes to the fore. Dostoevsky is inclined to generalize about the Russian people and to find the very essence of national mentality in its duality, its religiosity, and its longing for goodness, despite its contemptible appearance.

The scope of *The Humiliated and the Wronged* is wider than in the novels of his first period; the plot is decidedly more romantic and complex, with curious parallel subdivisions of action; but the book has many similarities to *Poor Folk* and particularly to *Netochka Nezvanova,* the last unfinished work before the exile. In *The Humiliated and the Wronged* the human wrecks, the defeated, the vanquished, are again in the foreground—all pure of heart. The old Ikhmenev after having listened to a young author (evidently a self-portrait of Dostoevsky), decides: 'We have learned from this manuscript that the most downtrodden man, the lowest of the low, is still a human being, and our brother.'

The story, which opens with the death of Smith, an old streetmusician (a Dickensian figure), is built around the adventure of Nellie, an abandoned child, who is mistreated by cruel masters and almost sold into a brothel. The image of an unfortunate, mistreated, and even violated child frequently recurs in the novels of Dostoevsky. (This has made some psychologists suspect that the writer himself had had a shameful experience with a child; in support of their theory they quoted some of his letters and offered an autobiographical interpretation of 'Stavroghin's Confession,' a chapter he omitted from the final edition of *The Possessed.* This method of identifying an author's plots and fictional incidents with his personal experiences is, however, a dubious one.)

What makes the melodramatic story of *The Humiliated and the Wronged* more than just another example of realistic humanism is the figure of the demoniac Prince Valkovsky, the forerunner of Stavroghin. He is evil and wicked because he is not bound by any moral code: he is the first Dostoevskian hero to assert his will and to treat other people as mere material for his experiences and desires. A daring individualist, Valkovsky does whatever he wants; his deeds are shameful and cruel, but he is a man of action, which differentiates him from all the other unhappy, frustrated, and delirious men of the underground.

The latter, however, are not only suffering creatures or weird maniacs: the hero of the *Notes from the Underground,* again a poor petty clerk, is capable of formulating a theory that serves as a rationalization of his state. A diabolical pride is hidden under his external submissiveness, and he turns into a bold Nihilist. He is no pure-heart; he is, rather, sheer mind, exploring reality and questioning the validity of creation. Intelligent men realize that life is an absurdity and refrain from action, leaving it to the stupid ones, to those who understand so little that they take pleasure in their senseless deeds. He goes even further and challenges the validity of reason and of rational solutions. Human beings are not rational; most of their motivations are irrational. Human beings are unstable, rebellious; they love chaos and destruction, seek variety, and flee from boredom into fantasy or cruelty. Thus the wise Seneca became involved in political intrigues, and the beautiful Cleopatra thrust golden pins into the breasts of her black bondswomen.

The hero of the *Notes* shies away from life. He is practically a human termite: in the darkness of his subterrane he gnaws at the foundations of society. Sometimes, distressed by loneliness, he crawls to the surface and tries to mix with humanity (the dinner scene), but is insulted and rejected. This makes him anti-social, a sort of obscure and evil anarchist. He behaves horribly with the only girl ready to love him; he destroys her and himself because of his mistrust and his desire for revenge, which take on a sadistic character. In no other work has Dostoevsky given a fuller interpretation of the morbid individualism, embittered philosophy, and twisted personality of the man from the underground than in the *Notes* whose hero marks the complete evolution of the type and proclaims the coming of Raskolnikov.

While creating Raskolnikov, Dostoevsky started another novel, *The Gambler*. Its autobiographical values are obvious. The imaginary town of Rulettenburg and all the details of gambling are drawn from the author's personal experiences in Wiesbaden and other German resorts, while the leading feminine character, Paulina, has a startling resemblance to Appollinaria Suslova. But *The Gambler* is more than a literary treatment of the author's life; it is even more than a 'tragedy of passion,' as Dostoevsky himself defined it. Its hero, Alexis Ivanovich, a young teacher, who loves Paulina with the devotion of a slave, is attracted by the green table because he believes in a 'stroke of luck.' Success at roulette would change his position, correct the injustice of his miserable existence, and give him happiness. The injustice is the result of a haphazard distribution of earthly goods. Everything—beauty, fortune, happiness, social standing—are bestowed upon man not rationally through merit and reward, but irrationally through chance. The whole world is an enormous gambling house. Gambling is one of the weapons in the struggle against the hazards of chance. The man of the underground comes to the light and wants to fight irrational injustice by irrational gambling.

Alexis Ivanovich is as obsessed by his idea as that other great gambler, Hermann in Pushkin's *The Queen of Spades*. Alexis' passion for gambling destroys his passion for Paulina, who rejects him just as he has won a hundred thousand florins—the price of her love—because she understands the law Dostoevsky cites in the novel: 'Two equally strong ideas cannot coexist simultaneously in human beings.' In other words, passion must be one and indivisible: gambling *or* love. Alexis Ivanovich spends all his winnings, which had failed to bring him happiness, on the shallow, greedy Blanche, a French cocotte, and then he returns to roulette.

It is not money that attracts him, but the element of chance. Gambling is akin to the initial chaos Tiutchev saw in nature and man, and Dostoevsky was discovering the strange attraction for it in himself and in the creatures of his imagination: they all revel in breathless seconds of hazard. Pushkin spoke about the rapture of danger; Dostoevsky felt that every 'storm of passion' gives a memorable elation. The irrational, which is almost catastrophic in mortals, always fascinated him. He caught a glimpse of some hidden truth in death, in supreme suffering, in the lightning illumination preceding an epileptic seizure—and in the delirium of gambling, the perfect example of passion and irrationality, which he knew so well and loved so intensely.

The hero of *The Gambler* is possessed by a passion; Raskolnikov, the hero of *Crime and Punishment,* is possessed by an idea that becomes a maddening passion. He is intelligent, handsome, generous—this poverty-stricken student eaten away with ambition and a guilty conscience about the sacrifices his mother and sister make for him; he also belongs to the men from the underground—those solitary individuals who remain outside of the group. In the silence of his garret Raskolnikov works out his theory. As a true Nihilist of the 'sixties, he despises conventional morals. They are good enough for ordinary mortals, for the millions of 'shivering creatures' forming the stupid, and passive masses, but the minority producing great men, the strong individuals of the world, can break with accepted rules of conduct. Everything is permissible for these supermen, as Nietzsche, greatly impressed by Dostoevsky, called them some twenty years later. They have the right to dispose of other peoples' lives and to place themselves above the law the multitudes obey.

According to this theory Raskolnikov feels himself entitled to kill Alena, the pawnbroker, an obnoxious harpy, an inferior creature. There is no wrong in suppressing a horrid hag and using her money for himself and his family. Far from being perverse or wicked, Raskolnikov in planning his crime thinks of money as a means of attaining freedom, almost as Alexis thought of his prospective gains from gambling. But the main incentive is not that of material gain. In his attempt to find a way out of the underground, he craves for action and self-assertion.

This act will be evidence of his superiority. By committing the crime with the same composure with which Napoleon sent thousands to be slaughtered, he will place himself definitely beyond good and evil, thus proving the validity of his rational theory. His crime therefore is purely intellectual, but its logical, abstract pattern does not correspond to irrational reality.

Raskolnikov's tragedy starts after the crime is committed, and Alena's sister, whom he has not even considered before, is also murdered. The double murder seems futile: it does not provide the proof he has expected. The disgust he feels after the horrible scene, the nightmares of his feverish sleep, his ensuing illness, the nervous exhaustion, and his unbearable spiritual isolation make him more of a 'shivering creature' than one of the elect. Everything intensifies his doubts. He helps the drunkard Marmeladov and his starving family in a spontaneous gesture, even though they most patently belong to the human vermin he despises: Marmeladov, whose death in a street accident fills him with pity, is nevertheless as contemptible in his eyes as the slain pawnbroker. Raskolnikov wonders whether there is something that bestows a supreme value on every human being—even the basest one. And his doubts are enhanced by Sonia, Marmeladov's daughter, who has turned prostitute to help her starving family.

She, too, is an outcast like himself in the eyes of society; she, too, has committed a crime—but her crime is one of self-sacrifice and not of self-assertion. If she has gone against the accepted moral code it has been from necessity—not through free will, as in Raskolnikov's case. He has chosen his fate; she has been driven to hers. And while the sufferings of Sonia, the dejection of Marmeladov's wife and children, and his own contradictions make Raskolnikov question the existence of God and the validity of the world's order, Sonia believes in Christ, and her simple faith gives her strength to endure her shame and pain. This wan, frail creature ignores sophistries, accepts suffering as a law of existence, and in her utter humility opposes faith to reason.

Raskolnikov ought to disdain this typical representative of submissive humanity, yet he cannot help loving her, and this again undermines his theory and his rational premises. In addition, he has less conviction in the quality of his own mind after his discussions with Porphyry, the District Attorney; their intellectual duel is not won by Raskolnikov, although for the sake of his ego he persists to the bitter end. His encounter with Svidrigailov, a man who has also chosen to be above the moral law, merely to satisfy his appetites and greed, and who tries to seduce Raskolnikov's sister, is another blow: Raskolnikov suddenly sees his own theory in the distorting mirror of the other's triviality.

Raskolnikov's final collapse, brought about by Sonia, is the result of his inner torments. It is not a conversion, although Dostoevsky intimates its future possibility, but simply the defeat of the man from the underground. The inevitability of such a solution is determined by the indivisibility of the irrational-emotional and the rational-intellectual elements in man. Raskolnikov attempted to build everything on logic and to disregard all the rest—and this provoked an unbearable conflict within him.

Crime and Punishment concluded the series of poor-folk types, who are isolated by poverty and social injustice, yet who try to overcome their circumstances by asserting themselves. Their rebellion—and Raskolnikov is a rebel—always ends in disaster: they are defeated by their passion (*The Gambler*), their egotism (*Notes from the Underground*), their transgressions (*Crime and Punishment*). The only 'exit from tragedy,' in Dostoevsky's opinion, is purity of heart and integrity of instinctive faith. This affirmation of the religious spirit as an antidote for isolation, depravity, and rebellion forms the main theme of Dostoevsky's writings in what may be called the third period of his evolution.

III   An attempt to present a positive approach to the moral problem raised by *Crime and Punishment* is made in *The Idiot,* the hero of which, Prince Myshkin, is in frank contrast to Raskolnikov. He has the purity and simplicity of those who are 'blessed, for they shall see God.' His mental disturbance and epilepsy —the sacred illness of prophets and mystics—necessitates his long sojourn in a Swiss sanatorium, from which he returns to St. Petersburg literally penniless. But material things are irrelevant to him: he asks for a place as a clerk as ingenuously as he speaks of the money he inherits a few months later.

He does not put himself above human law, as Raskolnikov does; he is within the divine law of Christian truth. Consequently his direct and artless behavior bewilders men and women whose lives are guided by revenge, pride, lust, avarice, and vanity. They look upon him as if he were from Mars and call him an idiot, yet they cannot help loving this kind, naive person, 'touched by God.' Myshkin is loved by Nastasia Philipovna, the ex-mistress of a heartless high official and a passionate woman tormented by pride and a sense of guilt, by a desire for domination, and by the need of self-sacrifice; he seems to her her only chance of salvation. Aglaia, the daughter of General Epanchin, also loves him— for he is unlike anyone else. Even Rogozhin, the rich merchant blinded by his mad passion for Nastasia, loves Myshkin, even though he is strongly tempted to kill this strange rival.

Unlike other innocents, who have nothing else to offer save their intuition and the 'main human virtues—compassion and mercy'— Myshkin has definite ideas. He blames Catholicism and Socialism for not answering the spiritual needs of a despairing world. Catholicism offers the domination of the Church and the rigidity of spiritual discipline; Socialism offers the domination of the State, maintained by oppression. Both rule through coercion, and both are anti-Christian. Only beauty is mercy and truth—and only beauty will save the world, since it implies harmony, order, and the resolution of all contraries through love. He is convinced that the Greek Orthodox faith is nearer than any other to the living, active concept of love; hence he believes in Russia and its universal mission. 'All Europe is amazed by our Russian fervor . . . we have passion.' The flame of life burns high in the country that is chosen to bring a new Gospel to weary mankind.

Myshkin is not able, however, to defend his ideas and—what is more—to make them effective in his own life. He cannot cope with the passions raging around him, revealing the crude and as yet unsublimated force of the Russian temperament. Those passions finally bring about the catastrophe: Rogozhin kills Nastasia, and Myshkin loses his mind altogether. This tragic end proves that Myshkin was wrong. Raskolnikov's individualistic solution, based on pride, rebellion, and crime, has led nowhere; but the individual solution of mercy, piety, and pity has been equally futile. Myshkin does not understand life because he underestimates the forces of evil and the destructive power of Russian fervor. He ignores the fundamental realities of human nature and, besides that, he is weak and passive. His example may be useful but he is not an agent for the betterment of man.

Dostoevsky saw two facets in the problem of evil: the metaphysical one—why does God, the symbol of goodness, mercy, and perfection, allow the existence of evil?; and the psychological one—why is man so attracted by it? He was keenly aware that human institutions are wrong and generate evil. In his youth he had gone through a period of utopian belief in the betterment of society through a radical change of its institutions. That faith he had lost completely in Siberia and upon his return to Russia. Even in the 'sixties he was firmly convinced that the roots of all evil lay in man alone; the reform of society was therefore impossible without the reform of the individual.

In *The Possessed* the revolutionaries have done away with the idea of God; they are anti-Christian and therefore strive for domination, as does Peter Verkhovensky. To him also, everything is permissible: he lies, cheats, ruins the lives of the young, and does not find it difficult to murder. He has no regrets or scruples: the end justifies the means.

Shigalev, one of his disciples, comes to the conclusion that one tenth of mankind is entitled to establish a dictatorship over the other nine tenths in order to force happiness upon them. His social paradise is based on obedience and equality in slavery. Freedom is barred from the state of the future (the same idea is found in the legend of the Grand Inquisitor in *The Brothers Karamazov*).

Verkhovensky organizes cells of five men, all of whom obey him blindly because he plays on their stupidity, cruelty, and vanity. He relies upon them to aid him during the unrest he plans to provoke by proclaiming a pretender to the throne who will defend the peasants' interests. The man he wants to place at the head of the movement as the Pretender is Nicholas Stavroghin, a rich and handsome nobleman and a much greater sinner than Prince Valkovsky.

Stavroghin, capable of anything and everything, is attracted equally by the monstrosities of vice and by acts of saintliness. His duality is frightening. Generous and reckless, he delights in excesses of degradation, in iniquity, and knavery. He marries a feeble-minded, crippled beggar girl merely to enjoy the atrocious contrast of her unsightliness, and later he lets her be murdered by an ex-convict. In the previously mentioned suppressed chapter, 'Stavroghin's Confessions,' published only half a century after Dostoevsky's death, the great sinner divulges to a priest one of the horrible secrets of his life: he has raped a poor child, who had then committed suicide. Stavroghin succeeds where Raskolnikov fails: he destroys other people easily and without scruple.

This demon of the revolutionary movement, which he regards with poorly concealed contempt, is a real superman; his strength is elemental and national. His is the stormy and disorderly energy of the Russian, who goes all the way in sins and excesses, until he strikes upon some great idea to harness and tame his forces. Whether a Russian becomes a saint or a sinner depends entirely on chance: he has both potentialities in him. This organic vitality turns into rebellion or useless outbursts in the Lucifer types of Dostoevsky's novels, (Ivan Karamazov, Stavroghin, Raskolnikov).

The tragedy of Stavroghin lies in his not knowing what to do with himself. He lives in a void, and his power is a burden to him—it is aimless and heavy. The world around him is boring, absurd, or gloomy, and he takes his life because there is nothing more left for him. His suicide does not resemble that of another hero of *The Possessed*, Kirilov, who wants to kill God by killing himself. He dreams of the time when man will overcome pain and fear and thus will become God. For him history is divided into two periods: from baboon to the destruction of God, and from the destruction of God to the physical change of earth and man. Instead of a God-man there will be Man-God, liberated from any submission to Providence or Death. To assert his own liberty and to give a proof of his aloofness to death, Kirilov shoots himself: suicide becomes for him the highest evidence of self-affirmation.

Raskolnikov tries to become a superior being through crime—and fails; Stavroghin, like Lucifer, succeeds in challenging the social, moral, and divine law—and fails. Kirilov tries to raise himself above the universal law, above God—and arrives at self-annihilation. This is the road of the proud candidates for supermen. They can not become masters of life. Neither, according to Dostoevsky, can a group of individuals who dream of transforming the world through blood and violence and who seek power in order to rule mankind: like the demons who were transferred into the Gadarene swine and then drowned, so will perish all those possessed of the idea of revolution.

In their rebelliousness, which stems from the Byronic tradition, all the strong heroes of Dostoevsky challenge accepted dogmas or strive for power. He felt that the need to rule, to control (to which Nietzsche later gave the name of *Wille zur Macht*), is as basic as any of the other instincts. The evil Verkhovensky is driven by the same lust for power as the young and kind Dolgorukii, the hero of *A Raw Youth*. Dolgorukii is a passionate dreamer with a strong character, ascetic tendencies, and an Oedipus complex, who decides to become a millionaire—not for the sake of money or material advantages, but to attain freedom through power. In our times it is money that buys power; therefore Dolgorukii wants to be rich. It is true that he is too involved in his emotional adventures and in his love-hatred for his father to follow his program of a gradual accumulation of wealth, but this relinquishment of his initial scheme results from a shift in his scale of values.

In *The Brothers Karamazov,* Dostoevsky's last novel, which sums up all his main themes and ideas, the problem of power and authority is discussed in the 'Legend of the Grand Inquisitor,' told by Ivan Karamazov to his brother Alesha. The 'Legend,' which has provoked hundreds of comments by Russian and European critics and philosophers, is of outstanding importance for an understanding of Dostoevsky. 'Without the "Legend," ' wrote Rosanov in his book on this remarkable story, 'not only *The Brothers Karamazov* but many of his other books could never have been written.' The modern reader of the 'Legend' is struck by its appearance of reality; the fantastic Grand Inquisitor who administers his State with an iron hand thoroughly formulates the philosophy of totalitarian government. He was intrepid enough to correct Jesus Christ and to rectify the shortcomings of Christianity.

The Son of God said that 'a man shall not live by bread alone,' yet

He ignored the fact that man cannot live without bread, either. He offered freedom, love, and renunciation as the way of salvation; but only the elect are capable of traveling that hard, uphill road. The average man is not fit for freedom. Afraid of freedom of choice or truth and having no need of them, he makes a mess of them if they are forced upon him. Society cannot be built on freedom, which is fit only for those who are chosen to enter the Kingdom of God; the sinful, childish, narrow-minded, rebellious multitudes need discipline and guidance. And the Grand Inquisitor, accepting the division of mankind into masters and slaves (the latter Raskolnikov wanted to exploit for his own sake, and Shigalev, for the sake of Socialism), builds a State that offers men an escape from the insufferable burden of freedom. He accepts the tenet that Christianity has set its ideal too high for the average mortal, and that it has therefore led to a double standard of morals and to social enmity.

The Grand Inquisitor has no illusions about human nature. Man is cruel, rebellious, ambivalent, destructive. It is difficult to make him happy, since he loves suffering. His longing for order and harmony is counterbalanced by his passion for chaos and destruction. He easily loses control and acts foolishly, forgetting all about duty and law. The desire for change and novelty feeds his instability; he is unreliable, prey to dangerous fancies, and never quite satisfied. In general, human nature is too expansive and too luxurious. To deal with mankind usefully one has to circumscribe the bounds of human behavior, to impose rules, to make men believe in infallible authority, to play on their love of awe-inspiring mystery and on their hope for miracles. The Grand Inquisitor's power is based on authority, mystery, and miracle. He gives mankind an obligatory religion—for men wish to believe and to adore collectively.

The Grand Inquisitor and his assistants rule through deceit; they are the only ones to know the whole truth and their shoulders are broad enough to bear the burden average mortals would not be able to sustain. In this theocratic State, administered by priests, the citizens are rewarded and punished like children, whom ignorance of the truth makes happy. When Christ descends upon earth again, the Grand Inquisitor puts Him in prison lest He destroy the existing order; then comes to His cell to explain why he had to amend Christianity: 'Didst Thou forget that men prefer peace, and even death, to freedom of choice in the knowledge of good and evil? Thou hast only the elect but we give rest to all.' This rest is offered here, on earth, and not in heaven. The Grand Inquisitor does not seem to believe in immortality of the soul—he does not think that man deserves it—and therefore his efforts are concentrated on the building of the City of God on this planet and not in the nebulous hereafter. Thus his State is only another version of the Socialist Utopia. Shigalev and the Grand Inquisitor, starting from opposite extremes, arrive at the same conclusions.

Ivan Karamazov, the author of the Legend, also denies the immortality of the soul: 'How can the existence of swine turn into eternal life?' He, too, is fain to build a City for mankind—but he rejects God. Like some of the other chief characters in the novel, he believes in a godless society, which will rise as a result of some revolution—'a geological earthquake,' as he calls it. Not unlike Kirilov, he sees the triumph of the future upheaval in the abolition of God, in the triumph of atheism. The denial of immortality of the soul brings him, by inference, to Raskolnikov's idea that everything is permissible. Ivan is beyond good and evil; his logic makes all moral restrictions crumble into dust. Smerdyakov, his double and half brother, listens to his pronunciamentos and arrives at the practical conclusion Ivan does not dare to draw: he murders old Karamazov and says: 'If God does not exist, there is no such thing as being virtuous; virtue is useless.' Smerdyakov's deed is Dostoevsky's answer to those who believe in the possibility of establishing a virtuous human society without a moral code based on religion.

Ivan Karamazov, a man with a strong logical mind, has only his intellect to hold on to, so long as he denies any 'outside frame of reference,' i.e. the Divinity. He tries to bridge the chasm between his emotional and rational selves—the same chasm that engulfed Raskolnikov—although his intellect burdens him. 'The more stupid one is, the clearer; stupidity is brief and artless,' he says to Alesha, practically repeating the arguments of the hero of *Notes from the Underground*. What makes him different from the latter or from Raskolnikov is that his rebellion against God derives from his non-acceptance of the discord between reality and his sense of justice. His orderly, Euclidean mind expects to find symmetry, clarity, and beauty in the external world, which is, on the contrary, confusing and horrible. Why does evil exist if the world was created by God? How can God, if he is Love and Mercy, make innocent children, who have committed no sin, suffer? And why does He punish man, who was created in His image? The hypothesis that all the revolting facets of life—evil, war, crime, abuse— are part of some larger unit, a necessary element of universal accord, does not comply with Ivan's longings for the happiness of mankind. He does not want cosmic harmony bought at the price of children's tears, of man's *Via Crucis,* and he 'respectfully returns his ticket' for the show.

Thus he underscores the rupture between the way the world is made and the moral judgments of men. Salieri, in Pushkin's poem, complains about the absence of justice not only on earth but in heaven too. Ivan feels that the human truth in his mind and heart and the inaccessible truth of God and Heaven, which he is unable to grasp, will never coincide, and one has to choose either what he knows and feels or what he does not understand. Almost like the Grand Inquisitor, he intimates that even if God exists, His order is not good for man. Human beings are basically dualistic. They are attracted equally by sin and depravity, symbolized in the Bible by the cities of Sodom and Gomorrah and by the dream of Beauty, Purity, and Harmony, as represented by poets and painters in the symbolic image of the Madonna. The Cities of the Plain and the Madonna are the two poles between which lie the varieties of man's potentialities. Man is capable of everything, he is 'too broad'—and therein is his tragedy.

Dimitri, Ivan's brother, is an example of that emotional extremism that Dostoevsky defines as a Russian national trait: he can commit a crime as well as perform an act of magnanimity and nobility. The angel and the devil who dwell in his heart pull him asunder. At Dimitri's trial the Prosecutor accuses him of wanting to 'leap across two precipices simultaneously.' 'We are both good and evil, blended in a most astonishing mixture,' says Dimitri. 'I was dissipated, yet loved the good.' Stavroghin did not see the difference between a 'bestially wanton jest and sacrificing one's life for the sake of another'—both seemed to him exhilarating.

The contradictions of nature are disclosed mainly in sensuality and sex; and Dostoevsky's heroes always obey the opposing impulses of attraction and repulsion, of voluptuousness and sublimation, of pride and self-abasement. This is even more marked in his feminine characters, such as Katerina Ivanovna, Grushenka, and Liza, in *The Brothers Karamazov,* Nastasia in *The Idiot,* or Lizaveta in *The Possessed.*

Duality and contradictions cause the final collapse of Ivan Karamazov, the intellectual instigator of a parricide that he cannot accept when it is finally perpetrated. Even as Raskolnikov is confronted with Svidrigailov, Ivan is confronted with Smerdyakov, that cheapened, vulgarized, and distorted replica of his rational self, that example of how, if widely spread and adapted to the mentality of the herd, his aristocratic concept of a superman would materialize. Ivan breaks down after a struggle between faith and disbelief, between analytical judgments and irrational emotions. In his hallucinations he sees his double (even as Golyadkin did), embodied in a shabby but neat and gentlemanly Devil, who talks like a sophist and temptingly presents insoluble contradictions.

Dostoevsky, tormented by the same doubts as his alter ego Ivan, took refuge in religion: not in the religious form the Grand Inquisitor contrived for mass consumption, but in true Christianity, leading to freedom through love and sacrifice. In *The Brothers Karamazov* this faith is embodied in Alesha, Ivan's younger brother, the disciple of Father Zossima, a former aristocrat who had become a monk and, later, the saintlike leader of a monastery. Alesha learns from him that suffering, repentance, and purification are natural stages of religious enlightenment. Even in the midst of sin and evil men look for spiritual help. Unlike Myshkin, whom he resembles to some extent, the youngest Karamazov is a robust though morbidly sensitive youth who loves life and tells his student friends: 'Don't be afraid of life. How good life is when one does something kind and right.' He is strong in faith, rich in love and compassion, friendly with all the tormented creatures who confide in him—and his love is active. Although he fails to prevent the crime—the killing of his father—for which he feels guilty, he usually acts as a force for good. To all of Ivan's arguments he opposes the simplicity of his answer: 'I accept the Divine Law, even though I do not know what it means.' He comprehends that faith should appear where reason fails, practically repeating the statement of Tertullian the African: 'I believe because it is absurd' (*credo quia absurdum est*): what can be proved by reason does not require an act of faith. Alesha has chosen Christ of his own volition and, without attempting to become a saint or to suppress his human instincts, he is guided by the supreme wisdom of tolerance and humility, pity and sacrifice, obedience and brotherhood, wisdom that had been rejected by all the rebels and proud sons of Lucifer, such as Valkovsky, Raskolnikov, Kirilov, Stavroghin, Ivan, and the Grand Inquisitor.

In this whole work of Dostoevsky's, which is a tragedy of passions and faith culminating in the undoing of those who have gone against divine law, Alesha, with whose name *The Brothers Karamazov* begins and ends, is the only hero who affirms positive values, accepts God's universe, and, in general, represents some hope in this maddening world of doubles, murderers, great sinners, men from the underground, refractory objectors, and spiritual convicts.

IV   None of Dostoevsky's novels presents a solution of the problems raised or expounds a doctrine; even Alesha is not fully convincing when confronted with his antagonists. Dostoevsky himself continually alternated between faith and disbelief,

sharing Ivan's dialectics or Stavroghin's temptations. His concept of true
Christianity as absolute freedom was heavily imbued with religious
anarchism. The very dynamism of his intellect and the intensity of his
emotions gave a revolutionary stamp to his writings. His power of
blasting accepted dogmas in order to arrive 'at the very roots of all
issues,' is more evident than his ability to reconstruct or to affirm. A
man of a complex inner fiber and of irreconcilable impulses, he was
himself afraid of the provocative and anarchical impact of his own work.
Just as the Grand Inquisitor attempts to quiet insubordinate mankind,
Dostoevsky tried to discipline his own nature, to penalize his own
rebellious spirit. He therefore genuflected before the Greek Orthodox
Church, professed his devotion to it, accepted its rituals, its regulations,
and its penances. This spiritual revolutionary, for whom the world was
in constant flux, who visualized life as a battle of ideas and temperaments, whose art registered, like a seismograph, all the subterranean
convulsions of the unconscious and all the eruptions of the passions—
this spiritual revolutionary worshiped at altars and knelt before thrones
to show his submissiveness.

No wonder that the Greek Orthodox dignitaries remained suspicious
of so strange a parishioner, whose ardent breath had a smell of brim-
stone about it. Seeking refuge from his restless mind in a surrender to
the State religion, this former political exile bowed also to absolutism,
blessing its firmness in restraining the anarchical disposition of the
Russian people. This, however, did not prevent him from furnishing the
atheists with their most effective arguments and from making equivocal
statements about Socialism, for which, despite his hatred, he felt a
sentimental affection.

Freud attributed this contradiction to the Oedipus complex: Dostoevsky had hated his father, with all the usual implications, including
a subconscious desire for his murder. The Viennese psychologist quotes
the sentence from *The Brothers Karamazov*: 'Who has not wished to kill
his father?' He also points out that parricide forms the crux of the
novel's plot and that *A Raw Youth* also deals with the problem of
father-and-son relations. When Dostoevsky's father was brutally slain
by his serfs in 1839, the eighteen-year-old youth suffered a tremendous
shock, and his remorse, enhanced by a sense of guilt, shaped the spiritual
and moral pattern of his future.

His rebellion against the Czar and God has its psychological explanation in his antagonism (projected politically and metaphysically) against
his father. His humble acceptance of punishment (the Siberian period)
and later of the Church and of absolutism are manifestations of guilt
accompanied by a desire for self-chastisement. His masochistic enjoy-

ment of submissiveness is another manifestation of the same psychological complex. In general, sadistic-masochistic impulsions are highly stressed in Dostoevsky: his interest in suffering, his descriptions of various characters who loved to inflict pain and to be tortured, are revelatory of the morbid acuteness of his basic psychopathological conflict.

One need not necessarily agree with this Freudian interpretation to discover that Dostoevsky's loyalty to God and Czar had the peculiar character of an escape from inner conflicts. This is probably the principal reason why his reactionary statements in *A Writer's Diary,* dealing with the problems current during the last years of his life, sound so strange, or suddenly take on an equivocal meaning. The creator of Alesha, the propounder of love and mercy, could not help but feel that the innate wickedness of man entitles society to take coercive measures. This led him to justify the brutal reprisals against revolutionaries resorted to by his most reactionary friend Pobyedonostzev—measures that were the mainstay of reaction and of the Czar's officialdom. Even as Gogol in his *Select Passages from Correspondence* had done, Dostoevsky defended repressions, despotism, and the 'hand of iron.' He who had been so attracted by the instability of human nature supported the conservatives in their efforts to maintain the stagnation of the *status quo.*

Yet Dostoevsky might easily be called the prophet of the Revolution: he felt the approach of a cataclysm, his whole conception of the universe was a catastrophic one, he constantly had apocalyptic visions of the future—and he dreaded what he foresaw in a mystical premonition. In the late 'seventies he thought that nothing could prevent an upheaval in Europe, but he hoped that the solid dam of absolutism would protect Russia against the flood.

Here again his political opinions reflected his duality. He criticized, in Slavophile terms, Roman Catholicism and Protestantism; in his letters from abroad he drew angry pictures of the meanness of petty-bourgeois France and of German smugness, brutality, and impertinence; he was angry about England and sarcastic about Italy. Yet at the same time he loved Europe. Ivan Karamazov called Europe his 'most cherished cemetery,' and promised to kiss its every tombstone. Versilov (in *A Raw Youth*) asserted that Europe was as close to the Russian heart as Russia itself, or even closer. In his speech on Pushkin Dostoevsky declared that Europe was a second fatherland for the Russians and he called his countrymen true Europeans.

He felt most poignantly the rift between the West and the East, often discussing it in his *Diary.*

We are the intruders and wanderers [he wrote in 1878] as new-comers, we have taken over from Europe only that which is most super-ficial. Europe laughed at us and despised us, but finally the Europeans understood that we coveted something dangerous and frightening, that there are hordes of us, that we know and understand all European ideas, while they ignore ours—and even if they were aware, they would not understand them. . . We speak all the languages, whereas they speak only their own.

But he warns the Russians against imitating the institutions of the West, prophesying that these institutions will be swept away by an imminent revolution, in which the bourgeois (contaminated by the Roman Catholic idea of power) and the proletariat (inspired by the Protestant idea of righteous law) will destroy each other in their vain attempt to bring about the unity of society by compulsory methods.

In his famous speech on Pushkin in 1880, which was interpreted as the termination of the old antagonism between the Slavophiles and the Westernizers, Dostoevsky formulated his messianic nationalism: Russia was destined to accomplish the union of all nations in a common cause, in a free accord of all peoples. The Russian national idea was not egotism or exclusiveness but, on the contrary, true universality. Two traits of Russian character made him believe in this Utopia. In the first place, he emphasized the capacity of his countrymen for assimilating the ideas and the spirit of other civilizations, for extracting the essence from all cultures. In *A Raw Youth* Versilov, who has a golden dream of the future of mankind, says: 'I am French in France, German with the Germans, Greek with the ancient Greeks—and thus am I most Russian and I serve Russia by stressing her main idea.' To be Russian meant to be universal; universality was Russia's national aim. On the other hand, the Russians were conscious of their sins and were eager for improvement, purification, and sacrifice. 'Our people, despite their apparent bestiality, have Jesus Christ in their hearts.' Therefore the reunion with the people was obligatory for the intelligentsia: Dostoev-sky's Populism had a definite religious basis.

The idea of Russian universality merging in his imagination with the role played by Greek Orthodoxy, Dostoevsky had a vague vision of a theocratic millenium and he prophesied the time when State would become Church—contrary to what had happened in Rome, where Church had turned into State.

Perhaps the Slavic idea is universal and final . . . bringing the end of all the previous history of European mankind. Yes, the destination of the Russians is undoubtedly all-European and world wide. To be a true Russian means to become brother to all men, to become All-Man.

It means the reconciliation of all European contradictions, the finding of an outlet for the anguish of Europe in the all-human and all-uniting Russian soul; it means, perhaps, the utterance of a final word of great total harmony, of definite brotherhood, and the concord of all nations in the law of Christ.

These statements of Dostoevsky tie in with his social, moral, and religious ideas. His political outlook is not merely an appendix to his *Weltanschauung*. It resumes the Slavophile tradition and attempts to accomplish in the religious domain what Herzen tried to do in the social and the political ones. The magnificent dream of Russia bringing universal peace and the reunion of all peoples as her national contribution to European civilization not only mirrors Dostoevsky's utopian nationalism, but also corresponds to the main directions of his thought and to his need of finding some hope for suffering and troubled humanity.

v   Dostoevsky's psychological novel of ideas, with all its insight into the crannies of the human mind and the almost unbearable intensity of its metaphysical and moral quest, has a specialized structure—that of the mystery or detective story. Russian critics have contended that this was owing to the influence of the French Romantics, whom Dostoevsky had admired in his formative years. He had avidly read Hugo, Soulié (*The Memoirs of the Devil*), Sand, Balzac, and Sue, the purveyor of thrillers for newspapers and the pulps. Horror tales also greatly appealed to him: his favorites include *The Mysteries of Udolpho* by Ann Radcliffe, Charles Robert Mathurin's *Melmoth the Wanderer,* T. A. Hoffmann's *The Elixir of Satan,* and other fantastic tales.

In Balzac, to whose writings he remained attached all his life, he appreciated the intricacies of plot and the characterizations, such as those of the ex-convict Vautrin (in *Père Goriot*). Later he was greatly impressed by Hugo's *Les Misérables*. Regardless whether the theory of literary influences is accepted or rejected, one fact is undeniable: Dostoevsky did not create in a void; he read books written in a specific style, discussed the principles and the practice of a school with definite connotations, and liked, or was attracted by, particular genres. His own novels have a startling external likeness to the Romantic adventure novels—chiefly those of the French.

Of course, next to the foreign authors whom Dostoevsky loved and translated, he was strongly influenced by Gogol as well as by certain other contemporaries, such as Alexander Weltman (1800-70), who wrote in a most fantastic vein. The influence of Gogol is easily perceived in *Poor Folk,* and particularly in the style of *The Double,* which

Ivan Aksakov called 'not an imitation, but simply a repetition, of Gogol.' At the same time *The Double* bears a resemblance to the tales of Hoffmann, as does *The Landlady* (1847), a fantastic story of ghosts, beautiful women, murder, and horror. But Gogol's influence on the plot and form of Dostoevsky's novels waned, whereas the pattern of the adventure and mystery story developed steadily. In most of his works we find the same ingredients as in the melodramatic tales of Sue or Soulié: children lost and recovered, false identity, blackmail, family skeletons in the closet, murders, demoniac villains, saintly prostitutes, noble beggars, escaping convicts. A garret, the death of a tubercular mad woman, a poor girl reared in a palace, an unrecognized genius, letters revealing a girl's family secret, a mysterious violin inherited by a poor musician, a court trial, a prison, a nocturnal serenade—these are some features in the story of *Netochka Nezvanova.* Thirteen years later in *The Humiliated and the Wronged,* there are similar romantic elements.

In other novels there are also weird madmen, rich aristocrats who go slumming (Stavroghin), paupers becoming millionaires (Myshkin), pure-hearted, remorse-tortured courtesans (Nastasia), illegitimate sons finding a lost document or discovering a secret that can ruin their fathers (Dolgorukii in *A Raw Youth,* Smerdyakov in *The Brothers Karamazov*). The core in the plot structure of most Dostoevsky novels is usually a crime, especially that of murder.

Dostoevsky deliberately wanted his novels full of incidents and intriguing episodes. He regretted that the ending of *The Idiot* was not 'sufficiently spectacular,' praised Alexander Dumas for his intricate plots and told young writers that 'a talented book means necessarily an exciting, thrilling book.' He abandoned the tradition of the realistic novel with its simplicity of plot and slow narrative style. He also opposed the purists or perfectionists, such as Turgenev, whom he styled a 'lubricated writer.' He loved Pushkin, as one loves an unattainable ideal that has nothing to do with reality. He repeated Tiutchev's dictum concerning the soothing effect of poetry which 'pours the oil of peace upon the stormy sea,' but he actually preferred ruggedness and stress to smoothness and equipoise. He wanted to shock, to surprise, and to puzzle the reader; he enjoyed tortuous paths in the development of a story, indulging in parallel situations, digressions, and complicated, dramatic climaxes.

Of course, Dostoevsky might have chosen this method of piling up romantic effects because he was by nature an extremist. A painter of passions, he reveled in the grotesque, in horrors and contortions: he needed unusual situations to release the hidden instincts and complexes of human beings. No wonder he was so fascinated by crime: it enticed all the Romantics who looked for 'strangeness,' deviations, contrasts, and emotional peaks, as well as for the ugliness in man.

Dostoevsky made it clear in the 'sixties why he was so interested in chronicles of crime: 'Court-room reports are more thrilling than all the novels, because they throw light on the dark facets of the human soul which art avoids touching upon, or touches only in passing.' Yet it is quite obvious that Dostoevsky belongs not to the Realistic but to the Romantic current in Russian literature, and an argument to the contrary based on the realistic details scattered throughout his work ignores the essentials of his art. Like all the Romantics he was interested in describing the monstrous and the rebellious, and the extreme of passion in extraordinary men—not in the daily existence of average men. The action of his novels takes place in a special world of the imagination, in which the earthly laws of gravity, time, and space assume a merely relative importance and in which feverish dreams and phantasms acquire a magnetic and troublesome reality. They are convincing within the borders of their world, which does not, however, mean that they are true to life.

Even his 'pure-hearted,' simple types—figures beloved of all Russian writers—are not at all simple. He may have preached humility and discovered that the watchword of national literature was 'be humble, ye proud man,' but he was irresistibly attracted by disdainful and self-exalted individuals. His heroes are involved, contradictory, and fantastically intense: all of them are like condensers of intellectual and emotional energy and catalysts of material and spiritual upheavals. It is quite possible that the intricacies of his plots and the spectacular dénouements of his wild stories corresponded to the inner strain of his characters, so that he created the only background in which they could seem convincing, while, on the other hand, they compensated for the abstract concepts forming the upper plane of his works. This theory is particularly sound in regard to the novels written after his Siberian exile.

The adventure story, coupled with metaphysical and moral pamphleteering, is transformed into something hardly known before in Russian —and perhaps in world—literature: it becomes a genre in itself, a new form following its own laws of composition. He proved that the principle of organic consistency may be a mere prejudice, and he used heterogenous elements as artistic material. This procedure, so typical of the modern novel, made him akin to the European and American writers of our times.

A cyclone with a zone of calm at its core: this is the impression created by most of Dostoevsky's novels. This core is not the story itself—it is an idea; and all the Romantic devices serve to embody this idea. This is the supreme contradiction of Dostoevsky's art: he writes a romance in the style of the pulps, in order to say the most complex and profound things. This wonderful storyteller who had a power of entrancing, of suspense and persuasion, transmuted the vulgar tricks, the conventional literary pattern, into a philosophical novel-drama.

The new form of the novel created by Dostoevsky, the most romantic of Russian prose writers, has many obvious defects. In the 'eighties, Vogué, in his book on the Russian novel, apologized for mentioning such a vague and confused writer as Dostoevsky, contending that even in his native land only a few could read *The Brothers Karamazov* to the end. Today, when Dostoevsky is recognized as one of the greatest masters in world literature, we can imagine how the uncouth qualities of his novels must have shocked Victorian tastes. He wrote hastily and often under the duress of harsh circumstances: always in debt, always taking advances for works he had no time to begin, publishing most of his writings in reviews, in monthly installments (which explains certain divisions in the structure of his novels and the sudden cliff-hanging breaks in action, intended to pique the curiosity to read the 'following issue').

The language is unseemly and loose, lapsing into journalese or the dryness of a report; it is devoid of poetic smoothness, with unnerving changes of pace and rhythm. The exposition is often lengthy and repetitious, although some of the repetitions have a distinct functional value. Unlike anything else in Russian prose (except for Narezhny, Pisemsky, and, to a slight extent, Lermontov), his novels are packed with action and crowded with dozens of protagonists. In *The Possessed* no less than thirty characters are directly involved in the plot. Events race along in an amazingly short span of time: the whole action of *Crime and Punishment* lasts only nine days—two of preparation, one for the murder, and the six leading up to Raskolnikov's surrender. Dostoevsky seems to be always in a hurry to unload all he has on his mind—hence all the many disgressions and stories-within-the-story. His novels are congested with incidents and ideas, passions and words, and each one contains enough material for several full-length novels. This profuseness is hardly ever resolved harmoniously, it is frequently on the verge of bad taste, just as his pathos is often dangerously close to bathos, and the high-pitched note of his narrative is ready to turn into painful shrillness.

In general, as Mikhailovsky has observed in his remarkable article, *The Cruel Genius,* Dostoevsky, who described the cruelty of his heroes, was himself none too easy on his readers and hardly spared their nerves. Reading Dostoevsky is an odd experience: one is forcibly dragged through breathtaking situations, shocked by daring ideas, hurt by out-bursts of emotion—yet at the same time held spellbound by this fantastic and often nightmarish world from which one awakens to reality with the sensation of having returned from another planet. What confers a magnetic attraction to these novels, which some conventional and genteel critics refuse to accept esthetically, is their intensity, a sort of frantic emotional drive which illuminates them all with a weird and sometimes lugubrious glare. They are ecstatic, and we know that parts of them were written ecstatically: Dostoevsky did fifty six pages of *The Humiliated and the Wronged* in one stretch of two days and two nights.

All his novels are built around a conflict—between man (Ivan Karamazov) and God; between a theory and the emotional self (*Crime and Punishment*); between love and hatred (*A Raw Youth*); between naive kindness and deadly passions (*The Idiot*); between the defence-less innocence of the individual and the brutality of society (*Poor Folk, The Double*). The main idea is dynamic: it is always embodied in a hero shown in action. All the characters are so completely absorbed by their thoughts and emotions that they seem to be lunatics. This mad-dening quality could hardly be rendered in a detailed narrative or in an epic unfolding of panoramic pictures. This is probably one of the reasons Dostoevsky chose the framework of confessions, diaries, or recitals in the first person.

If it is a confession, it may be delivered as a monologue—a high-strung, breathless speech by someone who is greatly perturbed intel-lectually or emotionally. The soliloquy, with all its subjective diversifi-cations, was used widely by Dostoevsky before 1849: *Poor Folk* is a double diary; *Notes From the Underground, The Gambler,* and *A Raw Youth* are told in the first person. Even in novels not written as such, confessions are inserted as separate chapters (that of Hyppolite in *The Idiot,* for example). *The Idiot, Crime and Punishment,* and *The Brothers Karamazov* are written as objective narratives. Other novels (such as *The Possessed* or *The Humiliated and the Wronged*) have a narrator whose role is to raise the curtain and to comment upon the action on the stage—while the stage itself is usually set on three or four levels, and the play is going on almost simultaneously on all of them. Only *Crime and Punishment* could be called a one-way novel, with a direct plot and with all the minor characters and incidents subordinated to the central conflict of the main hero. In almost all the others the ramifications of plot, the importance attached to secondary characters, the side-paths and back alleys of the action, all make the whole composition extremely complex.

In *The Brothers Karamazov,* however, this intricate structure is happily resolved in a symphonic unity of story and idea. The inner life of the chief characters is not rationalized by the author; it is shown in action or discussed in dialogues. The only exceptions to this rule are the speeches by the prosecution and the defense. But the court-room scene also has a dramatic quality which reflects the most essential trait of Dostoevsky's art. All his novels can be broken down to a succession of scenes, and their numbered parts correspond to the acts of a play. Each chapter begins with the entrance or exit of some protagonist and a new incident. The suspense is sustained by a swift, often surprising, shift in action and a change of setting. Something is happening every moment, and only the dialogue puts the brake on the terrific pace of the action.

The dialogue is not concerned with imitating the plain talk of real life: it has a dramatic function and is feverish and high-pitched, even when expository or when the hero has something to say—as when Myshkin gives his views on capital punishment, or Verkhovensky makes false revelations concerning Stavroghin. The action advances spasmodically, by explosions that often turn into minor catastrophes or *coups de théâtre.* Raskolnikov, on coming home and unexpectedly finding his mother and sister there, faints away; he is cornered in the District Attorney's office, when suddenly his dangerous opponent is informed that a workman has confessed to the pawnbroker's murder. The scenes where Nastasia (*The Idiot*) throws a hundred thousand rubles into the fire and where Stavroghin (*The Possessed*) is slapped in the face by Shatov, but restrains himself, are typical of such climactic surprises. Instead of carefully building up to one climax and one crisis, Dostoevsky uses a series of them, thus working his way toward the solution of the central conflict.

The plot is also not without dramatic surprises, like Stavroghin's secret marriage to the crippled, feeble-minded girl, or Smerdyakov's murder of old Karamazov, his father. The dramatic tension is enhanced by outbursts of temper, epileptic fits (Myshkin, Smerdyakov), duels, slapped faces (Myshkin, Stavroghin, Versilov), violent death, and public confessions. Heroes and heroines often break down and shout forth their self-accusations in front of others, who play the role of a chorus or act as judges. Proceeding by contrasts and assigning wraith-doubles to his important characters, Dostoevsky often shows the antipathy of ideas and temperaments by scenes in which people clash, quarrel, and insult each other (Katerina Ivanovna and Grushenka,

Dolgorukii and his father, Myshkin and Rogozhin, old Karamazov and Dimitri, *et al.*). Faithful to his dramatic techniques, he also observes, as far as he can, the unities of time and action, and even of place, so long as his settings are not too varied.

What makes these novel-dramas so powerful is the complete identification between the thoughts or passions of the protagonists and their behavior: they live as they think and feel. Nothing is ever abstract in this philosophical writer; the metaphysical and moral premises of his heroes are immediately materialized and enacted. Raskolnikov kills because everything is permissible; Verkhovensky makes preparations for revolution through deceit and crime, because there is no immortality of the soul.

The novel-drama with all its stage devices and its bare settings (few descriptions of environment and never a picture of nature) practically reaches the heights of a morality play or a tragedy. The complex of guilt and revenge, which forms the backbone in the plot of *The Gambler, The Idiot, Crime and Punishment, A Raw Youth, The Possessed,* and *The Brothers Karamazov,* is basically a tragic conflict. Some heroes of the tragedies, such as Raskolnikov, liberate their repentant egos through submission, thus initiating a process of regeneration. This sort of catharsis or purification, after the storm of action has subsided and the troublesome cycle of tension is closed, is indicated in the case of Alesha. But often the tragedy ends, as in a Greek drama, only in death and chastisement (*The Gambler, The Idiot, The Possessed*).

The particular feature of Dostoevsky's tragedies is the multiplicity of its planes: the various tiers could not be symbolized by spatial concepts, for they are not simply a structure of successive horizontal levels. For instance, the complexity of *The Brothers Karamazov* consists in the interrelation and interpenetration of its multiple planes, which in theory can be analyzed separately but in actuality present an inextricable maze. On the surface the novel is a murder mystery, based on parricide: old Karamazov is killed, the circumstantial evidence points to Dimitri and, less directly, to Ivan. The discovery of the true murderer and the incidents of the investigation form the vehicle of the plot and supply it with all the elements of movement and suspense. But within this melodramatic story there is the intermittent light of something else: the antagonism of the sons and the father, with strong undertones of sexuality, so that the parricide becomes both a psychological temptation and a basic crime.

At this new level the book may be analyzed as a family novel, concerned with the mystery of heredity: the vitality of old Karamazov, expressed in sex, has been transformed into intellectual force in Ivan, into an emotional urge in Dimitri, and into religious feeling in Alesha, while in Smerdyakov it has degenerated into servile baseness. Family relations and differences in the characters form a special plane connected with a purely psychological level: the four brothers, the women they love—Grushenka, Katerina Ivanovna, Liza—and all the minor characters reveal the fluctuations and twistings of human nature. Confronted by unusual situations, they all display a variegated gamut of motivations and complexes—from tenderness to murderous lust, from rational clarity to fantastic raving. This is the plane that is most apparent to the majority of critics and readers and that has given rise to the classification of Dostoevsky's work as purely psychological.

Yet each of his heroes is a thinking individual, acting according to his beliefs and expressing his opinions: these constitute a higher level of philosophical concepts, discussed by Father Zossima, Ivan, Alesha, Dimitri. These concepts deal with the basic problems of God, immortality, justification of evil, religion, freedom, and so forth. This is a metaphysical plane which is also alluded to throughout the work and which has a symbolic meaning; the death of old Karamazov, the suicide of Smerdyakov, the purification of Dimitri through suffering, and Alesha's submission to the Divine Will, while bringing us back to the plot—the first level—also serve to accentuate the whole significance of the tragedy and to unite all the planes in an artistic whole.

Naturally, only the most important levels are mentioned in this rough outline: the extraordinary wealth of the novel offers many other opportunities for study and discovery. The composite planes are augmented by parallel lines. Next to the main plot run the secondary ramifications: Father Zossima and the monastery (both of which also have a symbolic and religious meaning), the story of Ilya and other children, again functionally necessary to show that Alesha has disciples and that there is something to be hoped for after the tragedy is over.

Dostoevsky may be liked or disliked; he may, as he was by Joseph Conrad, be labeled dangerously morbid; or the reading of his novels may be painful, almost unbearable, more like a life experience than an esthetic one; but nobody can deny the terrifying power of this uncanny genius. A Titan who resorted to the pattern of second-rate melodrama, he made it the foundation of a literary school, fashioning that pattern into the original form of the novel-drama, the novel-tragedy. This extraordinary observer of the irrational in men, this analyst of unconscious urges and pathological complexes, certainly prophesied all the contradictory issues of our times and put questions that we are still unable to answer. That is why he appears so 'modern' and that is why his hypnotic art, filled with the pathos and fury, the delirium of his

imagination, the world of dreams, the intuitions and metaphysical passions, the moral doubts and sensuality—all of which he created—
remains unique in world literature.

VI   To the West Dostoevsky was a startling revelation and his influence was and continues to be enormous.
The study of the deep impression he left on European thought would
range from Nietzsche, who called him his master, to the French Exis-
tentialists, who see in him one of their forerunners. The list of European
and American writers who admired him to the extent of reflecting him
in their own works—and could not help but do so—is exceedingly
long, in fact too long to be given here. Dostoevsky gave rise to a
veritable literary current in many Western countries, and is today, next
to Leo Tolstoy, the most widely read, discussed, and imitated of all
Russian writers. A whole library could be easily built with books in
all languages offering diverse interpretations of his works—from the
Freudian analysis which reduces them to a transposition of the author's
complexes and psychopathological drives, to the exalted schemes of
mystics, who acclaim him as seer and prophet.

Psychiatrists, theologians, moralists, and scholars study Dostoevsky
and find him astonishingly instructive. The words of Goethe, *wer vieles
bringt wird jeden etwas bringen*—'he who brings much brings something for everybody'—can be fully applied to Dostoevsky.

In the 'forties Dostoevsky, linked with Gogol and the humanistic
trend, was called a Realist. In the 'sixties, when he resumed his writing,
he could hardly be fitted into any classification. The Raznochintsi welcomed him as 'the poet of the humiliated and the wronged.' He wrote
in the language of the middle class and of the professional intelligentsia,
introducing in prose the same sort of 'low' style Nekrassov had introduced in poetry. Of course he was not a writer from the nobility or
about the nobility: his heroes belonged to the underprivileged classes,
and even his noblemen, such as Myshkin or Stavroghin, despite their
titles and money, were more akin to bohemians than aristocrats. He
was also a writer of the city, breaking with the countryside tradition in
plot and in style and taking an almost hostile attitude toward 'manorial
literature,' which the Nihilists styled 'literature for esthetes.'

He continued plowing the ground broken by Pushkin with his
Bronze Horseman, and by Gogol with his St. Petersburg tales: Dostoevsky's only poetic descriptions are those of scenes set in St. Petersburg. To the radical Realists of the 'sixties, he seemed the poet of the
slums; yet they were puzzled by his reactionary philosophy. This philosophy brought him close to the circles of conservative noblemen; yet

the latter were disturbed by his vehemence and the disreputable environments in his novels.

Despite Dostoevsky's desire to catch up with his times and to write 'contemporary' stories, his work has no historical setting. Raskolnikov may be called a Nihilist while *The Possessed* is definitely a novel with a political tendency, but the contingencies of a given period seem irrelevant in comparison with the broad significance of the romantic drama of passions and ideas that he presents. The most patent pressure of his times could be found in Dostoevsky's desire to offer a message, in his rejection of the art for art's sake formula. All his novels are tendentious —from the moral, religious, social, and philosophical points of view— and in this he openly adhered to the general trend of the 'sixties and 'seventies.

In Russia his greatest fame began only after his death; however, during the Pushkin celebration of 1880, despite the controversial reaction provoked by his political statements, he was greeted by tremendous ovations which definitely put in the shade even Turgenev, who also delivered a speech at the unveiling of the Pushkin monument. Dostoevsky's popularity abroad grew steadily, while at home he was recognized by the end of the century as the greatest Russian novelist, equaled in stature only by Leo Tolstoy.

The conservatives tried to use him as an exponent of their political outlook, citing *A Writer's Diary* and passages from various novels of his in their struggle against the Revolutionaries. As a result of this, by the beginning of the twentieth century the name of Dostoevsky became identified in radical circles with morbid mysticism and anti-Liberalism. In 1906 Gorky refused to participate in the commemoration of Dostoevsky's death, declaring he hated the man who, although a literary genius, expressed reactionary views and wanted to support absolutism and clericalism. Socialists regarded Dostoevsky with suspicion and mistrust. His fame was greatly strengthened by the Symbolists, however, who studied the religious, moral, and artistic aspects of his work; Dimitri Merezhkovsky, Valery Briussov, and Viacheslav Ivanov wrote books and essays about 'this maddening convict, whose chains still jangle in Russian literature, which has been stunned by his raving invasion.'

Nationalists of various shadings hailed Dostoevsky as 'a great prophet, a great interpreter of national character, and a philosopher of the Russian idea.' Many liberals at home and abroad shared the opinion that Dostoevsky, as spokesman of Russian nationalism, voiced the very substance of 'Russia's dream.' T. Masaryk defined his works as 'the key to an understanding of the Bolshevik Revolution and of all Russian problems.' Dostoevsky as a religious writer was acclaimed by certain Church dignitaries as the 'obedient, though restless, son of the Greek Orthodox church.'

While Gorky and the Socialists were hostile to Dostoevsky on political grounds, a group of Realistic writers criticized him from a literary standpoint, castigating his fantastic Romanticism, his morbid imagination, and his disintegrating influence on young writers. The question of his morbidity was never allowed to rest. 'Pathological genius,' 'lover of the abnormal,' 'mad painter,' 'poet of madness'—these and similar epithets were widely circulated in press and conversation between 1900 and 1917. The Czarist authorities permitted only the most innocuous excerpts from his writings to be used in the curricula of the secondary schools.

Discussions of his works flared up with new vigor under the Soviet regime. The ambivalence in the attitude toward the great writer created a complex and puzzling situation. All the official mouthpieces of the Communist party, and consequently of the government, repeated Gorky's charges and affirmed Dostoevsky's complete incompatibility with Marxist ideology. They labeled him 'Promoter of the Russian imperialistic idea,' 'degenerate supporter of reaction, who did not believe in social progress and based his philosophy on pessimistic evaluation of human nature.' Dostoevsky the anti-Socialist, the monarchist, the Greek Orthodox Christian, the painter of the bestial, evil sides of man, was declared an enemy of Communism who ought not to be allowed to contaminate the minds and the hearts of the young. As a result of this tendency, until 1953, text books of literature authorized for the schools of the Soviet Union either completely omitted Dostoevsky, barely mentioned him, or discussed him sketchily in a page or two of small type. The students were left to wonder why a writer who (as some notes stated at the end) 'has received universal recognition as a master genius of the psychological novel' did not deserve more than a passing mention.

At the same time the State Publishing House did a superb job in editing and issuing the first complete annotated collection of Dostoevsky's works in thirteen volumes (1926-32), and in making available to the public, in the nineteen thirties a series of documents, letters, memoirs, notebooks, critical essays, and so forth, dealing with Dostoevsky.

A considerable amount of valuable literary material, including the writer's various drafts and outlines, was published between 1930 and 1940. Several books of interpretation, published in 1947-8, again provoked controversy and polemics. Exponents of the party line strongly objected to what they called 'an overestimation of Dostoevsky, with a deliberate refusal to analyze and criticize the reactionary, anti-Soviet essence of his ideology.'

The situation, however, improved greatly after Stalin's demise. In 1956, on the occasion of the 75th anniversary of Dostoevsky's death, large reprints of his writings, including a new edition of his collected works, and numerous critieal essays marked a change in the official attitude. Without retracting any of their derogatory statements, the Party leaders were compelled to accept the fact that Dostoevsky was a great novelist and classic. They also had to admit that quite a few Soviet writers could be called his disciples and that Soviet youth read eagerly all the novels and tales of the 'cruel genius.'

No overall figures on the circulation of Dostoevsky's works in the Soviet Union have ever been made available, although it is known that some novels, such as· *Crime and Punishment* (reprinted in 1945 and 1947), *Notes from the House of the Dead,* and his *Selected Works,* as well as illustrated editions of *The Gambler* and other minor tales, have sold well over 500,000 copies each. But even without any statistical charts, it would hardly be too much to assume that Dostoevsky remains one of the most widely read Russian classics in the Soviet Union.

15

LEO TOLSTOY

I   LEO TOLSTOY, one of the few men about whom a myth was created during his lifetime, was the first Russian writer to acquire world-wide fame. For many years he remained a central figure in European literature and thought; the voice of this man, who in his wrath resembled a Biblical prophet, resounded to the four corners of the earth; on all continents people who had read his works— and even those who had never looked at them—listened with wonder and awe to the echoes of his struggles with his own spirit, his family, his society; to the spiritual and bodily turmoils of a great writer who renounced art because he aspired to saintliness, of a count who threw away title and property because he wanted to lead the simple life of a peasant.

The grandiose scale of his activities also touched the imagination: his works were gigantic in scope and length—*War and Peace, Anna Karenina, Resurrection,* dozens of volumes of minor novels, tales, plays, and stories, and other dozens of religious and moral essays, of scholarly treatises and journalistic pamphlets. His moral preaching strove for nothing less than a renovation of Christianity and the establishment of his own brand of religion upon earth. He challenged everything—the family, marriage, morals, state, church, education—and some of his negations were like 'a moral earthquake, shattering the very foundations of our civilization.' Even his personal life was beyond all bounds, with his riotous passions and sudden conversions, his thirteen children, his domestic dramas (telegraphed or cabled all over the world by special correspondents), his longevity, his extraordinary vitality, and his pathetic death, which overtook the octogenarian as he fled from his ancestral home to appease his conscience.

Despite the variety of his activities, as moralist and religious reformer, and despite the fact that at the age of fifty-two he publicly repudiated his fictional works for the sake of spiritual regeneration, he was a writer first and last. On many occasions he denied it, sometimes out of snobbishness, sometimes in an attempt at understatement; he said that 'Lermontov and myself are not men of letters' to indicate that they both subordinated literary achievements to other, more important aims. But he was nonetheless primarily a writer. The urge to express himself in words, to encompass in phrases all that he had experienced and experimented with, to communicate to others the truths he believed he had found, was always predominant in him, and some ninety volumes of his writings (including 13 volumes of diaries and over 30 volumes of letters) clearly attest to this. Of course, Tolstoy had a complex and highly contradictory personality, a powerful mind, a hypersensitive conscience, a high moral awareness, and strong animal spirits: he was not merely a man with a great gift of words.

Every definition of his work outside this quality of writing is, however, incomplete: he was not a preacher, even though many of his articles sound like sermons; he was not the founder of a new sect, even though his disciples, the world over, from Europe to Japan, from India to South Africa, have launched a movement bearing his name; he was not a man of action, even though he had been an army officer, a judge, an educator, a landowner, a social worker; he was not a philosopher, even though in his writings he deals with the fundamental problems of abstract thinking. He was a man who loved to write and for whom writing was the most natural weapon in all his struggles, in all his affirmations and denials. If he was angry with himself he formulated his points of accusation on paper; if he was enchanted with life, he invented tales; when he was passing through a moral crisis he wrote books, and, to invoke God, to bring the Word to his fellow men, he used his pen over and over until his very death.

Many of Tolstoy's peculiarities, from his style to his ideology, stem from his background. In whatever he did and wrote he reflected the agrarian, paternalistic, almost feudal environment of the landed gentry to which he belonged. Born in 1828 at Yasnaya Poliana (Serene Meadow), the family estate, he was brought up in the best traditions of the nobility. He was a count, a member of a privileged class, descendant of those who had served the Czars and ruled the Empire: he always remembered that the Tolstoys had played a part in Russian history since the fourteenth century.

At the age of eighteen, as an odd, awkward youth, he dreamed of becoming an accomplished nobleman, *un homme comme il faut*. Even years later he could not help looking down at those of his countrymen who did not speak French perfectly and he was proud of his own Oxford English. In his youth he shared the prejudices of his caste, loved the easy-going life on his manorial lands, and found it quite natural to be served by a retinue of domestics or to be kowtowed to by deferential tenant farmers. He always styled himself a landowner, not a writer, as this was in better keeping with his title and his ideas of what was a proper occupation for an aristocrat.

In 1862, when a police search was ordered for Yasnaya Poliana during his absence, he wrote to the Czar about this injustice against a nobleman and even planned to emigrate to England: he would not admit that the authorities could behave toward him as they did toward ordinary citizens. He loved his ancient manor. 'It is difficult for me to represent Russia and my sentiment for her without my Yasnaya Poliana,' Tolstoy wrote even in his thirties. Of the two courses open to a nobleman, that of civil service or of managing his lands, Tolstoy much preferred the latter. 'To live as a landowner is in the nature of a nobleman, and he alone knows how to do it,' says Levin, Tolstoy's mouthpiece in *Anna Karenina*.

Tolstoy attended the University of Kazan but did not graduate, because he was bored by academic studies. In 1851 he enlisted as a volunteer in the Army, in which he served until 1854, fighting the guerrilla tribesmen in the Caucasus and, as an officer during the Crimean campaign, going through the dangers and privations of the siege of Sevastopol. In the years following he led the usual life of a young aristocrat, gambling, drinking, and making love in both capitals. Next he traveled abroad extensively, always remaining faithful to Yasnaya Poliana, however, and never giving up his idea of settling down as a landowner.

This he finally did, and, in 1862, at the age of 34 he brought to his ancestral home his eighteen-year-old bride, Sophie (née Behrs). From then on he spent almost fifty years on his estate, save for occasional trips to Moscow, to the Volga region, and to the Crimea. And, in accordance with his wishes, he was buried at Yasnaya Poliana.

Count Leo Tolstoy, the writer, who described himself under many guises, devoted the best years of his literary activity to picturing the milieu he knew and loved best—that of the Russian nobility. What is *War and Peace* if not a panorama of life and thoughts of the upper classes at the beginning of the nineteenth century? This novel was initially planned as a family chronicle with the suggestive title *All's Well that Ends Well,* clearly indicating its idyllic character and idealistic tendency. When the radicals of the 'sixties reproached him for not having paid enough attention to the lower classes, Tolstoy answered with scorn: 'The life of merchants, coachmen, seminarists, convicts, and muzhiks strikes me as monotonous and boring.' The setting of *Anna Karenina* is, again, that of high society; and the heroes of his other novels and tales, from the nineteen-year-old youth who decides to devote himself to his estate and the welfare of his serfs (*A Landowner's Morning,* in 1852), to Prince Nekhludov, who gives up his lands to turn them over to his peasants (*Resurrection,* in 1899), are all noblemen—either self-portraits or portraits of those he knew exceptionally well. It is impossible to understand the violence of Tolstoy's attacks against society without the realization that all his protests are a form of self-castigation, aimed at eradicating 'depravity and snobbishness' from his own nature. Tolstoy is the perfect examplar of the Repentant Nobleman, who severs his ties with his own class and even creates a doctrine of self-justification.

Another feature of his background is his closeness to all the processes of agrarian labor. His attitude toward the peasants may have gone through an evolution similar to that of all his opinions, but his background remained unchanged: from his childhood till his death he always saw in agricultural work a natural occupation providing man with all his needs. In an agrarian country like Russia, Count Tolstoy, the landowner, despite all his French and English governesses, felt very close to all the Ivans and Stepans, his least yeomen, whose work, language, and mentality were an open book to him. Thus, Tolstoy's aristocratic interests and tendencies were coupled with a strong attachment to the soil, and when in his revolt he rejected his society, he very naturally turned to the peasant huts which surrounded the manor house at Yasnaya Poliana.

On the whole, he could dwell either in the master's house or in the peasants' quarters of the same estate; yet all his quest for truth and wisdom amounted to no more than a trip around Yasnaya Poliana: after having duly admired its proprietors, he ended by idealizing its servants. In his contempt for civilization, in his denial of technical progress and science, and in his incessant war against the town, and the artificial life of great cities, he reflects the mentality of a peasant who is hostile to all the 'deviltry' of industry and obstinately defends his hoe and wooden plow.

The back-to-nature idea runs throughout the spiritual evolution of Tolstoy; it is his most stable principle, and he never deviated from it. A disciple of Rousseau, whom he had worshiped since his boyhood and a miniature portrait of whom he wore instead of a cross, Tolstoy was always attracted by the Natural Man and by the simplicity of an existence in close communion with Mother Earth. His anti-civilization feelings mirror the resentment of a farmer against the city slicker. In this he was completely opposed to Dostoevsky and other writers of the city. He is a nobleman with a peasant's mind, who epitomized in his person, his writings, and his philosophy the land of his ancestors and his serfs. In 1899, a man of seventy-one, he opens *Resurrection* with: 'Despite all the efforts of men gathered in hundreds of thousands to disfigure the patch of earth on which they were swarming, the spring remained spring even in the city.'

Gorky has noted that Tolstoy used in his conversation crude, blunt, sometimes shockingly frank peasant expressions in designating organic functions, sexual matters, or working habits. This agrarian mentality evinces itself even in his religious principles. This squire turned his back on other squires and looked for wisdom in peasant huts; he took to dressing like a muzhik, to working as a muzhik did, to living as the muzhik lived, and asserted that this lowly life was the only one conforming to the Divine Law. The repentant nobleman repudiated his class and the conventions and, fascinated by peasant ideology, he fought whatever threatened the peaceful existence of toil, procreation, humility, and resignation. He thus rejected state, church, military service, war, education, machines, and all the refinements of civilization, for the sake of primitive simplicity—the simplicity he wanted to assert in art as well as in daily life or religion.

This identification with peasant life had also deep biological roots. A man of great physical strength and prodigious vitality, Tolstoy was like a centaur, and both his sensuousness and sensuality were as well developed as his intelligence. From his childhood to his last day Tolstoy, the Barbarian, the Troglodyte (as the literati of St. Petersburg called him after his return from Sevastopol in 1855), felt himself a part of the universe, a product of nature, with its fields, forests, beasts, winds, smells, and colors. He was not like Turgenev, for whom nature served merely as a framework for his pastels, or loomed as a hostile force. Tolstoy, the admirer of Tiutchev, enjoyed nature and was happy whenever he was in contact with its elemental powers. His stamina and virility, the robustness of his body, the vehemence of his appetites, the keen alertness of his mind, all revealed the physical strength of his personality.

In the delightful novel *The Cossacks,* begun in 1852 when he was twenty-four and published in 1862, he described the wholesome life of primitive warriors as opposed to the sophisticated ways of civilization. Olenin, the autobiographical hero, spoiled by the inane and idle existence of the aristocracy, makes friends with Eroshka, an old Cossack hunter who looks like a forest deity. Eroshka loves all living creatures; a deer or a pheasant does not, to him, differ basically from a human being. He accepts everything, including bloodshed and death, and does not understand why men label certain deeds sinful. To this illiterate pantheist, hunting, fighting, and making love are not sins but natural manifestations of life. Olenin wishes he were able to emulate Eroshka, but he is already too corrupted by civilization, scruples, and introspection. Thus he fails in the rivalry for the love of Mariana, a buxom Cossack girl whose simple strength and bland sensuality are akin to the bravery and lust of young Lukashka, who finally wins her.

Tolstoy accepts the brutality, and even the cruelty, of the Cossacks, since he admires their naturalness, the unspoiled wholesomeness of their animal existence. This is the Russian version of the Noble Savage; what distinguishes it from its Romantic model is the stark realism of description: the simplicity of their life so fascinated Tolstoy that he had no need to adorn it. When he was nearing eighty he resumed the same theme in his tale of *Hadji Murat;* its psychological design is more complicated but it is again a treatment of the primitive man, a fighter and horseman as wild and strong as the Caucasian wind.

In general, those descriptions in Tolstoy's novels that convey a strong, animal sense of nature are extraordinarily vivid: the hunting scenes in *War and Peace,* the analysis of the pleasure Levin experienced from physical work (*Anna Karenina*), the story of *Yardstick,* the broken-down race horse. The pages about winter or spring (particularly in *War and Peace* and *Resurrection*) reflect nothing of the esthetic joys of a city dweller: they reveal the intimate link between the vital cycle of the seasons and the man who lives in the country.

This perception of the basic elements of life is also in all his portraits of human beings. A great master of physical portrayal, the 'seer of the flesh'—as Merezhkovsky defined him in contrasting the 'old wizard of Yasnaya Poliana' with Dostoevsky, 'the seer of the spirit'— he describes all the physical mannerisms of his heroes. For example, in *War and Peace* he repeatedly emphasizes the clumsiness of Pierre, his heavy gait, his bulky body, his babylike face and horn-rimmed spectacles; or the cold, alabastrine magnificence of his wife's shoulders; or Denissov's guttural enunciation (his *r* sounds like *g*); or the plump white hands of Napoleon; or the wrinkles on the forehead of the diplomat Bilibin. There are hundreds of such touches.

He knows all the secrets of the human body and he translates psychological nuances through their corresponding physical gestures. He even looks for some material expression to convey a moral idea. In *Resurrection* the heroine, Katiusha Masslova, is portrayed several times to indicate the results of her changing moral status: her fresh round face with charming, slightly squinting dark eyes becomes puffy, almost swollen, and acquires the sidelong glance of the prostitute; and then she becomes less fleshy when the forces of moral regeneration set in on the way to Siberia.

This is one of Tolstoy's most prominent traits: he sees, and strongly feels, all physical details in nature and man. With Théophile Gautier he could exclaim: 'I am one of those for whom the outward world does exist!' And he loves this world, and all that he finds in it appeals to his senses and enchants him. No other writer in Russian literature is as fundamentally realistic as this moral preacher, and nobody is so attached to the concreteness, the texture of earthly existence. The overflowing vitality of Tolstoy found its expression in the richness of all his art. When he became convinced of the necessity of renunciation for the sake of his soul, he had to wage a war against the foundations of his nature, against the temptations of the world he cherished with genuine passion. He loved the flesh, the senses, the joys of being, and they are what convey such a feeling of life to his novels.

Yet he did not want to accept blindly this vital force within and around him. He wanted to know the meaning of all this exuberance and to amend his own nature. This is probably the most important trait of his character: never satisfied with himself, he attempted to shape his life as well as everyone else's in accordance with the truth he was so eagerly seeking. This urge to improve himself and the world ran parallel to a strong tendency toward self-denial. He was a typical nay-sayer; his sharp critical sense compelled him to a ruthless analysis of what life had to offer him; and he enjoyed demolishing accepted dogmas, stripping off masks, digging to the very essence of things, and pitilessly casting aside what he considered of secondary or no importance. His style and artistic method sprang from the same attitude: his psychological realism was an attempt to get at the core of events and characters by piercing through the illusory appearance of conventions and patterns. He may have loved his heroes, but he nevertheless regarded them as would a relentless judge, never failing to castigate their weaknesses. He began by criticizing everything about him and finished by rejecting that which was strongest in himself: his art, his sex, his social background.

This was the cause of his tragedy. It conditioned his contradictions and the extraordinary variety and fullness of his work: he was wrestling with himself in his life and in his writings—and this struggle colored both his writings and his life. The struggle also bestowed upon him something exceedingly human: despite all the didactic bent of his mind, his rationality, his love of logic and glaring clarity; despite his innate puritanism made intransigent by its opposition to his innate paganism; despite the angry directness of his denial and the almost rigid firmness of his faith, he never dogmatized. He was neither a saint nor a hero on a pedestal—he was a great human being. When somebody reproached him one day that a recent statement of his was contrary to what he had affirmed the year before, he frowned and grumbled: 'I'm not a wood-pecker, to be making the same noise all my life long.'

II   The desire for self-perpetuation, so strong in Tolstoy and manifest in his eagerness for numerous progeny, was one of his main incentives in writing. Dostoevsky is usually labeled a subjective, and Tolstoy an objective, writer of epic magnitude, but nothing is more superficial than such generalizations. As a matter of fact, Tolstoy left much more autobiographical material in his novels than any other Russian novelist. Dostoevsky expressed his ideas and anxieties by describing other people, in a combination of reality and fantasy. Tolstoy, a thorough realist, described himself and all the actual incidents of his life, sometimes not even bothering to disguise them: he hardly changed the names of his relatives who served him as models for the characters in *War and Peace* (for example, his mother and her family, the princes Volkonsky, are called merely Bolkonsky).

He began his literary career with reminiscences: in *Childhood* (1852), *Boyhood* (1854), and *Youth* (1856), which, together with *Tales of Sebastopol,* laid the foundations of his fame, Tolstoy is repre-sented under the name of Nikolenka Irteniev. As well as reconstructing the domestic background of Yasnaya Poliana and describing his teachers and relatives, these three books are magnificent pieces of self-analysis and introspection. This first study of himself reveals how deeply he was concerned with his own spiritual development and the tumultuous con-tradictions of his temperament and mind—the struggle between Ego and Super-Ego in his efforts to attain sublimation. In *Sebastopol Tales,* written in a direct, realistic manner; in *Lucerne,* reflecting his moral indignation at the indifference of the idle rich to misery and suffering; in *A Landowner's Morning*—in *Family Happiness*—he always pic-tured himself. He is the Olenin of *The Cossacks,* and later the Levin of *Anna Karenina,* the Eugene of *The Devil,* and the Nekhludov of *Resurrection.*

At the same time this master of self-portraiture, who filled his books with all his personal and most intimate experiences, who never ceased using fiction as a means of perpetual confession and self-revelation (or self-accusation), had a tremendous power for impersonating and representing other people. He immortalized himself, but he also immortalized whomever he described, and such is his power of suggestion that all his fictional characters are as alive as the people we meet in life.

The scope and diversity of this artistic power are of gigantic proportions. Usually writers, like actors, are limited in the range of their impersonations: a tragedian does not often play comic roles, while a writer specializes in rendering a certain type of character. Only two literary geniuses of all literature seem to have fully possessed this unlimited range of characterization: Shakespeare and Tolstoy. There are 559 characters in *War and Peace,* and all of them—from the chief characters to the least important—are drawn with such vigor, precision, and realism that they are amazingly animated and individualized. Tolstoy's capacity of observing, memorizing, and understanding the essentials of bodily and mental characteristics and his power of rendering them so as to create a perfect illusion of life, are uncanny and unequaled. With the same ease and force he portrays emperors or peasants, old men such as Kutuzov, or fourteen-year-old girls like Natasha, and he knows exactly the feelings of each—Kutuzov's before yielding Moscow to Napoleon and Natasha's as she chats with her mother. There are no visible limits to his descriptions of the activities and various processes of life, from battles, which he makes us visualize with the precision of a military expert, to the prattle of children, from analytical pictures of the intricacies of diplomatic negotiations to the subtle shifts in mood of a man who has just fallen in love with a young girl.

His psychological insight also had an extraordinary range: his 'imaginary psychology' mirrors with equal penetration the thoughts of a commander-in-chief and the feelings of a debutante before her first ball. This diversity and fullness of insight reaches fantastic magnitude in *War and Peace,* where Tolstoy the creator is godlike in his fecundity. By an assemblage of realistic details and psychological traits he achieves an immediate illusion of the flow of time, of the daily growth of events, thoughts, emotions.

The completeness of detail that gave such power to the realistic narrative of Goncharov is amplified and deepened in Tolstoy. His realism has its own special features. First of all, he strictly observes the time element, the river-like quality of objective narrative; the even and majestic unrolling of his story which follows the natural sequence of events is completely contrary to the dramatic tenseness of Dostoevsky. The succession of scenes and dialogues gives each moment the illusion of fullness. Therefore the story, the incidents, serve only as a pretext or, to use the image of Ortega y Gasset, as a string that makes of the beads a necklace. But what is really important and makes the necklace priceless is the value of each bead: each is presented as an independent unit, and yet at the same time in relation to what has gone before and is to come.

Particularly in *Anna Karenina* Tolstoy shows how everything fits into a large pattern, so that each of Anna's words and actions acquires significance and gains momentum as the novel progresses. In Dostoevsky words and gestures serve to symbolize or illustrate a central idea, which is always identified with the plot. In Tolstoy the plot—as a combination of surprising incidents and accidents, as a complex entanglement of circumstances—hardly ever exists. For this anti-Romantic craftsman the processes of life, the progression of time, are in themselves sufficient vehicles for narration; a normal life-situation developing in a perfectly natural, almost banal, way offers him the pattern into which his exposition is woven. He narrates as life progresses, noticing all the visual and sensorial details of each moment, and his report on life never lapses into imagism or disconnected impressionistic flashes. On the contrary, the reader is led by the firm hand of the artist who knows very well where he is going and leaves little to be supplemented by the imagination.

There is a perfectly rational order in this preordained Tolstoyan universe. Characters and scenes, conversations and actions, are subordinated to a design, revolve around an invisible center as, according to his beliefs, the lives of men are directed by Divine Will. Tolstoy's world of fiction is a faithful image of God's universe, but the role of Providence is assumed by the author and, instead of complying with the Divine Law of the Lord, his heroes obey strictly the autocratic rules of the writer's composition, style, and moral vision. At the same time he always shows the fluidity of the psyche, the dynamics of our thoughts and emotions. Chernyshevsky called this method of psychological Realism 'the dialectics of the soul.' Tolstoy's heroes all go through various inner changes and Tolstoy the psychologist registers them all—even the most tenuous ones—describing their intricate courses with penetrating exactness and unsurpassed artistry.

The peculiarities of Tolstoy's art are most spectacularly revealed in *War and Peace,* the creation of which took seven years (1862-8). This work grew into its monumental shape like a living organism, expanding in scope during the process of writing. Initially begun as a novel about the Decembrists, it developed into simply a story of family life and later assumed the proportions of an epic, undergoing several transformations. Until 1865 the historic part was barely sketched out, and Napoleon and Alexander I did not figure in the initial drafts. No wonder that as a preliminary for the final Russian text of over 1800 pages, which was copied, recopied, and changed seven times, Tolstoy wrote more than a thousand pages of alternatives that he left out in the definitive edition.

As it stands now, *War and Peace* can be called a historical novel, since it unfolds the panorama of European events between 1805 and 1814, giving a particularly detailed picture of Napoleon's campaign in Russia in 1812. This vast canvas, which includes such historical figures as the French, Russian, and Austrian Emperors, Austrian diplomats, German strategists, and military leaders, is complemented by a theoretical treatise on the driving forces of history. Tolstoy believed that the sum total of what individuals feel and think forms the fabric of history, and he denied the concepts of progress and historical advancement. All the changes and evolution the historian talk about are illusory: 'heroes' who imagine they can shape events are fools doomed to failure, and their combined efforts are of no importance.

Thus Tolstoy, who had studied this period in documents, books, archives, memoirs, and even oral recollections of some survivors of this not too-distant past, and who wrote a glorified national epic of Russia's War for the Fatherland was eminently anti-historic. He laughed at the 'religion of progress' and saw life as an immutable mold of moral conflicts, and not in terms of fluent, changing scenes of historic mutation. Therefore, as a historical novel, *War and Peace* is as remote from the usual pattern of the genre as Tolstoy himself is from Walter Scott or Alexander Dumas. He is a historical novelist in the same way that Homer is the historian of the Trojan war. The Romantics enjoy the colorful, the picturesque, the involved, the heroic, and the ideal; Tolstoy takes a malicious pleasure in discovering triviality in the heroic, in reducing the involved to its most simple expression, in stripping materialistic motives of their ideal appearances, and in divesting the picturesque of its glamor. He struggles against the cult of heroes, against all pedestals and elevations.

The method he uses to uncrown history and to overthrow idols is one of derogatory realism, which often becomes satire. Napoleon is smug, pretentious, and believes he is a demigod; but he is also plump, short-legged, slightly ridiculous and has a runny nose before the Battle of Borodino—his courtiers are convinced that this indisposition impaired his military genius and therefore influenced the outcome of the fight. Alexander I comes out on the balcony to receive patriotic acclaim —and is munching a cookie. General Pfuhl is not so much interested in the upshot of the military operations he is directing as in the conformity of troop movements to his theoretical blueprint of military tactics—just as if he were playing with lead soldiers or having a game of chess. During the battles of Austerlitz or Borodino nothing develops according to the expectations of the strategists, no orders are really executed, all the attempts of leaders to guide the series of separate clashes constituting a battle are frustrated—yet everything happens as it was *bound* to happen, regardless of commanders-in-chief, head-quarters, and liaison officers. Pierre, at the Battle of Borodino, sees only a succession of senseless and disconnected feats of arms—just as does Fabrizio Del Dongo at the Battle of Waterloo in *The Charterhouse of Parma* by Stendhal, to whom Tolstoy paid the tribute of declaring that these few pages revealed to him the truth about war.

Kutuzov is a wise man because he does not try to intervene or to direct, merely 'helping' when he has a hunch how things are going and relying much more on the psychology of his soldiers than on the shrewd-ness of his general staff. In this he is the exact opposite of Napoleon, who takes himself seriously and makes others believe he is a superman. Napoleon's vanity and presumptuousness are disparagingly stressed, and his 'historic deeds and words' are ridiculed. It is not *War and Peace,* but simply a 'War against Napoleon' waged by Count Leo Tolstoy, to quote a *mot* that made the rounds of the St. Petersburg salons in the 'seventies. Contemporaries were puzzled by Tolstoy's unusual manner of presenting and interpreting historic events and by his deliberate tendentiousness. Turgenev called it 'comedy and charlatanism'; Saltykov said that the 'war scenes are a mess and a lie.' Subsequently Merezh-kovsky also reproached Tolstoy for resorting to tricks and lacking the 'atmosphere of history.'

The mistake that many critics made was in expecting a novel in the conventional pattern of Sir Walter Scott or other well-known his-torical novelists, of what was a new form in world literature. Today, after Tolstoy has influenced almost every writer of the historical novel, we are used to 'modernization of history,' to the presentation of the past with the sole aim of reference to the present, to the debunking of heroes and authorities. But almost a century ago Tolstoy's anti-Romantic, anti-heroic, anti-conventional approach was startling. That approach stemmed, of course, from a paradoxical situation: *War and Peace* was a historical novel that aimed at demonstrating the inanity of history. Facts and figures of the past were used by the author to emphasize the central idea of the whole work: 'true grandeur cannot exist without simplicity, goodness, and truth.' Actually the opposition of war to peace in the title of the epic had great significance: Tolstoy seemed to em-phasize that all the great events to which we usually attach so much importance and learn about in textbooks are of no consequence when compared with the only great facts of life—birth, work, love, death. True history consists of the lives of millions of people, with their worries and family troubles, their thoughts, emotions, faults, fears, and aspirations. All the rest is irrelevant, an evil illusion.

In the process of writing *War and Peace,* not only the historical part but also Tolstoy's general ideas underwent considerable changes. The most spectacular of these was the shift of his idealization of the nobility to an idealization of the *muzhik.* Although only 150 out of 1,820 printed pages of the first edition of the novel dealt directly with lower strata of Russia's population, and although the author avoided speaking about the ills of serfdom or corporal punishments in the Army—'I did not want to picture the brutality, the violence and abuses of serfdom'—he confessed that the novel turned out to be an apologia of the 'people who strove for the liberation of their country.' Tolstoy shows most convincingly that Napoleon was defeated because of the spontaneous and widespread patriotic resistance of the Russian masses, who organized guerrilla bands and drove the French out of their land. He describes how the cudgel of popular war smashed Napoleon's army, and he never fails to stress the simple heroism and the spirit of self-sacrifice in Russian soldiers.

Tolstoy, the officer who went through the humiliation of the Crimean defeat, took revenge and consoled himself with the vision of his country's glorious past. This was the significance of the novel for the whole generation of the 'sixties—a form of national self-satisfaction that consciously or unconsciously helped to make the book widely popular. It became the only epic of Russian literature expressing the national feeling in a dignified and simple manner, without aggressiveness or chauvinism, as well as without the usual bias and prejudices of the Slavophiles and the Westernizers. For the Russians *War and Peace* was and still is the glorification of the national spirit, the great symbol of the enduring qualities of the Russian people. In 1942, when Hitler's troops occupied more than half a million square miles of Russian territory, new editions of the novel were selling out as fast as they appeared: over 500,000 copies were sold in besieged Leningrad alone, everybody finding hope and faith in this majestic epic by Tolstoy, whom Turgenev called 'the great writer of the Russian land.'

The solid core of this monumental work consists of a family chronicle, a definite apologia of the way of life Count Leo Tolstoy knew and loved—an idealization he felt necessary to oppose to the radicals and Raznochintsi, who had been busy exposing the wrongs of pre-reform Russia. *War and Peace* had a slightly disguised polemical purpose, which Tolstoy bore in mind when he omitted chapters that might have played into the hands of the radicals by showing the seamy side of serfdom (the illegitimate children of old Bolkonsky sent to an orphan asylum; the serf-mistress of Prince Andrew; young Rostov and the Greek prostitute).

The composition of the family chronicle runs along three parallel lines: the Bolkonsky family, whose head, the old Prince, a former Field Marshal and Voltairean of Catherine's reign and a representative of the 'feudal opposition,' lives with his daughter Marie on his large estate of Bold Mountains, while his son, Prince Andrew, an ambitious officer of the guards, spends a great deal of time in the capital in Court circles. Next to these scions of high aristocracy comes the Rostov family of Muscovite gentry: Count Rostov is kind but limited, loving tradition and old-fashioned ways, and ready to do anything for his charming daughter Natasha and his son Nicholas, an unassuming army officer. The Rostovs are open-hearted, and hospitable, but they are going down hill financially. While the Rostovs mirror the simpler nobility, the Bezukhov family represents the wealthier stratum of high society. Old Bezukhov, a former court dignitary, leaves his huge fortune to his illegitimate son Pierre, an uncouth young man who does not want to serve his country and marries the splendidly beautiful, frigid, and none too faithful Helen. Then there are the relatives and friends: Prince Vassily, the servile courtier; the young and frivolous Anatole Kuraghin; the impecunious and intriguing Princess Drubezkoy and her career-making son Boris, and so on.

The family life is pictured in all its aspects, from dinner parties in the house of Count Rostov, where the young people play and dance, to the death of Old Bezukhov; from the balls at the Imperial Court to the Christmas entertainments with mummers and folk dances; from intricate maneuvers of social climbers to hunting parties; from the wild fun of drunken officers to the sentimental love affairs of adolescent misses—all aspects of life from birth to death are encompassed in Tolstoy's prodigious vision.

On the whole, the world he re-creates is a healthy world of sound physical reactions and human relations. There is nothing abnormal, tense, or particularly gloomy to catch the eye or to hurt the feelings. Even the appalling scenes of battles or of the Moscow fire are treated with such a sweep of epic grandeur that their horror becomes merely an organic part of a wider pattern. In general the 'climate' of *War and Peace* is serene and bright, an optimistic light illuminates its pages, and Tolstoy's zest for life, the pleasure he takes in picturing its details, is so contagious that all the trivialities of existence shine with a new poetic attraction. Over and above this he most obviously loves the impractical, good-natured Count Rostov, as well as the haughty, cranky Prince Bolkonsky, the lively, impulsive Natasha with all her affairs and pranks, and Princess Marie, with her beautiful, glowing eyes, big feet, and heavy gait; he is delighted with most of his chief characters as well as with their way of life.

His work thus becomes a challenge to the main tendency of Critical Realism. After Pushkin, it is in fact the first great affirmation of Russian literature—in the Apollonian sense, to use Nietzschian terminology. Here we are leagues removed from Gogol's grimacing masks, from men afflicted with oblomovism, from Stavroghins or other demons, from superfluous men and worthless citizens, and even from Bazarov, whose main virtue lay in his rejection of his surroundings. Instead of the Khlestakovs and Chichikovs, of unhappy clerks and raving students, *War and Peace* presents an assertion of life and portrays normal human beings. Whatever is critical in Tolstoy's realism is directed toward the psychological exposé, toward sifting the wheat from the chaff. He is constantly opposing the essence to the appearance of things, but he never turns to a questioning of reality. On the contrary, reality is glorified, and in this apotheosis the biological continuance of life assumes supreme radiance, finding in itself its own justification. Usually such exultations of existence are irrational and exclude any moral approach. The originality of Tolstoy consists exactly of the opposite: his pagan acceptance of the world is paralleled by a quest for the meaning of life, and his psychological analysis of individuals leads to indictment of false moral codes. He is sarcastic and almost ruthless about the pretensions and illusions he dislikes; he speaks with irony and hostility and even exposes the vanity of high society and the smallness of human ambitions; and he definitely opposes the 'humble ones' to the predatory types.

III   This moralizing tendency is represented by those characters who are dissatisfied with their lives and strive to change them for the sake of some higher ideal. Prince Andrew and Pierre seek their better selves. The first is ambitious but despises courtiers and an easy way of making a career: feeling himself to be intimately connected with all the heroes of the past, practically a witness to their development, he, also, wants to become a hero, a second Napoleon. His desire has nothing akin to Raskolnikov's theories or to the superman attitude of Ivan Karamazov; he is a strong individual, firm of will and with an acute intelligence backed by wide reading and original thinking. He is the only truly intelligent Tolstoyan hero, and the most complex: he changes according to the company he is in, showing the multiple facets of his personality—cold, self-possessed, proud in society, sensitive, frank, unassuming with his friends, irritable and unhappy with his charming, silly wife, stubborn and affectionate with his old father. Wounded at Austerlitz, he lies semi-conscious on the corpse-littered battlefield and, as he watches the limitless sky, realizes how vain and illusory all his ambitions were. In one supreme moment he glimpses a truth as eternal as the sky, and a whole phase of his life comes to an end.

After his recovery and return home, where his wife dies in childbirth, he tries to serve society, but fails to find satisfaction in political activity. He despairs but is regenerated by his love for Natasha, who brings him back to life but also inspires him with jealousy and disappointment. Wounded again in 1812, on his deathbed he comes to see the light, realizing that he must forgive everybody, that the law of God is self-sacrifice, self-denial—and he awaits the moment when all the earthly passions and attachments will dissolve in the eternal sea of Divine Love. He arrives at a theistic concept of Divinity and a condemnation of egotism: he suffered because he had attempted to assert himself; now he is happy because he is going to be reunited with the source of life which is God.

Pierre, the idealist with the heart of a child, is more matter-of-fact in his moral seekings. His uncouth vitality impels him towards sensuality (his marriage with the statuesque Helen) and toward such scandalous actions as tying together a police officer and a bear, or dueling with Dolokhov, the presumed lover of his wife. Highly emotional and spontaneous, he passes through several intellectual and moral crises, joins the Freemasons, becomes a mystic, resolves to kill Napoleon, whom he considers the Antichrist, and, taken prisoner by the French, discovers through a fellow prisoner, the simple-hearted soldier Platon Karataev, the truth he had so long been seeking. Platon is a simple soul, accepting with resignation whatever may come his way, since he believes in the Divine Will and tries to comply with it. He knows that all men are brothers and he tries to help everybody. Pierre realizes that the soul of millions was embodied in this man of medium height who looked like any average *muzhik*.

From a moral point of view Platon Karataev is the central figure of *War and Peace,* even though he is one of the book's least striking literary portraits. More of an abstraction, a symbol, than a living character, he is the incarnation of the Russian people, of their stamina, kindness, and silent heroism. Thousands of Platons died defending their soil; their combined efforts defeated the greatest army in Europe; they are the backbone and the hope of Russia, for they grasped intuitively what the intellectual noblemen failed to understand rationally: one must accept God's law and live in simplicity, peace, and brotherhood by the

labor of one's hands. There is no other wisdom, no other greatness—
and ultimately Napoleon is defeated because he put his own ambition
and egotism above God's will, and he was confronted by Kutuzov, who
derived his strength from his communion with thousands of Platons.

Thus the moral idea is identified with the basic meaning of the War
for the Fatherland—the Russians won because they defended a just
cause. The main theme of the epic—'True grandeur cannot exist without simplicity, goodness, and truth'—is embodied in Karataev: he im-
parts their full significance to all the other characters and incidents of
the novel. The epilogue—the picture of Pierre's happy marriage and
the indications of moral restlessness in Prince Andrew's son and the
other young men, who obviously will join the Decembrists together with
Pierre—shows that the moral search continues after the war and that
there is no pause in the eternal unfolding of the life forces. Whoever
splits Tolstoy into two halves and contends that the moral reformer
should be studied separately from the artist has missed the whole meaning of *War and Peace,* which formulates the main principles of Tolstoyan
doctrine with amazing completeness. It is true that the negative part of
this doctrine is less perceptible in this novel than in other succeeding
works (even than in *Anna Karenina*), but almost all of Tolstoy's philosophic concepts are contained in it.

War and Peace created its own epical form, that of the epic without
plot or a predominating hero, even though there are, in Peace, two
heroes (Pierre, Andrew) and two heroines (Marie, Natasha) and, in
War, three heroes (Napoleon, Kutuzov, and Karataev) and certain
secondary figures (Nicholas Rostov, Sonia, Denissov, and Helen) also
in the foreground. The composition defied all accepted patterns and bewildered the critics and writers. 'It is not a novel,' commented Turgenev,
'it is an elephant'; and Leontiev added, 'It is a Hindu idol, with three
heads and six arms.' Flaubert said he could not resist shouts of enthusiasm while reading *War and Peace* and he felt that all other writers
were like children playing silly little games in comparison with Tolstoy.
Many French literati, however, were disconcerted by Tolstoy's 'barbarian' autocratism in challenging all literary conventions. The complexity of structure, the mixture of historical and bucolic elements, the
complete disregard for literary effects, for sensation and suspense, the
abruptly didactic, almost scriptural tone in the midst of the most dramatic scenes, as if the author refused to take advantage of his art—
these and many other eccentricities upset all the rules of the writing
game.

It was fortunate, moreover, that the foreign critics could not read
Russian, for they thus were saved from being shocked by Tolstoy's

language—the style of the book was completely subdued in translation. All the translators of the nineteenth century tried to prettify Tolstoy, to make him presentable to the public, to tame his outbursts, to render 'milder' or 'more literary' his uncouth, crude passages.[1] Tolstoy had a way of writing all his own: anti-metaphoric, anti-Romantic, almost anti-poetic. Like the French bard he enjoyed 'wringing the neck' of rhetoric, dropping all the similes and conventions of literary art, reducing every-thing to bare essentials. This, in general, is his main tendency—in religion, morals, history, and art. He hated euphemisms, tropes, allu-sions; all he was interested in was semantics.

One must read his *Union and Translation of the Four Gospels* to grasp this fury of his in demolishing the ornate and the elusive. His sentences are written with an utter contempt for smoothness or pleasant musicality: he deliberately assembles asperities and makes the pace of his long periods uneven, compelling the reader to concentrate only on the meaning of words and not on their esthetic value. He repeats his prepositions, conjunctions, and adverbs; he does not give a rap for elegance or euphony or grace. A Tolstoyan sentence would, in a literal translation, read somewhat like this: 'She knew that it proved that in his secret heart he was glad that she had stayed home.' His grammar and syntax are often twisted or manhandled, and the irregularities of his phrases are more numerous than the reader usually notices—for that reader is swept along by the powerful swing of the narrative. The heavy, clumsy gait of Tolstoy's style has the impetuous power of an antediluvian monster.

Some writers work with ceramic chips to fashion bright mosaics, some prefer the regularity of bricks for balanced constructions, some use glazed tiles for carefully measured planes, while Tolstoy builds a huge edifice by piling up rocks and unpolished stones—one has to step back a certain distance to appreciate the imposing beauty of this cyclopic structure, for if one looks too closely each rock seems too rugged, almost formless.

Tolstoy pitted himself against the elegance of Turgenev as well as against the flowery verbosity of Gogol. This tendency is extremely typical of Tolstoy as man, as writer, and as philosopher, and in some way it corresponds to the anti-esthetic, utilitarian, nihilistic trend of the 'sixties. The kinship is, however, rather limited: Tolstoy objected to the 'bookish' terminology of the period, to words and turns or speech reveal-

---

[1] Almost all Russian writers have had to undergo much the same sort of beauty treatment at the hands of translators, and the processes of 'prettification' persist to this day.

ing intellectual or foreign origin, as well as to journalese, rhetoric, and sentimentality.

He was, however, very careful, in *War and Peace* as in his other books, to individualize the dialogue according to the social background of each of his protagonists. This explains the overwhelming proportion of French in the first edition of the novel, as well as the great number of gallicisms: Tolstoy mirrored the talk of the old aristocracy, which preferred French to its native tongue. The Rostov family, for instance, speaks differently from the Bolkonskys, using expressions popular in Moscow, while the children express themselves in a delightful 'family vernacular,' with all sorts of infantile words. Certain critics objected to such 'cacophony' and reproached Tolstoy for his 'naturalism of style.' But his language was always highly functional, with the emphasis on expressionism in which the preciseness of the term barred all other preoccupations: he says exactly what he wants to say without raising his voice, without metaphors or convolutions, in a direct, hard-hitting fashion. Sometimes this anti-genteel, anti-Romantic tendency borders upon brutality and crudeness, yet it always scores its point.

This directness of style becomes a potent weapon which Tolstoy handles with subtle skill and even shrewdness. By using ordinary or crude words he often achieves a caustic or forthrightly destructive effect —especially when he wants to discredit some phenomenon of life or to bare the true motivations of a person as distinct from his deluding trappings. For example, the description of the opera performance in *War and Peace* is often quoted as typical of this device:

In the second act there were backdrops representing monuments and there was a hole in the canvas representing the moon; the shades over the footlights were removed, the trumpets and double-basses struck up, and a lot of men in black capes trooped onto the stage from left and right. They began waving their arms about, with some kind of daggers in their hands, then some other men rushed on and started dragging off the damsel who had been dressed in white before but was now in a blue dress. They did not drag her off immediately, however, but first sang for a long time together with her; they finally did drag her away, however, and then somebody hit something metallic three times backstage, and all the people got down on their knees and chanted a prayer.

The anti-esthetes of the 'sixties were delighted by such mocking sketches. Tolstoy used the same critical and merciless method in analyzing emotions and thoughts, claiming that his only purpose was the truth: 'In art,' he wrote, 'a lie destroys all the connections between the phenomena and turns them into dust.' Stefan Zweig has said that Tolstoy

created a 'world without dreams or illusions, in which there is no other
light except merciless clarity of truth,' and complained that his art was
as transparent and sober as ice water.

IV   In *Anna Karenina* the analysis of
motivation and its moral impact are even more profound than in *War and
Peace*. The construction of this psychological family novel is more harmonious than that of the historical epic, and this is particularly perceptible in the first part, where Tolstoy unfolds his plot by gradually shifting
from secondary to more important incidents, changing the whole scene,
and planting at the very beginning all the concrete details that were to
play a part in the dénouement of the drama.

Tolstoy wrote *Anna Karenina* with great effort and labor; the idea
of the novel had come to him as early as 1870 but he did not start
actual work until 1873, after having made seventeen drafts of the beginning, and it was not finished until 1877. The writing of the novel
coincided with the intensification of his inner conflicts, and therefore the
identification of the story with the underlying moral idea is probably
more thorough and obvious than in *War and Peace*: it gives to *Anna
Karenina* a unity and a compactness that have made some critics pro-
claim it as Tolstoy's highest artistic achievement. Although the plot
again serves to show the flow of life, it is more of a story and so has
more of a dramatic quality than the author's other works.

Anna abandons her little son and her husband, the dry, formalistic
bureaucrat Karenin, for Count Vronsky, whom she loves with a pos-
sessive, jealous passion. The affair causes a scandal in high society;
Anna has a daughter by Vronsky; and the lovers go abroad. Upon their
return home Anna is ostracized; her struggle to obtain a divorce from
Karenin is a series of failures and humiliations; Vronsky, despite his
genuine love, becomes somewhat tired of his beautiful but exigent mistress; and Anna, driven by despair, throws herself under a train. The
incidents involving Anna's love for Vronsky form the main plot; while
a parallel story deals with a young landowner, Levin, who falls in love
with a charming young girl, Princess Kitty Shcherbatskaya, and finally
marries her. The contrast between the two love affairs underscores the
moral concept of the work. Anna is so absorbed by her egotistic, maddening love that she is blind to everything else—and this self-centered
concentration causes her own physical and moral undoing and ruins the
people around her. The life instinct in her case acquires a fatal glare;
her beauty is not only a promise of happiness but also a terrible force
of destruction.

Anna has no interest in God, or society, or human beings; she is aloof to duty, to intellectual aspirations, and to emotional complexities. The driving force within her is passion, combined with bodily charm and mitigated only by her Russian kindliness and straightforwardness: She lives only for herself, she sacrifices everything—her little son, her husband, her family, and even her lover—for the fulfilment of her desire, and this is the cause of her doom. Crime against the moral order leads to catastrophe, and Anna's violent death is a natural consequence of all her errors.

Tolstoy denies, however, the right of her contemporaries to judge or censure her. He pictures with scorn and irony the society Anna had challenged by doing openly what others were doing *sub rosa*. In the conflict between Anna and the world all of Tolstoy's sympathies are on the side of his honest but impulsive heroine. If he makes her die, it is because she has transgressed against the Divine Law, but her doom has nothing to do with human justice—for men, being fallible themselves, have no right to condemn others. This is the meaning of the epigraph to the novel, an epigraph usually omitted from English translations of *Anna Karenina* for reasons the present writer despairs of discovering: 'Vengeance is mine; I will repay, saith the Lord.' The negative idea, that no one ought to trespass the moral law lest he perish, is gradually converted into a positive one: salvation lies outside our ego, and those who seek a purpose in life above their own personality, attachments, or passions are complying with the moral precepts of Christianity.

Levin, a young landowner who does not want to introduce any radical changes on his estate, recognizes this moral law: he is tormented by the problem of the meaning of life and seeks the truth that would bestow enlightenment upon him and guide him through earthly existence. His search is identical with that of Tolstoy himself in the years he was writing *Anna Karenina,* and it is quite easy to recognize the actual details of the latter's life in the episodes of Levin's marriage, family happiness, and constant search for faith. A sentence he hears from a peasant acts as a catalyst for all his previous thoughts: he feels that reason, science, and intellectual activity in general cannot explain the meaning of life, while faith in the Lord and in the necessity of complying with His will offers a satisfactory answer. We have to live for something we do not understand, for God whom nobody can define or comprehend—and this faith in things that the mind is too weak to grasp yet which the conscience vaguely reflects is the true faith of peasants, of the great majority of mankind. Levin perceives what Anna ignores: one should live for others, for Truth, for God, not for oneself—and real love is self-sacrifice, never a predatory self-assertion.

V   The ideas formulated by Levin were
those Tolstoy was to express two years later in *My Confession* (1879).
Tolstoy himself, as well as his biographers, speaks of the crisis that took
place in his life between 1879 and 1882 and that led to his religious
conversion. It would be much more accurate to contend that by this
time all his previous doubts and moral torments had culminated, that
his anxiety about the meaning of life had assumed particular acuteness,
and that he was looking for a definitive solution to concepts he had been
familiar with since boyhood. By the time *My Confession* appeared, his
disappointment in science and philosophy as guiding forces had become
acute. The anti-scientific trend of Tolstoy's mind was not merely a result
of emotional attitudes or of speculation: he had studied a great deal in
Russia and abroad and was interested in various fields of knowledge,
from astronomy and physics to Greek and Hebrew (the latter he learned
in order to be able to read the Bible in the original). All his life he had
read widely; his library at Yasnaya Poliana contained almost 24,000
volumes, of which 14,000 show annotations in his own hand.

He kept abreast of modern thought and art, and at the age of
eighty used to surprise his guests by his up-to-date information. But all
his reading made him question the validity of scientific or philosophical
explanation of the meaning of life, and he abandoned the intellectual
efforts of the élite for the primitive faith of millions: here again his
religious search coincided with his populism, and his moral experience
bore the stamp of collectivism. He found the truth in the minds of the
peasants, just as he had discovered the right way of living in the habits
of working humanity. Union and communion with the working people
were Tolstoy's moral and religious solution to all problems—and Levin
intimated this even more than had Platon Karataev. This religious
populism—which ran parallel to the revolutionary socialist populism
predominating in the radical intelligentsia of the 'seventies and early
'eighties—did not stop at the Orthodox ritual, accepted by the Church
and shared by Russia's multitudes: obeying his critical, naturalistic, and
rationalistic bent, Tolstoy, by stripping popular religious convictions to
the bone, defined a clear, primitive, and rather revolutionary Christianity. Later this Christianity became to him the very substance of
all religious doctrines: he tried to distill it from all the great religions
of mankind, the basic kinship of which he always emphasized in his
writings.

From the point of view of this newly acquired Christian morality
Tolstoy examined his own life. By so doing he came to the conclusion
that ethical iniquity was inextricably bound with social evils. He has
told us that in his youth his passions met with the approval of his

family, that his aunts wanted him to have an affair with a married woman—'Because such a liaison helps to form a young man'—to be an aide-de-camp, to marry a rich heiress. Fornication, violence, lying, stealing were approved of by society, and nobody cared for the religious principles everybody was supposed to follow. This discrepancy between man's way of life and what is called his religion profoundly shocked Tolstoy, and he promised himself to be consistent and to live up to his ideas. Later he divided his own life into four periods: an innocent, poetic childhood; a youth filled with ambition, vanity, and lust; a happy, honorable family life; and the period after the conversion, when he concentrated on his service to God and humanity. Despite these sharp divisions, the perfectly consistent moral and religious development is easily distinguishable throughout all these phases, from early childhood when the boy played with his brothers, searching in the shrubs for the green stick that was to bring happiness to all men, down to the famous writer of fifty-two, who suddenly announced that he had found the truth for himself and for mankind.

His diaries, as well as his tales and novels, attest to the long and painful processes he had gone through before coming to the courageous, impressively written conclusions of *My Confession*. These conclusions have both general and personal implications. As a credo they affirm the necessity of faith as opposed to science, philosophy, or the Epicurean nonchalance and deliberate blindness of the upper classes. This faith in God and His moral law voiced by our conscience is identical with the humble, inarticulate religion of the people. During the three decades between *My Confession* and Tolstoy's death, he certainly fluctuated, changing his solutions to various problems and his opinions on secondary issues, but he always remained faithful to his main principles.

In 1901, replying to the edict of the Holy Synod of the Russian Orthodox Church, which had excommunicated him, he wrote:

I believe in God, whom I understand as Spirit, as Love, as the Source of All. I believe that He is in me and that I am in Him. I believe that the will of God is most clearly and intelligibly expressed in the teaching of the man Jesus, whom to consider as God and to pray to I believe to be the greatest blasphemy. I believe that man's true welfare lies in fulfilling God's will, and His will is that men should love one another and should therefore do unto others as they wish others to do unto them. . .

He believed that the Sermon on the Mount formulated all the essential moral rules, as the epitome of all religious strivings, and that the establishment of the Kingdom of God upon earth was possible if men would strive to replace discord, deception, and violence by free accord, truth, and brotherly love. He accepted the preachment, 'I say unto you, that ye resist not evil,' as a categorical imperative, and therefore condemned violence in any form. His was a Christian communism, bearing the marks of both the peasant democratic spirit and the disintegration of the aristocratic order. Equality, simplicity of life, anti-culture, and anti-Statism were combined with the concept of a benign Master of the Universe, of a God who was as simple, sober, and matter-of-fact as any toiling *muzhik*.

The second important feature of his system was its universality. Tolstoy aspired to a universal religion in which carefully chosen elements of Christianity were to correspond to the basic truth of other religions. In this he was very different from Dostoevsky or the Slavophiles, who wanted the national Church of Russia to expand into a universal church. Tolstoy was not a religious nationalist, for he denied the universal truth of Russian Orthodoxy—and of any Church as such. He was also keenly aware that the expansion of the world's frontiers had made more precarious the existence of various Christian denominations. Asia was not Christian, even though it is considered the cradle of religious thought; Africa was not Christian; and Europe was paying only lip service to Christianity. Tolstoy tried to build a system that would bring a compact Christianity to non-Christian peoples as well as to those who claimed to belong to the Christian world. This explains his interest in Buddhism, Judaism, Confucianism, and other religious faiths.

Tolstoy's tales and novels written before *My Confession* are remarkable for the almost complete dearth of villains. Even the most reprehensible characters are not fundamentally bad. This illustrates the main difference between Tolstoy the Realist and Dostoevsky the Romantic. The latter felt heavily the burden of Original Sin, which had corrupted human nature and branded it with depravity; Tolstoy, on the contrary, believed in the basic goodness of man and attributed man's ills to his illusions and weaknesses and the misleading effects of civilization. This attitude determined Tolstoy's peculiar views on education, which he styled the 'basic superstition of the religion of progress.'

During his own pedagogical experiments in the school for peasant children that he had founded at Yasnaya Poliana in 1860, he discovered that, rather than to try to mold children according to preconceived ideas, teachers ought to liberate them from all misconceptions and useless notions in order to bring out their hidden natural instincts, which are always good. Here again he displays his tendency to lay bare the essentials, to do away with illusions and appearances. His world is the Aristotelian universe of stabilized forms, of immovable patterns—and he rejects mysticism and metaphysics (although he loved Schopenhauer and his theory of the role played by will and illusion in the formation of our general concepts). He was a puritanic Protestant with a strong rationalistic bent, refusing to accept the Divinity of Christ, the seven sacraments, the ritual of worship, and the concept of the Trinity.

He dealt most realistically with the problem of mankind, without entering into historical or metaphysical discussions about its past and future. He simply acknowledged that men were chained by civilization, oppressed by the State, cheated by the Church, corrupted by lust and greed. The way of salvation was a return to man's primeval, instinctive goodness, simplicity, and purity, to the naive, spontaneous faith of poor folk. Individual improvement could lead to the common welfare: 'The Kingdom of God is within us.' Tolstoy censured those who expected miracles from a change in institutions and scoffed at the efforts of liberals and Socialists. The only transformation of environment he did accept was limited to the removal of evil, which prevented men from manifesting their goodness. But this transformation, in his opinion, had to come about as a result of moral conversion. And it was toward this goal that he worked, appealing to the conscience of the upper classes, which were the furthest removed from Divine Truth, helping those who had seen the light, and trying to save his own soul by incessant efforts at self-improvement.

A man of logical and moral integrity, Tolstoy decided, after having reached clear-cut solutions, to make them valid in his own case. He applied his doctrine to himself, and began the fight for the three renunciations his new faith implied. To concentrate on God and religion he had to sever his ties with the world—with art, sex, and society. The attempts to realize these three abnegations bred all the battles that for thirty years Tolstoy waged against himself, his wife, his family, the Russian government, the Orthodox Church, and aristocracy. His renunciation of art seemed the most astonishing in a man who had created *War and Peace* and *Anna Karenina*. The great writer suddenly proclaimed that all his works were no more than trifles and that, in general, literature and art were senseless or of little importance. Only in 1897 did he formulate his esthetic theories in a systematic way in his treatise *What is Art?*—but this book was an expression of ideas that had been maturing in him for a long time. At any rate, in the early 'eighties he was ready for the great sacrifice. With the wrath and power of an iconoclast and the almost phrenetic clarity of a stubborn rationalist, he analyzed and rejected contemporary esthetics based on the concept of beauty and gave his own definition of art.

The artist, according to Tolstoy, tries to transmit to others, by means of movement, line, color, sound or words, the feelings he has experienced so that others may be infected with them—and the stronger this power of infection is, the better is the art, as distinguished from those simulated feelings that Tolstoy denounced as one of the diseases of the time. Art is thus a means of communication or even of unity among men, forming a bond of identical feelings. These feelings could, of course, be good or bad; they could appeal to restricted groups or have a universal meaning.

Tolstoy found that 90 per cent of literature, music, painting, and other forms of art were intended for the upper classes, and, despite all their refinement and perfection, were limited to the themes of pride, sexual desire, and weariness of life. All such works of art ought to be discarded as obnoxious, dangerous, and useless. The only art having a right to exist is universal art—art accessible to the multitudes and comprehensible to everybody; sincere and pure art conveying religious emotions or those common to millions of men and women. Following this point of view Tolstoy made some highly controversial statements: he contended that Charles Dickens' *Christmas Carol,* Harriet Beecher Stowe's *Uncle Tom's Cabin,* and George Eliot's *Adam Bede* were supreme books; he attacked Shakespeare for his lack of moral sense, frowned upon Baudelaire as 'that riddle-maker,' ridiculed the Symbolists, jeered at Wagner's operas; declared that money spent on ballets, theaters, and most books of poetry was sheer waste; and claimed that most contemporary artistic activities—the dance, painting, writing—were practiced by idlers and meant for people who knew no other way to kill time.

Tolstoy loved music, for example, and not long before his death told Valerian Bulgakov: 'If all of Western civilization were to collapse, the only thing I would regret would be its music.' Nevertheless he reproached composers for stirring up dangerous emotions and sensuality. This esthetic puritanism was in complete accord with the stern utilitarian trend of the 'sixties. Tolstoy was saying the same things as Pisarev and the Nihilists, but with this difference: the Nihilists wanted art to serve public progress and social transformation, while he wanted it to serve moral and spiritual regeneration.

The didactic trend in Russian literature attained its highest point in Tolstoy: there is a straight line from the medieval preachers of Kiev and Moscow to Count Leo Tolstoy. Even as Savonarola compelled Botticelli to toss his pictures into the Bonfire of Vanities, so Tolstoy tossed all art into the flames of moral purgation. If Tolstoy's definitions are substituted for terms used by Communist ideologists in Soviet Russia, we discover a disturbing similarity: the artist who is asked to serve socialist society and make a conscious effort to help the new regime by educating the youth and bringing to the people a realistic, simple, deliberately tendentious work of art is performing a task very similar to what Tolstoy expected from an artist convinced of the all-embracing importance of regenerated Christianity.

The study of Tolstoy (who, incidentally is much quoted by Communist theoreticians) throws a great light on today's problems, for Tolstoy's theories of art certainly prepared the ground for the ideas that flourished in Russia after the Revolution of 1917. The irate accusations of the corruption of art in Europe and America made in the Soviet press after 1946 are almost identical to what Tolstoy said in 1897 about the decadent art of the upper classes. It would be instructive to compare the demands made upon artists by the late Soviet leader Zhdanov with Tolstoy's dictum that good art should be created for the people, to be understood by them.

Even in the late 'seventies, after the completion of *Anna Karenina,* Tolstoy examined his previous writings and condemned them as not falling into line with his newly formulated demands of moral asceticism. Ten years later, seeing *Anna Karenina* in the hands of a niece, he asked her: 'Why do you read such trash instead of something useful?' On the other hand, on coming one evening into the dining-room, where his children and some other young people were reading aloud a scene from *War and Peace,* he listened for a while without interrupting and then suddenly commented, 'That's not so very bad.' Although his literary activity after his conversion was channeled into treatises, pamphlets, letters, and propagandistic and moral essays, he was never able to give up fiction. From time to time he returned to writing tales and novels— either under the pretext of writing a useful piece of propaganda or simply yielding to the irresistible urge for self-expression.

In 1884, in 'The Death of Ivan Ilyich' he described the horror of physical annihilation in a man who had led a shallow and worthless existence. The almost unbearable details of bodily disintegration and the utterly realistic picture of the aloofness with which Ivan Ilyich's relatives and servants watch his vain struggle for life have strong moral undertones: Ivan Ilyich's complete solitude before his end symbolizes Divine Justice, the Law of retribution: everyone meets the death he deserves, and we die as we have lived, in despair or in humble acceptance of God's will.

This last idea Tolstoy had already expressed in his early story, 'Three Deaths' (1859), and repeated it in the popular tale 'Master and Man' (1895), which may be considered a counterpart to the gruesome 'Death of Ivan Ilyich.' The merciless realism of 'The Death of Ivan

Ilyich' is most impressive: it would be difficult to find in world literature another description of death as poignant and as tragic (except the
chapters on the father's death in Roger Martin du Gard's epical *The
Thibaults*). In his autobiographical *Notes of a Madman* (1881), re-
counting a harrowing experience he had had in Arzamas in 1869,
Tolstoy reveals that the idea of death, that 'white, red, square horror,'
drove him almost crazy and brought him to the verge of suicide.

In order to renounce art Tolstoy concentrated on propagandistic
works, but his long essays, such as *What I Believe* (1883) and *Union
and Translation of Four Gospels* (1881-2), and a series of articles on
religious and moral matters, alternate with tales for children and
peasants. Extremely simple in form and conceived as parables with
a straight didactic message, they form a separate section in his works,
beginning with 'What Men Live By' (1882), to the wellknown *How
Much Land Does a Man Need* (1886), and to the *Circle of Reading*
(1906-7)—a collection of thoughts, maxims, excerpts from the writers
and sages of all lands and times, interspersed with Tolstoy's own didactic
tales. Although Tolstoy considered his tales for the people an integral
part of his moral preaching, all of them nevertheless bear the stamp
of a great writer; their incisive simplicity has the persuasive force of
true art.

Time and again, the urge for writing fiction became so strong that
he reverted to the work he claimed to despise and to have abandoned,
hiding from his disciples what he considered the weakness of an old
man. Thus, in 1886, he wrote *The Power of Darkness,* a drama of
peasant life, in which an ignorant *muzhik* represented the voice of conscience which finally came to be heard by the greedy, the lustful, and
the violent and their victims. A few years later (*c.*1889) he wrote
several short stories (including 'The Devil'), *Fruits of Enlightenment*—
a satirical exposé, in the form of a comedy, of spiritualism and the
superstitions of high society—*The Kreutzer Sonata,* the short novel that
created such an enormous stir. Exactly ten years later, he wrote his last
novel, *Resurrection,* and in the last decade of his life returned several
times to writing fiction: *After the Ball* (1903), the delightful *Hadji
Murat* (1904), *The Living Corpse* (a drama, 1900), and several short
stories, all attesting to the artistic force and vigor of their octogenarian
author. He remained a writer to his last breath—despite all his denials
and his severe, inhuman self-discipline.

VI   The struggle between the creative
instinct and the demands of his conscience tormented Tolstoy for thirty
years; like Gogol, he sacrificed his art for the sake of faith. Yet this

was but one facet of the ceaseless conflict going on in his mind. Another was the struggle against his love of life and his vital force, as manifested in sex, which tormented him despite his years. He was sixty when he wrote 'The Devil,' in which he tells of Eugene, a happy husband and father, who is suddenly so overwhelmed by his desire for an attractive servant that the temptation assumes the form of an obsession, driving him to murder or suicide (there are two variants of the ending). He hid this story from his wife, lest she discover its autobiographical character: after his own marriage Tolstoy had been greatly troubled by the sight of his former mistress, Axinya Bazykina.

In his struggle for moral purity his sensuality proved to be the most discouraging obstacle; his sexual impulses were very powerful. From his early youth the violent demands of his flesh clashed with the puritanical bent of his mind. He believed in purity and chastity, yet could be neither pure nor chaste. For reasons we can only guess he felt that the flesh was the Devil himself and he fought against it with exasperation, always resenting his own frailty. It is quite probable that, as in other matters, he was happy only when he could yield to his desires in the simple, primitive way of an Eroshka, whose naturalness stripped physical love of its hideous moral connotations. This was perhaps one of the reasons why simple, unsophisticated women, like Mariana in *The Cossacks,* attracted him so strongly.

Just before he married Sophie Behrs, while having an affair with Axinya Bazykina, a peasant who bore him a son, he confessed in his diary that he had never been so much in love. The importance of this sexual experience lies probably in the physical accord of the participants: Tolstoy found in Axinya the same elemental urge, the same force of nature beyond morality, that he admired in Eroshka or Mariana but tried to discipline in himself. Tolstoy's tragedy was, in the opinion of several of his biographers, caused by a lack of real physical happiness in marriage. His wife, a 'Porcelain Doll,' as he called her, could not understand or share his physical passion, regarding sexual intercourse as a painful duty and reproaching her husband with being oversexed— thus driving him unconsciously toward feelings of guilt and disgust.

Whatever the origin of his complexes and inhibitions, the fact remains that Tolstoy always looked for a moral justification of sex; however, he always wanted to justify all the manifestations of life. At one time he felt very strongly that marriage was the only honest solution, and *War and Peace* is a glorification of family life. Sexual intercourse in marriage, besides its salutary effects, was sanctified as long as it had an aim—procreation. His faith in the sanctity of marriage was, however, shattered even before his conversion of 1880. His wife and children did not share his opinions, and his God-seeking alienated them from him. They could put up with his writing moral essays or getting religious, but they were quite shocked and horrified when he renounced the way of life of his own class, turned vegetarian, wore boots he cobbled himself and a peasant blouse (now called *tolstovka* in the Soviet Union), did manual labor (farm work, mostly), reduced his material needs to a strict minimum, relinquished all his property to his wife (after a painful struggle), and renounced his copyrights. In the last case he had to compromise again with his loudly protesting wife: she retained the right to all his works produced before 1881, and only his writings after this date were in the public domain and could be published without any royalties.

Tolstoy resented being isolated in the midst of his own household, attacked as an eccentric by his wife, or having to encounter the sullen opposition of his sons and daughters. The incessant disputes and quarrels arising from his renunciations made him feel like a stranger in Yasnaya Poliana, although all on the estate were part of himself, flesh of his flesh. The rift and the family squabbles were also complicated by his marital habits. At sixty his virility was exactingly vigorous, and he felt ashamed of it. All the painful complexities of his family drama may be guessed from a dictum recorded in Gorky's *Reminiscences:* 'Man lives through earthquakes, epidemics, the horrors of disease and through all sorts of torments of the soul, but throughout all times, the most excruciating tragedy for him has been, is, and shall be the tragedy of the bedroom.' [2]

The Kreutzer Sonata (1889) was a violent attack against sensuality and an exposé of the usual hypocrisy in sexual matters. Tolstoy spent over two years writing and revising this work, of which he has left us 9 different versions, 16 variants, and 25 manuscripts. The *Afterword* summed up his moral conclusions: Christ was not and could not be married; consequently complete chastity was the ideal state, and all the rest was but concession to our frailties.

The form of this short novel is unusual for Tolstoy: the story is told during a train journey in a feverish monologue by Pozdnyshev, who, after killing his wife in a fit of jealousy, was tried and acquitted by a jury. Now he tells his casual companions of the circumstances that led to the tragedy, making angry, bitter remarks about love and women. Society, in his opinion, is to blame for glorifying sexuality and spreading wrong ideas in regard to the relations of the sexes. Among the upper classes love is either violence or fraud. He laughs to scorn the mere

[2] *The Portable Russian Reader*, The Viking Press, New York. Quoted by permission of the publishers.

mention of such euphemisms as 'spiritual bonds' and 'twin souls.' 'Spiritual affinity!' he exclaims coarsely. 'Identity of ideals, indeed! But in that case, why do they go to bed together?' Sensuality reigns among the upper classes; polygamy is generally practiced; lust is favored; sexual feats are glorified; art, food, dances, parties—all serve to provoke lechery. Women favor dresses designed to allure men; music titillates the senses; the theater and literature deal with nothing but kisses and embraces; men kill themselves or destroy others for the possession of women; millions of workers supply females with articles of luxury and rubbish for the adornment of their bodies; and sexual gratification is the only pivot on which the life of the so-called cultured society turns. Marriage itself has lost its meaning; it is a thing of convenience or a blind for vice, fostering quarrels, jealousy, lies, and criminal passions. Evil generates evil—and Pozdnyshev, who, obeying the code of his social group, had looked upon his wife as an object for carnal pleasure, who corrupted her by his attitude and had unconsciously pushed her toward flirtation with other men, finally became a murderer.

The thoroughly negative point of view of *The Kreutzer Sonata* could not be explained simply by a sour-grapes attitude of the aging Tolstoy. His wife was right when she jotted down in her diary after reading the novel: 'What an obvious link connects Leo's old diaries with his *Kreutzer Sonata*.' Tolstoy had taken his revenge against the torments of sex and indicated his decision to make a definitive renunciation in this field as well. No art, no love: the Seer of Yasnaya Poliana announced to the world his rejection of both.

Although *The Kreutzer Sonata,* that impassioned, harsh and gloomy story, made a tremendous impression in Russia as well as abroad, the war Tolstoy was waging against State and society had even more far-reaching repercussions. This was his third renunciation—and it challenged all institutions, accepted conventions, and the way of life of his own class. He questioned the very foundations of society and reproached the State for its lust for power, its ignorance of Christian principles, and its use of force. He affirmed that a democratic republic was no better than an autocratic monarchy: the only difference lay in the degree of brutality and ruthlessness in oppressing the individuals. Using an expression by Herzen—whom he highly praised—he called the modern State 'Genghis Khan with telegraph wires.' The Mongolian barbarians based their domination on the same disregard of truth, love, and mercy as do modern politicians, prime ministers, or chiefs of staff. The essence of the State is coercion; therefore the State is anti-Christian. As a consistent religious anarchist, Tolstoy repudiated military service and helped all conscientious objectors, proclaiming any war an insane and absurd offense against God; he was horrified by legalized 'wholesale murder' as well as by 'retail murder,' as he defined capital punishment. He declared that laws protecting property were stupid and that the whole capitalist system, with its competition and its cult of money, was senseless and disgusting.

He could never understand why men were so boastful of their technical inventions: no machine could make the human race better or happier. On the contrary, so-called progress was an enormous sham, the printing press was an instrument for spreading lies, big cities were prisons for the multitudes, breeding disease and depravity; education reared morons, hypocrites, and mountebanks; justice aimed only at the preservation of the *status quo* and was a shameful farce. Prevalent throughout the world were crime and misery, coarseness and bestiality, an insane waste of energy, and a colossal attempt to disguise the horrible truth under all sorts of masks and high-sounding words. This tempestuous attack against modern reality reverberated all over the world, but its impact was mostly felt in Russia. Tolstoy, faithful to the Evangelical precept of nonresistance to evil, disapproved of any revolutionary activity. But in his violent denunciations of the Czarist political and religious repressions, administrative injustices, and ecclesiastical abuses he found himself on the side of the radical opposition, which acclaimed this unexpected ally.

Particularly violent were his attacks against the oppression of the working masses and the economic-political regime which ruined the peasants and caused their misery. By a strange paradox the apostle of nonresistance became one of the most efficient forerunners of the Russian Revolution. He dealt mortal blows to Czarism and started a wide movement of protest, criticism, and opposition.

From his open letter to the Czar in 1881, imploring mercy for the terrorists who had assassinated Alexander II, to 'I Cannot Keep Silent,' his famous pamphlet against the mass executions of revolutionists in 1907, he remained for almost thirty years the mouthpiece of the Russian conscience, stricken by the inhuman ways of autocracy. Whenever and wherever some particularly appalling case of maltreatment occurred, Tolstoy launched appeals to the Emperor or wrote incensed articles which usually aroused general indignation. Most of such writings—and there were scores of them—were banned or heavily mutilated by the censors; nevertheless they had a great circulation, in editions put out by the underground press in Russia, or in copies smuggled in from abroad, where Tolstoy's followers and disciples were publishing all his works. The government, the police, the Church seemed helpless against this old man who sat like a judge in Yasnaya Poliana, defying everybody and pointing out the evils of his time.

This was a unique situation. At the turn of the century Alexis Suvorin, the well-known publisher, wrote in his diary: 'We have two czars in Russia: Nicholas II and Tolstoy.' The government did not dare to take repressive measures against the Seer of Yasnaya Poliana, whose moral authority was tremendous and who repeatedly asked to be treated in the same way as his persecuted disciples. The guardians of the regime found themselves in an absurd position: people found in possession of Tolstoy's pamphlets, such as 'Restoration of Hell' and 'An Open Letter to the Emperor,' were jailed or exiled, while the author of these subversive writings, protected by his fame at home and abroad, was left unharmed. 'A prison big enough to put Tolstoy in hasn't been built yet,' a peasant answered triumphantly when an irate monarchist claimed that the 'old Count' ought to be arrested. The administration had to be content with watching every step Tolstoy took, tailing his visitors, tapping his telephone, opening his mail, and surrounding his estate with secret agents.

Tolstoy waged war against himself, against his family, and against the world—and it was a stunning and pathetic sight, that of the white-bearded, bushy-browed man with piercing ursine eyes, fearless in the solitude of his revolt, never missing an opportunity to repeat the principles of purified Christianity.

As *The Kreutzer Sonata* had proclaimed his renunciation of sex and epitomized all his moral ideals, *Resurrection,* his last novel, reflected his negative attitude toward society. He had had the first outline of this novel in his mind ever since 1887, when A. Koni, a liberal lawyer, had told him a striking incident taken from life. The writing of the novel was begun in 1889, but was not finished until 1899, when Tolstoy decided to publish a book to help the sect of the Doukhobors and finance the migration of these Spirit-Wrestlers to Canada, that they might escape the persecutions they were undergoing in their homeland. The process of writing was, as usual, painful and laborious (he has left 6 manuscripts and 150 partial variants) but also joyful: Tolstoy said that he had never felt such creative elation since *War and Peace.*

Resurrection appeared serially in the popular weekly *Niva* (*The Fallowland*) and its text was telegraphed and cabled for translation to dozens of foreign lands (despite this popularity, there is not a single good translation of *Resurrection* in English). The hero of the novel, Prince Nekhlyudov, a natural man of good qualities, but corrupted by money and the idleness of his class, is drawn as a juryman in a Moscow court. While the boring legal proceedings are under way, he recognizes in the defendant, Katiusha Masslova, accused of being an accomplice in the murder of a merchant, a former protegée of his aunt, a sort of privileged chambermaid whom he had seduced in his youth. She had become pregnant and had been turned out from his aunt's house; desperate and losing faith in good, she had by degrees sunk into a life of prostitution. Now this drink-sodden creature was facing penal servitude. Nekhlyudov understands clearly that she is not guilty and feels that it was his irresponsible action that had been the initial cause of her downfall. Moved by remorse and compassion, and wanting to atone for his fault, he visits Katiusha in prison and offers to marry her. Even after she turns down his strange proposal with mistrust and hostility, he still tries to help her.

In visiting the jail Nekhlyudov becomes acquainted with the other prisoners, and learns with horror mixed with astonishment that most of them are the victims of circumstance, intrigue, or miscarriage of justice. He attempts to assist them as well as to protect Katiusha, who, despite her innocence, has been sentenced to hard labor because of a legal muddle. Nekhlyudov intercedes for her with lawyers, senators, and influential administrators and is shocked by his discoveries: the legal machinery of the state is blindfolded, inhuman, formalistic; the reign of red tape is as stupid as it is omnipotent; the top men of the government are indifferent and drugged by a sense of unlimited power. The worst thing is that the judges are often on a lower moral plane than those they condemn and punish: if the judges had been placed in similar positions and exposed to the same passions of jealousy, anger, greed, or drink, they would have acted exactly as the defendants upon whom they looked down from their high benches. What strikes Nekhlyudov is the common acceptance by high society of the double standard: nobody really cares about the misery, pains, and sufferings of the people, and nobody cares for truth or religion. 'They all cared only for themselves, for their pleasure, and all their talk about God and goodness was simply a lie.'

When Katiusha is sent to Siberia, Nekhlyudov follows her, comes in contact with political exiles, becomes interested in revolutionaries, witnesses Katiusha's moral regeneration under their influence, and finally understands that the Sermon on the Mount contains the complete moral code. The only way to live an honest life is to comply with the will of the Master, as written in our conscience, and to repudiate the shams and lies of modern civilization.

While in Siberia he receives the news that his appeal on Katiusha's behalf has been heard and that her sentence is being commuted. We do not know, however, whether Nekhlyudov is going to stay on with her in

Siberia or how deep and stable his religious conversion is. Tolstoy always wanted to write a sequel to *Resurrection* to show Nekhlyudov's struggle for complete regeneration, with all his errors, temptations, and dearly won victories.

Although the sweep of the novel and its vivid characterizations attest to the art of the septuagenarian master, who was still using his method of translating the inner emotions of his heroes through concrete external traits, *Resurrection* differs in form and spirit from the other great works of Tolstoy. Of course, the power of representation is still there: the portraits of the St. Petersburg bureaucrats, the descriptions of wardens, peasants, prisoners, Siberian officials, or ladies of high society, the contrasting scenes showing sharply the gulf between the upper classes and the oppressed, second-class citizens are all true to life and highly impressive. No less extraordinary is the artistry with which he depicted young Nekhlyudov's love for Katiusha, the spell of an Easter night, the poetic charm of first intimacy: here Tolstoy merged in a stupendous unity the art of objective narrative and his memories of the heart and the senses.

Resurrection is, however, a didactic and tendentious novel filled with editorial asides, moralizing sentences, and deliberately emphasized incidents. Even its structure, its constant use of contrasting scenes (the clean, luxurious house of Nekhlyudov against the foul, stifling prisons; the beautiful drawing rooms of the St. Petersburg belles against the infernal prison camps in Siberia), had a definite moral purpose. Nekhlyudov, the repentant nobleman, Katiusha, the victim of social injustice, whose basic goodness does emerge at last, and finally the idle and reprehensible way of life of the ruling classes: these, the three main lines in the development of the plot, served the same end—the proving of a thesis—an end Tolstoy never lost sight of. When showing one of the judges speeding up the trial proceedings because he has a date with his mistress, or when making a Mass at the prison chapel seem like an opera performance (using his old trick of a derogatory tone and plain words), he intends to indict society, to declare that justice is merely an instrument to protect the upper classes, that religion is the slave of the state and as hypocritical as everything else.

He never missed an opportunity to stress that men live and act contrary to the teachings of Christianity, that a society based on hypocrisy, injustice, and inequality can be maintained only by coercion and lies which lead to turpitude. The Greek Orthodox Church could excommunicate Tolstoy for his scene in the prison chapel (a scene omitted together with many other passages from Russian editions until 1917), the government could declare that his attacks against aristocracy and bureaucracy were biased or insane, but the Russian intellectuals and the majority of the reading public were profoundly impressed by the blasting onslaught of *Resurrection* and acclaimed it one of the greatest exposés of modern civilization. Even those who did not feel inclined to accept the author's doctrines could not deny their critical impact.

Tolstoy taught humility, yet it was with incensed fury that he dealt his formidable blows against the world he lived in. He resembled that old, shaggy ferryman whom Nekhlyudov met on the bank of a Siberian river and who was so angry at all things and all men that he refused to bear a name, to recognize any authority, or to bow to any man. Tolstoy's rejection of current institutions, morals, and ways of life was complete and categoric, and he made it with Biblical wrath. And in this, again, lay Tolstoy's tragedy: the efficiency of his rejection, of his denunciation, was much stronger than his appeals for love and mercy. Nonresistance was the cornerstone of his moral code; yet he waged a ceaseless war against the ills of his time and, although he dreamt of ascetic serenity toward earthly passions and illusions, he felt them intensely and described them with the zest of a true lover of life.

Thus his inner struggle never ceased—until the moment he left his house in order to be alone and to reach a supreme reconciliation with himself and, after catching pneumonia on the road, died at Ostapovo, an obscure railroad station, on 20 November, 1910, still true to the spirit of his own words: 'Why do you say that I am a teacher? I am not; I am simply your brother in sin and resurrection.'

VII   Various tendencies of Russian literature converge in Tolstoy—didactic extremism, moral restlessness, preoccupation with social issues, a desire to bring a universal message, a revolutionary boldness of ideas and forms. Like the majority of Russian writers, he was opposed to art for art's sake and yearned to use literature as a weapon for molding souls. But he was, first of all, a Realist intent on utilizing material true to life and interpreting it in the light of his moral convictions. Russian Realism, whose roots go deep not only in literature but also in the national character, reaches its zenith in Tolstoy and its further development is marked by his influence. His literary domination has weighed so heavily that since the 'eighties hardly a novelist has been able to escape the gravitational attraction of his works: acceptance of Tolstoy, his methods, forms, and attitudes, or revolt against him, seemed to have been an inevitable phase in the evolution of many major and minor novelists. This phenomenon is evident even today.

It would be impossible to trace in this book the total impress left by Tolstoy upon all areas of Russian art, thought, and life. He was, without any doubt, the only man in Russian history of the nineteenth century whose activity—in literature, morals, and politics—has had such a tremendous impact on several generations. He was born three years after the Decembrist uprising and he died seven years before the downfall of Czarism: thus the beginning of the development of modern Russia was encompassed during his lifetime, and all its intellectual, artistic, literary, and philosophic currents were reflected or commented upon in his works. At the same time they, as well as their author, have become an organic part of Russia's history. His books—from *Childhood* to *Resurrection*—have been such powerful sources of emotions, imitation, and controversies; his statements on economics, religion, and politics were so provocative and original; his attitudes toward art, marriage, justice, and morality caused such interminable discussions—that for more than half a century Tolstoy remained the center of Russia's spiritual life, like a heart whose pulsations send blood to all the organs and vessels. Never in the history of letters do we find a similar case: a writer who for more than fifty years was recognized both by admirers and foes as an authentic representative of the whole nation, as its voice, its conscience, and its greatest artist.

The fact that this leadership was assumed by a moralizing realist had numerous implications for Russian literature. Their full impact became completely realized, however, only in the Soviet era. It was to be expected that Tolstoy's religious doctrines and, particularly, his theory of nonresistance to evil, his appeals for resignation, and his aloofness to institutional changes, would not gain top rating in a Communist society. As a matter of fact, the majority of Soviet critics preferred to dismiss or ignore them. Whenever it became necessary, Tolstoy's 'subversive' opinions were labeled 'reflections of the crisis in the disintegrating class of landholders' or were attributed to the contradictions in his environment and in his nature. At one time, in the 'twenties, most critics played variations on the theme of Lenin's article, 'Tolstoy as a Mirror of the Russian Revolution,' written in 1908 and practically repeating Mikhailovsky, who discussed Tolstoy's contradictory tendencies in his famous essay, 'The Left Hand and the Right of Count Tolstoy.'

But Tolstoy the novelist and Tolstoy the critic of Czarism were accepted with enthusiasm from the first days of the Revolution of 1917. Lenin, who loved Tolstoy, qualified his works as 'a step forward in the artistic development of all mankind,' and often called him Russia's greatest genius. These statements, as well as Gorky's epithet of Tolstoy the Colossus, became slogans for the Communist party. The official line regarding Tolstoy was firmly established and remained unchanged for years. It coincided with the feelings of the general public, for whom Tolstoy had always been the uncrowned ruler of national literature.

Thus the Communist party and the average citizen of the Soviet Union found a meeting ground in the cult of Tolstoy, which has lately taken on extraordinary proportions. Even between 1888 and 1917 Tolstoy was, next to Pushkin, Russia's leading best seller: over ten million copies of his works were sold during that period. In Soviet Russia, between 1917 and 1947, the circulation of his works (some of them published in 65 languages) reached 26,500,000 copies. These figures included the magnificent monumental Jubilee Edition of Tolstoy's collected works in 90 volumes. Carried out by the State Publishing House, this critical unabridged edition, with all the variants and numerous comments, presents a definitive text of all of Tolstoy's writings.

The literature on Tolstoy—bibliographies, memoirs, biographical studies, critical and philosophical essays, and so on—runs to many thousands of titles and is being constantly augmented by documentary material published regularly by such special institutions as the Tolstoy Museums, particularly those of Moscow, Leningrad, and Yasnaya Poliana. Tolstoy's estate and his grave are considered national shrines, to which the people make pilgrimages. Desecrated by the Germans during World War II, they were restored by the government in 1945.

Most significant is Tolstoy's direct influence upon Soviet writers. It is not limited to the Tolstoyan School alone, which became very strong in the 'thirties and which will be examined in the volume on modern Russian literature. A group of writers (Sholokhov and Fadeyev among them) has been formed in the Tolstoyan tradition, and critics always point to Tolstoy as a great model for Soviet novelists. The followers of Socialist realism are advised to learn how to write and how to tell the truth about men and women from the master of psychological realism. Tolstoy's methods, and even his mannerisms, are devoutly studied (and imitated), and his 'stripping off of all masks' is quoted as a guiding principle of the new Communist literature. All this proves that Tolstoy's cult is devoid of academic stiffness and does not stem from official veneration: it is spontaneous, organic, and sincere, and as such is subject to growth and expansion. Today in the Soviet Union Tolstoy is not merely a glorious figure of the past: he is still alive and he forms an integral part of the Russian contemporary scene.

Notes

THERE ARE several anthologies of Russian prose (or prose and verse), ranging from the rather dated and fragmentary but still useful *Anthology of Russian Literature* by Leo Wiener (Putnam, New York, 1902-3), 2 vols. (Part I, from the tenth century to the close of the eighteenth; Part II, dealing with the nineteenth), to more recent collections such as Bernard G. Guerney's *A Treasury of Russian Literature* (Vanguard Press, New York, 1943) and *The Portable Russian Reader* (Viking Press, New York, 1947); *A Treasury of Russian Life and Humor* by John Cournos (Coward-McCann, New York, 1943); *Best Russian Short Stories* by Thomas Seltzer (Modern Library, New York, 1923); *Great Russian Short Stories* by Stephen Graham (Liveright, New York, 1929); and *A Treasury of Great Russian Stories* by Avrahm Yarmolinsky (Macmillan, New York, 1944).

Among various collections of Russian poetry published since 1917 (mostly of the nineteenth century) the following may be found useful: *Russian Lyrics* by James Duff (Cambridge, 1917); *Russian Poets and Poems* by Jane Harrison (Longmans Green, New York, 1917); *Modern Russian Poetry* by Babette Deutsch and Avrahm Yarmolinsky (John Lane, New York, 1923); *Verse from Pushkin and Others* by Oliver Elton (E. Arnold, London, 1935); *Have You Anything To Declare?* by Maurice Baring (Knopf, New York, 1937); *A Book of Russian Verse* by C. M. Bowra (Macmillan, London, 1943); *Poems from the Russian* by Frances Cornford and Esther Polianowsky-Salaman (Faber & Faber, London, 1943); *Three Russian Poets, Selections from Pushkin, Lermontov and Tiutchev* by Vladimir Nabokov (New Directions, Norfolk, Conn., 1944); *The Wagon of Life* by Sir Cecil Kisch (Oxford University Press, New York, 1947); *A Treasury of Russian Verse,* edited by Avraham Yarmolinsky (Macmillan, New York, 1949); *The Penguin*

Book of Russian Verse, edited by Dimitri Obolensky (London-Baltimore, 1962); and numerous translations in the *Slavonic Review,* London.

A large number of titles mentioned in these Notes can be obtained in paperback editions, mainly in Vintage, Modern Library, Signet, Mentor, New American Library, Dell, Laurel, Bantam, Anchor, and other collections. For the list of current paperbound books in the field see the June 1963 issue of *Slavic Review,* published at the University of Washington.

INTRODUCTION: THE BEGINNINGS

Quotations from various writers of the tenth to the seventeenth centuries may be found in the *History of Early Russian Literature* by N. Gudzy (Macmillan, New York, 1949), and in the *History of Russian Literature from the Eleventh Century to the End of the Baroque* by D. Cizevskij (Mouton, The Hague, 1960). Also *Medieval Russia's Epics, Chronicles and Tales* (XI-XVII centuries), an anthology edited by S. Zenkovsky (Dutton, New York, 1963).

For Russian folklore see: *Russian Fairy Tales* by A. Afanasiev, translated by N. Guterman (Pantheon, New York, 1945); *The Epic Songs of Russia* by Isabel Hapgood (Scribner's, New York, 1886); *Russian Heroic Poetry* by N. Kershaw Chadwick (Cambridge University Press, 1932); also numerous quotations in *Russian Folklore* by Y. Sokolov (Macmillan, New York, 1950).

"The Russian Primary Chronicle" is translated by Samuel H. Cross *(Harvard Studies and Notes in Philology and Literature,* vol. II, Cambridge, 1930).

A complete English translation by Samuel H. Cross of *The Lay of the Host of Igor* is included in the French volume on *The Lay (La Geste du Prince Igor,* New York, 1948); also translations by V. Nabokov (Vintage Books, New York, 1960), A. Petrunkevich *(Poet Lore,* vol. 30, Boston, 1919), and by L. Magnus: *The Tale of the Armament of Igor* (Oxford University Press, 1915); there are prose versions in Wiener's and Obolensky's anthologies and a translation in verse of a part of *The Lay* in Guerney's *Treasury.*

The Life of the Archpriest Avvakum by Himself was translated by Jane Harrison and Hope Mirrlees (L. & V. Woolf, London, 1924, reprinted by Archon Books, Hamden, Conn., 1963).

CHAPTER 1: POETS, PLAYWRIGHTS, AND SATIRISTS OF THE EIGHTEENTH CENTURY

Poems by Derzhavin and other poets of the period can be found in vol. I of *Specimens of the Russian Poets* by John Bowring (London, 1821), and throughout other anthologies of Russian verse. (See *Anthology of Eighteenth Century Russian Literature* edited by C. Manning, 2 vols. (Columbia University Press, New York, 1951-53.)

Fonvizin's *Hobbledehoy* is included, under the title *The Young Hopeful*, in *Masterpieces of the Russian Drama*, selected and edited by G. R. Noyes (Appleton, New York, 1933); C. E. Beechhofer gives a version of *The Choice of a Tutor* in *Five Russian Plays* (Keegan Paul, London, 1916).

Radishchev's *A Journey* has been published by Harvard University Press in Leo Wiener's translation (Cambridge, 1955).

CHAPTER 2: THE NEW ERA

Karamzin's *Travels from Moscow Through Prussia, Germany, France and England* has been translated (from the German), 3 vols. (John Badcock, London, 1803); his tales were translated in the same year, under the title *Russian Tales*, by J. B. Elvington (London, 1803). Poems of Zhukovsky and Batiushkov are to be found in Bowring's *Specimens* and throughout other anthologies of Russian verse.

Fables by Ivan Krylov has been translated by Sir Bernard Pares (Cape, London, 1926). An earlier version is by Henry I. Harrison: *Kriloff's Original Fables* (Remington, London, 1883).

CHAPTER 3:
FROM THE NAPOLEONIC INVASION TO THE DECEMBRISTS

Poems by Voyeikov, Shakhovskoy, Bobrov, and Dmitriev are given in vol. II of Bowring's *Specimens*.

Griboyedov's *'Tis Folly To Be Wise* has been translated by Sir Bernard Pares, under the title *Wit Works Woe*, in *Masterpieces of the Russian Drama;* see also *The Mischief of Being Clever* in *Slavonic Review*, London, June-December 1924.

CHAPTER 4: PUSHKIN

The most complete collection of Pushkin's works in English is *The Poems, Prose, and Plays of Alexander Pushkin*, selected and edited by Avrahm Yarmolinsky (Random House, New York, 1936, also in the Modern Library series). See also Oliver Elton's translation of *Evgeny Onegin* (Pushkin Press, London, 1937); the same scholar's versions of Pushkin's poems and fairy tales in *A Sheaf of Papers* (Liverpool

University Press, 1932) and *Verse From Pushkin and Others* (E. Arnold, London, 1935). There are translations of *Evgeny Onegin* by E. Kayden (Antioch Press, Ohio, 1964) and W. Arndt (Dutton, New York, 1964) and a version by V. Nabokov due for publication in 1964. Poems by Pushkin were translated by T. Keane (1894), C. E. Turner (1899), M. Baring (1931), W. Morison (1945) and many others, and his prose by T. Keane (Bell, London, 1916) and N. Duddington, also his poetic dramas in E. Kayden's version (Antioch Press, Ohio, 1964). (*The Captain's Daughter,* Dent, London, 1938). For a bibliography see *Pushkin in English,* a publication of the New York Public Library (1937).

CHAPTER 5: LERMONTOV

A Sheaf from Lermontov by J. Robbins (Lieber & Lewis, New York, 1923); *The Demon,* translated by Gerard Shelley (Richards Press, London, 1930): this version, however, has been excoriated by Russian critics. The same poem has also been translated by R. Burness (Edinburgh, 1918).

The Prophet and Other Poems, translated by E. N. Kayden (Sewanee, Tennessee, 1944); *A Song About Tsar Ivan Vassilievich,* translated by John Cournos (Dial Press, New York, 1928). See also anthologies by Yarmolinsky, Obolensky, Bowra, Nabokov, and *The Demon and other Poems,* translated by E. Kayden (Antioch Press, Ohio, 1964).There are versions of *A Hero of Our Times* by J. H. Wisdom and May Murray (Knopf, New York, 1916) and by R. Merton (Allen, London, 1928). The best translation of this book is by V. and D. Nabokov (Anchor, New York, 1958).

For a bibliography see *Lermontov in English,* compiled by Anna Heifetz (New York Public Library, 1942).

CHAPTER 6: DREAMERS AND PHILOSOPHERS

Except for a few casual translations from Baratynsky, Khomiakov and Koltzov in anthologies, a translation of Bulgarin's novel *Ivan Veejeeghin, or Life in Russia,* which appeared in London in 1831, and one of Zagoskin's *Tales of Three Centuries,* translated by J. Curten (Little, Brown, Boston, 1891), few writings of this period are available in English. See *Belinsky, Chernyshevsky, Dobroliubov,* selected criticism edited by R. Matlaw (Dutton, New York, 1962). Belinsky's *Letter to Gogol* is translated by Guerney in his *Treasury.*

CHAPTER 7: WESTERNIZERS AND SLAVOPHILES

Quotations from the writers of the period may be found in *The Spirit of Russia* by T. G. Masaryk, 2 vols., translated from the German (Macmillan, New York, 1918).

My Past and Thoughts by A. Herzen, translated by Constance Garnett, 6 vols. (Chatto & Windus, London, 1924-7); the first two parts have been translated by J. Duff under the title *The Memoirs* (Yale University Press, New Haven, 1928).

CHAPTER 8: GOGOL

The Constance Garnett translations of Gogol were published in London and New York at various dates (mainly by Chatto & Windus, and Knopf). More recent versions of *Dead Souls* are recommended: by G. Reavey (Pantheon, New York, 1949), and under the title *Chichikov's Journey,* by G. B. Guerney (Rinehart, New York, 1948); also by D. Magarshack (Penguin, London, 1961). See also *Tales of Good and Evil,* translated by D. Magarshack (Anchor, New York, 1957) and *Diary of a Madman and Other Stories,* translated by A. McAndrew (Signet, New York, 1961).

CHAPTER 9: CRITICAL REALISM: GONCHAROV AND GOGOL

The only unabridged versions of Goncharov's novels in English are: *A Common Story,* translated by Constance Garnett (Heinemann, London, 1890); *Oblomov,* translated by Natalie Duddington (Allen & Unwin, London, 1929; also Dutton, New York, 1960); *The Precipice,* translated by M. Bryant (Knopf, New York, 1916).

Ostrovsky has been translated by G. R. Noyes: *Plays by Alexander Ostrovsky: Poverty is No Crime, Sin and Sorrow Are Common to All, It's a Family Affair* (Scribner's New York, 1917); also *At the Jolly Spot* and *Bondwoman (Poet Lore,* Boston, 1925-6, vol. 36); *The Forest* (French, New York, 1926); *A Last Sacrifice, A Cat Has Not Always Carnival* and *Fairy Gold (Poet Lore,* Boston, 1928-9, vols. 39 & 40); *The Thunderstorm* (French, New York, 1927), also translated by Constance Garnett under the title *The Storm* (Duckworth, London, 1899), available in anthologies of world drama. *The Poor Bride,* translated by J. L. Seymour and J. R. Noyes, in *Masterpieces of the Russian Drama;* see also *Easy Money and Other Plays,* translated by D. Magarshack (Allen & Unwin, London, 1944).

CHAPTER 10: THE CRITICS AND THE NIHILISTS

Fragmentary excerpts from critical essays of the 1860's in Wiener's *Anthology;* see *Belinsky, Chernyshevsky, and Dobroliubov,* edited by R. Matlaw (Dutton, New York, 1962). *What's To Be Done? A Romance by N. G. Chernyshevsky,* translated and published by B. R. Tucker (Boston, 1886), revised and abridged by L. Turkevich (Vintage, New York, 1961).

Apollon Grigoryev's *My Literary and Moral Wanderings,* translated by R. Matlaw (Dutton, New York, 1962), is good reading.

CHAPTER 11: LITERARY TRENDS OF THE 'SIXTIES

A. Pisemsky's *One Thousand Souls,* translated by Ivy Litvinov (Grove Press, New York, 1959); his play *A Bitter Fate* in *Masterpieces of Russian Drama. Krechinsky's Wedding* by A. Sukhovo-Kobylin, translated by R. Magidoff (Michigan University Press, Ann Arbor, 1961).

The Fishermen, a novel by D. Grigorovich, has been published by Stanley Paul (London, 1916). The best version of Aksakov is *Chronicles of a Russian Family* by M. Beverly (Routledge, London, 1924, reprinted by Dutton, New York, 1961), also *Years of Childhood,* translated by A. Brown (Vintage, New York, 1960).

Saltykov-Shchedrin's novel, *Golovlyov's Family,* has been translated by N. Duddington (Macmillan, New York, 1931), by A. Yarmolinsky (under the title *A Family of Noblemen,* Boni & Liveright, New York, 1917), and by A. McAndrew (under the title *The Golovlovs,* Signet, New York, 1962).

CHAPTER 12: NEKRASSOV, TIUTCHEV, AND THE MINOR POETS

Nekrassov's Poems, translated by D. Prall (University of California, Berkeley, 1944); *Poems by Nekrassov,* translated by Juliet Soskice (Oxford University Press, New York, 1929); *Who Can Be Happy and Free in Russia?* translated by Juliet Soskice (Oxford University Press, London, 1917); *Red Nosed Frost* (Ticknor, Boston, 1886).

Poems by Tiutchev, Alexis K. Tolstoy, A. Maikov, and L. Mey in verse anthologies, also *Versions from F. Tiutchev* by C. Tomlinson (Oxford University Press, New York, 1960).

A. Tolstoy's dramas *The Death of Ivan The Terrible* in *Masterpieces of the Russian Drama,* and the second part of the trilogy *Tsar Fedor Ivanovich,* translated by Jennie Cowan (Brentano's, New York, 1923).

CHAPTER 13: TURGENEV

While the collected works of Turgenev have been translated by Constance Garnett in seventeen volumes (Heinemann, London, 1920-21) and by Isabel Hapgood in fourteen volumes (Scribner's, New York, 1903), there are many good and more recent versions of his novels and stories: *Fathers and Sons,* translated by George Reavey (Noonday,

New York, 1958), by R. Hare (Hutchinson, London, 1947), and by B. Makanowitzky (Bantam, New York, 1960); *A Nobleman's Nest,* translated by R. Hare (Hutchinson, London, 1947), *Rudin,* translated by A. Brown (Hamilton, London, 1950), *Smoke,* translated by N. Duddington (Dutton, New York, 1950); *On the Eve,* translated by M. Budberg (Cresset Press, London, 1950). A Turgenev "omnibus," four novels and three novelettes, translated by H. Stevens (Knopf, New York, 1950). See also *Five Short Novels,* translated by F. Reeve (Bantam, New York, 1960) and *Selected Tales of Ivan Turgenev,* translated by D. Magarshack (Anchor, New York, 1960). *The Plays by Ivan Turgenev,* translated by M. S. Mandell (Macmillan, New York, 1924).

For a bibliography see *Turgenev in English,* compiled by R. Yachnina and D. H. Stam (The New York Public Library, 1962).

CHAPTER 14: DOSTOEVSKY

The works by Dostoevsky, in Constance Garnett's translation, have been published at various dates in numerous reprints. Dostoevsky's novels are available in various editions, including the Modern Library classics (Random House, New York) and different paperbacks. *The Short Novels, The Short Stories,* and *A Raw Youth* were reprinted several times (Dial Press, New York, 1945-7). To these standard editions should be added *The Diary of A Writer,* translated by B. Brasol, 2 vols. (Scribner's, New York, 1949); *Dostoevsky's Letters to His Wife,* translated by E. Hill and D. Mudie (Constable, London, 1930); *Dostoevsky's Letters,* a selection, translated by E. Lehrman (Knopf, New York, 1960). New versions of Dostoevsky's major novels were offered by D. Magarshack in Penguin editions (1951-60), and by M. McAndrew in the Signet series (New York, 1959-62).

CHAPTER 15: LEO TOLSTOY

The best translation of Tolstoy's collected works is that in the Centenary Edition, by Aylmer and Louise Maude, 21 vols. (Oxford University Press, London, 1928-37); the *Complete Works,* 29 vols., have also been translated by L. Wiener (Dana Estes, Boston, 1904-12); *Posthumous Works* (Dodd, Mead, New York, 1912); *Dramatic Works,* translated by N. H. Dole (Crowell, New York, 1923); *Diaries,* translated by C. J. Hogarth and A. Sirnis (Dutton, New York, 1917); *Journals,* translated by Rose Strunsky (Knopf, New York, 1917).

For a bibliography see *Tolstoy in English,* compiled by A. Yassukovitch (The New York Public Library, 1929) and a comprehensive list in *Tolstoy* by E. J. Simmons (Little, Brown, Boston, 1947).

Index